Cold Peace

Dr. Garner,

With great admiration!

Cold Peace

China-India Rivalry in the Twenty-First Century

Jeff M. Smith

LEXINGTON BOOKS

Lanham • Boulder • New York • Toronto • Plymouth, UK

Published by Lexington Books
A wholly owned subsidiary of Rowman & Littlefield
4501 Forbes Boulevard, Suite 200, Lanham, Maryland 20706
www.rowman.com

10 Thornbury Road, Plymouth PL6 7PP, United Kingdom

British Cataloging in Publication Information Available

Library of Congress Cataloging-in-Publication Data

Smith, Jeff M.
  Cold peace : China-India rivalry in the twenty-first century / Jeff M. Smith.
     pages cm
  Includes bibliographical references and index.
  ISBN 978-0-7391-8278-9 (cloth) — ISBN 978-0-7391-8279-6 (electronic)
  1. China—Foreign relations—India. 2. India—Foreign relations--China. I. Title.
  DS740.5.I5S55 2014
  327.51054—dc23

                                                                    2013039847

Printed in the United States of America

Contents

Section 5: Turf

Section 6: Trade

Acknowledgments

My deepest gratitude goes to the American Foreign Policy Council (AFPC), my employer for the last six years, and specifically the council's founding president, Herman Pirchner, Jr. From the moment he welcomed me to AFPC fresh out of graduate school, he supplied wisdom, encouragement, support, and independence—all a young analyst could ask for. Let me also thank Annie Swingen, Ilan Berman, and Rich Harrison, and the dozens of fellows, coworkers, and interns who have served as my friends and family at AFPC.

Special thanks is due to the Smith Richardson Foundation, whose support was crucial to the success of this project. The foundation has consistently demonstrated foresight in funding cutting-edge foreign policy scholarship in general, and advancing the field of Sino-Indian relations in particular. Notably, the foundation was among the supporters of Dr. John Garver's *Protracted Contest*, which set the benchmark for contemporary Western scholarship on China-India relations. Special thanks is also due to the Veale Foundation, without whose support this project would not have been possible.

Perhaps most of all I want to thank the incredibly gifted young interns and research assistants who deserve a large share of the credit for bringing this project to fruition in the allotted timeframe. They include: Anuysha Ramaswamy, Sarah McKeever, Kunal Mehta, Amanda Sawit, Joshua Truman, Darren Fazzino, Jared Swanson, Tom Wilson, Harrison Menke, and Megan Carey, among others.

Foreword

This book proceeds from the premise that the twenty-first century will witness China and India reclaim their positions atop the global hierarchy of nations, where they spent the better part of the first and second millennia. It's not a particularly controversial proposition: by 2012, China ($12.7 trillion) and India ($4.7 trillion) were already the second- and third-largest economies in the world measured by purchasing power parity (PPP), a popular technique that adjusts for variations in price levels. Given projected growth rates, both economies may surpass the United States by mid-century, even if they will continue to *feel* a great deal poorer owing to their massive populations.

If—as economists, demographers, and political scientists—the two Asian giants continue their rapid ascent, the relationship among China, India, and the United States will emerge as among the most important and consequential set of relationships in the twenty-first century. And while the fields of Sino-U.S. and Indo-U.S. relations are being capably served by analysts and scholars here in Washington, considerably less analytic attention has been applied to the third leg in this strategic triangle.

METHODOLOGY

This book represents an attempt to update and strengthen our understanding of the contemporary Sino-Indian relationship by examining the Sino-Indian rivalry through a security studies paradigm. This book makes no value judgment on whether "rivalry" is the most apt description of the China-India relationship. It simply recognizes that elements of rivalry constitute an important, and at times predominant, dimension of bilateral relations. And it finds merit in exploring the sources, the contours, and the implications of those points of discord.

It pursues this task through two principal avenues. The first major objective of the book is to collect, organize, and present an objective and nuanced picture of the Sino-Indian rivalry in a manner that is both valuable to the veteran analyst and accessible to the laymen. In some respects, this contribution is as important as the presentation of new ideas and analysis, as discussions of the Sino-Indian rivalry often get bogged down in a sea of contradictory and biased reporting, and arcane historical facts.

Second, the book contributes new insights and analyses through over one hundred interviews with senior Chinese, Indian, and U.S. policymakers, scholars, and military officials in Washington, Beijing, and Delhi between November 2011 and July 2013. The interviews were complemented by field research at the disputed China-India border in Ladakh and Arunachal Pradesh; in Dharamsala where the Tibetan Government in Exile resides; in the Andaman and Nicobar Islands, India's sentinel outpost in the eastern Indian Ocean; and on Hainan Island, the Chinese province that administers China's South China Sea territories.

Critical to the success of this project, I participated in a handful of AFPC delegations to China with fellows and staff, as well as former Chairman of the Joint Chiefs of Staff Richard "Dick" Myers, former Under Secretary of Defense Dov Zakheim, former Under Secretary of State Paula Dobriansky, and former Under Secretary of State William Schneider.

On these delegations I was afforded access to senior Party leadership, including nearly a dozen meetings with cabinet-level ministers and vice-ministers in the Chinese Foreign Ministry and the International Department of the CPC, as well as multiple briefings from scholars at China's top think tanks. During the delegations, there was often time for candid exchanges of views and ideas outside the confines of the formal meeting, as senior and junior officials accompanied us on travel and shared drinks and dinner. Equally important, the AFPC delegation received comprehensive, in-depth briefings from the U.S. Embassy team in Beijing during these trips, and met with the U.S. ambassador to China.

In each case I was able to stay in Beijing after the delegation had departed to schedule individual meetings with some of China's top India scholars with the assistance of AFPC Senior Fellow in China Studies Joshua Eisenman, an accomplished author with years of experience living and teaching in China. These one-on-one, in-depth interviews, including with Hu Shisheng and Li Li (CICIR), Zhao Ganchen (Shanghai Institute for International Studies), Ma Jiali (China Reform Forum), and Ye Hailin and Zheng Ruixiang (CASS), among others, provided crucial insights into China's perspective on a wide range of issues in Sino-Indian relations.

FIGURE 0.1.   Foreign Travel and Institutions Visited

India, November 2011	*Delhi:* Ministry of External Affairs, Observer Research Foundation, Institute for Defense Studies and Analysis, Indian World Affairs Council, United Services Institute, interviews with Indian Members of Parliament.
China, February 2012	*Beijing, Hainan Island:* Foreign Ministry, International Department of the CPC, Chinese Institutes of Contemporary International Studies, Chinese Academy of Social Sciences, China Institute for International Studies, China Institute for International Strategic Studies, China Reform Forum, National Institute for South China Sea Studies, U.S. Embassy in Beijing.
PACOM, April 2012	*Honolulu:* Pacific Command Headquarters, East-West Center, Asia-Pacific Center for Security Studies, CSIS Pacific Forum.
India, August 2012	*Delhi, Dharamsala, Srinagar-Kargil-Leh, Pangong Lake:* Observer Research Foundation, Institute for Defense Studies and Analysis, United Services Institute.
India, Nov/Dec 2012	*Delhi, Port Blair, Tawang:* All individual interviews.
China, April 2013	*Beijing, Jinan:* Foreign Ministry, International Department of the CPC, Chinese Institutes for Contemporary International Studies, China Reform Forum, Chinese Academy for Social Sciences, U.S. Embassy in Beijing.
PACOM, May 2013	*Honolulu:* China-India-U.S. Track 1.5 Maritime Security Dialogue, sponsored by Asia Pacific Center for Security Studies.

Through three trips to India between November 2011 and December 2012, I conducted dozens of interviews with senior officials and analysts, including the Joint Secretary for East Asia in the Ministry of External Affairs, the serving Indian ambassador to China (twice in China), two former commanders of India's Andaman and Nicobar Command, two former Indian foreign secretaries, a former Indian Army chief, a former Indian intelligence chief, a former Indian National Security Advisor, several serving Members of Parliament from both of India's mainstream political parties, the directors of several Indian think tanks, and a number of India's most prolific strategic affairs analysts from the United Services Institution, the Institute for Defense Studies and Analysis, the Observer Research Foundation, and the Indian World Affairs Council (all former officials interviewed served in government or the military after 2000).

I

THREAT PERCEPTIONS

Chapter 1

A Civil Rivalry

It was a remarkable achievement: two of the largest and oldest civilizations in the world, living side by side in almost uncontested harmony for two millennia. Through centuries of conflict, conquest, defeat, subjugation, and colonization, the Himalayan frontier that separates the Chinese and Indian people went largely undisturbed.

Yet it took only fifteen years after the creation of the People's Republic of China and the Republic of India in the late 1940s to squander this legacy. Distant neighbors for over twenty centuries, the allure of conflict proved irresistible in 1962 when China and India fought the first, last, and only war in their long shared history.

A decade of open rivalry followed the 1962 border war before the two sides gradually slipped into the confines of a Cold Peace that has proven remarkably durable in the intervening half century, offering the Asian giants a foundation to build a robust diplomatic and economic relationship. But despite a series of important breakthroughs in bilateral relations in the 1980s and 1990s, in many respects the lure of rivalry stands undiminished in the twenty-first century.

* * *

If China and India are indeed rivals, as the title of this book implies, they are not rivals by any traditional definition of the word.

In 2006, Chinese President Hu Jintao declared: "To enter into strategic partnership with India is not an expedient. Rather, it's a strategic decision and firm goal of the Chinese government."[1] A year earlier, Indian Foreign Secretary Shyam Saran insisted China and India "do not look upon each other as adversaries but we look upon each other as partners."[2]

The statements are symbolic of the warmth that underscores official diplomatic exchanges in the twenty-first century. Ma Jiali of the Beijing-based China Reform Forum claims Chinese President Hu Jintao and Indian Prime Minister Manmohan Singh had twenty-six face-to-face meetings during Hu's term in office (2002–2012), "far more than the leaders of the U.S. will ever meet with the leaders of Britain or Japan."[3] According to India's ambassador to China, S. Jaishankar, the two countries now have thirty-six separate dialogues and diplomatic mechanisms in place, a large share of which were created only in the last decade.

The reality is, thirteen years into the new century China and India are more politically engaged and economically interdependent than at any time since their birth as modern nation-states in 1949 and 1947, respectively. Bilateral trade expanded an astonishing 67-fold from 1998 to 2012, and the Chinese and Indian armies held joint exercises for the first time in history in 2007, 2008, and again in 2013. The two capitals have begun to cooperate on global issues of mutual interest, most notably on world trade talks, climate change negotiations, the primacy of state sovereignty, and the need to reform global governance institutions.

Perhaps most important, the leaders of both countries have demonstrated a firm commitment to mitigating tensions in the relationship and restraining reactionary elements at home. When minor disputes do arise—as was the case with the "intrusion" of a Chinese patrol across their disputed border in April 2013—the political leadership in both capitals respond with calm and patience, utilizing the elaborate diplomatic mechanisms in place to dissolve the crisis. At the government-to-government level relations are, in a word, civil.

All of which has led a number of Chinese scholars—and a smaller group of Indian scholars—to contest the proposition that China and India are rivals at all. Western analysts and some Indian hawks, they say, have fabricated a narrative of Sino-Indian rivalry in an effort to sow discord among Asia's two great powers and draw India into a U.S.-led alliance to contain China.

"Western media hype 'the competition between the dragon and the elephant,' trying to provoke China-Indian relations," argued a commentary the Communist Party mouthpiece, the *People's Daily*, in May 2013.[4] Chinese analysts frequently blame the Indian media for playing up the "so-called China threat" in order to "avoid domestic problems, bolster up national morale and raise votes."[5] The bottom line, they suggest, is that some provocateurs are trying to create a false narrative of rivalry to describe a relationship that is fundamentally characterized by cooperation, elevating the views of a few vocal hawks at the expense of the silent majority.

This book finds flaws in that line of reasoning. The hostile opinions they speak of do not merely represent the views of a vocal minority;

they give voice to widely shared sentiments in both countries that are artificially suppressed for the sake of diplomatic comity. And while it's true that disputes in the Sino-Indian relationship are often amplified and dramatized by the Indian and Western media, the elements of rivalry that have shadowed the relationship for almost six decades are not only genuine and deep-seated, they are largely intrinsic to the bilateral relationship. And they are growing in number.

"India has a good reason to adopt the policy of containing China," admitted an article in the *People's Daily*, in January 2013.[6] The "structural disputes" that are undermining the Sino-Indian relationship, it said, include "territorial disputes, the issues of Tibet, Pakistan, and the Indian Ocean and even the difference about the adjustment of the world political and economic order." "These disputes," the article concluded, "cannot be solved fundamentally through a slight friendliness and interaction in diplomatic or military circles."

For their part, Indian officials and analysts bear less reservations about couching the relationship in the language of strategic rivalry. Serving Indian politicians have publicly described China as a "threat and a challenge" and serving Indian military commanders have publicly implicated China as their country's top external security threat. An informal survey conducted for this book suggests that for many in India's national security establishment, China has replaced Pakistan as their country's principal long-term national security threat. In Delhi, negative views of China are not only well within the mainstream, they are incredibly popular and supremely profitable.

This is not to suggest that the aforementioned elements of cooperation are an illusion. Rather, it is a recognition that Sino-Indian relations do not exist in a zero-sum universe: cooperation and competition coexist side by side, at times advancing in tandem on parallel tracks. The phenomenon should be familiar to those in Washington. U.S.-China relations operate in a similar framework: deeper integration in the diplomatic and economic sphere accompanied by strategic mistrust in the security arena. And while the cooperative track in Sino-Indian relations has proceeded at an accelerated rate since the turn of the century, the strategic competition between the two countries has kept pace, and in some arenas advanced even faster.

THREAT PERCEPTIONS IN SINO-INDIAN RELATIONS

If there is one characteristic that most defines the Sino-Indian rivalry, it is the recognition that this is not a rivalry of equals. Thirteen years into the new century, the strategic gap between China and India is as large, or larger, than the gap between China and the United States.

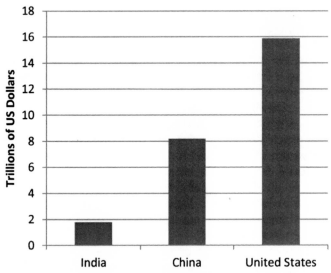

Figure 1.1. China, India, U.S. Nominal GDP 2012
Source: CIA World Factbook

Measured by Gross Domestic Product (GDP), China's economy was over four times the size of India's in 2012, and over eight times the size when adjusting for purchasing power parity (PPP). This is a relatively new phenomenon. As late as 1990 the Chinese and Indian economies were virtually at parity. But as figure 1.2 shows, by the mid-1990s the Chinese economy began racing ahead, and the gap has only widened in every year since.

In the military arena, India's $38 billion defense budget in 2013 was just a fraction of China's official military budget of $119 billion (excluding the additional $124 billion for internal security).[7] India has over double the poverty rate (29.8 percent versus 13.4 percent) and only two-thirds the literacy rate (61 percent versus 92 percent). In life expectancy, infant mortality, and higher education, the gap between China and India is wide and in many cases growing wider in China's favor.

Most economists expect these divides to narrow before mid-century if India can leverage favorable demographics. In 2012 India's working-age population grew by twelve million while China's shrank by three million.[8] A June 2013 UN report on world population prospects predicts India's population will surpass China's by 2028.[9]

But for the immediate future, China's comprehensive national power will exceed India's by a wide margin, and this disparity is matched, unsurprisingly, by a stark asymmetry in threat perceptions. Put simply, most Indian strategists today view China as their country's principal security threat, and for many that threat has grown more severe in the twenty-first century. In contrast, India ranks somewhere in the middle of

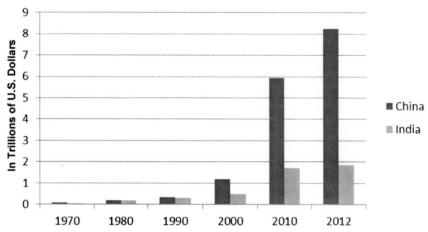

Figure 1.2. China, India Nominal GDP 1970–2012
Source: World Bank World Development Indicators (accessed August 5, 2013). http://databank.world
bank.org

the pack in China's matrix of strategic priorities: "To be frank, somewhere above Brazil but below Germany," says Ye Hailin, the deputy director for South Asia at the Chinese Academy of Social Sciences (CASS).[10]

This disparity in threat perceptions underscores one of the iron laws of Sino-Indian relations: "China can threaten India more than India can threaten China, which limits India's ability to influence Chinese behavior."[11]

Chinese Threat Perceptions

Traveling to Beijing, Jinan, Xi'an, Tianjin, and Sanya on a series of delegations organized by the American Foreign Policy Council between 2010 and 2013, this analyst was afforded the opportunity to solicit Chinese views of India from a wide variety of Party officials, think-tank scholars, and common Chinese citizens. Chinese perceptions of India appeared to be colored by two distinct themes—disdain and disinterest—and Chinese threat perceptions toward India focused around four areas, which are covered in greater detail in subsequent chapters of this book: Tibet, the Indo-U.S. relationship, India's military modernization, and India's Look East policy.

Talking Nice

Since the late 1970s successive generations of Chinese leadership have been remarkably consistent in their diplomatic approach to India. They have all promoted a harmonious bilateral relationship defined by cooperation and conciliation. Even during periods of heightened discord they have rarely strayed from this narrative, leaving it to state propaganda organs to voice their disapproval with Indian policies. Chinese leaders have gone to great lengths to stress China's "civilizational bonds" with India, and every generation since Mao has articulated a variation of the line most recently given by Premier Li Keqiang in May 2013: "without the simultaneous development of China and India, there won't be prosperity in Asia."[12]

It was China that offered the first diplomatic overture to India eight years after the traumatic 1962 border war. In 1970 Chairman Mao Zedong famously told India's charge d'affairs, Brajesh Mishra, that the two sides should put their troubled past behind them. "We cannot go on quarrelling like this. We must become friends again. We will become friends again."[13] Diplomatic ties were restored six years later, and the emergence of more liberal-minded party leadership under Deng Xiaoping in 1978 heralded a new era of engagement.

"Based on the Dengist perspective, China started to seek a new-type security partnership with India," writes Chinese scholar Dr. Li Li. "It defined India as neither an ally nor an enemy but a partner with which China might have both cooperation and competition at the same time."[14] Deng's successors assumed this broad template for Sino-Indian relations. During his visit to New Delhi in 1996, Chinese President Jiang Zemin proclaimed: "Our common interests far outweigh our differences, as neither of us poses a threat to the other. . . . We, the two great nations of broad-mindedness and wisdom that pioneered human civilization, will surely bring a cooperative and constructive partnership into the twenty-first century."[15]

Under the Hu Jintao administration (2002–2012) Chinese leaders began using the phrase "long-term constructive partnership" to define the China-India relationship.[16] "Mutually beneficial cooperation (between China and India) will change the look of Asia and the world at large,"[17] said Chinese President Hu Jintao in 2006. The new Chinese administration under President Xi Jinping has given little indication that it will deviate from the template set by its predecessors. During a visit to India in May 2013, Chinese Prime Minister Li Keqiang described the two sides as "strategic partners and good friends" and spoke of the "unprecedented and enormous opportunities for opening a new chapter in China-India relations." "Amicable relations, deeper cooperation and common development between China and India are a true blessing for Asia and the world at large . . . without the common development of China and India, Asia won't become strong and the world won't become a better place."

Disdain

Yet these public professions of friendship belie less charitable views of India held by many Chinese elites and the Chinese public at large, views rooted in geopolitics but nurtured and reinforced by cultural and racial stereotypes.

In an extensive 2011 study of the views of Chinese Web users, Simon Shen of Hong Kong's Institute of Asia-Pacific Studies observed: "many Chinese people (the ethnic Han in particular) perceive Indians as being racially inferior to themselves."[18] In China, "India is stereotyped by terms such as 'curry,' 'dirty,' and 'poor'"[19] and the "nine-tenths majority view" of China's online community is that India is the "yellow sick man of Asia. . . . In all [online] forums, racist sentiments towards the Indian are overwhelming."[20] To be sure, a survey of Web users—even one that includes both liberal and nationalist websites—is not representative of the Chinese public at large. This author found the average Chinese citizen most likely to be indifferent or uninformed about India. Yet where Chinese do express opinions about India, it is rarely in a positive light. A 2012 Pew Research poll found 62 percent of Chinese respondents with an unfavorable view of India versus only 32 percent reporting a favorable view. Less than a third thought bilateral ties were defined by cooperation.[21]

And while the grossly negative sentiments captured by Shen's study may not be representative of the Chinese public at large, they *are* representative of an influential strain of *Chinese nationalist* perceptions of India. During periods of heightened Sino-Indian tensions, as in 2009, Party censors have permitted these less flattering views of India to be aired openly. As later chapters will show, Chinese nationalists wrote critically about a country plagued by weak growth, a fragmented political system, internal ethnic and religious strife, a feudal caste system, dilapidated infrastructure, endemic corruption, and a country paralyzed by rivalry with a smaller, weaker neighbor, Pakistan. Indian democracy was portrayed not as a model to be studied or emulated but as an example of the pitfalls of popular governance.

Disinterest

"Objectively speaking, China does not spend much time guarding against India, while India focuses a lot of attention on China."[22] This observation, by China's nationalist *Global Times* in the spring of 2012, accurately summarizes the second defining feature of Chinese perceptions of India: disinterest. A cursory summary of media coverage in both countries underscores this point. The *New York Times* notes that India's largest English-language newspaper, the *Times of India*, carried fifty-seven articles on China in a single month in 2011, for an average of almost *two articles a day*.[23] In contrast, in the first seven months of 2011, the English-language version of the *People's Daily* carried just twenty-four articles mentioning India, averaging just over *three articles a month*.

This lack of interest extends to the elite halls of power in Beijing, where there remains a glaring lack of expertise and interest in Indian affairs. Andrew Small, an expert on China's South Asia policy at the German Marshall Fund, says that aside from a handful of veteran analysts in Beijing and Shanghai there is "too thin a sliver of experts on South Asia in China. There is not always the sophistication on South Asia that China has cultivated in other regions. . . . They have a legacy of not taking India very seriously."[24]

Ye Hailin of the Chinese Academy of Social Sciences concurs, pegging the number of South Asia scholars in China at no more than fifty. Among that small club is Dr. Zhao Ganchen of the Shanghai Institute for International Studies, who admitted in an interview that "India study is marginalized in China" and expressed frustration at the failure of the small South Asia studies community to compel China's leadership to take India more seriously. "The 'Center' is not paying enough attention to India. If China wants a stable periphery, India is a decisive factor. If India wants to become troublesome, Chinese policy faces a very serious test."[25]

Climbing the Ranks

There are indications, however, that at least since 2005 India's budding strategic partnership with the United States, its deepening engagement with East Asia, Chinese insecurities in Tibet, and India's growing military capabilities have raised India's profile within China's threat matrix.

Dr. Mohan Malik notes that an internal study on India by China's top South Asia experts in 2005—the year India signed a defense pact and civilian nuclear deal with the United States—concluded that China "should not take India lightly any longer" and suggested Beijing should take all measures to maintain its current strategic, diplomatic, and economic leverage over India.[26] "Chinese strategists and technical experts have been devoting more attention to Indian capabilities since 2005," concludes M. Taylor Fravel, although the Indian military continues to receive far less coverage than the U.S., Japanese, or Russian militaries in Chinese military journals.[27]

Indian Threat Perceptions

Does China constitute India's greatest security threat? A survey of official Indian statements would suggest not. In 2012, the "Year of China-India Friendship and Cooperation," Indian Prime Minister Manmohan Singh praised the "wisdom and sagacity of the Chinese leadership," and commented on how greatly he valued China-India friendship.[28]

Yet, even more than in China, the diplomatic language that pervades official Sino-Indian discourse does not accurately reflect elite *or* public opinion about China in India. A 2010 survey by the Pew Research Center[29] found just a third of Indians holding favorable views of China, with a simple majority (56 percent) expressing an unfavorable view. A Lowy Institute Poll[30] released in May 2013 found just 31 percent of Indians surveyed felt China's rise had been good for India, while 65 percent felt India should "join other countries to limit China's influence." Some 73 percent of Indians surveyed thought war with China was a "big threat" and 70 percent thought China's aim was "to dominate Asia."

At the elite level even India's trained diplomatic corps has struggled at times to portray the relationship in a positive light. In 2009, Indian Foreign Secretary Nirupama Rao was taxed to put a positive spin on the relationship, describing ties as "complex, but growing variegated in texture and substance."[31] A year earlier, Foreign Minister Pranab Mukherjee broke protocol and publicly described China as a "challenge and a priority." India, he said, would have to develop "more sophisticated ways of dealing with these new challenges posed by China."[32]

It is telling that, in private, the debate in India is not over whether China is viewed as a security threat, but whether it has surpassed Pakistan as India's *principal* security threat. Several recent studies by Western scholars[33] have concluded that "the vexatious relationship with Pakistan still dominates [Indian] military thinking."[34] And polling suggests Pakistan still narrowly edges out China as the top threat in the eyes of the Indian public.[35] However, this analyst found that among many in Delhi's national security establishment, China has comfortably surpassed Pakistan as the India's principal national security concern.

The matter was publicly addressed in May 2009 by then–Indian Air Force Chief Fali Homi Major when he stated "China is a totally different ballgame compared to Pakistan. . . . They are certainly the greater threat."[36] And Defense Minister A. K. Antony reportedly told the Indian armed forces that same year that "they should consider China rather than Pakistan the main threat."[37] Members of the India Special Focus Group at the headquarters of U.S. Pacific Command in Honolulu stressed that "India now sees China as its main adversary—its whole nuclear, trade, defense modernization strategy is now geared toward China. No one stays awake at night worried about Pakistan anymore."

This assessment is corroborated by India's evolving twenty-first-century defense posture: India is now the world's largest importer of arms, despite its unchallenged conventional military superiority over Pakistan. Nearly all the major initiatives to improve India's military infrastructure are taking place at India's border with China, not Pakistan. In 2009 India added two new mountain infantry divisions near the Line of Actual Control, followed by an announcement in 2013 that India would raise a 50,000-man offensive Strike Corps for the China border, the first of its kind.[38]

India's naval modernization, meanwhile, is geared toward power projection capabilities and the ability to meet a challenge from a large conventional force. In the strategic arms arena, India is developing longer-range ballistic missiles capable of reaching targets upward of 5,000 kilometers, despite having all of Pakistan covered by its short- and medium-range missile arsenal.

Threats Far and Wide

According to Ambassador Ranjit Gupta, a member of India's National Security Advisory Board until 2010, a wide variety of Chinese policies are responsible for triggering Indian threat perceptions. China, he said at a public speech at the Kerala International Center in November, 2011, was trying to

> weaken India by consciously undermining its internal and external security; to nurture and promote anti-Indian sentiment amongst India's neighbors in particular and other countries in general; to obstruct and undermine India's regional and global aspirations; [and] to pursue the establishment of an assertive strategic presence in the Indian Ocean.[39]

For India, Chinese security threats can be broadly grouped into two tiers. The first tier regards two longstanding core concerns over the unresolved territorial dispute and China's strategic partnership with Indian rival Pakistan. A second tier of concerns regard China's growing sphere of influence in continental South Asia and a parallel—and much newer—set of concerns about China's growing maritime presence in the Indian Ocean.

Moving Forward

In sum, the Sino-Indian rivalry continues to be fueled by a set of core issues in which there exists a fundamental conflict of interests—or what Chinese analysts are fond of calling the "Five Ts" of Sino-Indian relations: Territory, Tibet, Third Parties, Threat Perceptions, and Tawang.

The core friction points—the territorial dispute and the conflict of interests in Tibet—predate, and were permanently enshrined by, the 1962 border war. Since the turn of the century these "legacy disputes," which also include China's partnership with Indian-rival Pakistan, have been joined by others: India's strategic collaboration with the United States, a yawning trade imbalance, a growing conflict of interests in the maritime

Table 1.1.

Indian Threat Perceptions	Chinese Threat Perceptions
1st Tier	*1st Tier*
border dispute	Tibet
Sino-Pakistan relationship	Indo-U.S. relationship
2nd Tier	*2nd Tier*
China's "String of Pearls"	India's "Look East" policy
trade, cyber, water	Indian military modernization

arena, and friction at multilateral forums (UN Security Council, Asian Development Bank, Nuclear Suppliers Group) and the global commons (trade, cyber, water).

In the meantime, contemporary developments have reaggravated the legacy disputes. The transition of power to an elected prime minister in the Tibetan Government in Exile and a new Indian assertiveness on issues relating to Tibet come at a time when Chinese sensitivities on the plateau have been heightened by a series of riots in 2008 and a wave of over 100 self-immolations by Buddhist monks protesting Chinese rule beginning in 2009.

Developments along the disputed border have been even more problematic. The stalling of the border negotiations process in the mid-2000s, China's renewed claims to the strategically sensitive border town of Tawang, a military and infrastructure buildup along both sides of the Line of Actual Control, Chinese intrusions across the disputed border, the political use of visas to challenge Indian sovereignty in Kashmir and Arunachal Pradesh, and the visit of Indian officials to the disputed border territories have kept the border dispute at center stage in bilateral relations in recent years.

And just as the contemporary Sino-Indian relationship seemingly begins and ends with the border dispute, so too will this book. As one reviewer for this book noted, the border dispute is a particularly tricky subject to master because it is so often drenched in a reservoir of arcane and misleading facts of a historical variety. The following chapter attempts to cut through this dense maze to provide a factual foundation to examine the role of the border dispute in contemporary Sino-Indian relations. Without relitigating the 1962 border war, we will use the dispute as a prism through which to view the general evolution of bilateral relations from the 1940s to the turn of the century.

The third chapter, "Return to Rivalry," continues in a similar vein, examining how a series of advancements in bilateral relations from 2000 to 2005 were ultimately undermined by a series of disputes from 2006 to

2013. The final chapter on the border dispute, "The Elusive Settlement," examines why a settlement to the world's largest ongoing border dispute has eluded the two sides for over a half century, and why the window to reaching a settlement may be closing.

Following that, the book will proceed to more conventional examinations of specific issues, including: Tawang, Tibet, the Dalai Lama succession question, the role of the United States and Pakistan in Sino-Indian relations, China's Indian Ocean policy, India's Necklace of Diamonds, India's Look East policy, and trade and the global commons.

NOTES

1. Hu Jintao, "Working Together to Expand Cooperation and Create a Bright Future," *Embassy of the People's Republic of China in India*, November 22, 2006 (Accessed 10 April 2013): http://in.china-embassy.org/eng/embassy_news/2006en/t282088.htm.

2. John Lancaster, "India, China Hoping to 'Reshape the World Order' Together," *Washington Post*, April 12, 2005 (Accessed July 24, 2013): http://www.washingtonpost.com/wp-dyn/articles/A43053-2005Apr11.html.

3. S. Jaishankar, Indian Ambassador to China. Author interview. Beijing, April 2013.

4. "China, India have great wisdom to handle sensitive issues," *People's Daily Online*, May 10, 2013 (Accessed June 12, 2013): http://english.peopledaily.com.cn/90883/8239797.html.

5. "Border Conflict Stirs Old Resentments Over 'Incursions' in Indian Media," *Global Times*, May 13, 2013 (Accessed June 12, 2013): http://www.globaltimes.cn/content/781259.shtml.

6. "Will India Join Strategic Containment of China?" *People's Daily Online*, January 22, 2013 (Accessed April 18, 2013): http://english.peopledaily.com.cn/102774/8102712.html.

7. Dean Cheng, "China: No Sequestration for Chinese Military Spending," *The Heritage Network, The Foundry Blog*, March 6, 2013 (Accessed June 12, 2013): http://blog.heritage.org/2013/03/06/no-sequestration-for-chinese-military-spending/.

8. "What a Waste," *The Economist*, May 11, 2013 (Accessed July 8, 2013): http://www.economist.com/news/leaders/21577372-how-india-throwing-away-worlds-biggest-economic-opportunity-what-waste.

9. The *2012 Revision* of the *World Population Prospects* is the twenty-third round of global demographic estimates and projections undertaken by the Population Division of the United Nations Department of Economic and Social Affairs of the United Nations Secretariat: http://esa.un.org/wpp/.

10. Ye Hailin. Author interview. Washington, DC, June 27, 2013.

11. M. Taylor Fravel, "China Views India's Rise: Deepening Cooperation, Managing Differences," *Strategic Asia* 2011–2012: 97.

12. Saibal Dasgupta, "India, China Decide to Ramp Up Ties," *The Times of India*, May 11, 2013 (Accessed June 12, 2013): http://articles.timesofindia.indiatimes.com/2013-05-11/china/39185699_1_khurshid-border-dispute-recent-chinese-incursion.

13. B. Raman, "An Assessment: Brajesh Mishra (1928–2012)," *OutlookIndia.com*, September 29, 2012: http://www.outlookindia.com/article.aspx?282419.

14. Li Li, *Security Perception and China-India Relations* (New Delhi: KW Publishers, 2009), 85.

15. "India Ready to Work for a Fair and Reasonable Solution to Border Dispute with China," *Rediff on the Net*, 1997 (Accessed April 14, 2013): http://www.rediff.com/news/1996/2811chin.htm.

16. Zhou Ganchen. Author interview. Washington, DC, May 16, 2012.

17. "India's Gandhi Calls for Dialogue with China," *Reuters*, October 27, 2007 (Accessed April 10, 2013): http://www.reuters.com/article/2007/10/27/us-china-india-gandhi-idUSPEK13281820071027.

18. Simon Shen, "Exploring the Neglected Constraints on Chindia: Analysing the Online Chinese Perception of India and Its Interaction with China's Indian Policy," *The China Quarterly*,Vol. 207, September 2011: 542.

19. Simon Shen, "Exploring the Neglected Constraints on Chindia: Analysing the Online Chinese Perception of India and Its Interaction with China's Indian Policy," *The China Quarterly*, Vol. 207, September 2011: 548.

20. Simon Shen, "Exploring the Neglected Constraints on Chindia: Analysing the Online Chinese Perception of India and Its Interaction with China's Indian Policy," *The China Quarterly*, Vol. 207, September 2011: 547.

21. "Growing Concerns in China about Inequality, Corruption," *Pew Research Global Attitudes Project*, October 16, 2012 (Accessed April 10, 2013): http://www.pewglobal.org/files/2012/10/Pew-Global-Attitudes-China-Report-FINAL-October-10-20122.pdf.

22. "India Being Swept Up by Missile Delusion," *Global Times* April 19, 2012 (Accessed April 10, 2013): http://www.globaltimes.cn/NEWS/tabid/99/ID/705627/India-being-swept-up-by-missile-delusion.aspx.

23. Vikas Bajaj, "India Measures Itself against a China That Doesn't Notice," *New York Times*, August 31, 2011 (Accessed April 13, 2013): http://www.nytimes.com/2011/09/01/business/global/india-looks-to-china-as-an-economic-model.html?_r=2&.

24. Andrew Small. Author interview. Washington, DC, March 14, 2012.

25. Dr. Zhao Ganchen. Author interview. Washington, DC, May 16, 2012.

26. Mohan Malik, "India-China Competition Revealed in Ongoing Border Disputes," *Power and Interest News Report*, October 9, 2007 (Accessed April 10, 2013): http://www.gees.org/documentos/Documen-02608.pdf.

27. M. Taylor Fravel, "China Views India's Rise: Deepening Cooperation, Managing Differences," *Strategic Asia* 2011–12, September 2011: 74.

28. Naveen Kapoor, "PM Manmohan Singh Says India Greatly Values Friendship with China," *Yahoo News*, November 19, 2012 (Accessed April 10, 2013): http://in.news.yahoo.com/pm-manmohan-singh-says-india-greatly-values-friendship-070223951.html.

29. "America's Image Remains Strong: Indians See Threat from Pakistan, Extremist Groups," *Pew Research Global Attitudes Project,* October 20, 2012 (Accessed April 10, 2013): http://www.pewglobal.org/2010/10/20/indians-see-threat -from-pakistan-extremist-groups/.

30. The Lowy Institute New India Poll 2013, May 20, 2013: http://www.lowy institute.org/publications/india-poll-2013.

31. "'Bilateral Relations with the U.S. Truly Multi-Faceted,'" *Deccan Herald,* April 13, 2013: http://www.deccanherald.com/content/36818/bilateral-relations -us-truly-multi.html.

32. Indrani Bagchi, "Finally, Pranab Calls China a Challenge," *Times of India,* November 5, 2008 (Accesed April 10, 2013): http://articles.timesofindia.india times.com/2008-11-05/india/27900493_1_india-and-china-india-china-chinese -president-hu-jintao.

33. Jonathan Holslag, *China and India: Prospects for Peace* (New York: Columbia University Press, 2010), 139.

34. "Know Your Own Strength," *Economist,* March 20, 2013 (April 10, 2013): http://www.economist.com/news/briefing/21574458-india-poised-become -one-four-largest-military-powers-world-end?zid=306&ah=1b164dbd43b0cb27ba 0d4c3b12a5e227.

35. Lowy Institute for International Policy India Poll 2013, May 20, 2013 (Accessed June 12, 2013) http://www.lowyinstitute.org/publications/india -poll-2013.

36. Rahul Singh, "China Now Bigger Threat than Pakistan, Says IAF chief," *Hindustan Times* May 23, 2009: 10 (Accessed April 2013): http://www.hindustan times.com/News-Feed/India/China-now-bigger-threat-than-Pakistan-says-IAF -chief/Article1-413933.aspx.

37. "Know Your Own Strength," *Economist,* March 20, 2013 (Accessed April 10, 2013): http://www.economist.com/news/briefing/21574458-india-poised -become-one-four-largest-military-powers-world-end?zid=306&ah=1b164dbd43b0 cb27ba0d4c3b12a5e227.

38. There were already three Strike Corps positioned at the Indo-Pakistan border but this will be the first at the Sino-Indian border.

39. Public Lecture by Ambassador Ranjit Gupta. At Thiruvananthapuram TMCA Hall hosted by Kerala International Center, November 9, 2011.

II
TERRITORY

Chapter 2

Defining the Dispute

The Republic of India and the People's Republic of China emerged from the ashes of World War II determined to reclaim their roles atop the Asian hierarchy after extended periods of foreign domination.

Communist China's founding father, Mao Zedong, was committed to restoring the Middle Kingdom to its previous greatness and atoning for the preceding "century of humiliation," when a weakened China had become a playground for foreign powers. China was to be the vanguard of a communist revolution he believed would soon sweep Asia, and within a year of assuming power, his People's Liberation Army (PLA) had invaded Tibet and was battling American forces on the Korean peninsula.

Modern India, in contrast, joined the world traumatized by the creation of Pakistan via Partition,[1] still widely regarded as one of the largest forced migrations in recorded history. When the smoke cleared from the first Indo-Pakistan War of 1948, India emerged a fragile nation struggling to forge a national identity amongst a myriad of ethnic, linguistic, religious, and social divisions. Faced with this ambitious democratic experiment, Delhi was determined to remain above the political and ideological conflicts of the Cold War.

Despite these seemingly incompatible national narratives, the leadership of both countries committed themselves, at least initially, to pursuing an amicable relationship. India was the first non-socialist country to establish diplomatic relations with the PRC in April 1950, and later that year Delhi advocated for China's membership in the United Nations. Indian Prime Minister Jawaharlal Nehru received a grand reception on a trip to Beijing four years later, marking the climax of a short-lived honeymoon now epitomized by a popular phrase of the time, "Hindi Chini Bhai Bhai" ("China and India are brothers").

This early bout of comity was all the more remarkable because aside from their philosophical differences, in 1950 China invaded Tibet (which had declared independence from China in 1911), occupying the buffer state that separated the Chinese and Indian heartlands for millennia. No less important, the two states had inherited a comparatively large territorial dispute from their predecessors along their undemarcated Himalayan border.

For the time and the region, the absence of a defined border was not particularly uncommon, as buffer states and zones of influence long substituted for the fixed borders of the Westphalian nation-state. The unforgiving Tibetan plateau had performed admirably as a natural boundary between the Chinese and Indian civilizations for millennia, depriving the two sides of the urgency to demarcate a border.

The origins of the territorial dispute trace back to the late nineteenth century, when the British colonialists that ruled India made several attempts to fix new borders in the undefined frontier between India and Tibet. The Tibetan plateau had drifted in and out of the sovereign orbit of various Chinese empires over the preceding seven centuries, and in the late 1800s Britain saw an opportunity to extend India's borders northward in the form of a weakened Qing Dynasty in Peking.

There were two separate "sectors" along the Indo-Tibetan frontier where the British sought to fix new boundaries, but in both cases their efforts went unrewarded. In the "Western Sector," along Kashmir's border with Tibet and Xinjiang, British proposals to set a border near the Karakoram mountain range went unanswered, and no formal agreement was ever reached with China or Tibet, leaving the border undefined through Indian independence. In the "Eastern Sector," where India's greater northeast meets the underbelly of Tibet, the British coaxed an agreement on a new border out of Tibetan officials at a conference in Simla in 1914, but this new "McMahon Line" was quickly repudiated by China and in practice never enforced by Tibet or the British Raj.

Upon independence India inherited these unsettled borders and, despite its relative weakness, assumed the most expansive of the British Raj's claims in both sectors. And China, at least initially in the Eastern Sector, appeared willing to accommodate India's claims. The "Pansheel Agreement" signed during Nehru's visit to Beijing in 1954 outlined "Five Principles of Peaceful Coexistence" and contained what Delhi believed to be an equitable quid pro quo: India endorsed Chinese sovereignty over Tibet, which the PLA had invaded four years earlier, in return for Chinese assurances that the border would be settled on terms favorable to India. The key difference was that India's concession was explicitly written into

Table 2.1. Timeline of Major Events, 1947–1962

1947	Indian independence (August 15, 1947)
1947–1948	First Indo-Pakistan War (October 22, 1947–December 31, 1948)
1949	Birth of Communist China (October 1, 1949)
1950	Chinese invasion of Tibet (October 7, 1950)
1951	Seventeen-point agreement between China and Tibetan representatives on Tibetan autonomy (May 23, 1951)
1954	Panscheel Agreement, Nehru trip to China (April 19, 1954)
1956	Tibetan/Khampa resistance begins in Kham province (June 1956)
1957	China announces completion of road through disputed Aksai Chin (September 2, 1957)
1958	Indian patrol sent to investigate road in Aksai Chin captured and released (September 1958)
1959	Tibetan uprising in Lhasa (March 10, 1959)
1959	Dalai Lama flight to India (March 17–March 31, 1959)
1959	First deadly clashes at the Sino-Indian border (August 1959)
1961	India formally adopts "forward policy" of border patrolling (November 2, 1961)
1962	Sino-Indian Border War (October 20–November 21, 1962)

the text of the Panscheel Agreement, while the Chinese commitment on the border was *implicit* in a series of verbal and written exchanges between Nehru and Chinese Premier Zhou Enlai.

When Nehru broached the subject of the McMahon Line with Zhou two years after the Panscheel Agreement, the Chinese premier said the line was "still undecided and unfair to us," but admitted it had become an "accomplished fact." "We should accept it . . . there is no better way than to recognize this Line."[2] Beijing was willing to treat the border dispute with magnanimity, it seemed, so long as its position in Tibet was secure.

But Tibetans had a voice in this drama too. In 1956 the martial class of Tibet, the Khampas, began a campaign of armed resistance against Chinese rule that snowballed into a wider uprising over the ensuing three years. As tensions on the plateau surged, Beijing grew outraged by the moral support being offered to the Tibetan resistance by the Indian media (which they believed acted as an extension of the Indian government) and by the presence of Tibetan resistance camps inside India's borders, many of which appeared to be getting support from the U.S. Central Intelligence Agency.[3]

Beijing began to walk back its conciliatory language on the McMahon Line and the gentlemen's agreement on the border was put in doubt. In 1957 India learned that China had constructed a road through a part of the Western Sector claimed by India. The following year an Indian patrol sent to investigate the road was captured by Chinese forces and subsequently released.

The two sides maintained a veneer of diplomatic comity through this turbulent period but events in the spring of 1959 would eventually push the two sides toward armed conflict. By then the revolution in Tibet had expanded both geographically and ethnically from a localized Khampa rebellion to a much wider uprising that reached the Tibetan capital of Lhasa. In March of that year, the supreme spiritual leader of Buddhism, the Dalai Lama, fled Lhasa amid an escalating bout of violence between protesters and government security forces. Beijing was incensed when the Buddhist leader emerged in India weeks later to great fanfare and suspected India of orchestrating the Dalai Lama's flight into exile.

That same year, under orders from Delhi, India's border guards grew more aggressive in their patrolling along the unmarked border, leading to the adoption of a provocative "forward policy" in 1961. China ordered the PLA to resist advances by Indian border patrols as it continued to pursue a diplomatic resolution to the dispute. Deadly clashes between armed border patrols first erupted in 1959 and grew in frequency and lethality until the dangerous game of brinksmanship spilled into open conflict in the fall of 1962.

It took the PLA only thirty-two days after the launch of its surprise invasion on October 20, 1962, to deal India an embarrassing defeat and secure control over the disputed territory in the Western Sector, where China had constructed a strategically vital highway linking Tibet to Xinjiang. In the Eastern Sector, China advanced some 160 kilometers into Indian territory before Beijing called a unilateral ceasefire on November 21 and withdrew its forces twenty kilometers *behind* the prewar line of control, leaving India all the territory it was claiming in the Eastern Sector south of the McMahon Line.[4] The status quo established by the war—China in possession of the disputed Western Sector and India in possession of the disputed Eastern Sector—has endured for over fifty years.

DEFINING THE DISPUTE

The China-India border dispute is better described as an amalgamation of separate territorial disputes occupying multiple, noncontiguous sections of territory on both sides of the Line of Actual Control.

Even the length of the border is disputed: media reports and authoritative figures in India and the West frequently peg the length of the Sino-Indian border at 4,057 kilometers[5] but the official estimate used by the Indian government is 3,488 kilometers, which is roughly equivalent to the estimate in the CIA World Factbook, 3,380 kilometers.[6]

In contrast, the Chinese media and analysts[7] refer to a 2,000 kilometer Sino-Indian border. Chinese scholar Hu Shisheng explained to *The Hindu*[8]

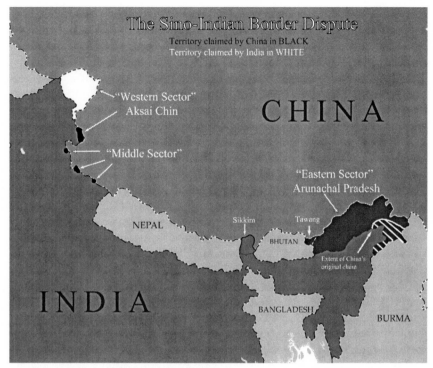

Map 2.1. The Sino-Indian Border Dispute
Source: American Foreign Policy Council

in 2010 that India's figures improperly include the boundary of Indian-administered Kashmir (which China recognizes as disputed) and add the length of the curved border of Aksai Chin, which is claimed by India but controlled by China.[9]

Western Sector

The Western Sector refers to a dispute over a thumb-shaped swath of territory straddling the Indian state of Kashmir and the western edge of the Tibetan plateau. The territory is commonly referred to as Aksai Chin ("desert of white stones") though the sector hosts two separate disputes. India claims 38,000 square kilometers of icy desert controlled by China since the 1962 war, while China claims a much smaller, roughly 1,500 square kilometer, piece of territory controlled by India to the south surrounding Demchock.

Pangong Lake, the largest brackish water body in Asia, stretching 135 kilometers east to west, crosses the Line of Actual Control in Aksai Chin, and is controlled in part by both India (western one-third) and China (eastern two-thirds). A section of the lake approximately twenty kilometers east of the Line of Actual Control is controlled by China but claimed by India; the rest is not disputed. A ten-kilometer stretch of the much smaller Spanggur Lake fifteen kilometers to the south is also disputed.

Both sides have offered evidence of historic trading records, tax collection receipts, and survey missions into the obscure territory to support their claims to the desert of white stones, but history offers only limited and ultimately inconclusive evidence on the validity of each side's claim.

A 1683 treaty between the rulers of Tibet and Ladakh, at the time quasi-independent kingdoms, fixed the border at "the Lhari stream at Demchok" but was silent on the border north of Demchok, the area in dispute today.[10] A letter of agreement and a treaty between representatives of Kashmir, the Dalai Lama, and China in 1842 committed the parties to not "interfere at all with the boundaries of Ladakh and its surroundings as fixed from ancient times."[11] An 1852 treaty between Ladakh and Tibet reads: "The boundary between Ladakh and Tibet remains the same as before."[12]

The contemporary dispute essentially derives from a disagreement over whether the Ladakh-Tibet boundary belongs at the crest of the Karakoram mountain range, as China claims (and where the Line of Actual Control runs today), or at the crest of the Kun Lun range some 200 kilometers to the north and east, as India claims.

It was a British surveyor, W. H. Johnson, who initially proposed the more expansive claim at the Kun Lun range. The "Johnson Line" produced by his oft-criticized 1865 survey of the region would have given all of Aksai Chin to Kashmir. A competing proposal in 1899 by Sir Claude MacDonald, a former British Minister to China, was far less expansive. The "MacDonald Line" traced the border at the crest line of the Karakoram mountain range, roughly conforming to China's claim today.

British officials vacillated between the two options and when they finally made a formal proposal to China, they deferred to the less-expansive MacDonald Line, which would have left all of Aksai Chin to China. Yet Beijing never formally responded and when India inherited the unsettled boundary from the Raj, Delhi assumed a modified version of the Johnson Line.

China gained control over Aksai Chin during the 1962 border war and has administered the region as part of the Hotan prefecture of the Xinjiang Autonomous Region.[13]

Shaksgam Valley

Technically not a part of the Sino-Indian border dispute, the 5,180 square kilometer Shaksgam Valley was ceded to China by Pakistan in

Map 2.2.   The Shaksgam Valley
Source: Wikimedia Commons

March 1963 after four years of closed-door negotiations. As part of the deal, China ceded to Pakistan some 1,942 square kilometers in the Oprang Valley and dropped its claims to an additional 1,554 square kilometers in Kashmir. [14] India, which still claims the Shaksgam Valley, insists that Pakistan lacked the authority to transfer the disputed territory to China. Beijing maintains that the 1963 agreement remains subject to change pending any final agreement between India and Pakistan over Kashmir.

Middle Sector

The Middle Sector is the least volatile of the three main "sectors" with the smallest amount of territory under dispute. In 1959 a Chinese note to India stated, "the boundary line in the middle sector is relatively close to the delineation of the Chinese maps, but still a number of areas which have always belonged to China are included in India." [15] China claims some 2,100 square kilometers of territory controlled by India including several noncontiguous pockets of territory in the Indian states of Himachal Pradesh (303 square kilometers total) and Uttarakhand (1,818 square kilometers total). [16] The Middle Sector is viewed by both sides as the sector most ripe for compromise, and remains the only sector where China and India have exchanged maps, in 2001, outlining their claims.

Sikkim

Technically a "protectorate" under the British Raj, the tiny Buddhist enclave of Sikkim wedged between India and Tibet voted against joining the Indian Union when the British left the subcontinent in 1947. A 1950 Indo-Sikkim treaty restored the kingdom to a protectorate under the

Republic of India and in 1975 Sikkim's parliament passed a proposal to join the Indian Federation. At the time China protested vigorously, accusing Delhi of political interference and stage-managing the initiative, and refusing to recognize India's "illegal annexation of Sikkim."[17]

Sikkim is not one of the major "sectors" of the border dispute, though Beijing does claim a tiny, one-kilometer sliver in the north of the state commonly referred to as the "Finger Area." Sikkim was also the site of the last major clash at the border after the 1962 war. Several hundred casualties resulted from six days of border skirmishes and artillery exchanges at Nathu La in September 1967.

In 2003 the Sikkim issue was ostensibly resolved when China seemed to drop its challenge to Indian sovereignty over the territory by agreeing to reopen a historic trading post at the Sikkim-China border at Nathu La that had been closed since the 1962 war. The move was received by Delhi as an implicit Chinese recognition of Indian sovereignty; however, as the next chapter will demonstrate, there is more ambiguity to China's position on Sikkim than is commonly accepted.

Eastern Sector

The Eastern Sector constitutes the most volatile and strategically significant of the territorial disputes. The irony of the largest ongoing border dispute in the world is that a majority of the territory under dispute is barren, mountainous terrain to which both capitals have little historical attachment.

Not so in parts of the Eastern Sector, which is comparatively rich in terms of population, natural resources, hydropower, and infrastructure. Alone the town of Tawang—positioned along the main strategic corridor into India's northeast from Tibet and host to an important Buddhist monastery—carries more political, strategic, and religious value than is found in any of the other disputed sectors.

The origins of the dispute in the Eastern Sector, crystallized in the 1914 Simla Accord, are covered in greater detail in the dedicated Tawang chapter. For now suffice it to say that India claims its northeastern border with Tibet lies at the crestline of the Himalayas (roughly approximate to today's Line of Actual Control), while China perceives the border to be 100–200 kilometers south, in the Himalayan foothills.

In nearly all contemporary discussions of the Eastern Sector, China is said to claim 90,000 square kilometers roughly approximate to the Indian state of Arunachal Pradesh (AP). That figure is widely perceived as authoritative and has been used by both Indian[18] and Chinese[19] officials. However this analyst found ample reason to doubt the integrity of this figure.

At one time China's claim in the Eastern Sector appeared to be straight-forward. *The Sino-Indian Boundary Question,* published by Beijing in 1962, included detailed maps outlining China's perception of the Sino-Indian border (as seen below).

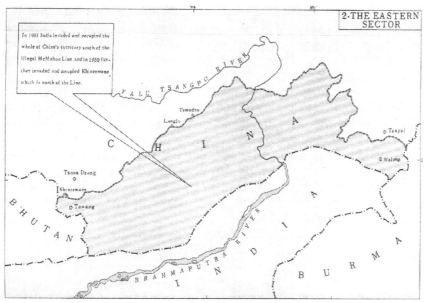

Map 2.3.   China's Claim in Arunachal Pradesh
Source: "The Sino-Indian Boundary Question" Foreign Langauage Press, Peking, 1963 (Official government publication).

Though not readily apparent in the above map, the first notable feature about China's claim line is that it *does not* include the entire state of Arunachal Pradesh (as better seen in map 2.1). China's claimed border stops at the eastern end of the state, just north of the Indian town of Changlang, where the state bends sharply to the south and west.

The other notable feature of China's claim line is that it includes a narrow sliver of the Indian state of Assam north of the Brahmaputra River. This tract of claimed land in Assam appears to be roughly 180 kilometers long and fifteen kilometers wide at its widest point.[20]

If this is an accurate representation of China's claim (it is still used today on various maps issued by the Chinese government, and by Western media outlets,[21] the Chinese version of Google Maps,[22] U.S. think tanks,[23] and several Indian media outlets[24]) it raises doubts that China could possibly be claiming 90,000 square kilometers of Indian territory. The total area of Arunachal Pradesh is only 84,000 square kilometers. If China is only claiming 80 to 85 percent of the state and a 1,500 square kilometer sliver of Assam, its claim in India's northeast appears to be closer to 70,000 square kilometers.

However, our understanding of China's claim was further put into doubt by China's ambassador to India, Sun Yuxi, in 2006. Speaking to the Indian media, he said: "In our position the *whole of the state of Arunachal Pradesh is Chinese territory*. And Tawang is only one of the places in it. We are claiming all of that. That is our position [emphasis added]."[25] While a substantial body of evidence suggests the ambassador's remarks were *not* cleared with Beijing beforehand, Chinese officials never publicly repudiated his statement.

So is China claiming all of Arunachal Pradesh, as the ambassador claimed, or only 80 to 85 percent of the state, as most Chinese maps claim? And how does one arrive at the 90,000 square kilometer figure if AP is, in total, only 84,000 square kilometers?

We simply don't know because China has refused to exchange maps with India outlining its specific claims. "China does not accept AP as a legitimate establishment, it is therefore unnecessary for China to clarify which part of AP is claimed and which part is not by China. This is precisely the area the two sides need to discuss," Dr. Zhao Ganchen of the Shanghai Institute for International Studies explained to this author in a written response.[26] Indian analyst Mohan Guruswamy says China has "never been quite explicit on how much of Arunachal they seek," noting that he has seen official maps in Lhasa portraying only the narrow Tawang tract twenty kilometers south of the border as Chinese territory and others displaying all of Arunachal Pradesh as Chinese territory.[27]

COMING TO TERMS

Fifteen years of open hostility followed the 1962 China-India border war. Beijing and Delhi found themselves locked in a competition for influence among the Non-Aligned nations of the world and supporting competing insurgent and separatist movements. In 1969, China set up a Coordination Bureau with Pakistan to coordinate and oversee "the supply of arms, training, and funding to Indian northeastern insurgencies."[28] And through the 1960s India offered material support to the Tibetan resistance, air-dropping arms and supplies to fighters inside Tibet and coordinating activities with the CIA as Tibetans continued their low-intensity struggle against Chinese rule.[29]

These Machiavellian strategies were abandoned in the 1970s, when Chinese diplomatic overtures to India eventually opened the door for the restoration of diplomatic ties in 1976. India's only precondition to renewed diplomatic engagement was that the two sides immediately turn their attention to resolving the border dispute.

In the intervening three and half decades the Sino-Indian relationship has been largely defined by the "longest continuing frontier talks between any two countries since the end of the Second World War."[30] Formally initiated in 1981, the process has spanned eight rounds of initial border talks, a further fourteen meetings of the Joint Working Group (JWG), and sixteen rounds of Special Representatives meetings as of July 2013.

Table 2.2.   China-India Border Negotiations

Event	Date
1st Round of Border Talks	December 10–14, 1981
2nd Round of Border Talks	May 2–20, 1982
3rd Round of Border Talks	January 28–Februaray 2, 1983
4th Round of Border Talks	October 25–30, 1983
5th Round of Border Talks	October 17–22, 1984
6th Round of Border Talks	November 4–10, 1985
7th Round of Border Talks	July 21–23, 1986
8th Round of Border Talks	November 16–18, 1987
Rajiv Gandhi State Visit to Beijing	December 23, 1988
Establishment of the Joint Working Group (JWG)	
1st Round of JWG	June 30–July 4, 1989
2nd Round of JWG	August 30–31, 1990
Established periodic meetings between military commanders	
3rd Round of JWG	May 13, 1991
4th Round of JWG	February 20–21, 1992
5th Round of JWG	October 28–29, 1992
Agreement on the Maintenance of Peace and Tranquility along the Line of Actual Control	September 7, 1993
6th Round of JWG	June. 25–26, 1993
1st Meeting of the Experts Group	February 2–4, 1994
2nd Meeting of the Experts Group	April 21–22, 1994
7th Round of JWG	July 6–7, 1994
3rd Meeting of the Experts Group	March 2–4, 1995
8th Round of JWG	August18–19, 1995
Agreement to dismantle some military posts	
9th Round of JWG	October 1996
Agreement on Confidence-Building Measures in the Military Field along the Line of Actual Control	November 29, 1996
10th Round of the JWG	August 4–5, 1997
11th Round of the JWG	April 27–28, 1999
12th Round of the JWG	April 2001

(continued)

Table 2.2.

Event	Date
13th Round of the JWG	July 31, 2001
14th Round of the JWG	November 21, 2002
Declaration on Principles for Relations and Comprehensive Cooperation (Appointment of Special Representatives)	June 23, 2003
1st Special Representative Meeting	October 26, 2003
2nd Special Representatives Meeting	January 12–13, 2004
3rd Special Representatives Meeting	July 26, 2004
4th Special Representatives Meeting	November 18–19, 2004
5th Special Representatives Meeting	March 10–12, 2005
15th Round of the JWG	March 30–31, 2005
Protocol on Modalities for the Implementation of Confidence Measures in the Military Field	April 11, 2005
6th Special Representatives Meeting	September 26–28, 2005
7th Special Representatives Meeting	March 11–13, 2006
8th Special Representatives Meeting	June 25–27, 2006
9th Special Representatives Meeting	January 17–19, 2007
10th Special Representatives Meeting	April 24–27, 2007
11th Special Representatives Meeting	September 24–26, 2007
12th Special Representatives Meeting	September 18–19, 2008
13th Special Representatives Meeting	August 7–8, 2009
14th Special Representatives Meeting	November 29–30, 2010
15th Special Representatives Meeting	January 16–17, 2012
Agreement on the Establishment of a Working Mechanism for Consultation and Coordination	
1st Meeting of the Working Mechanism	March 5–6, 2012
2nd Meeting of the Working Mechanism	November 29–30, 2012
16th Special Representatives Meeting	June 28–29, 2013
Border Defense and Cooperation Agreement	October 23, 2013

Measuring the success of this elaborate process depends very much on the criteria used. The two sides can boast of at least one major achievement: thanks to a complex set of confidence-building measures and border management initiatives there has not been a major clash at the border since the 1967 skirmish at Nathu La.

The second achievement of the border talks was to break the postwar diplomatic ice between China and India, allowing them in the 1980s to reach common ground on an important principle: the broader development of the bilateral relationship would no longer be held hostage to the unresolved territorial dispute. This "delinking" marked a significant concession from India, which had since the 1960s insisted that a border settlement was an absolute precondition to the normalization of relations.

The concession was prompted in part by a realist appraisal of the changing geopolitical landscape. By the late 1980s India's superpower patron, the Soviet Union, was in decline. Chinese scholar Li Li notes that in a 1986 visit to India, Soviet Premier Mikhail Gorbachev "conveyed a very clear message to [Indian Prime Minister] Rajiv Gandhi . . . that India should not expect as before the Soviet Union to extend its unqualified and categorical support in any possible conflict between China and India."[31] A year later, when an arms buildup in the Eastern Sector nearly sparked a shooting war between China and India, the Soviet Union "withdrew an Armored Division from Mongolia at the height of the Sumdorong Chu confrontation. The Chinese," says Indian analyst R. S. Kalha, "felt reassured that Soviet support for India would not be forthcoming."[32]

Just one year after the Sumdorong Chu incident, Ravij Gandhi made a historic visit to China, and a new border resolution mechanism was agreed in the form a Joint Working Group which met fourteen times between 1988 and 2003. The Joint Working Group was criticized as a "largely bureaucratic exercise," but it established the foundation for a pair of landmark border agreements signed in 1993 and 1996.[33]

Under the September 7, 1993, "Agreement on the Maintenance of Peace along the Line of Actual Control in the India-China Border,"[34] both sides agreed the boundary question would be resolved through "peaceful and friendly negotiations," and they pledged to never use force against one another. The agreement, described by scholar Tan Chung as the "first Magna Carta" of Sino-Indian confidence-building measures at the border, committed both sides to "strictly respect and observe the Line of Actual Control."

The deal quickly produced tangible results: after the eighth round of the Joint Working Group in 1995, troops from both sides disengaged from several provocatively positioned border posts near the Walong area of Arunachal Pradesh, where the two sides nearly went to war in 1987.

The pact was followed three years later by the November 29, 1996, agreement on "Confidence-Building Measures along the Line of Actual Control in the India-China Border Areas."[35] The text of the agreement offered specific provisions for reducing or limiting military forces along the border: Large-scale exercises at the border involving more than one division were to be avoided, with prior notification given for any exercises involving more than one brigade.

For the first time since the 1962 border war, the two sides had an elaborate and durable framework for managing their territorial dispute. Entering the twenty-first century, two important questions confronted China and India faced. First, would the agreements of 1993 and 1996 offer them the political space to advance their stagnant diplomatic and economic relationship? Second, could the dual agreements serve as a springboard to reach a final settlement to the border dispute?

NOTES

1. Partition refers to the partition of India based on religious demographics and the formation of the state of Pakistan (then East and West Pakistan), resulting in the deaths of as many as one million people and the displacement of as many as twelve million.

2. Zorawar Singh, *Himalayan Stalemate: Understanding the India-China Dispute* (London: Straight Forward Publishers, 2012), 13.

3. See "The CIA's Secret War in Tibet" by Kenneth Conboy and James Morrison (University Press of Kansas, 2002).

4. Scholars still debate the reasons behind China's decision to call a ceasefire and unilaterally withdraw behind the McMahon Line. The most compelling argument, to this author, is the realization of the logistical difficulties China would have faced in trying to sustain a campaign across the Himalayas after the onset of winter, in which most of the mountain passes close for three to four months.

5. This writer assumes this number is derived from those who include the border of Pakistan-occupied Kashmir with Tibet.

6. "The World Factbook: India," *Central Intelligence Agency*, January 29, 2013 (Accessed February 6, 2013): https://www.cia.gov/library/publications/the -world-factbook/geos/in.html.

7. "China, India Hold Border Talks, Pledge to Safeguard Peace," *English .news.cn.*,March 3, 2012 (Accessed February 6, 2013): http://news.xinhuanet.com/english/china/2012-03/06/c_131450604.htm.

8. Ananth Krishnan, "Officials Dismiss China's Kashmir Border Claims," *The Hindu*, December 20, 2010 (Accessed February 6, 2013): http://www.thehindu .com/news/national/article963655.ece.

9. Claims of a 2,000 kilometers China-India border also appear in Western and Indian press, though some are undoubtedly honest errors, as the traditional 3,400 kilometer estimate translates to roughly 2,000 *miles*.

10. Giriraj Shah, *Tibet: Himalayan Region: Religion, Society, and Politics* (Delhi: Kalpaz Publications, 2003), 281.

11. W. D. Shakabpa, *Tibet: A Political History* (New Haven: Yale University Press, 1967), 327–28.

12. Byron Tzou, *China and International Law: The Boundary Disputes* (New York: Praeger Publishers, 1990), 65.

13. "Aksai Chin," *Princeton.edu*, February 6, 2013: http://www.princeton .edu/~achaney/tmve/wiki100k/docs/Aksai_Chin.html.

14. Ananth Krishnan, "Month after Border Talks, Chinese Paper Says Aksai Chin is a Closed Chapter," *The Hindu*, February 16, 2012 (Accessed February 6, 2013): http://www.thehindu.com/todays-paper/tp-international/article2898189.ece.

15. John B. Allcock, *Border and Territorial Disputes*, 3rd Ed. (Harlow: Longman Current Affairs, 1992).

16. "Round Table Discussion on Indo-China Border Impasse," *Observer Research Foundation*, August 6, 2007 (Accessed February 6, 2013): http://www. observerindia.com/cms/sites/orfonline/modules/report/ReportDetail .html?cmaid=9806&mmacmaid=9807.

17. Li Li, *Security Perception and China-India Relations* (New Delhi: KW Publishers, 2009), 163.

18. Kuna, "China Illegally Claiming 90,000 km of Our Territory—India," TwoCircles.net, February 28, 2008: http://twocircles.net/node/50808.

19. "India Should Not 'Stir Up' Border Trouble, Says PLA General Ahead of Antony Visit," *The Hindu*, July 4, 2013: http://www.thehindu.com/news/international/world/india-should-not-stir-up-border-trouble-says-pla-general-ahead-of-antony-visit/article4881266.ece?mstac=0.

20. Author estimation using Google Maps.

21. "Indian, Pakistani, and Chinese Border Disputes: Fantasy Frontiers," *Economist Online*, February 8, 2012 (Accessed February 6, 2013): http://www.economist.com/blogs/dailychart/2011/05/indian_pakistani_and_chinese_border_disputes.

22. Stefan Geens, "Google Maps' Arunachal Pradesh Place Names Turn Chinese, Google Admits Error," *Ogle Earth*, August 9, 2009 (Accessed February 6, 2013): http://ogleearth.com/2009/08/google-maps-arunachal-pradesh-place-names-turn-chinese-google-admits-error/.

23. Lisa Curtis and Dean Cheng, "The China Challenge: A Strategic Vision for U.S.-India Relations," *Heritage Foundation*, July 18, 2012 (Accessed February 6, 2013): http://www.heritage.org/research/reports/2011/07/the-china-challenge-a-strategic-vision-for-us-india-relations.

24. "Now India, China in Map Row over Arunachal Pradesh, Aksai Chin," *India Today*, November 6, 2012 (Accessed February 6, 2013): http://indiatoday.intoday.in/story/india-china-map-row-arunachal-pradesh/1/230544.html.

25. "Arunachal Pradesh Is Our Territory: Chinese Envoy," *Rediff*, November 14, 2006 (Accessed July 8, 2013): http://www.rediff.com/news/2006/nov/14china.htm.

26. Dr. Zhao Ganchen. Email correspondence. January 16, 2013.

27. Mohan Guruswamy. Email correspondence. December 5, 2012.

28. John W. Garver, *Protracted Contest: Sino-Indian Rivalry in the Twentieth Century* (Seattle: University of Washington Press, 2001), 93.

29. John W. Garver, *Protracted Contest: Sino-Indian Rivalry in the Twentieth Century* (Seattle: University of Washington Press, 2001), 62–3.

30. Francine Frankel and Harry Harding, *The India-China Relationship: What the United States Needs to Know* (Washington DC: Woodrow Wilson Center Press, 2004), 48.

31. Li Li, "Security Perception and China-India Relations," (KW Publishers New Delhi, 2009), 56.

32. R. S. Kalha, "The Chinese Message and What Should the Reply Be?" IDSA Comment, May 21, 2013: http://www.idsa.in/idsacomments/TheChineseMessageIndiareply_rskalha_210513.

33. Zorawar Singh, *Himalayan Stalemate: Understanding the India-China Dispute* (London: Straight Forward Publishers, 2012), 27.

34. "Confidence-Building Measures along the Line of Actual Control in the India-China Border Areas," *The Stimson Center*, 2013 (Accessed February 6, 2013): http://www.stimson.org/research-pages/confidence-building-measures-along-the-line-of-actual-control-in-the-india-china-border-areas/.

35. "Confidence-Building Measures along the Line of Actual Control in the India-China Border Areas," *The Stimson Center*, 2013 (Accessed February 6, 2013): http://www.stimson.org/research-pages/confidence-building-measures-along-the-line-of-actual-control-in-the-india-china-border-areas/.

Chapter 3

Return to Rivalry

Buoyed by the dual border agreements of 1993 and 1996, China and India were poised to enter the twenty-first century on the best footing since the "Hindi Chini Bhai Bhai" days of the 1950s. The improvement in bilateral ties from the restoration of diplomatic relations in 1976 had not been linear. China's invasion of Indian ally Vietnam in 1979, a crisis and near-shooting war in the Eastern Sector in 1987 at Sumdorong Chu, and an Indian nuclear weapons test in 1998 all provided temporary setbacks to the relationship. But each step back was followed by two steps forward.

It was only two years after China's invasion of Vietnam that the two sides agreed to establish the first border talks, in 1981. Rajiv Gandhi's historic 1988 visit to Beijing took place just one year after the war drums started to beat in Sumdorong Chu. And India's 1998 nuclear test, for which India's prime minister and defense minister indirectly implicated China, preceded the most substantive period of engagement in contemporary Sino-Indian history.

The early 2000s were "characterized by frequent high-level visits by civilian and military leaders; increasing cooperation on bilateral, regional, and international issues . . . and economic cooperation in areas such as energy, agriculture, education, and technology."[1] Chinese Premier Zhu Rongji called on New Delhi in January 2002, and Indian Defense Minister George Fernandes reciprocated in early 2003, receiving more (and more favorable) press coverage in Beijing "than that for all visits [of Indian officials] in the previous years put together."[2]

An alphabets soup of new multilateral mechanisms offered the senior leadership of both countries frequent venues to interact, including RIC, BRICS, BASIC, SCO, The Developing Five, EAS, and ARF, to name a few. This engagement was further buoyed by the exponential expansion of bilateral trade: between 1998 and 2006 bilateral trade surged twenty-four-fold, from barely $1 billion to $24 billion.[3] "Cooperation is just like two pagodas, one hardware and one software. Combined, we can take the leadership position in the world," Chinese Premier Wen Jiabao announced on a trip to Delhi in 2005.[4]

In the more sensitive military-strategic arena, the early and mid-2000s saw China and India witness a litany of firsts: first Strategic Dialogue; first joint naval exercises; first Memorandum of Understanding (MOU) on defense exchanges; first Annual Defense Dialogue.

Table 3.1. Notable Military Exchanges 1996–2013

March 1996	Indian Chief of Naval Staff Admiral V. S. Shekhawat to China
May 1998	Chinese Chief of General Staff Gen. Fu Quanyou to India
May 2001	Indian Chief of Air Staff Anil Yashwant Tipnis to China
April 2003	Indian Defense Minister George Fernandes to Beijing
March 2004	Chinese Defense Minister Gen. Cao Gangchuan to Delhi
December 2004	Indian Chief of Army Staff Gen. N. C. Vij to Beijing
May 2005	Chinese Chief of General Staff Gen. Liang Guanglie to India
May 2006	Indian Defense Minister Pranab Mukherjee to China
October 2006	Commander of PLA Air Force Gen. Qiao Qingchen to India
May 2007	Indian Army Chief Gen. J. J. Singh to China
November 2008	Indian Air Force Chief Fali Homi Major to China
November 2008	PLA Navy Chief Admiral Wu Shengli to India
April 2009	Indian Chief of Naval Staff Admiral Sureesh Mehta to China
September 2012	Chinese Defense Minister Gen. Liang Guanglie to Delhi
July 2013	Indian Defense Minister A. K. Antony to China

Source: Embassy of India in Beijing http://www.indianembassy.org.cn/DefenseRelations.aspx

VAJPAYEE TO CHINA

A landmark trip to Beijing in June 2003 by Indian Prime Minister Atal Bihar Vajpayee saw the two sides take a significant step toward resolving the longstanding border dispute. A major protocol signed during Vajpayee's visit provided for the appointment of "Special Representatives" tasked with finding an "agreed framework" for a final border settlement.

Previous border negotiations had been handled by India's joint secretary (East Asia) and a vice-minister in China's Foreign Affairs Ministry. With the appointment of Special Representatives, China passed the negotiating portfolio to the State Councilor, whose rank inside China's bureaucracy exceeds the foreign minister's. In India, the mandate was assigned to the relatively new position of National Security Advisor with the Prime Minister's Office seizing the initiative of reaching a border settlement from the Ministry of External Affairs.

In addition, Vajpayee's trip to Beijing saw each side offer a carrot to assuage the "core concerns" of the other. Vajpayee reaffirmed Chinese sovereignty over Tibet (as multiple Indian prime ministers had done before him), while China for the first time offered indirect recognition of Indian sovereignty over the Himalayan kingdom of Sikkim.

That recognition had been withheld by China since 1975, when Sikkim voted to join the Indian Union amid what China saw as political interference from Delhi. During Vajpayee's visit, Beijing did not explicitly reverse its position, but it did sign an agreement to reopen border trade at Nathu La, an ancient trading post at the Sikkim-China border that had been closed since the 1962 war.[5] Since then, Indian officials have deemed Sikkim to be a "closed chapter."[6] However, a careful reading of Beijing's position suggests otherwise.

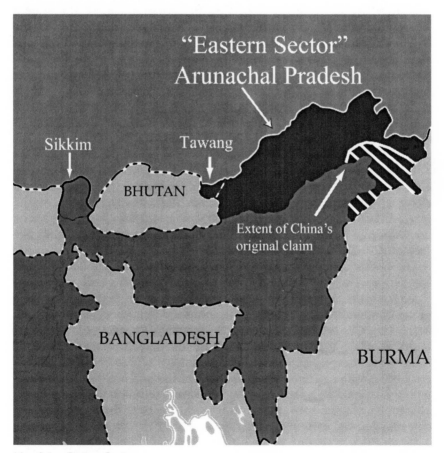

Map 3.1. Eastern Sector
Source: American Foreign Policy Council

On one hand, in China's "World Affairs Year Book 2003–04" Sikkim was, for the first time, absent from the list of countries of the world.[7] And in October 2003,[8] the Chinese Foreign Ministry removed Sikkim from a list of "Countries in the Region" on its website.[9]

On the other hand, to date no Chinese official has ever publicly recognized Indian sovereignty over Sikkim. When a foreign ministry official was questioned on the matter shortly after Vajpayee's visit, he answered equivocally: "The question of Sikkim is left over from history. . . . I believe that the question will be solved gradually with the improvement and development of Sino-Indian relations."[10] Most surprising to this author, still active on the Chinese foreign ministry's website (as of November 2013) is a page titled "China and Sikkim." It is dated August 25, 2013—two months after Vajpayee's visit—and contains one line of text: "The Chinese Government does not recognize India's illegal annexation of Sikkim."[11]

For the time being, however, the Sikkim-Tibet exchange was overshadowed by optimism surrounding the appointment of the Special Representatives. Upon returning to Delhi, Vajpayee announced that the new border talks would start immediately. "The aim is to end this dispute. So far, the talks were limited between officials who could not take decisions. It will not be so now and representatives of the two countries will resolve this issue."[12]

WEN JIABAO TO DELHI

The Special Representatives first met in October 2003 and thrice more in 2004 and 2005. They were complemented by visits to Delhi by Chinese Defense Minister Cao Gangchuan (March 2004) and the PLA's chief of general staff, Liang Guanglie (May 2005), who laid the groundwork for a breakthrough in the military-to-military relationship and eventually the first joint Sino-Indian army exercises.

The next major diplomatic exchange occurred in April 2005, with a trip to New Delhi by Chinese Prime Minister Wen Jiabao. In the run up to Wen's visit, some in Delhi were speculating about the possibility of a grand bargain "package deal" on the border dispute and two weeks before he arrived, the two sides quickly organized a meeting of the Special Representatives to try and reach a last-minute agreement on the border.

The snap meeting of Special Representatives ultimately failed to produce the coveted package deal, but the Chinese premier did leave Delhi with a less ambitious border agreement that "substantially bridged and accommodated the positions of both sides."[13] Under the *Political Parameters and Guiding Principles for the Settlement of the India China Boundary Question* the two agreed to "seek a fair, reasonable and mutually acceptable solution to the boundary question through consultations" and "make meaningful and mutually acceptable adjustments to their respective positions on the boundary question, so as to arrive at a package settlement."

RETURN TO RIVALRY

The signing of the 2005 border agreement likely marked the pinnacle of post–Cold War Sino-Indian relations. Barely five years into the new century, the two sides had averted a potential crisis over India's nuclear tests, signed two critical agreements on their longstanding border dispute, significantly expanded trade relations and paved the way for the first substantive bilateral military-to-military exchanges in Sino-Indian history.

Then, just one year after the 2005 border protocol was signed, India was preparing for a highly anticipated visit by Chinese President Hu Jintao, the first by a Chinese head of state in sixteen years, when disaster struck. Under questioning from the Indian media on the border dispute, Chinese Ambassador to India Sun Yuxi declared, "In our position, the whole of the state of Arunachal Pradesh is Chinese territory. And Tawang is only one of the places in it. We are claiming all of that. That is our position."[14]

To India's media the statement was akin to a diplomatic act of aggression. "Autocratic China becoming Arrogant" and "Arunachal Belongs to Us!" read a pair of Indian headlines. "What is new is not China's claim to Tawang or to the whole of Arunachal Pradesh but its brassy assertiveness in laying out in public its territorial demands," opined Indian analyst Brahma Chellaney.[15] As a matter of fact, the ambassador's position was new—insofar as China's previous claim in the Eastern Sector included only large portions of Arunachal Pradesh, not "the whole of the state."

Many in Delhi assumed Sun's statement was part of a premeditated strategy to reaggravate the border dispute, an assumption fed by the Chinese foreign ministry's refusal to distance itself from the ambassador's remarks. Questioned on the episode, a ministry spokesman responded simply that China's position on the border dispute "has been clear" and that the two sides could resolve the dispute through friendly consultations.[16]

In hindsight, the ambassador's remarks look less like a coordinated provocation than an ill-timed and poorly worded outburst from an excitable official. Diplomatic correspondence between U.S. and Indian officials reviewed by this author suggest Sun's remarks had not been cleared with Beijing and had embarrassed the Chinese foreign ministry. Chinese analysts interviewed for this book offered expressions of regret over the episode, suggesting "the ambassador's statement was wrong and it was not government policy."[17] One scholar at the Shanghai Institute for International Studies put blame with the Ministry of Foreign Affairs for not publicly refuting Sun's claim or recalling him (though he was transferred to Italy several months later).[18]

SETTLED POPULATIONS

The controversy over the Chinese ambassador's remarks was the first of two major blows to the border negotiations process in 2006 and 2007. Indian optimism about the prospects for a final border resolution in 2005 was driven in part by a seemingly obscure article in the *Political Parameters and Guiding Principles* agreement that read: "In reaching a boundary settlement, the two sides shall safeguard the due interests of their settled populations in the border areas."

To India, the text implied that China had agreed to exclude from future negotiations any area along the disputed border with a "settled population" and there was only one place where this language carried clear implications: the tiny Buddhist enclave of Tawang. Hugging the China-India-Bhutan tri-border in India's Arunachal Pradesh, Tawang is home to a famous Buddhist monastery and birthplace of the sixth Dalai Lama. China's claims on the town had contributed to a stalling of the border negotiations in the mid-1980s, but the "settled populations" language, noted the *Economist*, "implied that China had dropped its historical demand for Tawang."[19]

Beijing saw things differently. At the seventh round of Special Representatives talks held in March 2006, China insisted that the Eastern Sector of the territorial dispute, *including* Tawang, be the focal point in border negotiations. A year later China's new foreign minister, Yang Jiechi, told Indian Foreign Minister Pranab Mukherjee in Hamburg that the "mere presence" of settled populations would not affect China's claims to disputed territory along the border.[20]

Indian analyst Zorawar Daulet Singh concluded that China "no longer holds sacrosanct the settled principles for boundary demarcation agreed upon in 2005."[21] And interviews with multiple Indian officials revealed that for New Delhi, China's "duplicity" on the settled populations/Tawang issue emerged as a major factor in the stalling of the border negotiations.

The effect was undeniable. After the agreements of 2003 and 2005, the dozen rounds of border talks held after the 2005 protocol offered no new breakthroughs or substantive initiatives. Chinese scholar Hu Shisheng told this analyst that since 2005 the India-China border negotiations have moved in the opposite direction: "We have now switched from dispute settlement to crisis management."[22] Indian officials interviewed for this book concurred, warning not to expect any settlement at the border "in the next fifteen years."[23]

AN ARMS BUILDUP AT THE BORDER

Precisely as the Special Representatives talks ground to a halt over Chinese claims to Tawang, China and India began quietly sliding into a new arms race at the disputed border.

Throughout the 1990s and early 2000s, India watched as China added thousands of kilometers of new road and rail across Tibet, constructing the most elaborate infrastructure links between the western frontier and the Han heartland in China's history. China had always enjoyed logistical advantages atop the Tibetan plateau but by the mid-2000s the widening infrastructure gap was bringing renewed scrutiny to India's *intentional* neglect of its own border areas.

In May 2006 (six months before the Sun Yuxi controversy), India's Cabinet Committee on Economic Affairs approved the construction of a network of "strategic roads" along the border with China. The announcement marked a paradigm shift in a decades-old Indian border doctrine that counseled against building infrastructure along the Line of Actual Control. Indian strategists long argued that improved infrastructure in the border regions would only facilitate a Chinese invasion. The downside, of course, was that it made rapidly supplying and defending forward positions at the border nearly impossible (Even today many of the India's remote Himalayan outposts can only be supplied by air or through a grueling mountain trek on foot).

Addressing India's Border Roads Organization (BRO) in 2010, Defense Minister A. K. Antony explained: "earlier the thinking was that inaccessibility in far-flung areas would be a deterrent to the enemies."[24] However, Antony now judged that mindset—which several Indian scholars described to this writer as "very foolish and naïve"[25]—to be "incorrect."[26] "In the past we did not perform our duty. That is our mistake. Now we have learnt our lessons."

"There are plans for seventy-three roads on the Indo-China border . . . of total length of 3,394 kilometers in Jammu and Kashmir, Himachal Pradesh, Uttarakhand, Sikkim, and Arunachal Pradesh,"[27] Antony announced. India planned to build eleven tunnels near the Chinese and Pakistan borders, including a tunnel to bypass the treacherous Zoji La Pass in Ladakh and two tunnels on the equally dilapidated road to Tawang in the Eastern Sector.[28] Home Ministry officials told the Deccan Herald in 2012 it would take between three and eight years to "match" Chinese infrastructure on the other side of the border.[29] Delhi even recalled BRO employees from Afghanistan to assist in the massive undertaking.[30]

In the years following the 2006 decision, the infrastructure modernization package was joined by the largest permanent buildup of Indian military forces at the border since the 1960s. A steady stream of assessments of China's superior capabilities atop Tibetan plateau prompted India's Cabinet Committee on Security (CCS), the country's top national security policymaking body, to approve a major initiative in May 2009 to upgrade India's military capabilities at the border.

Two new independent infantry divisions (35,000 soldiers and 1,260 officers) were raised and deployed to Assam, bringing total Indian troop strength in the eastern sector to over 120,000.[31] Delhi further announced plans to upgrade a dozen airports and advanced landing grounds in the eastern sector, station new light-weight radars in Ladakh, and deploy three wings of India's most advanced fighter jets, the Sukhoi-30MKI, and four regiments of the advanced Brahmos cruise missile to the northeastern border with China. In tandem, the announcements constituted the most significant permanent buildup of Indian forces along the Line of Actual Control since the 1960s.

CHINA RESPONDS—A WAR OF WORDS

By the summer of 2009 the Chinese Communist Party had seen enough. India's military deployments to the border were perceived as a direct provocation that merited a response.

Party censors unshackled the nationalist commentariat, permitting a rare public broadside against New Delhi. "In an era when precision-guided weapons are developing rapidly, everyone with common sense knows that concentrated troops could be eliminated easily," noted the *People's Daily*.[32] Excerpts from an article carried jointly by the *Global Times* and *People's Daily* in June 2009 titled "India's unwise military moves" merit reprinting.

> The tough posture Singh's new government has taken may win some applause among India's domestic nationalists. But it is dangerous if it is based on a false anticipation that China will cave in. . . . Indian politicians these days seem to think their country would be doing China a huge favor simply by not joining the "ring around China" established by the U.S. and Japan. . . . which has led India to think that fear and gratitude for its restraint will cause China to defer to it on territorial disputes. But this is wishful thinking, as China *won't make any compromises in its border disputes with India*. And while China wishes to coexist peacefully with India, this desire isn't born out of fear. India's current course can only lead to rivalry between these two countries. . . . *India needs to consider whether or not it can afford the consequences of a potential confrontation with China* [emphasis added].[33]

The same day the article was released, the *Global Times* printed the results of an "online poll" in which ninety percent of respondents saw India as a "big threat" after the new troop deployments to AP.[34] Later that month an article on China.org warned that "India has been ignoring China's sovereignty these days" and that India's actions had "destroyed the trust" between the two countries.[35]

Throughout 2009 four of the most commented opinion pieces on the *People's Daily Online* were about India and nearly all the comments were highly critical.[36] In August 2009, an article appeared on a private Chinese website suggesting "the Great Indian Federation can be broken up" with just "a little action" from China. Officials distanced themselves from the attack on the "Hindu Religious State," but the article was reprinted on several more authoritative Chinese websites.[37]

A month later a legitimate public opinion survey conducted by the Sydney-based Lowy Institute gauged the opinions of 1,200 Chinese citizens regarding the greatest threats to China. The United States ranked first, while India was tied for second with China's historic rival, Japan.[38] An oft-quoted article in Britain's *Sunday Times* noted "not everyone in Beijing speaks in the silky language of the foreign ministry . . . the enemy most often spoken of is India."[39]

Confrontational language was escalating on the Indian side too, and it wasn't confined to the excitable media. In May 2009, Indian Air Force chief Fali Homi Major stated "China is a totally different ballgame compared to Pakistan. . . . they are certainly the greater threat."[40] At a closed-door seminar six months later, Indian Army Chief General Deepak Kapoor talked of changes to India's military doctrine to better prepare for a "two front war," stating "there is now a proportionate focus toward the western and northeastern fronts."[41]

The year 2009 marked a nadir in post–Cold War Sino-Indian relationship. The dominant theme of bilateral relations had again shifted from tentative cooperation to direct competition. The thirteenth round of Special Representatives talks on the border were held in August 2009, but the only meaningful outcome was an agreement to set up a hotline between leaders in both capitals—an agreement that, to date, has not been implemented. The stalling of the border negotiations, the Chinese ambassador's expanded claims on Arunachal Pradesh, the Indian arms and infrastructure buildup at the border, and China's "duplicity" on the settled populations/Tawang issue combined to undermine the diplomatic progress of the early 2000s. Those irritants were soon joined by others.

STAPLED VISAS

In May 2007 Indian Administrative Service (IAS) Officer Ganesh Koyu applied for a Chinese visa to visit Beijing and Shanghai as part of a delegation of IAS officers sent to study Chinese economic growth. His visa was denied. Arunachal Pradesh, Beijing reasoned, was Chinese territory, and no visa was needed for Koyu to visit his own country. New Delhi responded by calling off the entire delegation, and the Indian media seized on the development as a provocative new affront to Indian sovereignty.

China's visa policy was not, in fact, new. In 2007 the *Times of India* admitted that China had in the past "cancelled the visas of several Arunachalees, including ministers," taking the position that "indigenous inhabitants of Arunachal did not need [a] visa to visit" China.[42] Indeed, as far back as October 1981 "an Indian parliamentary delegation cancelled a proposed visit to China . . . after the Chinese authorities refused to issue a visa to a delegate from Arunachal Pradesh."[43] A compromise was reached in 1981: Indians from Arunachal were given visas not on their passports but stapled to separate pieces of paper.

By the late 2000s, China was offering these stapled visas to *citizens* of Arunachal Pradesh, while denying visas altogether to *officials* in the AP government. However, the policy was inconsistent. In 2006 Vishal Nabam, later an advisor to the chief minister of Arunachal Pradesh, was granted a normal month-long tourist visa to China.[44] And months after Ganesh Koyu was denied a visa, an academic from Arunachal Pradesh, Marpe Sora, was granted a normal visa to tour China with twenty-one other Indian academicians for nearly two weeks.[45]

The Indian government seemed willing to accept the subtle challenge to its sovereignty over AP, but in 2008 China began applying the same policy to residents and officials from Kashmir, and the dispute suddenly escalated into a genuine crisis. Delhi responded with a travel advisory in November 2009 stating that the "paper visas stapled to the passport are not considered valid for travel outside the country"[46] though the issue managed to avoid the Indian headlines until July 2010. That month, China issued Lt. Gen. B. S. Jaswal, commander of India's Kashmir-based Northern Command, a visa stapled to a separate sheet of paper, sparking a crisis in military-to-military relations.[47]

Delhi canceled Gen. Jaswal's delegation to China and, rather dramatically, put a freeze on the entire defense relationship. Indian officials made it clear that for defense ties to resume, the visa-stapling for Kashmiris would first have to come to an end. "The ball is in their court. There is no doubt about that," Indian Foreign Secretary Nirupama Rao said during Wen Jiabao's visit to India in December 2010.[48]

The stapled visas issue cooled after an April 2011 BRICS summit meeting in Sanya, Hainan Island. Four Indian journalists from Kashmir were granted normal visas to attend the summit,[49] and a discussion between Manmohan Singh and Hu Jintao on the sidelines of that meeting appears to have put the issue definitively to rest. Later that year China was again issuing regular visas to military officers and civilians from Jammu and Kashmir.[50]

The controversy over Arunachal visas, on the other hand, has endured. In January 2011, the Chinese embassy in India indicated that officials from AP would continue to be denied visas while residents would continue getting stapled visas.[51] In January 2012, China issued stapled visas to two Indians destined for China's Weightlifting Grand Prix. Indian immigration officials declared the visas invalid and prevented the sportsmen from traveling to China.[52]

Again in January 2012 Chinese officials denied a visa to an Indian officer from AP, Captain Mohonto Panging, who was traveling to China as part of a thirty-member tri-service delegation. "Suppose we have a Prime Minister who belongs to Arunachal Pradesh, should the government drop him from a China-bound delegation? Will China now decide India's foreign policy?" asked Bharitiya Janata Party spokesman and Member of Parliament Tarun Vijay.[53] In the end, Delhi chose to "split the difference," allowing the delegation to proceed but cutting its size in half. Since then, some retired Indian officials have proposal stapling visas to Chinese citizens from Tibet, Xinjiang, Gansu, and Qinghai.

ARUNACHAL VISITS

Keeping Arunachal Pradesh the focal point of Sino-Indian tensions in the late 2000s were a series of visits to the disputed territory by Indian officials. In October 2008, just two weeks after returning from a trip to Beijing, Prime Minister Singh toured AP ahead of local elections there, declaring "The sun kisses India first in Arunachal Pradesh. It is our land of rising sun."[54] It was the first visit to AP by an Indian prime minister in a decade and during his stay Singh announced a $2.5 billion development plan including a 2,000 kilometer Trans-Arunachal highway, a new airport for the state capital of Itanagar, and the reopening of four state airports.

On October 13 a Chinese foreign ministry spokesman demanded "the Indian side address China's serious concerns and not trigger disturbance in the disputed region."[55] The Indian Ministry of External Affairs responded hours later: "Arunachal Pradesh is an inalienable part of India and China is aware of this."[56] The following day another "online poll" from the *Global Times'* Chinese-language website, huanqui.com, indicated that 96 percent of polled Web users were opposed to frequent visits to disputed areas by Indian officials.[57]

Undeterred, Delhi dispatched External Affairs Minister Pranab Mukherjee to visit AP just a few weeks later in a trip that included a stop at the strategically sensitive Buddhist monastery at Tawang. Ahead of Mukherjee's visit China's foreign ministry warned that India "takes no regard of the historical facts . . . the current Chinese government, as well as previous ones, has never recognized the illegal [border between China and India]. India knows this."[58]

Yet it was an altogether separate visit to Arunachal Pradesh a year later by the Dalai Lama that truly provoked China's ire. The Dalai Lama, who permanently resides in Dharamsala, India, had publicly announced plans to visit AP in 2008, but his request was denied by New Delhi, ostensibly to avoid complicating local elections. Yet, in 2009, amid a peak in Sino-Indian tensions, New Delhi issued the Dalai Lama the necessary permits to visit AP and the famed Tawang Monastery. On September 9, the Dalai Lama arrived by helicopter to a grand reception of thousands of Tibetan monks and residents.

Ever since he fled Tibet for India in 1959, Beijing has reserved unique disdain for the fourteenth Dalai Lama. By the mid-2000s, the Communist Party's hatred for the Buddhist leader had reached hysteria. The state-run Xinhua labeled the Dalai Lama a "serf owner" and a "tricky liar skilled in double-dealing," comparing him to the "uncontrolled and cruel Nazi during the Second World War."[59]

"India may have forgotten the lesson of 1962, when its repeated provocation resulted in military clashes. . . . India is on the wrong track again," warned a *Global Times/People's Daily* article, citing an "anonymous scholar." [60] In the same article, Hu Shisheng, one of China's few noted India specialists, suggested the Dalai Lama's trip was taken "probably because of pressure from India." "When the conflict gets sharper and sharper, the Chinese government will have to face it and solve it in a way that India has designed."[61]

INDIAN ASSERTIVENESS

Deferential to China's sensitivities in Tibet, Delhi had traditionally treated the Dalai Lama and the Tibetan exile community with caution, keeping a careful lid on activities deemed provocative to Beijing. In 2008 the Indian government faced a groundswell of domestic criticism for imposing a virtual lockdown on the Tibetan exile community in Delhi during a ceremony celebrating China's hosting of the 2008 Olympics. Permitting the Dalai Lama to visit Tawang a year later was a reflection of a new Indian assertiveness toward China's "core interests."

This assertiveness was again on display in 2010. At a foreign ministers meeting in Wuhan, China that year, Indian External Affairs Minister S. M. Krishna told Chinese Foreign Minister Yang Jiechi[62] that just as Delhi had been sensitive to Chinese concerns over Tibet and Taiwan, India now "expect[s] China to be sensitive to our core concerns. That is how relationships are built, relations are nurtured."[63] Kashmir, he said, was a "core issue" for India in the same way Tibet and Taiwan were "core issues" for China.[64]

I. Quik Tabs
w/ Kashmir

2010

Premier Wen Jiabao visited New Delhi a few months later. Dating back to the 1950s every joint statement issued after a high-level bilateral exchange included mention of China's "One China" policy. However, during Wen's visit for the first time India demanded a reciprocal gesture, in writing, with China affirming Indian sovereignty over Kashmir. Wen Jiabao declined and for the first time a Sino-Indian joint statement made no reference to the "One China" policy[65] (in back-to-back diplomatic exchanges in 2013. India again declined to reaffirm the "One China" policy, setting a new precedent).

In November 2011, India and China were scheduled to conduct the fifteenth Round of Special Representative talks on the border. Shortly before the talks Chinese officials noticed the Dalai Lama was scheduled to address a major Buddhist conference in New Delhi the same week Chinese State Councilor Dai Bingguo was due to visit the Indian capital. China contacted the Indian Ministry of External affairs and demanded India move the Buddhist conference to another date. Delhi refused. China then demanded the Buddhist conference be scrapped altogether.

This author was in Delhi at the time, and the response of a senior MEA official intimately involved in the affair was: "Are you crazy? All of our leaders are on the same page on this: We're not going to budge. There are some fundamental values we won't change for some bloody Chinese delegation."[66] He added that Australia, South Africa, and other countries had been "pressurized" by China into canceling visits with the Dalai Lama but that India "wouldn't be doing the same." Beijing responded by calling off the fifteenth round of Special Representatives talks.

Chandan Mitra, an Indian MP and editor of the popular newspaper the *Pioneer*, told this author the move was "typical of China. No one in India is shedding any tears over the canceled border talks."[67] Another Indian official insisted the Chinese embassy was to blame for catching the scheduling conflict only at the last minute. "We went out of our way to ensure [Dai Bingguo and the Dalai Lama] wouldn't be talking at the same time," he said. "China kept changing the goalposts."

Chinese analysts saw things differently. The scheduling conflict was "not really a coincidence. It could be regarded as a purposed arrangement," Hu Shisheng told the *Hindu* in an interview the following week.[68] Beijing was particularly irritated by the fact that the governor of West Bengal, M. K. Narayanan, broke protocol and joined the Dalai Lama on stage in Kolkata just days after the canceled border talks.[69]

THE STORM SUBSIDES

The years 2011 and 2012 saw a moderation of the excesses of the Sino-Indian rivalry that trebled in 2009. The Annual Defense Dialogue that had been frozen in 2010 met again in 2012, and the Kashmir stapled visa

Not forget I +
J at same time.

Cant I

issue was put to rest after the BRICS summit in 2011. That year the two sides held their first Strategic Economic Dialogue. Chinese nationalists began directing their attention east, toward China's maritime territorial disputes with the Philippines, Vietnam, and Japan as party propaganda began emphasizing cooperation with India again.

The canceled fifteenth round of Special Representatives talks were rescheduled for January 2012, where the two sides reached a modest agreement on a "Working Mechanism for Consultation and Coordination on India-China Border Affairs"[70] to meet once or twice a year.[71] However, the *Daily Mail* reported that the talks ultimately "went off track following some hard bargaining by China," which insisted on discussing the Eastern Sector, including Tawang, first.[72]

The periodic sparring that occupied so much of 2009 also surfaced in 2012 after India conducted the first test of its Agni-V Medium Range Ballistic Missile. It was an open secret that the Agni-V was built with China in mind: India's robust arsenal of short- and medium-range ballistic missiles are already capable of reaching every part of Pakistan. With a 5,000 kilometer range, the Agni-V, however, would be the first missile in India's arsenal with the capability of striking anywhere in China from multiple locations in India.

The nationalist *Global Times* ridiculed the "dwarf missile"[73] and said that India's strategic missile force was in "early childhood" and the Agni V demonstrated the "backwardness of Indian missiles."[74] "India should not overestimate its strength," warned another editorial. "Even if it has missiles that could reach most parts of China . . . India should be clear that China's nuclear power is stronger and more reliable. For the foreseeable future, India would stand no chance in an overall arms race with China."[75]

However, heading to China's once-in-a-decade leadership transition in the fall of 2012, officials in India were cautiously optimistic that the incoming administration under Xi Jinping would prioritize better relations with Delhi. Though President Xi skipped India on his first few visits abroad, he sent a letter to Indian Prime Minister Manmohan Singh in January 2013 stating: "China will, as it has been doing, pay great importance to developing relations with India and expects to carry out close cooperation with India to create a brighter future of their of their bilateral relations."[76] Chinese Prime Minister Li Keqiang reportedly phoned Prime Minister Singh within hours of being sworn into office, and many in Delhi applauded his decision to make India his first visit abroad in May 2013.

Then, just as it had in 2006, weeks before Chinese President Hu Jintao's first visit to India, disaster struck in the weeks before Prime Minister Li's visit to Delhi. On April 20 it was revealed that a week earlier, a forty- to fifty-strong Chinese patrol had ventured nineteen kilometers across the Line of Actual Control and set up five tents at the Depsang Bulge near where the Chinese, Indian, and Pakistani borders meet in Ladakh.

That a Chinese border patrol had crossed the Line of Actual Control was not exactly novel: transgressions across the LAC are all too common along the undemarcated border where there are at least a dozen sections where there is no mutual agreement on where Indian and Chinese troops have the legal right to be positioned. Indian media reports suggested there had already been more than 100 PLA transgressions across the LAC in the first quarter of 2013, which tracks with Indian Home Ministry figures citing 228 transgressions in 2010 and 213 in 2011.[77] In 2008 reports of Chinese border incursions in the Finger Area of Sikkim[78] prompted India to move T-72 battle tanks to the area in response.[79]

However, most of the transgressions are innocent violations of an unmarked border, and it's unclear how guilty Indian patrols are of similar violations because China doesn't keep count. According to the *Economist* there are

> in all a dozen stretches of frontier where neither side knows where even the disputed border should be. In these "pockets," as they are called, Indian and Chinese border guards circle each other endlessly while littering the Himalayan hillsides—as dogs mark their lampposts—to make their presence known. When China-India relations are strained, this gives rise to tit-for-tat and mostly bogus accusations of illegal border incursions—for which each side can offer the other's empty cigarette and noodle packets as evidence.[80]

The Indian government generally downplays these innocent "transgressions" of the LAC, in which Chinese border patrols briefly cross into Indian territory before returning to their forward operating base on the Chinese side. But the April 2013 episode wasn't an innocent transgression by the Indian government's own definition, it was an "intrusion"—an intentional and provocative breach of the LAC. Instead of returning to their forward base at night, the Chinese patrol stayed put.

Three border personnel meetings over the course of three weeks failed to dislodge the Chinese patrol, whose intrusion was a daily feature in the Indian headlines and a source of outrage for the Indian opposition. A former defense minister, Mulayam Singh Yadav, accused the government of being "weak and cowardly" and called for the Indian Army to evict the Chinese positions. "[China] insulted us in 1962. They are insulting us now in the world fora."[81] "A bully will back off the moment it realizes that it's dealing with a country which will not submit to its will,"[82] opined former External Affairs Minister Yaswant Sinha.

Nevertheless, the Indian Army was not deployed, and the government's China Study Group advised restraint. Prime Minister Manmohan Singh downplayed the intrusion, saying it was a "localized problem" and that India did not want to "accentuate the situation."[83] External Affairs Minister Salman Khurshid called the intrusion "acne" that "can be addressed by simply applying an ointment."[84] On May 6, three days ahead of a planned trip to China by Khurshid and two weeks before Chinese Premier Li Keqiang was to visit India, the Chinese patrol withdrew without warning or explanation.

Dozens of devoted articles and dozens more interviews with Indian officials produced no consensus on China's motive. "We were incredibly puzzled by all this," Commodore C. Uday Bhaskar told this writer. "The one conclusion we drew is: 'we know even less about the workings of the Chinese system than we think we do.'"[85]

The event was variously described as part of a broad trend of heightened Chinese assertiveness; an effort by incoming President Xi Jinping to consolidate authority over the PLA; a response to several new provocative Indian deployments at the border; and the result of an adventurous and unsanctioned move by a local official.

However, the most convincing explanation was that Beijing intended to apply pressure on Delhi to sign a Border Defense and Cooperation Agreement (BDCA). China began floating a draft BDCA in late 2012 with the intention of improving border management and instituting a freeze on military and infrastructure projects along the Line of Actual Control. Recognizing that such a freeze would enshrine China's substantial advantage along the LAC, India resisted the proposed freeze.

As if to underscore this point, in July 2013, just months after the Depsang Valley incident, Delhi approved a long-gestating proposal to raise a new Strike Corps for the Eastern Sector of the LAC. Specializing in offensive operations and high-altitude mountain warfare, the 50,000-strong offensive formation would be raised over a period of seven years. Most important, it would constitute the first offensive Strike Corps to be stationed at the LAC (India's three other Strike Corps are all positioned at the Indo-Pakistan border).

It was no surprise then, when the BDCA was eventually signed during Prime Minister Manmohan Singh's last visit to China in October 2013, the draft omitted any language of a freeze. Instead the BDCA merely re-stated previously agreed-to principles and introduced modest border management reforms, including a commitment to set up a new military hotline and an agreement not to have each side's border patrols "tail" the patrols of the other country.

FULL CIRCLE

This abridged history of the twenty-first-century Sino-Indian rivalry demonstrates how relations remain, in the words of Prime Minister Wen Jiabao, "very fragile, easily damaged and very difficult to repair."[86]

The events of 2013 demonstrate how, despite the dramatic progress wrought through dozens of rounds of border negotiations and confidence-building mechanisms, the two sides remain oceans apart from resolving the largest ongoing border dispute in the world. The next chapter will examine why a settlement has proven so elusive in the past, why practical challenges and domestic constraints may make a settlement even less likely moving forward, and will review the costs and benefits to both parties of maintaining the status quo.

NOTES

1. Murray Scot Tanner, *Distracted Antagonists, Wary Partners: China and India Assess Their Security Relations* (Alexandria: Center for Naval Analyses, 2011), 1.

2. Jonathan Holslag, *China and India Prospects for Peace* (New York: Columbia University Press, 2010), 56.

3. "Background Note: India," U.S. Department of State, 2012 (Accessed April 22, 2013): http://www.state.gov/r/pa/ei/bgn/3454.htm.

4. "China Aims to Dominate Tech Industry; Asks for India's Help," *Newsmax .com*, April 10, 2005 (Accessed April 2013): http://archive.newsmax.com/archives/articles/2005/4/10/82600.shtml.

5. The border post opened for trade on July 6, 2006.

6. "China Incursion to Be Raised, Sikkim Is a Closed Chapter: India" *Indian Express*, June 20, 2008 (Accessed June 12, 2013): http://www.indianexpress.com/news/china-incursion-to-be-raised-sikkim-is-a-closed-chapter-india/325132/.

7. Suryanarayana, "China's Gesture," *Frontline*, Vol. 21 No. 11, April 22, 2013 (Accessed June 15, 2013): www.frontlineonnet.com/fl2111/stories/20040604001905100.

8. Alexa Olesen, "China, India Resolving Sikkim Dispute," *Associated Press*, October 8, 2003 (Accessed April 22, 2013): www.tibet.ca/en/newsroom/wtn/arhive/old?y=2003&m=10&p=8_4.

9. "Countries in the Region," *Ministry of Foreign Affairs of the People's Republic of China*, 2005 (Accessed April 22, 2013): www.fmprc.gov.cn/eng/wjb/zzjg/yzs/gjlb/default.htm.

10. "Foreign Ministry Spokesperson Liu Jianchao's Press Conference on May 18, 2004," *Ministry of Foreign of Affairs of the People's Republic of China*, May 18, 2004 (Accessed April 22, 2013): www.fmprc.gov.cn/eng/xwfw/2510/t112578.htm.

11. "China and Sikkim," *Ministry of Foreign Affairs of the People's Republic of China*, August 25, 2003 (Accessed April 22, 2013): www.fmprc.gov.cn/eng/wjb/zzjg/yzs/gjlb/2772/t16190.htm.

12. "China Rules Out Early Sikkim Resolution," *Dawn the Internet Edition*, June 27, 2003 (Accessed April 22, 2013): http://archives.dawn.com/2003/06/28/top6.htm.

13. Zorawar Singh, *Himalayan Stalemate: Understanding the India-China Dispute* (London: Straightforward Publishers, 2012), 28.

14. "Arunachal Pradesh Is Our Territory: Chinese Envoy," *Rediff India Abroad*, November 14, 2006 (Accessed April 2013): http://www.rediff.com/news/2006/nov/14china.htm.

15. Brahma Chellaney, "Tibet Is at the Core of the India-China Divide," *Stagecraft and Statecraft*, April 2, 2007 (Accessed April 22, 2013): http://chellaney.net/2007/04/02/tibet-is-at-the-core-of-the-india-china-divide.

16. "China Reiterates Its Claim to Arunachal Pradesh," *Dawn the Internet Edition*, November 15, 2006 (Accessed April 22, 2006): http://archives.dawn.com/2006/11/15/top7.htm.

17. Chinese analysts. Author interview. Beijing, February 2012.

18. Scholar at the Shanghai Institute for International Studies. Author interview. Washington, DC, May 2012.

19. "A Himalayan Rivalry," *Economist*, August 19, 2010 (Accessed April 2013): http://www.economist.com/node/16843717.

20. Jo Johnson and Richard McGregor, "China Raises Tension in India Dispute," *Financial Times*, June 10, 2007 (Accessed April 22, 2013): http://www.ft.com/cms/s/0/2606bb64-176e-11dc-86d1-000b5df10621.html#axzz27snGlnfl.

21. Jagannath P. Panda, "China's Designs on Arunachal Pradesh," *Institute for Defence Studies and Analyses*, March 12, 2008: 1.

22. Hu Shisheng. Author interview. Beijing, February 2012.

23. Indian officials. Author interview. Washington, DC, March 2012.

24. Vivek Raghuvanshi, "India to Modernize Road Networks in Border Areas," *Defense News*, May 7, 2010 (April 22, 2013): http://www.defensenews.com/article/20100507/DEFSECT02/5070304/India-Modernize-Road-Networks-Border-Areas.

25. Lydia Polgreen, "India Digs Under Top of the World to Match Rival," *New York Times*, July 31, 2010 (April 22, 2013): http://www.nytimes.com/2010/08/01/world/asia/01pass.html?pagewanted=all.

26. Vivek Raghuvanshi, "India To Modernize Road Networks in Border Areas," *Defense News*, May 7, 2010 (April 22, 2013): http://www.defensenews.com/story.php?i=4616391.

27. "Government to Expedite Road Infrastructure Works along China Border," *Economic Times*, September 8, 2010 (April 22, 2013): http://articles.economictimes.indiatimes.com/2010-08-11/news/27589064_1_road-infrastructure-border-areas-km.

28. Dipak K. Dash, "Govt Plans 11 Tunnels on Pak, China Borders," *Times of India*, January 6, 2012 (Accessed April 22, 2013): http://articles.timesofindia.indiatimes.com/2012-01-06/india/30597365_1_tunnels-strategic-roads-highways-ministry.

29. Deepak K. Upreti, "LAC Airbases to Be Upgraded," *Deccan Herald*, March 11, 2012 (April 22, 2013): http://www.deccanherald.com/content/233718/lac-airbases-upgraded.html.

30. Vivek Raghuvanshi, "India To Modernize Road Networks in Border Areas," *Defense News*, May 7, 2010 (April 22, 2013):http://www.defensenews.com/story.php?i=4616391.

31. Saurabhi Joshi, "India to Double Troops in Arunachal," *StratPost*, June 8, 2009 (Accessed April 22, 2013): http://www.stratpost.com/india-to-double-troops-in-arunachal.

32. He Zude and Fang Wei, "India's Increasing Troop May Go Nowhere," *People's Daily Online*, November 15, 2011 (Accessed April 10, 2013): http://english.people daily.com.cn/102774/7644826.html.

33. "India's Unwise Military Moves," *Global Times*, June 11, 2009 (Accessed April 2013): www.globaltimes.cn/opinion/editorial/2009-06/436174.html.

34. Zhu Shanshan, "90% in Online Poll Believe India Threatens China's Security," *Global Times*, June 11, 2009 (Accessed April 22, 2013): www.globaltimes .cn/china/top-photo/2009-06/436320.html.

35. Li Xiaohua, "India's Provocation Irritates Chinese Netizens," *China.org. cn*, June 15, 2009 (Accessed April 22, 2013): http://www.china.org.cn/interna tional/2009-06/15/content_17951232.htm.

36. Mohan Malik, "War Talk: Perpetual Gap in Chindia Relations," *Association for Asian Research*, October 7, 2009 (Accessed April 22, 2013): http://www.asian research.org/articles/3224.html.

37. D. S. Rajan, "China Should Break Up the Indian Union, Suggests a Chinese Strategist," *Chennai Centre for China Studies*, August 9, 2009 (Accessed April 22, 2013): http://www.c3sindia.org/india/719.

38. "Many Chinese Think India Greatest Security Threat after US: New Poll," *Indian Express*, December 2, 2009 (Accessed April 22, 2013): http://www.indian express.com/news/many-chinese-think-india-greatest-security-t/548808/.

39. Michael Sheridan, "Chinese Sure No One Will Rain on Their Parade," *The Australian*, September 28, 2009 (Accessed April 22, 2013): http://www.theaustra lian.com.au/news/world/chinese-make-sure-no-one-will-rain-on-their-parade/ story-e6frg6so-1225780181859.

40. Rahul Singh, "China Now Bigger Threat than Pakistan, Says IAF Chief," *Hindustan Times*, May 23, 2009 (Accessed April 22, 2013): http://www.hindu stantimes.com/News-Feed/India/China-now-bigger-threat-than-Pakistan-says -IAF-chief/Article1-413933.aspx.

41. Rajat Pandit, "Army Reworks War Doctrine for Pakistan, China," *Times of India*, December 30, 2009 (Accessed April 2013): http://articles.timesofindia .indiatimes.com/2009-12-30/india/28104699_1_war-doctrine-new-doctrine -entire-western-front.

42. "China Grants Visa to Arunachal Pradesh Academician," *The Times of India*, December 6, 2007 (Accessed April 24, 2013): http://articles.timesofindia.india times.com/2007-12-06/india/27984868_1_ganesh-koyu-visa-arunachal-pradesh.

43. John B. Allcock, *Border and Territorial Disputes*, 3rd Ed. (Longman Current Affairs, 1992), 433.

44. "China Says No Change in Its Arunachal Pradesh Policy," *Economic Times*, January 17, 2011 (Accessed April 24, 2013): http://articles.economic times.indiatimes.com/2011-01-17/news/28432458_1_stapled-visas-weightlifting -grand-prix-indian-immigration-officials.

45. "China Grants Visa to Arunachal Pradesh Academician," *Times of India*, December 6, 2007 (Accessed April 24, 2013): http://articles.timesofindia.india times.com/2007-12-06/india/27984868_1_ganesh-koyu-visa-arunachal-pradesh.

46. C. Raja Mohan, *Sumdra Manthan: Sino-Indian Rivalry in the Pacific* (Washington, DC: Carnegie Endowment for International Peace, 2012), 222.

47. Murray Scot Tanner, *Distracted Antagonists, Wary Partners: China and India Assess Their Security Relations* (Alexandria: Center for Naval Analyses, 2011), 16–17.

48. "No Mention of 'One China Policy' in India-China Joint Statement," *Phayul .com*, December 17, 2010 (Accessed April 24, 2013): http://www.phayul.com/news/article.aspx?id=28767&t=1.

49. "China 'Ready to Work' on Stapled Visa Issue with India," *Indian Express*, April 12, 2011 (Accessed April 24, 2013): http://www.indianexpress.com/news/china-ready-to-work-on-stapled-visa-issue-with-india/775244/.

50. Ananth Krishnan, "Chinese Visa Policies Cast a Shadow over Ties," *Hindu*, July 22, 2011 (Accessed April 24, 2013): http://www.thehindu.com/news/national/article2282599.ece.

51. "China: Visa Regime Unchanged for Arunachal Pradesh," *Stratfor*, January 14, 2011 (Accessed April 24, 2013): http://www.stratfor.com/sitrep/20110114-china-visa-regime-uchanged-arunachal-pradesh.

52. China will not issue visas to any officials from AP, nonofficials will receive a stapled visa according to the Chinese Embassy. "China Issuing 'Invalid' Stapled Visas to Arunachal Pradesh Residents," *Times of India*, February 25, 2012 (Accessed April 24, 2013): http://articles.timesofindia.indiatimes.com/2011-01-12/india/28374355_1_stapled-visas-techi-china-weightlifting-grand-prix.

53. "BJP National Spokesperson and MP, Shri Tarun Vijay," *Bharatiya Janata Party*, January 8, 2012 (Accessed April 2013): http://www.bjp.org/index .php?option=com_content&view=article&id=7526:press-bjp-national-spokesperson-and-mp-shri-tarun-vijay&catid=68:press-releases&Itemid=494.

54. "China Retorts to India on Arunachal Issue," *News Track India*, November 12, 2008 (Accessed April 24, 2013): http://www.newstrackindia.com/news details/3664.

55. "China Voices 'Strong Dissatisfaction' over Indian Leader's Visit to Disputed Region," *China View*, October 13, 2009 (Accessed April 24, 2013): http://news.xinhuanet.com/english/2009-10/13/content_12222106.htm.

56. "Gov't Says Arunachal Integral Part of India after Chinese Protest," *Times of India*, October 13, 2009 (Accessed April 24, 2013): http://articles.times ofindia.indiatimes.com/2009-10-13/india/28077010_1_china-claims-arunachal -pradesh-ma-zhaoxu.

57. "96% Chinese against Indian Visits to Arunachal," *NDTV*, October 14, 2009 (Accessed April 24, 2013): http://www.ndtv.com/article/india/96-chinese -against-indian-visits-to-arunachal-10025.

58. Pranab Mukherjee, ". . . Arunachal Pradesh Is an Integral Part of India," *Outlook India*, November 11, 2008 (Accessed April 14, 2013): http://www.outlook india.com/article.aspx?238923.

59. Lu Hui, "Commentary: Seven Questions to the 14th Dalai Lama," *Xinhua*, February 24, 2012 (Accessed April 2013): http://news.xinhuanet.com/english/indepth/2012-03/24/c_131487143.htm.

60. "India covets Dalai Lama's visit" *People's Daily Online English*, November 9, 2009 (April 24, 2013) http://english.people.com.cn/90001/90776/90883/6807180 .html

61. "India Covets Dalai Lama's Visit," *Global Times*, November 9, 2009 (Accessed April 24, 2013): http://world.globaltimes.cn/asia-pacific/2009-11/483521 .html.

62. Siddharth Vardarajan, "India Tells China: Kashmir Is to Us What Tibet, Taiwan Are to You," November 15, 2010 (Accessed April 24, 2013): http://www .thehindu.com/news/national/article886483.ece.

63. "China Should Respect India's Sensitivities: SM Krishna," *Daily News and Analysis*, October 15, 2010 (Accessed April 14, 2013): http://www.dnaindia.com/india/report_china-should-respect-india-s-sensitivities-sm-krishna_1452946.

64. Indrani Bagchi, "Keep Off Pok, India Warns China," *Times of India*, September 16, 2011 (Accessed April 16, 2013): http://articles.timesofindia.indiatimes.com/2011-09-16/india/30164512_1_stapled-visas-karakoram-highway-china-issues.

65. Indrani Bagchi, "India Declines to Affirm 'One China' Policy," *Times of India*, December 17, 2010 (Accessed April 24, 2013): http://articles.timesofindia.indiatimes.com/2010-12-17/india/28261765_1_stapled-china-india-india-and-china.

66. Ministry of External Affairs New Delhi. Author interview. South Block, New Delhi, November 2011.

67. Chandan Mitra. Author interview. New Delhi, November 2011.

68. Ananth Krishnan, "China Sees a Newly Assertive India," *Hindu*, November 30, 2011 (Accessed April 24, 2013): http://www.thehindu.com/news/national/article2672222.ece.

69. "West Bengal Governor Ignores China's 'Advice,' attends Dalai Lama Meet," *Times of India*, December 1, 2011 (Accessed April 24, 2013): http://articles.timesofindia.indiatimes.com/2011-12-01/india/30462526_1_dalai-lama-west-bengal-governor-spiritual-leader.

70. Xinhua reported that under the agreement, a Chinese official at the director general level will meet with a joint secretary from India. Both sides would be accompanied by military delegations. The first meeting was held March 6, 2012, though China was represented by a vice minister in the Foreign Ministry, not a director general.

71. "India, China to Set-Up Border Mechanism," *Hindustan Times*, January 17, 2012 (Accessed April 24, 2013): http://www.hindustantimes.com/India-news/NewDelhi/India-China-sign-border-management-pact/Article1-798623.aspx.

72. Saurabh Shukla, "China Plays the Bully on Arunachal: Beijing tells Delhi to Work Out Eastern Sector Formula," *Mail Online*, January 20, 2012 (April 24, 2013): http://www.dailymail.co.uk/indiahome/indianews/article-2092841/China-plays-bully-Arunachal-Beijing-tells-Delhi-work-Eastern-sector-formula.html.

73. Manpreet Sethi, "The Agni-V: A Dragon's Response," *Diplomat*, April 10, 2013 (Accessed April 2012): http://the-diplomat.com/flashpoints-blog/2012/04/27/the-agni-v-%E2%80%93-a-dragons-response/.

74. "Chinese Media Mock India's 'Dwarf' Missile," *BBC News Asia-Pacific*, April 10, 2013 (Accessed April 20, 2012): http://www.bbc.co.uk/news/world-asia-pacific-17784779.

75. "India Being Swept Up by Missile Delusion," *Global Times*, April 19, 2012 (Accessed April 10, 2013): http://www.globaltimes.cn/NEWS/tabid/99/ID/705627/India-being-swept-up-by-missile-delusion.aspx.

76. "China to Pay Great Importance to Ties with India: Xi Jinping," *Times of India* January 14, 2013 (April 10, 2013) http://articles.timesofindia.indiatimes.com/2013-01-14/china/36330737_1_india-china-border-talks-china-india-relations-dai-bingguo.

77. "China Violated LAC 505 Times since January 2010," *Tribune*, May 16, 2012: http://www.tribuneindia.com/2012/20120517/main6.htm.

78. "India to Raise Sikkim Incursions with China" *Times of India,* June 19, 2008 (Accessed June 13, 2013) http://articles.timesofindia.indiatimes.com/2008-06-19/india/27742766_1_incursions-into-indian-territory-finger-area-pla.

79. "Indian Tanks Move in Sikkim after Chinese Activities," *India Today,* July 28, 2009 (Accessed June 12, 2013): http://indiatoday.intoday.in/story/Indian+tanks+move+in+Sikkim+after+Chinese+activities/1/53856.html.

80. "India and China: A Himalayan Rivalry," *Economist,* August 19, 2010 (Accessed June 19, 2013): http://www.economist.com/node/16843717.

81. "India and China: A Himalayan Rivalry," *Economist,* August 19, 2012 (Accessed June 18, 2013): http://india.nydailynews.com/politicsarticle/32439 a4b041e4c7af5c321904de0b568/china-biggest-enemy-of-india-pakistan-no-threat -mulayam.

82. Narmala George, "Chinese Incursion Leaves India on Verge of Crisis," *Associated Press,* May 2, 2013: http://world.time.com/2013/05/02/chinese-incur sion-leaves-india-on-verge-of-crisis/.

83. "China Biggest Enemy of India, Pakistan No Threat: Mulayam" *Daily Press,* April 29, 2013 (Accessed June 18, 2013): http://india.nydailynews.com/politic sarticle/32439a4b041e4c7af5c321904de0b568/china-biggest-enemy-of-india-paki stan-no-threat-mulayam.

84. Roy Subhajit, "Incursion an Acne, Can Be Cured with Ointment, Says Kurshid," *Indian Express,* April 26, 2013 (Accessed June 18, 2013): http://www .indianexpress.com/news/incursion-acne-can-be-cured-with-ointment-says -khurshid/1107855/.

85. C. Uday Bhaskar. Author interview. May 22, 2013, Honolulu, Hawaii.

86. "China-India Ties Fragile, Need Special Care: Chinese Envoy," *Times of India,* December 14, 2010: http://articles.timesofindia.indiatimes.com/2010-12-14/india/28213836_1_chinese-envoy-zhang-yan-china-india.

Chapter 4

The Elusive Settlement

The senior leadership in China and India have publicly touted their commitment to a settlement of their territorial dispute for over three decades,
investing no shortage of time and resources into an elaborate negotiation
process. So why has a resolution to the dispute proven so elusive, and to
whom should we assign blame for this failure?

There are two competing narratives. One, proposed by India's critics,
suggests Delhi is to blame for a uniquely uncompromising approach to
the border dispute. This line of reasoning gained favor following the publication of British journalist Neville Maxwell's 1971 tome, *India's China
War*. Maxwell challenged the dominant narrative at the time portraying
India as the victim of Chinese aggression via a thoroughly documented
and biting criticism of the Nehru administration's myriad missteps, mis-
calculations, and provocations in the months and years leading up to the
war. Forty years later, Maxwell maintains that the burden of blame for the
failure of the border negotiations falls to Delhi:

> It is the Indian refusal to negotiate that created the boundary dispute, that
> makes it impossible to resolve it, and will make it always impossible until
> some Indian government appears, and as Gorbachev once did, says 'we've
> got it wrong, you're right.' We're ready to sit down and negotiate."[1]

Together with many Chinese scholars, Maxwell implicates Delhi for repeatedly rejecting an equitable "package deal" offered by Beijing on no
less than four occasions between 1960 and 1980; a deal that would have
enshrined the status quo along the Line of Actual Control, with China
retaining Aksai Chin in the Western Sector, India keeping Arunachal

Pradesh in the Eastern Sector, and the two sides making minor adjustments in the relatively less contentious Middle Sector.

Some scholars have also pointed out that Beijing has proven prag-
matic—even magnanimous—in its efforts to settle the majority of its continental land border disputes (China's approach to its *maritime* territorial
disputes is an entirely different matter). MIT Professor M. Taylor Fravel
documents how, of the twenty-three territorial disputes the People's
Republic of China initiated or inherited, Beijing "offered substantial compromises in seventeen" of the twenty-three, "often agree[ing] to accept
less than half of the territory being disputed."[2] Many of the disputes were
settled only recently, including deals with Kyrgyzstan and Kazakhstan in
1996 and 1998; with Russia and Vietnam in 2008; and with Tajikistan in
2011. Indian analyst Srikanth Kondipalli admits that overall China "has
been liberal in border dispute resolution."[3]

Of China's six remaining territorial disputes, four are offshore or maritime disputes and one is a relatively minor dispute with the tiny Himalayan kingdom of Bhutan. That leaves India as the only country with which
China has a substantial unresolved land border dispute, a fact wielded by
India's critics as proof of Delhi's intransigence.

Some Indian and Western analysts have posited an alternative theory.
What makes the Sino-Indian border unique, they say, is not India's in-
flexible negotiating posture, but its unrivaled leverage in Tibet. China
only settled its land border disputes with its other neighbors because it
either wanted something or no longer saw a need to maintain a point of
strategic leverage over them. In contrast, India is situated along China's
"soft underbelly" and host to the Tibetan Government in Exile, and is
therefore in a unique position to stir trouble for China in Tibet should it
feel compelled to do so.

Dr. Mohan Malik, author of *China and India: Great Power Rivals,* has
argued that Beijing's insecurities in Tibet—and its recognition of Indian
influence there—has made China reluctant to settle the border dispute
"until Tibet is pacified in the same way Inner Mongolia has been pacified."[4] "China's strategy is evident," says Indian analyst Ajai Shukla, "to
confine Indian strategic attention to the Sino-Indian border, preventing
New Delhi from looking beyond at Tibet and Xinjiang, China's most sensitive pressure points."[5]

Both narratives carry some elements of truth: a preponderance of evidence points to a strategic connection Beijing has made between the border
dispute and the Tibet issue. On the other hand, even today some Indian
scholars lament the fact that they repeatedly rejected what is increasingly
acknowledged as a reasonable package deal offered by Beijing. However,
as the following section will show, since the mid-1980s both countries' position on a desirable final settlement have undergone substantial evolutions.

THE FAILURE OF THE SWAP PROPOSAL

The outlines of a grand bargain swap proposal were first offered, unofficially, by Chinese Premier Zhou Enlai in 1960. Visiting New Delhi in a last-ditch attempt to resolve the border dispute diplomatically, Zhou outlined the contours of an "East-West Swap" and "offered to recognize India's position in the eastern sector if India accepted China's sovereignty over the Aksai Chin area in the west."[6] The proposal was ultimately rejected by New Delhi, which insisted on negotiating the dispute "sector-by-sector."

It was twenty years before the package deal was publicly revived by Deng Xiaoping in 1980.[7] In a June 21 interview with Krishna Kumar, editor of the *Vikrant*, Deng suggested that India would benefit from a "package deal" as it was "in possession of the territory that was larger, inhabited and endowed." And again India demurred in favor of a "sector-by-sector" approach.

"The Indian side," says analyst Zorawar Singh, "could never get itself to equate the two disputes."[8] The country's leaders were convinced of the historical and legal legitimacy of India's ownership of Arunachal Pradesh; by Delhi's account the border there had been settled by the 1914 Simla Accord. Ownership of Aksai Chin, on the other hand, had never been specified by any treaty, therefore the territory was seen as more genuinely disputed. India wanted China to first concede its claims to the Eastern Sector before moving to authentic negotiations on the Western Sector—i.e., the "sector-by-sector" approach.

Off the record some Indian officials suggested Delhi was "foolish" for not having accepted the initial package deal, though such opinions are rarely voiced in public. Dr. Mohan Malik suggested to this writer that India had "missed the bus" on the package deal. "Now that door may be closed."[9]

China Rescinds the Swap Proposal

Indeed, that door did seem to close in the mid-1980s, when China's position on the swap proposal underwent a noticeable shift. While still seeking a territorial swap roughly conforming to the Line of Actual Control, Beijing began to specifically demand that any package deal would have to include the transfer of the strategically prized town of Tawang in Arunachal Pradesh to China.

Shyam Saran, a former Indian Foreign Secretary, says it was in 1985 that China "began to signal the so-called 'package proposal' for resolving the border issue . . . was no longer on offer." He continues: "It was conveyed to us that at a minimum, Tawang would have to be transferred to the Chinese side. When we pointed out that just three years back in 1982

Deng Xiaoping had himself spelt out the package proposal as we had hitherto understood it, the response was that we may have read too much into his words."[10] In 1988 Chinese Vice-Premier Wu Xueqian clarified that "Comrade Deng's" package proposal only referred to "principles" and only when those principles were settled could "specific concessions . . . be dealt with by the delegations."[11]

Why did Beijing seemingly amend its package proposal and emphasize a demand on Tawang that Chinese scholars admit is "non-negotiable" for India? "I can't answer that," said Dr. Zhao Ganchen of China's Shanghai Institute of International Studies. "All I can tell you is that China's enthusiasm for a package deal has declined dramatically."[12]

Some have speculated that Beijing's new emphasis on Tawang was simply a response to India's repeated rejections of its original package proposal. It is a timeless negotiating tactic: by escalating its claims on Tawang, China has effectively shifted the equilibrium of the border negotiations. Any grand bargain in which India is able to keep Tawang is now likely to be viewed as a substantial Chinese concession. "China's strategy has always been to put unreasonable positions down then come a bit to the middle and sound reasonable," Kanwal Sibal, a former Foreign Secretary of India, explained to this writer.[13]

Look to Tibet

An alternative explanation points to the strategic connection China has made between Tibet and the border dispute. There is evidence to suggest that just as tensions over Tibet aggravated the border dispute in the late 1950s, Tibet may also be responsible for the hardening of China's position on the package deal.

Deng Xiaoping's rise to power in the late 1970s ushered in a new era of Chinese foreign policy that included several conciliatory gestures to the Tibetan exile community. He invited Tibetan exiles to return to the plateau and offered the Dalai Lama "a symbolic post in Beijing" as well as "the right to visit Tibet when he wanted, and freedom to speak to the press."[14] He requested that the Dalai Lama "send fact-finding delegations to Tibet and said that apart from the question of total independence all other issues could be discussed and settled."[15] Two rounds of secret talks between representatives of the Dalai Lama and the Communist Party in China followed in 1982 and 1984.

The initiative ended in failure. The Dalai Lama refused to return from exile and the two sides were unable to reach agreement on an acceptable level of autonomy for Tibet. The fact-finding missions to Tibet backfired, "expos[ing] the nationalist sentiment among Tibetans in the region, causing Beijing to reassess its strategy toward both Tibet and the Dalai Lama."[16] "By 1984,"—around the time China's position on the swap deal evolved—"the door to dialogue [between Beijing and the Dalai Lama] was no longer open."[17]

The fissures only grew deeper in the late 1980s. In 1987 the Dalai Lama launched an international campaign to garner support for the Tibetan cause in the United States and Europe, traveling to the West for the first time as a "political leader." That year he made his first address to the U.S. Congress, outlining a five point plan for Tibetan peace in a speech to the Congressional Human Rights Committee. The following year he offered a similar proposal to the European Parliament in Strasbourg, and in 1989—seven months after massive demonstrations against communist rule on the Tibetan plateau—the Dalai Lama was awarded the Nobel Peace Prize.

"By the end of the 1980s," Patricia Marcello writes, "the Dalai Lama had become more than a religious icon and the political leader of a distressed nation; he had become a celebrity. His international profile upset the Chinese government, for not only was he a thorn in their side, but also his popularity served to embarrass them before the world."[18]

Did China's heightened sense of insecurity in Tibet and growing disdain for the Dalai Lama prompt a decision to raise the bar for a settlement of the border dispute? Did Beijing conclude that the Dalai Lama and the Tibetan independence movement were long-term problems and that control of Tawang, with its famous Buddhist monastery, would be necessary to secure a greater foothold over Tibetan Buddhism?

DOMESTIC CONSTRAINTS

We may never know why China began to place greater emphasis on its claim to Tawang in the 1980s. What we do know is that despite the border agreements of 1993, 1996, 2003, and 2005, the border negotiations have fallen painfully short of their mandate. Today China and India are, in the words of a senior official in India's Ministry of External Affairs, "no closer [to a border resolution] than we were forty-five years ago."[19] Hu Shisheng of the Chinese Institutes for Contemporary International Studies bluntly admitted to this analyst in Beijing that "there is no prospect for a border resolution in the near term . . . *or in the long term* [emphasis added]."[20]

More troubling are signs that the window to reaching a border resolution may be closing even if the leadership in China and India find the urgency to reach a settlement. Present trends in both countries suggest domestic constraints are likely to materially restrict the ability of the leadership in Beijing and Delhi to make territorial concessions in the future.

Both capitals share common restraints stemming from the relative weakness of the political leadership, and the relative unwillingness of both publics to stomach concessions. "Neither India nor China is now ruled by imperious Emperors, like Nehru and Mao were. In their place we have timid bureaucrat politicians, vested with just a little more power than the others in the ruling collegiums. Collegiums are cautious to the point of being bland and extremely chary of taking risks," observes Indian analyst Mohan Gurusawmy.[21]

The greater constraints exist on the Indian side, both politically and institutionally. Any deal on the border dispute—however small or favorable to Indian interests—would have to be sold to a highly skeptical public, an opportunistic political opposition, and a sensational media in a country where anti-China sentiment is politically and financially profitable.

Perhaps most important, any Indian territorial concessions would almost certainly require an amendment to the Indian Constitution. That document gives the power to "diminish the area" or "alter the boundaries" of any state to parliament, not the government.[22] However, the First Schedule of the Indian Constitution, which defines India's territory, would likely have to be amended, a process that would require passage in both houses by a two-thirds majority of present members, and no less than a simple majority of the entire house. Consent would also almost surely have to be obtained from the relevant state governments where concessions were being made.

However, there are no indications that the political conditions in India are ripe for territorial concessions; quite the opposite. In June 2009, B. S. Raghavan, a columnist and former Indian Administrative Service officer, urged Delhi to consider concessions on Tawang as a means of breaking the impasse at the border: "There can be no definitive solution without give-and-take of territories on either side. The formula that has the best chance of success is accepting the status quo in the western and northern sectors, and ceding Tawang to China."[23]

The reaction of Admiral Arun Prakash, only recently retired as India's chief of naval staff, was typical: "Does no one remember history and the wages of appeasement? Let there be no doubt that China is a hegemon which wants to give India another knock to ensure we know our place in Asia. Give away Tawang today and they will demand Arunachal and Ladakh tomorrow."[24]

It is noteworthy, however, that Indian officials are at least now talking publicly about the possibility of concessions. General J. J. Singh, former Indian Army chief and governor of Arunachal Pradesh, told a seminar in the state's capital in March 2012 that on the border dispute "some give and take is necessary . . . India will have to move away from our position that our territory is non-negotiable."[25] And B. Raman, the former head of India's external intelligence agency, argued in a 2013 article that India "should be exploring the possibility of mutually acceptable border adjustments in the Arunachal Pradesh Sector instead of depending on an eternal status quo."[26]

It is, however, too early to tell whether this public debate will gradually degrade the stigma attached to the concept of territorial concessions, or whether the backlash against these proposals will make territorial concessions even less palatable to Indian politicians in the future. Early indications point to the latter.

China Too . . .

While an autocratic communist country may seem less susceptible to the whims of public opinion, there are signs that Chinese officials face domestic constraints of their own on the issue of territorial concessions. There is a rather spirited debate underway among China watchers regarding the ability of increasingly vocal nationalist groups to restrict the freedom of China's leadership to maneuver on politically sensitive issues like territorial concessions. The most influential of these groups remains active and retired members of the People's Liberation Army, whose brand of militaristic nationalism has been embraced by a new generation of vocal, digitally-savvy nationalist Chinese youth.

In today's China both groups have new outlets to contribute to a national debate that remains tightly restricted—but also closely watched—by the Party leadership. Active or retired PLA officers who previously lacked a platform to publicly air their views are now regularly featured in television shows and on the OpEd pages of China's nationalist press. China's leaders ignore these voices when they must, and exploit them when it's useful, but they are being heard.

Many in the West remain skeptical that this nationalist commentariat is capable of applying decisive pressure to the Chinese leadership. However, the body of contradictory evidence is growing larger with each new year. China's former ambassador to India, Zheng Ruixang, says that when he was a young diplomat "there was no difference of opinion in our country—no distance between the leadership and the people or between leaders themselves. That is not the case today and people who don't see that don't understand today's China." One scholar from the Chinese Academy of Social Sciences (CASS) explained to this writer:

> Chinese nationalism can't be ignored anymore. The elite—most of which are pro-globalization, pro-trade, pro-enrichment—think the nationalists are a burden. You assume that the government can silence some hawkish general if they don't like what he's saying. Wrong. He may have a million followers on his personal blog. He can embarrass the leadership if he likes.[27]

In April 2013 Lt. Gen. Wang Hongguang, the vice president of the PLA's Academy of Military Science, seemed to address this issue head-on in a rare rebuke to the professional PLA commentariat. "In recent years, military affairs experts have frequently appeared on TV and in all kinds of publications," he said, warning that "some have said off-key things, things that have misled the audience and been irresponsible." Some of their commentary was "inciting public sentiment and *causing some interference with our high-level policy decision-making and deployments* [emphasis added]."[28] C. Uday Bhaskar of India's National Maritime Foundation worries that the Chinese have "ginned up" so much nationalism that they are now "on top of the tiger and don't know how to get off."[29]

While this is representative of a systemic evolution in China, it's likely to have direct implications for the Sino-Indian border dispute. Simon Shen's 2011 study of Chinese nationalist blogs finds that "as Beijing has granted more room to anti-Indian netizens . . . it will be impossible to maintain anti-Indian activism totally within governmental control."

> India is perhaps the only major nation which is perceived as culturally and socially inferior on one hand, but capable of offering a legitimate challenge to China—with proven realist intention—on the other. Because of this, any economic, military or territorial defeat by the Indians would be seen as an unacceptable face-loss for the online Chinese nationalists and could have fatal consequences for the party-state. As a result, concessions are less likely to be made by Beijing towards Delhi than towards Washington, Tokyo or any developing nation in Africa.[30]

In *Distracted Antagonists, Wary Partners*, Murray Tanner of the Center for Naval Analysis cites Chinese diplomats explaining how "the role of nationalist internet opinion was putting pressure on Chinese officials and was an important obstacle to progress on the border."[31] Dr. Zhao Ganchen suggests the public is "not ready to offer any major concession on Arunachal. It would virtually mean that China acknowledges the legitimacy of the McMahon Line, and that China made a very important mistake in 1962."[32]

THE COSTS AND BENEFITS OF THE STATUS QUO

It is increasingly difficult to conceive of a settlement to the border dispute outside the confines of a grand bargain swap; increasingly difficult to envision a grand bargain without China abandoning its claim to Tawang; and increasingly difficult to envision either of these things happening in the current political environment.

A few imaginative alternatives have been proposed. Wu Yongnian of the Shanghai Institute for International Affairs has suggested creating an economic development zone linking Arunachal Pradesh with Tibet, with the boundary dispute being temporarily shelved.[33] And Ram Jethmalani, a former minister of law and justice and BJP parliamentarian, has argued that the border dispute could be settled by the International Court of Justice "unless the Chinese are prepared to accept arbitration by some world dignitaries enjoying the confidence of both countries."[34]

Neither these, nor other equally creative proposals, have found much traction in either country. Indian professor Mira Sinha Bhattacharjea says, "It is inevitable that the LAC must eventually become the border as neither country is in a position to wage war. [But] not doing anything is also a possible solution. It has to be noted that the relationship has progressed despite the border dispute. *So what is wrong with the status quo?* [emphasis added]."[35]

Perhaps nothing. The border has been free from violence for forty-five years and both Chinese and Indian analysts assess the risk of an inadvertent conflict at the border to be low. Ajai Shukla, a noted Indian defense correspondent who lived and served in the border areas told this author that the Sino-Indian border "could be a model for international border disputes."[36] "While resolutely stonewalling the exchange of signed maps, the PLA has never militarily violated the status quo."[37]

The stable maintenance of the status quo does in fact seem to be the route preferred by the Chinese leadership. Visiting India in December 2010, Chinese Premier Wen Jiabao suggested it would take a "very long time" to settle the border dispute, echoing a line favored by Chinese officials about leaving the border dispute to "future generations" to resolve.

However, numerous Indian scholars have interpreted this posture as a sign China has no intention of pursuing an early resolution to the border dispute. In his refreshingly candid manner, Ye Hailin of CASS says they might be right. "Frankly speaking, China has no intention to solve the border dispute. It's simply not worth trying. . . . Even if we somehow miraculously get a resolution, we still have problems in Tibet, in Pakistan, in the Indian Ocean. So why try so hard to resolve this dispute? It seems every time we try and solve the dispute it only makes things worse."[38]

Ironically, some Chinese scholars believe that it is India that lacks the desire to resolve the dispute, and ultimately benefits from the status quo. Several Chinese scholars told this analyst that India had traditionally just used its claims on Aksai Chin as a "bargaining chip."[39] The disputed territory under India's possession in Arunachal Pradesh, says Hu Shisheng, is more populated, richer in natural resources, and carried more religious and political value than the disputed territory under China's possession.[40] India, in his estimation, was the great beneficiary and proponent of the status quo.

If this belief is widely held, it would seem to be a miscalculation on China's part. For India the border dispute is an open wound; a constant reminder of a traumatic military defeat suffered at the hands of China fifty years ago. Moreover, the disputed border remains a point of profound strategic vulnerability for New Delhi. Already facing a nuclear-armed antagonist on its western front with which it has fought four wars, Delhi is severely overstretched defending a second disputed border with a second nuclear-armed antagonist.

The cost to India of the status quo is that it must continue diverting precious resources, attention, expertise, and manpower to the defending of a disputed border at a time the country needs to be devoting its attention and energy toward development. India is, by all indications, desirous of a swift resolution to the border dispute, albeit not one that includes the loss of Tawang.

The costs to China of the status quo are no less consequential, though Beijing's incentive structure is more complex and its calculation at the border more difficult to decipher. Like India, China is also operating in a hostile neighborhood, ringed by Asian powers aligned to the United States and grappling with a series of escalating maritime territorial disputes in the Pacific. Yet with the balance of power across the Himalayas tilted so heavily in China's favor, Beijing does not fear aggression from India, and the border does not evoke a comparable sense of vulnerability for China. Most important, the unresolved border *does* give China an explicit point of strategic leverage over India; an asset Beijing may not be willing to part with until it is sufficiently convinced India has neither the desire nor the capability to undermine Chinese rule in Tibet.

NOTES

1. "China Was the Aggrieved; India the Aggressor in '62," *OutlookIndia.com*, October 22, 2009 (Accessed June 13, 2013) http://www.outlookindia.com/article .aspx?282579.

2. M. Taylor Fravel, "Regime Insecurity and International Cooperation: Explaining China's Compromises on Territorial Disputes," *International Security*, Vol. 30 Issue 2, 46–83, fall 2005 (Accessed February 8, 2013): http://belfercenter .hks.harvard.edu/files/is3002_pp046-083_fravel.pdf.

3. Sudha Ramachandran, "China Plays Long Game on Border Disputes," *Asia Times Online*, January 27, 2011 (Accessed February 8, 2013) http://www.atimes. com/atimes/China/MA27Ad02.html

4. Dr. Mohan Malik. Author interview, Honolulu, April 2012.

5. Ajai Shukla, "China's Third Confrontation with India's Border Build Up," *Broadsword*, April 26, 2013 (Accessed June 13, 2013): http://ajaishukla.blogspot .com/2013/04/chinas-third-confrontation-with-indias.html.

6. M. Taylor Fravel, "Regime Insecurity and International Cooperation: Explaining China's Compromises on Territorial Disputes," *International Security*, Vol. 30 Issue 2, 46–83, fall 2005 (Accessed February 8, 2013): http://belfercenter .hks.harvard.edu/files/is3002_pp046-083_fravel.pdf.

7. Indian scholars who have done archival research on the subject suggest Chinese officials offered a package deal through various channels no less than four times between 1960 and 1984.

8. Zorawar Singh, *Himalayan Stalemate: Understanding the India-China Dispute* (London: Straight Forward Publishers, 2012), 14.

9. Dr. Mohan Malik. Author interview. Honolulu, April 2012.

10. Shyam Saran, "China in the Twenty-First Century: What India Needs to Know about China's World View," Second Annual K. Subrahmanyam Memorial Lecture, 9.

11. A. G. Noorani, "Only Political Leaders Can Resolve the Boundary Dispute between India and China, Not Officials," *Frontline*, Vol. 25, Issue 21, October 11–24, 2008 (Accessed February 6 2013): http://www.frontlineonnet.com/fl2521/stories/20081024252108000.htm.

12. Dr. Zhao Ganchen. Author interview. Washington, DC , May 16, 2012.

13. Ministry of External Affairs New Delhi. Author interview. South Block, New Delhi, November 2011.

14. Patrick French, *Tibet, Tibet: A Personal History of a Lost Land* (Random House Digital Inc., 2009). 109–112.

15. Melvyn Goldstein, "The Dalai Lama's Dilemma," *Foreign Affairs*, Vol. 77, No. 1, 86, January/Febuary 2008 (Accessed Febuary 6, 2013): http://c2.hbs.boell -net.de/downloads/Link_Goldstein.pdf.

16. Tashi Rabgey and Tseten Wangchuk Sharlho, "Sino-Tibetan Dialogue in the Post-Mao Era: Lessons and Prospects," *East-West Center*, Policy Studies No. 12, February 2004 (Accessed June 13, 2013): http://www.eastwestcenter.org/publi cations/sino-tibetan-dialogue-post-mao-era-lessons-and-prospects.

17. Tashi Rabgey and Tseten Wangchuk Sharlho, "Sino-Tibetan Dialogue in the Post-Mao Era: Lessons and Prospects," *East-West Center*, Policy Studies No. 12, February 2004 (Accessed June 13, 2013): http://www.eastwestcenter.org/publi cations/sino-tibetan-dialogue-post-mao-era-lessons-and-prospects.

18. Patricia Cronin Marcello, *The Dalai Lama: A Biography* (Greenwood Publishing Group, 2003), 137.

19. Ministry of External Affairs New Dehli. Author interview. South Block, New Delhi, November 2011.

20. Hu Shisheng. Author interview. Beijing, February 2012.

21. Guruswamy Mohan, "50 Years After 1962: Will India and China Fight a War Again," *South Asia Monitor*, 1–3.

22. Indian Constitution, Schedule 1.

23. B. S. Raghavan, "India China Confluence, Ushering in a New Golden Era," *Hindu Business Line*, July 6, 2009 (Accessed February 6, 2013): http://www .thehindubusinessline.in/bline/2009/07/06/stories/2009070650390900.htm

24. Ram Narayanan, "Should Indian Make Up with China Now?" *Freedom First*, Monthly No. 513, March 2010 (Accessed February 8, 2013): http://www .wired.com/beyond_the_beyond/2010/02/freedom-first-and-china-last/.

25. "JJ Clarifies: Remarks on India-China Border Personal," *Indian Express*, April 21, 2012 (Accessed February 8, 2013): http://www.indianexpress.com/news/jj-clarifies-remarks-on-indiachina-border-personal/939599\.

26. B. Raman, "Dragon's New Face," *OutlookIndia.com*, 2013 (Accessed February 27, 2013): http://www.outlookindia.com/article.aspx?283780.

27. Author interview in Washington, DC, June 27 2013

28. "Lieutenant-General Wang Hongguang Blasts PLA Pundits' 'Interference' in Decisions and Deployments," *South Sea Conversations*, April 29, 2013: http://southseaconversations.wordpress.com/.

29. C. Uday Bhaskar. Author interview. New Delhi, August 2012.

30. Simon Shen, "Exploring the Neglected Constraints on Chindia: Analysing the Online Chinese Perception of India and Its Interaction with China's Indian Policy," *China Quarterly* Vol. 207, September 2011, 560.

31. Murray Scot Tanner, "Distracted Antagonists, Wary Partners: China and India Assess Their Security Relations," *CNA*, September 2011 (Accessed February 8, 2013): http://www.cna.org/sites/default/files/research/Distracted%20Antagonists%2C%20Wary%20Partners%20D0025816%20A1.pdf.

32. Dr. Zhao Ganchen. Author interview. Washington, DC, May 16, 2012.

33. Ananth Krishnan, "China Will Not Accept LAC as Solution for Border Dispute, Says Commentary," *Hindu* citing *Jiafang Daily/Liberation Daily*, October 25, 2012 (Accessed February 8, 2013):http://www.thehindu.com/news/national/china-will-not-accept-lac-as-solution-to-border-dispute-says-commentary/article4031786.ece.

34. Ram Jethmalani, "China Threat Cannot Be Ignored," *Sunday Guardian*, February 8, 2013 (Accessed June 13, 2013): http://www.sunday-guardian.com/analysis/china-threat-cannot-be-ignored.

35. Srikanth Kondapalli, "Military Seminar Report #204," Institute of Peace and Conflict Studies, December 27, 2006 (Accessed February 8, 2013):http://ipcs.org/seminar/military/india-china-border-issue-763.html.

36. Ministry of External Affairs New Delhi. Author interview. South Block, New Delhi November 2011.

37. Ajai Shukla, "The LAC Is Not the LoC," *Broadsword*, September 19, 2012 (Accessed February 8, 2013):http://ajaishukla.blogspot.com/2012/09/the-lac-is-not-loc.html.

38. Ye Hailin. Author interview. Washington, DC, June 27, 2013.

39. Author interview with Dr. Zhao Ganchen at Center for Strategic and International Studies, Washington, DC, May 16, 2012.

40. Hu Shisheng. Author interview. Beijing, February 2012.

III

TAWANG AND TIBET

Chapter 5

Tawang

At the intersection of the two most intimate disputes in the Sino-Indian rivalry—Tibet and the border dispute—lies the tiny Buddhist enclave of Tawang, arguably the most strategically valuable real estate along the Sino-Indian border. Cherished by India and coveted by Beijing, Tawang is also arguably the single biggest obstacle to a final settlement of the largest ongoing border dispute in the world.

Just ten kilometers east of the Bhutan border and twenty kilometers south of the China border, Tawang is perched on a Himalayan mountainside some 8,000–10,000 feet above sea level. Located at the western extreme of the Indian state of Arunachal Pradesh, the Tawang district is home to 50,000 people spread across 2,000 square kilometers, making it one of the least populated districts in India.

Since helicopter service was suspended a few years ago, reaching Tawang necessitates a 500-kilometer, nineteen-hour journey from Guwahati, Assam[1] on a single, primitive road prone to landslides and frequent winter closures. The mud and gravel zig-zag road that climbs 14,000 feet to the Se La Pass offers large civilian and military vehicles a dangerously thin margin of error.

Traveling to Tawang in December 2012, it was quickly apparent that the much-touted border infrastructure modernization plan announced for Arunachal Pradesh in 2006 remains a distant promise. Manned crews with pitchforks and a small army of tractors and heavy machinery work around the clock just to keep the road passable, which may be little more than half the year.

A report by India's comptroller and auditor general in 2010 found that the Home Ministry failed to spend over 90 percent of the funds

71

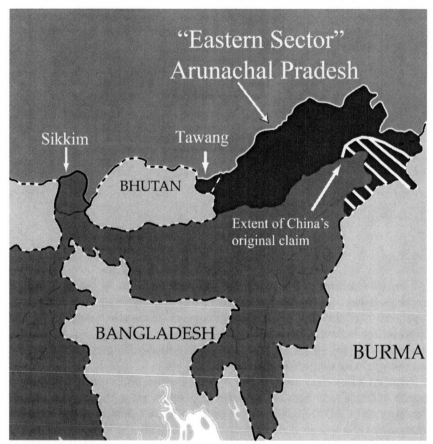

Map 3.1.   Eastern Sector
Source: American Foreign Policy Council

allocated for road projects in each of the four years between 2006 and 2009.[2] Namrata Goswami, an expert on India's northeast, puts the bulk of the blame for this failure with the bureaucracy, which she says has dithered on issuing the necessary environmental and interministerial clearances. Local protests, a lack of skilled engineers and modern equipment, and corruption have also been blamed for the glacial pace of progress in building infrastructure.

Several hours from the nearest internet connection or central heating system, the town itself remains largely untouched by modernity. In searching for the next possible flashpoint in the China-India relationship, this sleepy Buddhist enclave would seem an unlikely candidate. But Tawang's rustic charm belies a town with outsized religious and geopolitical value.

Tawang sits astride an old trade route[3] that constitutes one of the shortest and least hazardous paths from the Tibetan plateau to India's northeast. This quickly became evident during the 1962 war, as the People's Liberation Army (PLA) seized Tawang less than four days after the outbreak of hostilities, providing China an ideal staging ground to push further south to Bomdila and beyond.

For India, Tawang thus represents the potential frontline in any future conflict with China at the border, a firewall between the PLA and the foothills and plains to the south. For China, however, the town's military value may be overshadowed by its significance to Tibetan Buddhism.

Like a sentinel overlooking the town from above, the Tawang Monastery is the largest Buddhist monastery in India and, outside of Tibet, one of the largest in the world. The physical size of the complex—with some sixty-five buildings housing several hundred monks—is commensurate with its standing in Tibetan Buddhism.

According to legend, in 1681 the fifth Dalai Lama dispatched an emissary to locate a site for a new monastery. Sidetracked from his journey, the emissary was tracking the hoofmarks of his stray horse when he stumbled upon the site of an ancient palace. The grounds were selected for the new Tawang (literally, "chosen by horse") Monastery.[4] The fifth Dalai Lama died the following year, but for over a decade his death remained a secret while a Regent searched for his reincarnation. In 1697 the reincarnation was found in Tawang, a fourteen-year-old boy born at the tiny Urgelling Monastery just a few kilometers from the Tawang Monastery.

Still the most controversial of the Dalai Lamas, the sixth reincarnation famously disavowed monastic life to indulge the guilty pleasures of wine and women. He nevertheless enshrined Tawang's place in the religious history of Tibetan Buddhism: it was, and remains, only the second time a Dalai Lama had been born outside the confines of Tibet proper (the fourth Dalai Lama was born in Mongolia).

Over three centuries later, the fourteenth (and current) Dalai Lama made his own contribution to the legend of Tawang. It was the first Indian town in which he took refuge on his fifteen-day journey into permanent exile from China in March 1959. Though he later went on to establish the Tibetan Government in Exile some 1,500 kilometers away in Dharamsala, the Dalai Lama has returned to Tawang no less than five times, and the town retains an influential place in the minds of Tibetan Buddhists and the Tibetan exile community at large.

TO WHOM DOES TAWANG BELONG?

China's claim on Tawang has the virtue of being straightforward. Beijing argues Tawang was historically a part of Tibet, and Tibet is historically a part of China. Full stop. The claim has not gone unchallenged by scholars. As the following chapter will demonstrate, for 700 years Chinese authority over the Tibetan plateau "waxed and waned with the changing fortunes of the central government at Peking. When that government was strong, their authority was real; when weak, it was nominal."[5] Because Tibet drifted in and out of China's sovereign orbit multiple times after the Mongol invasion in the fourteenth century, many scholars have found the term *suzerainty* a more apt description than *sovereignty* to describe the nature of China's relationship with Tibet.

In much the same way, evidence suggests that Lhasa's authority and influence in Tawang fell short of full sovereignty. Tawang was historically "Tibetan" insofar as it paid fealty to the Tsona Dzongpons, secular administrators from Lhasa who "periodically toured the [Tawang] area to collect taxes and settle disputes."[6] In 1936 the chief secretary of Assam documented how the Tawang Monastery was paying 5,000 rupees tribute annually to Tibet, split between officials in Lhasa, the Drepung Monastery (of which the Tawang Monastery is a "daughter institution"), and the Tibetan administrators of Tawang.[7]

However, positioned as it was on the southern slope of the Himalayas and on the outer fringe of Tibet's sphere of influence, Tawang always retained a substantial degree of autonomy. Nain Sing of the Trigonometrical Survey of India visited Tawang in 1874–1875 and concluded that the district was run by a "sort of Parliament termed Kato" populated by Lamas from the Tawang Monastery, which in his words was "entirely independent of the . . . Lhasa Government."[8]

Claude Arpi argues that by the time Communist China invaded Tibet in 1950, Tawang was under "some vague Tibetan administration, with the [local Tibetan officials] collecting 'monastic' taxes from time to time."[9]

The Tibet-Tawang connection is further weakened, some scholars argue, by an ethnic, cultural, and geographic divide. While the Monpa people that constitute the majority of Tawang's population are fervent followers of Tibetan Buddhism, they are "racially, linguistically, and culturally different from the mainstream of the Tibetan population."[10] They "always stood somewhat apart from the Tibetans of the plateau, despite sharing their religious and cultural outlook," says Ishaan Tharoor. "In the days when political power was concentrated in Lhasa, Tibetans would look down upon the Monpa almost as if they were a tribe of southern barbarians." [11]

The British Raj and Tawang

India's historical attachment to Tawang rests on even looser foundation than China's. According to Dr. John W. Garver, prior to British rule no Indian kingdom was able to assert authority over the primitive and warlike tribes of India's northeast.[12] Indeed, it was not until the early nineteenth century, when local tribes sought British protection from Burmese invaders that the footprint of the British Raj reached Assam. Assam was formally annexed in 1838, but Tawang, positioned to the north in the nebulous Himalayan buffer zone between the Indian empire and Tibet, remained an afterthought.

As it consolidated its control over India's northeast, by the late nineteenth century the British Raj became seized with the idea of opening Tibet to British trade and influence, and defining a new Indo-Tibetan frontier favorable to British interests. The endeavor received added urgency as London watched, with great alarm, the slow expansion of the Russian empire south and east into Xinjiang.[13]

When China's last imperial dynasty, the Qing, collapsed in 1911, British officials jumped at the chance to negotiate a new border with a newly independent Tibet, which was now desperate for allies and international recognition. Despite treaties with China (1906) and Russia (1907) committing London not to disturb Tibet's territorial integrity, a tripartite conference was convened at Simla on October 6, 1913 that gathered representatives from Tibet (Lonchen Shatra), China (Ivan Chen) and Britain (Sir Henry McMahon).

The Tibetans sought recognition of their declaration of independence-from China in 1911, while China wanted to station 2,000 troops on the plateau and control Tibet's military and foreign affairs.[14] To split the difference, McMahon proposed a division of Tibet into two distinct zones, as had happened when Mongolia declared independence in 1911: an "Inner Tibet" would fall under China's full administrative authority while an "Outer Tibet" would enjoy substantial autonomy.

China flatly rejected the proposed division of Tibet but as the meetings stretched into 1914, a series of parallel and private negotiations between McMahon and Lonchen Shatra produced an exchange of notes[15] and a map.[16] Drawn by McMahon and included as an appendix to the final agreement, the map outlined a new Indo-Tibetan boundary twenty kilometers north of Tawang. When the "Simla Accord" was tabled on April 27, 1914, Chinese representative Ivan Chen initialed—but did not sign—the draft, and Beijing repudiated the agreement two days later.[17]

To this day China maintains that Tibet lacked the sovereign authority to renegotiate its borders in 1914. Beijing considers the "so-called McMahon Line" to be a "predatory and imperialist imposition of the British government . . . when China was weak, divided and under the domination of foreign imperialist powers."[18]

Beijing's opposition to the Simla Accord was not surprising, but London's opposition was. British officials were concerned the accord violated their earlier treaties with China and Russia, and were convinced

McMahon had exceeded his mandate. "A consideration of the north-eastern frontier did not form part of the functions of the conference, and the views and proposal put forward might be regarded as personal to Sir Henry McMahon," read a message passed to London by the Indian Viceroy, Lord Hardinge.[19] For the next two-plus decades official British maps and documents made no mention of the McMahon Line and no effort was made to enforce the agreement or extend British administration to Tawang.

In 1935 a pioneering officer in the Foreign and Political Department of India, Olaf Caroe, unexpectedly "unearthed" the proceeds of the Simla Accord and orchestrated a campaign for British reaffirmation of the McMahon line. However, he met resistance in London and Delhi, while Tibetan officials "made clear that their acceptance of the McMahon border was not firm."[20] Caroe did succeed in having the McMahon Line included in the 1937 *Survey of India* and 1938 volume of *Aitchison's Treaties, Engagements and Sanads*, the official record of all treaties entered into by the government of India.[21] But British officials made no practical effort to enforce their writ in Tawang.

An expedition to Tawang led by Captain G. S. Lightfoot in 1938 again produced calls for Britain to extend its administrative control over the town and evict Tibetan officials. And again caution prevailed and the proposal was mooted in deference to Beijing and Lhasa. When British colonialists ultimately left India to its freedom in 1947, "no final provision was ever made for Tawang. The future of the town and the issues associated with it would depend on the evolving decisions of a new India and the policies of the new (Communist) China."[22]

India Takes Tawang

The great irony of China's claim to Tawang is that the prized town was in Beijing's possession not once but twice in the twentieth century, and in both cases Tawang was lost or ceded without a fight.

When Mao Zedong ordered the People's Liberation Army into Tibet in 1950 in one of his first acts in office, Tawang was still loosely administered from Lhasa, and thus nominally brought under Chinese control.

The governor of Assam had other plans. Unaware to Delhi, in 1950 Governor Jairamdas Daulatram organized an unauthorized mission to capture Tawang. "Neither [the federal government] nor I have the ability to get the Commander-in-Chief, Field Marshal Roy Boucher, to agree to a military expedition for this task," Daluatram told the decorated World War II veteran he commissioned to lead the expedition, Major Ralengnao "Bob" Khating.[23]

In the winter of 1950 and 1951, Khating marched for Tawang with several hundred soldiers from the Assam Rifles, reaching his destination in February 1951. After several days camped out on a ridge overlooking Tawang, Khating led his troops into town with fixed bayonets and planted the Indian flag in front of the Tawang Monastery.

On March 20, Khating entered the palace of the local Tibetan administrator accompanied by Major T. C. Allen, a relic of the British Raj and one of the last colonial officials left in the region. "Since India is a republic now, you really have no business here," Allen told the local Tibetan official. Sidharth Mishra colorfully recounts what happened next: "Because of the awkwardness in sitting on the cushions . . . and because his pistol butt was poking his hip, Allen suddenly took out his Smith and Wesson pistol and placed it on the ground in front of him."

Unsurprisingly, the Tibetan official immediately signed a document transferring sovereignty of Tawang to India. Allen was handsomely rewarded, later appointed to be the lieutenant governor of India's Northeast Frontier Agency. However, according to Mishra's account Indian Prime Minister Jawaharlal Nehru was beside himself after learning of the expedition: "I wish you had the good sense to consult me before you commissioned this colossal stupidity," he told Assam's governor. "I want a complete blackout."[24]

Delhi was shocked to learn of the Tawang expedition, but the reaction in Beijing was even more surprising: "studied and significant silence."[25] The mission to Tawang "drew no protest from China," whose "presence in Tibet still barely extended beyond Lhasa."[26] Chinese officials admit it was not until 1953 or later that they realized Tawang had changed hands, an admission wielded by Indian and Tibetan analysts as evidence of China's tenuous claim of sovereignty over the town.

Less than a decade later Tawang would again swing back in the Chinese orbit during the 1962 border war. Within a week of the outbreak of hostilities the PLA seized Tawang in a pincer movement from the east and west. And yet again Chinese rule over Tawang proved short lived. After driving 160 kilometers into Indian territory, on November 21, 1962, China unilaterally declared a ceasefire and withdrew its troops twenty kilometers north of the McMahon line. Voluntarily, unexpectedly, Tawang was returned to India.

Tibetans and Tawang Today

Long after the Dalai Lama and the Tibetan Government in Exile accepted India's hospitality, they maintained that Tawang was historically Tibetan, not Indian. This was publicly expressed by the Dalai Lama as late as 2003 when he was questioned on the matter during a trip to Tawang. Then, in 2008 the Dalai Lama reversed his longstanding position. For the first time since arriving in India fifty years before, the Dalai Lama acknowledged that Arunachal Pradesh (of which Tawang is a part) was historically a part of India in an interview with the *Navbharat Times*. During a trip to Tawang the following year, the Dalai Lama reaffirmed his change of heart, stating "Tawang is an integral part of India."[27]

Officials of the Tibetan Government in Exile now argue that despite Tawang's historic links to Tibet, the town today is indisputably Indian. The director of the Tibet Policy Institute in Dharamsala, Karma Yeshi, maintains that Tawang was "legally ceded to India in 1914" and Tibetans "have to respect [the Simla] treaty; it was signed by our officials." Yeshi lamented the fact it had taken this long to acknowledge Tawang's place in India. "This displeased India and may have caused them to be less supportive of Tibet's cause. While China was the real threat we were quibbling about small things."[28]

THE FUTURE

As this book shows, the seemingly unbridgeable gap between China and India over Tawang has repeatedly surfaced to undermine efforts at achieving a final settlement of their territorial dispute. In the mid-1980s China's insistence that any grand bargain on the border dispute include the transfer of Tawang ultimately poisoned the "package deal" China had been informally proposing since 1960. In the mid-2000s, a surge of optimism about the prospects for a comprehensive settlement to the border dispute were underpinned by the Indian assumption that China had dropped its claim to Tawang as part of the "settled populations" provision of the 2005 border protocol. When that assumption proved false, the border negotiations ground to a halt and, as of 2013, appear hopelessly deadlocked.

It is difficult to imagine a normalization of the Sino-Indian relationship without the border dispute being resolved, and it is difficult to envision a resolution to the border dispute without significant—and hitherto inconceivable—concessions from one or both sides on Tawang. Yet today there appears to be little appetite on either side to find mutual accommodation. The domestic political environment in both countries has put significant constraints on the Chinese and Indian leadership to make any material concessions, were they so inclined. But they are not. On the contrary, both sides' position on Tawang have hardened since the turn of the century.

Chinese scholars have suggested that any concessions on Tawang would represent an unacceptable failure to protect "Tibetan interests." Wang Yiwei, an associate professor at Fudan University explains: "Tawang goes beyond a territorial issue. We want to win the hearts of Tibetans."[29] Similarly, the China Reform Forum's Ma Jiali has argued "Tawang is central to the resolution of the Sino-Indian border issue."[30] Only if India returns Tawang, he said, could China be "magnanimous" in settling the Middle and Western sectors. During a visit to the China Reform Forum in April 2013, Ma suggested (in a personal capacity) that perhaps China could drop its claims to "big Tawang" (i.e., the Tawang district), if India would concede "small Tawang" (i.e., the town of Tawang).

Such a proposal is unlikely to find many takers in Delhi. India's commitment to Tawang today is firmer than it's ever been. When the Sino-Indian rivalry sharpened in 2009, Delhi dispatched three senior government officials to Tawang—the Defense Minister, Home Minister, and Prime Minister—in a span of fifteen months. While visiting the town in April 2010, Home Minister P. Chidambaram stated "Tawang and all of Arunachal Pradesh are part of India *and will always remain a part of India* [emphasis added]."[31] Indian diplomats interviewed for this book echoed that sentiment, explaining that Tawang was now an inseparable part of the Indian Union with representatives elected to the Indian parliament. "We will never give it up," was a promise made by more than one official. Mohan Guruswamy insisted to this author that India's claim to Tawang was as legally and historically valid as China's claim to Tibet: "China occupied Lhasa in 1951, and we occupied Tawang in 1951. If [they] want to discuss Tawang, fine. We want to discuss Lhasa."[32]

Tawang is in many ways the axis on which the Sino-Indian rivalry pivots. The border dispute, the Dalai Lama, the McMahon Line, the Simla Accord, the legacy of Western imperialism, and the conflict of interests in Tibet, all intersect at this tiny Buddhist enclave. If the China-India relationship is to evolve beyond the confines of strategic rivalry in the twenty-first century, they will first have to reach an accommodation on Tawang.

NOTES

1. Tawang is roughly 400 kilometers from Guwahati and Itanagar, the capitals of Assam and Arunachal Pradesh, the closest transport hubs. Flying into Tezpur can cut a few hours off of the drive.

2. Rajeswari Pillai Rajagopalan and Kailash Prasad, "Sino-Indian Border Infrastructure: Issues and Challenges," *ORF Issue Brief*, August 2010 (Accessed January 30, 2013): http://www.observerindia.com/cms/sites/orfonline/modules/issuebrief/attachments/Ib_23_1283150074942.pdf.

3. Julie Marshall, *Britain and Tibet: 1765–1947* (New York: Taylor and Francis, 2007), 245.

4. "Arunachal: Tawang Trek," *Wild World India*, January 28, 2013: http://www.wildworldindia.com/treks/tawang.asp.

5. Prithwis Chandra Chakravarti, *India's China Policy* (Bloomington: Indiana University Press, 1962), 15.

6. T. V. Rajeswar, "India-China Border Dispute: What Can Be a Possible Solution," *The Tribune*, January 30, 2013 (Accessed June 13, 2013): http://www.tribuneindia.com/2012/20121103/edit.htm#4.

7. Claude Arpi, "A New Road to Bhutan," *Claude Arpi's Blogspot*, November 24, 2012 (Accessed January 30, 2013): http://claudearpi.blogspot.com/2012/11/a-new-road-to-bhutan.html.

8. Manilal Bose, *History of Arunachal Pradesh* (New Delhi: Concept Publishing Company, 1997), 140.

9. Claude Arpi. "Thoroughly Unscrupulous, Unreliable and Determined Power at Our Doors," *Claude Arpi's Blogspot*, May 21, 2012 (January 30, 2013) http://claudearpi.blogspot.com/2012/05/thoroughly-unscrupulous-unreliable-and.html

10. Manilal Bose, *History of Arunachal Pradesh* (New Delhi: Concept Publishing Company, 1997), 140.

11. Ishaan Tharoor, "Beyond India vs. China: The Dalai Lama's Agenda," *Time World*, Novemeber 5, 2009 (Accessed January 30, 2013): http://www.time.com/time/world/article/0,8599,1934948,00.html.

12. John W. Garver, *Protracted Contest: Sino-Indian Rivalry in the Twentieth Century* (Seattle: University of Washington Press, 2001), 92.

13. Moscow eventually gained a major foothold in the Xinjiang when the local warlord, Sheng Shicai, became a client of the Soviet Union in the 1930s and 1940s.

14. Manilal Bose, *History of Arunachal Pradesh* (New Delhi: Concept Publishing Company, 1997), 133.

15. The exchange of notes were attached to the agreement in the appendix.

16. Xuecheng Liu writes: "Three maps are related to the Simla conference. One is attached to the March 24 notes; one to the April 27 convention, and the third to the July 3 convention. As far as the Tawang Tract is concerned, the three maps show the McMahon line quite differently. On the first map, the McMahon Line was shown running along south of the Thagla range far north of Tawang; on the second map, it is not shown in the Tawang tract; and on the third one, it is superimposed on the word "Tawang." Xuechang Liu, "Look Beyond the Sino-Indian Border Dispute," *China Institute of International Studies*, August 11, 2011 (Accessed January 30, 2013): http://www.ciis.org.cn/english/2011-08/11/content_4401017.htm.

17. China's main contention, it should be noted, was not the new Indo-Tibetan boundary, but the new Sino-Tibetan boundary and the bifurcation of Tibet.

18. Li Hongmei, "What Is Beyond the Physical Line?" *English People's Daily Online.* August 21, 2009 (Accessed January 30, 2013): http://english.people.com.cn/90002/96417/6726134.html.

19. Xuechang Liu, "Look Beyond the Sino-Indian Border Dispute," *China Institute of International Studies*, August 11, 2011 (Accessed January 30, 2013) http://www.ciis.org.cn/english/2011-08/11/content_4401017.htm

20. Steven A. Hoffman, *India and the China Crisis* (Los Angeles: University of California Press, 1990), 21.

21. British officials also retroactively amended the 1929 version of Aitchison's Treaties to reflect the McMahon line, making no mention of the revision in the document.

22. Steven A. Hoffman, *India and the China Crisis* (Los Angeles: University of California Press, 1990), 22.

23. "Forgotten: The Man Who Won Us Tawang," *Pioneer*, March 10, 2012 (Accessed January 30, 2013): http://www.dailypioneer.com/home/online-channel/top-story/48702-forgotten-the-man-who-won-us-tawang.html.

24. "Forgotten: The Man Who Won Us Tawang," *Pioneer*, March 10, 2012 (Accessed January 30, 2013) http://www.dailypioneer.com/home/online-channel/top-story/48702-forgotten-the-man-who-won-us-tawang.html

25. A. G. Noorani, "The Truth," *Frontline*, November 30, 2013 (Accessed January 30, 2013): http://pay.hindu.com/ebook%20-%20ebfl20121130part1.pdf.

26. Neville Maxwell, "Whose Tawang? A Dispute within the Sino-Indian Boundary Dispute," January 30, 2013 (Accessed June 13, 2013): http://chinaindiaborderdispute.files.wordpress.com/2010/07/nmaxwelltawangsevensisterspost nov2011.pdf.

27. "After Dalai Lama's Rebuke, China Breathes Fire," *Times of India*, November 9, 2009 (Accessed January 30, 2013): http://www.timesnow.tv/After-Dalai-Lamas-rebuke-China-breathes-fire/articleshow/4331672.cms.

28. Karma Yeshi. Author interview. Dharamsala, India, August 2012.

29. Sudha Ramachandran, "China Toys with India's Border," *Asia Times Online*, June 27, 2008 (Accessed January 30, 2013): http://www.atimes.com/atimes/South_Asia/JF27Df01.html.

30. "Return Tawang to China to Resolve Boundary Dispute," *Rediff News*, March 7, 2007 (Accessed January 30, 2013): http://www.rediff.com/news/report/china/20070307.htm.

31. "Tawang, Other Areas of Arunachal Integral Parts of India: Chidambaram," *Daily News and Analysis, India.com*, April 2, 2010 (Accessed January 30, 2013): http://www.dnaindia.com/india/report_tawang-other-areas-of-arunachal-inte gral-parts-of-india-chidambaram_1366623.

32. Mohan Guruswamy. Author interview. Delhi, November 2011.

Chapter 6

Tibet

Bound by one of the longest shared borders in the world, China and India should be the most intimate of neighbors. Yet the two civilizations spent most of their long histories as distant relatives, separated by some of the most unforgiving terrain on the planet.

When plate tectonics thrust the Indian subcontinent into the underbelly of Asia fifty million years ago, the collision created the world's most imposing mountain chain, the Himalayas, and the barren, icy plateau we now call Tibet. Long considered a model "strategic buffer" between the Han Chinese heartland and the Indo-Gangetic plains, it would be hard to conceive of a more perfect natural barrier. It is thus ironic that Tibet, which was largely responsible for the absence of conflict between China and India for two millennia, ultimately helped propel the two countries to war in 1962.

When the People's Liberation Army (PLA) invaded Tibet in 1950, Mao intended to return the plateau to what he saw as its rightful place in the Chinese empire. But the invasion had the unintended side effect of "shrinking the strategic distance between India and China,"[1] bringing the first permanent Chinese military presence to India's northern border. From that point forward, Tibet ceased to be a strategic buffer between China and India and instead became a source of leverage and vulnerability for both countries.

Separated as they were by the Himalayas, India's relationship with Tibet never reached the intimacy of China's. Indo-Tibetan ties were historically confined to the cultural and religious arenas. Most notably, in the seventh century Buddhism made the voyage from its birthplace, India,

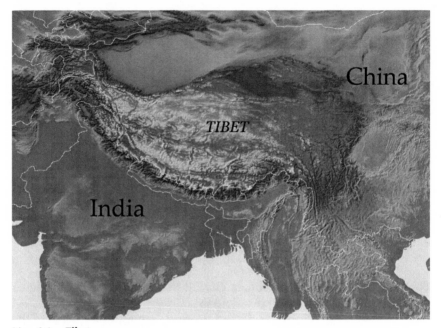

Map 6.1. Tibet
Source: American Foreign Policy Council

across the Himalayas into Tibet, in what is arguably India's most influential contribution to the region. However, central Indian empires never became enmeshed in the politics of the plateau and never wielded direct influence in Lhasa on the same level as the Chinese.

The nature of China's more expansive relationship with Tibet remains a complex and controversial subject still debated by scholars. Beijing claims that following an invasion of Tibet by the Mongol rulers of China in 1240 A.D., Tibet was "organically included as an administrative unit"[2] in the Chinese empire.[3] This is the basis for the oft-quoted Chinese claim that "for more than 700 years the central government of China has continuously exercised sovereignty over Tibet, and Tibet has never been an independent state."[4]

There are three principal criticisms leveled at this claim of continuous sovereignty. First, while scholars uniformly agree that Chinese authority over Tibet grew substantially under the (Mongol) Yuan—and later the (Manchu) Qing—dynasties, a majority contend that even during these periods of heightened Sino-Tibetan engagement, Tibet retained a degree of autonomy that rendered Chinese authority on the plateau considerably short of full sovereignty.

China's Mongol rulers ultimately became fervent followers of Buddhism,[5] creating a politico-religious connection that Tibetans say was more akin to a "priest-patron" relationship than one between subject and ruler. Dr. John W. Garver argues this religious bond made Chinese rule "less intrusive and coercive" than was found in China's other tributary relationships,[6] with the Mongols leaving Tibet to manage its own religious and local political affairs. "China's version of history often deliberately blurs the distinction between what was no more than hegemonic influence, tributary relationships, suzerainty, and actual control," argues Dr. Mohan Malik of the Asia-Pacific Center for Security Studies.[7]

The second criticism of China's claim of 700 years of continuous sovereignty over Tibet is that the periods of more intense Sino-Tibetan engagement under the Yuan and Qing Dynasties were bracketed by eras in which Chinese authority in Tibet was virtually nonexistent. The Mongols were succeeded by the (Han) Ming Dynasty (1368–1644), which Beijing claims continued to manage Tibetan affairs "according to conventions and customs, granting titles and setting up administrative organs."[8] However, non-Chinese scholars agree that in practice, the Ming oversaw a dramatic cessation of Chinese interest in, and influence over, the plateau. Tibetologist Melvyn Goldstein argues,

> the Ming emperors exerted no administrative authority over [Tibet]. Many titles were given to leading Tibetans by the Ming emperors, but not to confer authority as with the Mongols. By conferring titles on Tibetans already in power, the Ming emperors merely recognized political reality.[9]

Like the Mongols, the (Manchu) Qing Dynasty (1644–1912) that followed the Ming embraced Buddhism and reasserted Chinese authority in Tibet, including eventually stationing a military garrison on the plateau. And again this period was followed by an abrupt retraction of Chinese authority on the plateau when Tibetans evicted Chinese forces and declared independence in 1911. For the next forty years Tibet remained a nominally independent country, denied formal recognition by the international community but engaging in acts befitting a nation-state.[10]

Finally, some scholars have questioned the validity of the Han-led Peoples Republic of China laying historical claim to all of the territory conquered by the non-Han empires of China's past. The Mongols and, to a lesser extent the Manchus, were not at the time viewed as "Chinese rulers," but as foreign barbarians ruling over a weakened Chinese people. Again, Mohan Malik argues:

> Official Chinese history today often distorts this complex history, however, claiming that the Mongols, Tibetans, Manchus, and Hans were all Chinese, when in fact the Great Wall was built by the Chinese dynasties to keep out the northern Mongol and Manchu tribes that repeatedly overran Han China . . . China laying claim to the Mongol and Manchu empires' colonial

possessions would be equivalent to India laying claim to Afghanistan, Bangladesh, Burma, Malaysia (Srivijaya), Nepal, Pakistan, and Sri Lanka on the grounds that they were all parts of either the Maurya, Chola, or the Moghul and the British Indian Empires.[11]

NOT JUST A BORDER DISPUTE

In an ideal world, Tibet would find its historic role as the bridge between the Chinese and Indian civilizations. In the real world, though, Tibet is likely to be at the very core of an unending tension between China and India in the coming years.

—C. Raja Mohan, *Samudra Manthan: Sino-Indian Rivalry in the Pacific*[12]

The origins of the conflict of interest in Tibet draw from the same colonial machinations that preempted the border dispute in the late nineteenth and early twentieth century. As the British maneuvered to negotiate a new Indo-Tibetan border in the late nineteenth century, they were also working to secure from the Qing Dynasty a series of special privileges on the Tibetan plateau. After a military expedition to Tibet in 1903–1904, the British opened trade offices in several towns and eventually a diplomatic mission in Lhasa. From Beijing they won several trade advantages and the right "to maintain escort troops at the specified trade marts."[13] When the British left the subcontinent in 1947, many of these special privileges were inherited by a newly independent India.

However, China's 1950 invasion of Tibet put these privileges at risk and threatened to remove the historic buffer between the Chinese and Indian civilizations. Instead of attempting to challenge China's entry onto the plateau, Indian Prime Minister Nehru pursued a more limited goal of preserving domestic autonomy for Tibet and, by consequence, India's privileges there. By affirming Chinese sovereignty over Tibet in the 1954 Panscheel Agreement, Nehru hoped to create an environment in which Beijing would be amenable to granting Tibet a substantial degree of autonomy. However, those hopes were permanently quashed when the PLA re-invaded Tibet in 1959 to crush a popular rebellion.

Beijing came to suspect India of complicity in the 1959 uprising and Beijing's suspicions were seemingly confirmed when the Dalai Lama fled to India in March 1959. That the Buddhist leader was welcomed by Indian government officials and provided the political space and physical territory to establish a Tibetan Government in Exile was further proof to Beijing of nefarious Indian intentions.[14]

The rift over Tibet aggravated the territorial dispute China and India had inherited from their predecessors. It was just months after the Dalai Lama's flight to India that the first deadly clashes at the border were reported in 1959. After the war, Chinese Premier Zhou Enlai told an assembly of socialist countries in Beijing that "center of the Sino-Indian conflict" was not the border dispute but India's efforts to "oppose reform in Tibet" and its desire to keep Tibet as a "buffer state."[15] Dr. John Garver recounts a tense exchange on the causes of the 1962 war between Mao Zedong and Soviet leader Nikita Khruschev in which the Chinese president insisted that "the Hindus acted as if [Tibet] belonged to them."[16]

And yet, despite their continuing impasse over India's hosting of the Dalai Lama, in the decades following the border war Tibet ceased to be an immediate source of hostility. In 1988, Indian Prime Minister Rajiv Gandhi offered Beijing an olive branch by reaffirming Chinese sovereignty over Tibet, as Nehru had done before him. When a violent uprising did coalesce in Lhasa a year later, in March 1989, Sino-Indian relations were not adversely affected.

But a deterioration of conditions in the Tibet Autonomous Region in the latter half of the 2000s; the rising international profile of the Dalai Lama; the political transition to an elected prime minister of the Tibetan Government in Exile; and the escalating battle over the Dalai Lama's succession have in recent years added complex new layers to the Sino-Indian rivalry.

Two Steps Back

When Mao Zedong ordered the People's Liberation Army into Tibet in 1950, he saw the campaign not as an invasion but a liberation. In the eyes of China's leadership, pre-Communist Tibet was a backward society trapped in an "abusive feudal system" and in desperate need of "revolutionary social change."[17] In his eyes, the Chinese invasion was an attempt not only to return Tibet to its rightful place as an autonomous region of China, but to free the Tibetan proletariat from the tyranny of a privileged theocratic elite. Any resistance to this effort, particularly from India, reflected "an effort to uphold a backward way of life" typical of the "reactionary class nature" of India's rulers.[18]

Mao was right about one thing: the Tibet of the nineteenth and early twentieth centuries was a far cry from a Buddhist utopia. Melvyn Goldstein laments the "socially regressive system"[19] of pre-1950 Tibetan society and Ellen Bork describes it as an "isolated theocracy perched on the 'roof of the world.'"[20] It was a society where some 95 *percent* of Tibetans were illiterate "hereditary serfs and slaves owned by monasteries and nobles"[21] and gruesome mutilations and decapitations were common forms of punishment.

Under sixty years of communist rule, the most regressive practices have vanished, and the average Tibetan has experienced a material improvement in living standards. Beijing can boast of the provision of free schooling, complimentary medical care, a virtually tax-free environment, free leases of land to Tibetan citizens, and an urban unemployment rate under three percent.[22] Billions of dollars in infrastructure investment have poured into the TAR, with some $47 billion more earmarked for the 2011–2015 Five Year Plan.[23] Lhasa, Chinese officials are quick to point out, was voted the "happiest city in China" four out of five years between 2008 and 2012.[24]

However, outside the halls of the Communist Party, Beijing is seen as "ruling over a sullen Tibetan populace deeply resentful of China's takeover of their ancestral homeland."[25] Tibetan exiles insist that residents of the TAR are regularly subject to coercion and fear, and that cooperation with Party officials is done "only to survive; not out of loyalty to the Communist Party."[26] Navi Pillay, the UN high commissioner for human rights, has condemned reports of "detentions and disappearances, of excessive use of force against peaceful demonstrators, and curbs on the cultural rights of Tibetans." "Social stability in Tibet," she told the UN General Assembly in November 2012, "will never be achieved through heavy security measures and suppression of human rights."[27]

International human rights organizations and Tibetan exile groups have highlighted and condemned a litany of repressive Chinese practices:

- "Patriotic education" has been introduced in every Tibetan monastery that requires students to denounce their spiritual leader, the Dalai Lama.[28]
- Fluency in Mandarin remains a "passport for success" in Tibet, and higher education is taught almost exclusively in Mandarin. "While Tibetan language learning is encouraged and facilitated at school, it is, professionally, of little use to anyone with a career in anything other than teaching or editing."[29]
- Tibetans are excluded from positions of political power. No Tibetan has ever served as party secretary of the Tibet Autonomous Region (TAR). And in Tibetan-majority areas only 20 percent of businesses are controlled by Tibetans.[30]
- The fear of "ethnic dilution" has become paramount, as a large influx of migrant Han Chinese workers could one day make Tibetans a minority in their own homeland. The speaker of the Tibetan Parliament in Exile compares what's happening in Tibet today to the Han

migration to Inner Mongolia thirty years ago, with natives of Inner Mongolia now comprising only 20 percent of the province.[31]

In the latter half of the 2000s, widespread discontent directed at Chinese rule culminated in a sporadic outpouring of violence and a haunting campaign of protest suicides.

2008 Protests

In March 2008—on the anniversary of the 1959 and 1989 Lhasa uprisings—the Tibetan capital erupted in violence, with native Tibetans targeting Han citizens and businesses, setting fire to homes and storefronts. Nineteen people were reported killed and over 300 injured in the worst outbreak of violence on the plateau since 1989.[32] The rioting quickly spread to Gansu, Qinghai, and Sichuan provinces, where thousands of ethnic Tibetans destroyed government buildings and set fire to police vans.

James Miles, a reporter from the *Economist* on location in Lhasa, was shocked by the "outpouring of ethnic violence." He surmised that Tibetans were likely trying to take advantage of China's hosting of the 2008 Olympics to raise international sympathy for their cause but ultimately attributed the uprising to "festering grievances."[33]

Chinese officials, on the other hand, saw the unrest as an orchestrated plot from the "Dalai Lama clique" based in India. The Buddhist spiritual leader was directly blamed for the violence by Chinese Premier Wen Jiabao, and Tibet Party Chief Zhang Qingli called the Dalai Lama a "wolf in a monk's robe, a monster with a human face but the hearts of beast."[34]

Self-Immolations

More unsettling to Beijing than the riots of 2008 has been the wave of self-immolations that first began in February 2009 and accelerated dramatically in 2011 and 2012. As of October 2013, over 100 Tibetans had set fire to themselves with over eighty-two fatalities in what one official from the Tibetan Government in Exile calls the "ultimate extreme expression of nonviolent protest."[35]

Beijing has dismissed the immolations as "premeditated political moves"[36] and Chinese scholar Hu Shisheng told this author that the immolators "aren't really monks but unemployed youth dressed up as monks who realized they can gain attention through sensationalism."[37] As in 2008, Chinese officials have been quick to blame the Dalai Lama for instigating the immolations. "His prayers for those self-immolators amount to encouragement of the violent deed," a Chinese Embassy official wrote to the *Hindu*.[38]

CHINA'S VIEW OF INDIA AND TIBET

In theory the Tibet issue is settled . . . in practice it is not settled.

—Zheng Ruixiang, former Chinese ambassador
to India, interview with author, April 2013

The Chinese leadership has reserved a unique disdain for the Dalai Lama. The vitriol directed at the Buddhist leader by Party officials and propaganda organs is almost unmatched in contemporary China. But why?

We do know that China feels betrayed by the Dalai Lama's flight to India in 1959. The circumstances surrounding that turbulent episode are still debated, but Beijing has held up as evidence of the Dalai Lama's duplicity an exchange of letters between the His Holiness and General Tan Kuan, the acting representative of the Central People's Government in Tibet, between March 10 and March 16, 1959.

As the Tibetan uprising gathered steam in early March, the Dalai Lama wrote a series of conciliatory letters to General Tan insisting the protests had been "instigated by a few evil elements" and they had put the Buddhist leader to "indescribable shame." The Dalai Lama was "immediately overjoyed" after learning the general had not been disturbed by the unrest and argued that "reactionary, evil elements are carrying out activities endangering me under the pretext of protecting my safety."[39]

It was thus a great surprise to Beijing when a few days after the exchange of letters the Dalai Lama suddenly disappeared, only to reemerge in India two weeks later condemning Chinese repression in Tibet. The Dalai Lama later explained that the letters to General Tan "were written to disguise my true intentions." In his autobiography, *My Land and My People*, he explains that he thought it would be "foolish to argue with the general" and only wanted to "calm him down . . . by seeming to accept his sympathy and welcome his advice."[40]

Ever since that episode China has cast suspicion on India's relationship with the Dalai Lama and its intentions in Tibet. China's foremost demand on Delhi is that it prevent the Dalai Lama from engaging in "political activities." While India has in principle agreed to those terms, the two sides have never properly defined—and they clearly have different perceptions of—what constitutes "political activities." This author asked several Chinese officials and analysts to define a "political activity" by the Dalai Lama, and a number responded that *any* public activities by the Dalai Lama are inherently political.

Others, including Dr. Zhao Ganchen, insisted this was an unreasonable criteria but said: "It is impossible for China to define political activities just as it is impossible for India to define this. . . . This was a verbal agreement based on mutual trust. Unfortunately, there is not a lot of mutual trust right now." Dr. Zhao was convinced, however, that wherever this nebulous line belonged, the Dalai Lama and India had repeatedly crossed it. "India let him visit Arunachal Pradesh and give a press conference in Tawang! This is the People's Republic of China!"[41]

Over lunch at the China Institute for Contemporary International Relations, Deputy Director Hu Shisheng explained that "India is purposely not doing much work to control the 'Free Tibet' movement in New Delhi." "Indian scholars," he said, "are still talking about linking Tibet to Kashmir. . . . Any violations related to our sovereignty could have very, very negative implications." Ambassador Zheng Ruixiang offered a similar take. India, he said, "has not completely put down the burden of the Tibet issue."[42] "The Indian side has only kept part of the promise . . . the [TGIE] has never stopped its anti-China activities. Until now some Indians are still clamoring for playing the 'Tibet Card.'"[43]

INDIA AND TIBET

> Tibet is virtually the only effective mechanism of leverage India has against Beijing. China's vulnerability in Tibet is to India what India's vulnerability vis-à-vis Pakistan is to China.
>
> —Dr. John Garver, *Protracted Contest*[44]

Playing host to the Dalai Lama and the Tibetan Government in Exile was never part of India's plan. When tensions between China and the local Tibetan populace turned violent in the mid-1950s, Indian Prime Minister Jawaharlal Nehru desired above all to foster an accommodation between the Dalai Lama and Beijing which preserved Tibetan autonomy and allowed the spiritual leader to remain in Lhasa. When the Dalai Lama visited Delhi on a state-sanctioned trip in 1956 and 1957, he sought Nehru's permission to remain in India amid the first signs of Tibetan resistance to Chinese rule. His request was rebuffed. Allowing him to stay, Nehru felt, would have needlessly aggravated Beijing and created a more repressive environment in Tibet proper.

By the time the Dalai Lama fled to India in 1959, public sympathy for the Tibetan struggle—and outrage at the Chinese crackdown—forced Nehru's hand. Considerations of realpolitik were now overwhelmed by domestic political pressures, and Nehru welcomed the exiled Tibetans with open arms, allowing them to establish a Tibetan Government in Exile in Dharamsala.

After China's 1962 invasion of India, Delhi expanded the political space afforded to the TGIE, no longer fearful of offending Chinese sensibilities. The TGIE opened representative offices in New York and Geneva in the

1960s. In the fall of 1965, officials in New Delhi even toyed with the idea of withdrawing recognition of Chinese sovereignty over Tibet. "The conditions under which we recognized China's suzerainty no longer exist," opined Indian Home Minister M. C. Chalga. However, the idea, Dr. John W. Garver notes, was quickly dropped and has not been subsequently revived by any serving Indian official,[45] though there are signs it is again gaining traction among experts and the Indian public.

In 1965 India voted at the UN General Assembly to condemn Chinese repression on the plateau (after abstaining from similar votes in 1959 and 1961), criticizing China for the "miserable plight and terrible suppression" of the Tibetan people. India's Ambassador to the UN argued: "Ever since Tibet came under the stranglehold of China, the Tibetans have been subjected to a continuous and increasing ruthlessness which has few parallels in the annals of the world . . . the Chinese have indulged in the worst kind of genocide and the suppression of a minority race."[46] Most important, he reiterated that India would "continue to give the Dalai Lama and his simple and peace-loving people . . . all our hospitality."

Nearly sixty years later, Delhi can confidently assert it has kept that promise. Today the Dalai Lama is a quasicelebrity figure in India, revered by the public and granted privileged access to the country's top political leadership. According to the Dalai Lama's own website, recent meetings with Indian officials include the President of India (April 2012), the Minister of Labor (December 2009), and the country's most powerful politician, Congress Party President Sonia Gandhi (July 2009). His Holiness is a frequent guest of former Indian President Dr. Abdul Kalam,[47] and Indian Foreign Secretaries Ranjan Mathai and Nirumpama Rao met with the Dalai Lama in July 2010 and June 2011 for hour-long meetings at his palace in Dharamsala.[48]

When asked directly about the Dalai Lama, Indian officials and analysts are prone to describe him as a "clever fellow" who has "frequently outsmarted the Chinese." They seem privately amused that the giant power to the east is so easily excited by the activities of a seventy-six-year-old Buddhist monk. "This guy has no army, no party, and yet few countries in the world have this much power over China. So long as he controls the minds of Tibetans, he is a threat to Beijing," says Sanjoy Hazarika, director of India's Center for Northeast Studies.[49]

Despite their public ambivalence, Indian strategists are well aware that the Dalai Lama and the Tibet issue in general constitute a rare point of strategic leverage over China. Brahma Chellaney argues, "As long as the Dalai Lama remains in Dharamsala, it is a great strategic asset for India."[50] Hazarika told this author in Delhi that His Holiness was India's "trump card." "We would be stupid to do anything to give that up."

Yet it is a trump card India has been cautious about playing. Only once has India sought to apply direct pressure to China in Tibet, when it tacitly facilitated assistance to Tibetan rebels in the late 1950s and 1960s.[51] The mission was ultimately unsuccessful, a fact lamented by one prominent Indian analyst who wished to go unnamed: "I wish we would've played the card better at the time. . . . If so we wouldn't be dealing with this monster today."

Since that failed experiment, India has seemed content to hold the Tibet card close to the vest, keenly sensitive to the risk of unnecessarily provoking Beijing. "The Tibet weapon doesn't need to be wielded and branded in public," says defense analyst Ajai Shukla. "The Chinese know it's there and that's sufficient."[52]

True to form, since the 1950s multiple Indian leaders have expressed their unequivocal recognition of Chinese sovereignty over Tibet. The most recent reaffirmation came during Prime Minister Vajpayee's 2003 visit to China, in which he affirmed that "the Tibet Autonomous Region is a part of the territory of the Peoples' Republic of China." Chinese scholar Li Li concluded that of all the Indian statements on Tibet, Vajpayee's language "is the closest to China's stance," which is that "Tibet is an inalienable part of Chinese territory."[53]

Ironically, while the change in terminology reportedly came at China's behest, some Indians have noted that Vajpayee's language was also the most limited in scope. He referred not to *China* but the *People's Republic of China*, implying that India's recognition extends only back to 1949 (not, as Beijing claims, since the Yuan Dynasty). Second, the endorsement referred to the *Tibet Autonomous Region*, a much newer and more narrow geographic construct than "Tibet," which notably excludes China's claimed territory in Arunachal Pradesh as well as large parts of Tibetan-populated areas in other Chinese provinces.

Indian Assertiveness

There are signs that if the Sino-Indian competition continues to sharpen in the decades ahead, Delhi may increasingly look to Tibet to balance perceived Chinese aggression. "It is in our interest to keep the Tibetan heart beating in this region," former Indian intelligence chief B. Raman wrote in February 2013. "Decades of suppressive policy . . . have not been able to crush the independent spirit of the Tibetan youth and monks and their desire for the return of His Holiness the Dalai Lama to Lhasa. The self-immolations since 2009 are an indication of the total failure of the Chinese suppressive policy in the Tibetan areas."[54]

While such views are rarely aired in public by serving Indian officials, since 2006 India has afforded the Dalai Lama greater space to engage in activities deemed provocative by Beijing. India allowed the spiritual leader to visit Arunachal Pradesh and the Tawang Monastery in 2009 during a peak in Sino-Indian tensions and later declined to reaffirm Beijing's "One China" policy in the joint statement following Chinese Premier Wen Jiabao's visit to New Delhi in December 2010, and again during Li Keqiang's visit to Delhi in May 2013 and Prime Minister Manmohan Singh's visit to Beijing in October 2013.

The Indian policy document *NonAlignment 2.0* suggests India's Tibet policy needed to be "reassessed and readjusted." The authors urge India to prepare for a potential Chinese invasion by "acquir[ing] intelligence of all logistic and supply routes from Tibet" and "develop[ing] the capabilities to interdict China's logistics and operational infrastructure in Tibet." Delhi, the report said, should "persuade" China to "seek reconciliation with the Dalai Lama and the exiled Tibetan community. . . . The Dalai Lama's popular legitimacy among his own people is a fact that the Chinese government must acknowledge."[55]

This chapter is a reminder that discussions about Tibet in Sino-Indian relations always come back to the Dalai Lama. He is, in many ways, the embodiment of India's leverage in Tibet and, from China's perspective, the principal source of tension in the bilateral relationship. While the level of Indian influence in Tibet is subject to debate, no one doubts the substantial following the Dalai Lama still maintains on the plateau, though it remains difficult to quantify as credible public opinion data inside the TAR is virtually nonexistent. However, that influence can no longer be taken for granted, for as the next chapter will show, one of the greatest uncertainties—and potential flashpoints—in the Sino-Indian relationship regards who will succeed the seventy-six-year-old Dalai Lama.

NOTES

1. Srinath Raghavan, "The Fifty Year Crisis: India and China Since 1962," *India Seminar*, January 2013 (Accessed April 15, 2013): http://www.india-seminar.com/2013/641/641_srinath_raghavan.htm.

2. "History of Tibet," *China.org.cn.*, March 21, 2008 (Accessed January 28, 2013): http://www.china.org.cn/china/2008-03/21/content_13268563.htm.

3. The basis for the oft-quoted Chinese claim that they have "exercised full sovereignty over Tibet for the past 700 years."

4. "Origins of So-Called 'Tibetan Independence,'" January 28, 2013 (Accessed June13, 2013): http://english.peopledaily.com.cn/whitepaper/6%282%29.html.

5. Buddhism was declared the state religion by Kublai Khan in 1253.

6. John W. Garver, *Protracted Contest: Sino-Indian Rivalry in the Twentieth Century* (Seattle: University of Washington Press, 2001), 34.

7. Mohan Malik, "Historical Fiction: China's South China Sea Claims," *World Affairs Journal*, May/June (2013): 86.

8. Dinesh Lal, *Indo-Tibet-China Conflict* (Delhi: Kalpaz Publications, 2008), 45.

9. Melvyn Goldstein, *The Snow Lion and the Dragon* (Berkeley: University of California Press, 1997) 4–5.

10. The legality of Tibet's declaration of independence is still a hotly debated topic. No capital recognized Tibet as an independent country, though the United States seemed inclined to do so, drafting a diplomatic memorandum proposing that "consideration could be given to recognition of Tibet as an independent state" if "developments warrant" it. In 1978 the United States adopted the position that Tibet was a part of China.

11. Malik, Mohan. "Historical Fiction: China's South China Sea Claims." *World Affairs Journal*, May/June 2013: 85.

12. C. Raja Mohan, *Samudra Manthan: Sino-Indian Rivalry in the Pacific* (Washington DC: Carnegie Endowment for International Peace, 2012), 20.

13. Melvyn Goldstein, *A History of Modern Tibet: The Calm Before the Storm: 1951–1955* (Los Angeles: University of California Press, 2009), 469.

14. Beijing further charged India with helping to facilitate CIA assistance to Tibetan rebels. It is still a matter of debate among historians whether Indian Prime Minister Jawaharlal Nehru was fully aware of the nature and extent of these operations.

15. Zheng Ruixiang, "China-India Relations: Course of Development and Prospects," *China International Studies* November/December 2011: 152–70.

16. Zheng Ruixiang, "China-India Relations: Course of Development and Prospects," *China International Studies* November/December 2011: 152–70.

17. John W. Garver, "The Security Dilemma in Sino-Indian Relations," *India Review*. Vol. 1, No. 4 (2012): 33.

18. John W. Garver, "The Security Dilemma in Sino-Indian Relations," *India Review*. Vol. 1, No. 4 (2012): 33.

19. Shree Pandya and Kevin Wallentine, "An Interview with Melvyn Goldstein," *Claremont Mckenna University*, January 30, 2013.

20. Ellen Bork, "Tibet's Transition: Will Washington Take a Stand?" *International Campaign for Tibet*, September 26, 2012 (February 27, 2013): http://www.savetibet.org/media-center/tibet-news/tibets-transition-will-washington-take-stand.

21. Peter Hessler, "Tibet through Chinese Eyes," *Atlantic*, January 30, 2013 (Accessed June 13, 2013): http://www.theatlantic.com/magazine/archive/1999/02/tibet-through-chinese-eyes/306395/?single_page=true.

22. Hannah Beech, "As Tibetans Burn Themselves to Protest Chinese Rule, Communists in Beijing Stress Happiness in Tibet," *Time World*, November 10, 2012 (Accessed January 30, 2013): http://world.time.com/2012/11/10/as-tibetans-burn-themselves-to-protest-chinese-rule-communists-in-beijing-stress-happiness-in-tibet/.

23. "China to Pump $47 Bln into Tibet to 2015," *Reuters*, September 14, 2011 (Accessed January 20, 2013): http://www.reuters.com/article/2011/09/14/china-tibet-idUSL3E7KE24W20110914.

24. Hannah Beech, "As Tibetans Burn Themselves to Protest Chinese Rule, Communists in Beijing Stress Happiness in Tibet." *Time World*, November 10, 2012 (Accessed January 30, 2013) http://world.time.com/2012/11/10/as-tibetans -burn-themselves-to-protest-chinese-rule-communists-in-beijing-stress-happi ness-in-tibet/

25. John W. Garver, "The Security Dilemma in Sino-Indian Relations," *India Review* Vol. 1, No. 4 (2012): 33

26. Karma Yeshi. Author interview. Dharamsala, India, August 2012.

27. Central Tibetian Administration, "UN Urges China to Urgently Address Longstanding Grievances of Tibetans," *Central Tibetan Administration,* November 2, 2012 (January 30, 2013): http://tibet.net/2012/11/02/un-says-china-must -urgently-address-longstanding-grievances-of-tibetans/.

28. Dennis J. Burke, "Tibetans in Exile in a Changing Global Political Climate," *Economic and Political Weekly*: 81.

29. Dennis J. Burke, "Tibetans in Exile in a Changing Global Political Climate," *Economic and Political Weekly*: 80.

30. Jesper Svensson, "Managing the Rise of a Hydro-Hegemon in Asia: China's Strategic Interests in the Yarlung-Tsangpo River," *IDSA Occasional Paper No. 23*: (April 2012). 1.

31. Speaker of Tibetan government. Author interview. Dharamsala, India, August 2012.

32. Marc Blecher, "China in 2008: Meeting Olympian Challenges," *Asian Survey*, Vol. 49, No. 1, 2009: 74–87.

33. James Miles, "Transcript: James Miles interview on Tibet," *CNN Asia,* March 20, 2008 (Accessed January 30, 2013): http://www.cnn.com/2008/WORLD/ asiapcf/03/20/tibet.miles.interview/.

34. Ching Ching Ni, "China Steps Up Criticism of Dalai Lama over Tibet." *Los Angeles Times,* March 20, 2008: http://articles.latimes.com/2008/mar/20/world/ fg-tibet20.

35. One official from the Tibetan government-in-exile. Author interview. Dharamsala, India, August 2012.

36. Tom Lasster, "Chinese Officials Blame Dalai Lama for String of Self-immolations," *Miami Herald,* March 7, 2012 (Accessed January 30, 2013): http:// tibetreporter.blogspot.com/2012/03/chinese-officials-blame-dalai-lama-for.html.

37. Hu Shisheng. Author interview. Beijing, February 2012.

38. Li Xiaojun, "Muddying the Waters," *Hindu,* July 10, 2010 (January 30, 2013): http://www.thehindu.com/opinion/letters/article3621384.ece.

39. "Kuan-san, Tan, and Dalai Lama," 1959 (Accessed January 30, 2013): http:// www.claudearpi.net/maintenance/uploaded_pics/Letters_Tan_Dalailama.pdf.

40. Dalai Lama, *My Land and My People* (New York: Warner Books, 1997), 186–88.

41. Dr. Zhao Ganchen. Author interview. Washington, DC, winter 2012.

42. Cdr Gurpeet and S. Khurana, "China-India Maritime Rivalry," *Indian Defence Review*, Vol. 23, No. 4.

43. Cdr. Gurpeet and S. Khurana, "China-India Maritime Rivalry," *Indian Defence Review*, Vol. 23, No. 4.

44. John W. Garver, *Protracted Contest: Sino-Indian Rivalry in the Twentieth Century* (Seattle: University of Washington Press, 2001), 75

45. John W. Garver, *Protracted Contest: Sino-Indian Rivalry in the Twentieth Century* (Seattle: University of Washington Press, 2001), 62.

46. "Statement of the Indian Government," *Indian Government,* January 30, 2013: http://fnvaworld.org/download/india-tibet/1965IndianStatementatUN.pdf.

47. "Dignitaries Met: 2005–2010," *Dahlilama.com.* 2012 (Accessed January 30, 2013): http://www.dalailama.com/biography/dignitaries-met.

48. ET Bureau, "Beijing Uneasy as Rao Meets Dalai Lama," *Economic Times (India Times),* July 14, 2010 (January 20, 2013): http://articles.economictimes.indiatimes.com/2010-07-14/news/28400948_1_tibet-related-issues-dalai-lama-china-political-activities (accessed January 30, 2013).

49. Sanjoy Hazarika. Author interview. New Delhi, August 2012.

50. Brahma Chellaney, "Tibet Is at the Core of the India-China Divide," *Chellanay.net,* 2007 (Accessed January 30, 2013): http://chellaney.net/2007/04/02/tibet-is-at-the-core-of-the-india-china-divide/.

51. See Kenneth Conboy, James Morrison, *The CIA's Secret War in Tibet,* University Press of Kansas 2002.

52. Ajai Shukla. Author interview. New Delhi, November 2011.

53. Li Li, *Security Perception and China-India Relations* (New Delhi: KW Publishers, 2009), 163.

54. B. Raman, "Dragon's New Face," *Outlookindia.com,* 2013, (Accessed February 27, 2013): http://www.outlookindia.com/article.aspx?283780.

55. Kumar Khilnani et al., "Non-Alignment 2.0: A Foreign and Strategic Policy for India in the 21st Century," 2012: http://www.cprindia.org/sites/default/files/NonAlignment%202.0_1.pdf Pg. 14.

Chapter 7

The Rise of the Sikyong
and the Succession
of the Dalai Lama

The Tibetan Government in Exile (TGIE), also known as the Central Tibetan Administration (CTA), was established in Dharamsala, Himachal Pradesh, in 1960. It consists of a prime minister (Sikyong), a forty-odd-member parliament (Assembly of the Tibetan People's Deputies) and seven-member cabinet (Kashag) serving the roughly 150,000 Tibetans living outside of China (including over 120,000 in India and 15,000 in Nepal).

Delhi seems content to keep the details of its relationship with the TGIE obscure. Jagannath Panda, coauthor of a rare and exhaustive report[1] on the Tibetan exile population in India from the Institute for Defense Studies and Analysis (IDSA), says that Delhi exerts indirect but considerable influence over the TGIE. "Little is done without approval or at least knowledge of the Indian government," says Panda, who claims the Home Ministry and the Ministry of External Affairs are assigned primary responsibility for interacting with the TGIE, with the former taking precedence in any disagreement on policy.[2]

The major Tibetan secondary education institutes—including the Central University of Tibetan Studies and the Central Institute of Higher Tibetan Studies—receive funding from the Indian Ministry of Education and local governments. India's Human Resource Development Ministry (HRD) long managed and funded the sixty to seventy Central Tibetan Schools serving 10,000 students[3] across India before transferring management to the TGIE in 2011.[4] However, the full extent of Indian financial support to the TGIE remains a matter of speculation.

The TGIE enjoys only limited jurisdiction over the Tibetan community inside India. It has no law enforcement authority and depends entirely on the Indian government for policing and to enforce administrative decisions. It was only in recent years the TGIE adopted a justice system with the authority to try civil—though still not criminal—cases.

While the Tibetan exile community in India remains largely segregated into forty-odd approved settlements,[5] the largest of which is in Dharamsala, Tibetans in India generally enjoy a higher socioeconomic status and quality of life than other refugee communities in India and, for that matter, many Indians. Tibetans residing in India "do not have the rights of Indian citizens such as voting or carrying an Indian passport but they are free to work on the Indian economy or in the numerous Tibetan settlements established by the Indian Government. They can marry Indian citizens, although few do."[6] The IDSA task force report, among others, has applauded the Indian government for the general lack of socioeconomic friction generated by the presence of over 120,000 Tibetans exiles living in India. "Giving shelter to them," the report states, "is inherent to our strategic culture based on soft power."[7]

THE RISE OF THE SIKYONG

> This is not only my own retirement but also that of a four-century-old Tibetan tradition. Now that has ended. Proudly, voluntarily, happily.
>
> —The Dalai Lama, Interview with the *Hindu*, July 9, 2012[8]

The TGIE lacked even a nominal political figurehead until 2001, when a poll was held to elect the movement's first prime minister.[9] Lobsang Tenzin, the fifth Samdong Rinpoche, won the first of two successive five-year terms in 2001, but was vested with largely symbolic powers, and parliament was seen as little more than a rubber stamp for decisions made by the ultimate Tibetan authority, the Dalai Lama. Tibetan apathy toward the political process was reflected in the fact that only 26.8 percent of registered voters participated in the 2006 election.[10]

All of this changed in 2011. In the run-up to the 2011 election, the Dalai Lama made a dramatic announcement: he was renouncing the supreme political authority held by every Dalai Lama since the reign of the fifth Dalai Lama 400 years prior. While he would remain the spiritual leader of Buddhists worldwide and would retain the authority to appoint special envoys and sit in on parliament meetings,[11] the Tibetan Charter was amended to give the office of the prime minister final executive authority.[12]

After the Dalai Lama's announcement, interest in the 2011 election surged, with 60 percent of registered voters participating in the March 2011 poll.[13] Lobsang Sangay, a Harvard-educated Boston native, bested his nearest competitor 55 percent to 37 percent, riding a wave of support among Tibetan youth.

Now in his mid-forties, Sangay was born in a Tibetan refugee camp in Darjeeling, India in 1968. In 1995 he earned a scholarship to study at Harvard where he received his doctorate, earning him the label of a "Western-leaning liberal" in the press. In a pair of meetings with Sangay in Washington and Dharamsala, this writer found the prime minister to be thoughtful and unassuming, whose calm demeanor masks the fighting spirit that was foreshadowed in his inaugural speech.

In his first year in office Sangay established the Tibetan exile movement's first think tank, the Tibet Policy Institute. He also addressed a longstanding grievance among Tibetan refugees in India by extending the valid term of the identity permits all Tibetans must carry from one year to four.

However, the prime minister is under no illusions about the challenges he faces. He is, in the words of the *Sydney Morning Herald*, the "prime minister of a government that doesn't exist, claiming a land that he has never seen."[14] His first task is to emerge from the shadow of the Dalai Lama—with whom he travels frequently and has a good personal rapport—providing substance to a position that until now was little more than a symbolic figurehead. The Dalai Lama, Sangay admits, is a "a global phenomenon and is highly respected and revered by Tibetans and people around the world, so there is no way a single person can fill his shoes."[15] "Our challenge now," Sangay told this author, "is whether we can rally around a system and a principle, rather than the cult of a leader."

In the long term, Sangay faces a much bigger challenge. The pool of world leaders willing to host the Dalai Lama is dwindling under the weight of Chinese pressure. In November 2012 South Africa's Supreme Court of Appeal censured their government for denying the Dalai Lama a visa under Chinese pressure.[16] Closer to home, the Dalai Lama was denied a request to meet with President Barack Obama in 2010, ahead of the U.S. president's first visit to Beijing. When he obtained a meeting with the U.S. president a year later, he was hurried out of the back door of the White House, famously sidestepping several piles of garbage on his way out.[17]

Yet, rather than striking an accommodative tone with China, Sangay has adopted a more combative posture than the Dalai Lama. To be sure, he remains unequivocal in his commitment to the Dalai Lama's "Middle Way." "We have two uncompromising principles: nonviolence and democratization," Sangay argues. However, the prime minister has not shied away from directly criticizing China in OpEds and public interviews. Excerpts of Sangay's August 8, 2011, inaugural speech merit reprinting:

The results of this election should send a clear message to the hardliners in the Chinese government that Tibetan leadership is far from fizzling out . . . The ongoing political repression, cultural assimilation, economic marginalization and environmental destruction in occupied Tibet is unacceptable. . . . After sixty years of misrule, Tibet is no Socialist Paradise that Chinese officials promised. There is no "Socialism" in Tibet, but rather Colonialism . . . As long as Tibetans are repressed, there will be resistance . . . While I live I am determined to fight for our freedom.[18]

Unsurprisingly, the rise of a new Tibetan prime minister has been received very differently in China and India. "Terrorist poised to rule 'Tibetan government in-exile'?" asked a headline in the *People's Daily*.[19] A Chinese official of the United Front Work Department, which is responsible for dialogue with the Dalai Lama, denounced the election of Sangay as a "show" that "happens every year without any political significance. The Dalai Lama and his clique lost political power ever since he went to India in 1959."[20]

In contrast, the election of Sangay has largely been welcomed in India. Press coverage of the new prime minister is almost universally positive, and Indian officials interviewed for this book spoke favorably about the prime minister. The IDSA task force report insists "India will have to facilitate assumption of leadership role by the Prime Minister of the [TGIE]."[21]

THE OPENING VOLLEY

The devolution of political power to an elected prime minister is reverberating across the Tibetan community inside and outside of China. But the rise of the Sikyong is only one chapter of a story of far greater consequence to the China-India relationship. At stake is nothing short of the future of a global religion.

The question now foremost on the minds of Tibet-watchers in Beijing and New Delhi is: what happens when the seventy-six-year-old Dalai Lama dies? It is a question that has prompted a fierce competition between China and the institution of the Dalai Lama for the right to name a successor to the Buddhist religious leader; a struggle that will have major implications for Sino-Indian relations in the twenty-first century.

The opening shots were fired back in 1989, with the sudden death of the tenth Panchen Lama, second only to the Dalai Lama in the Buddhist religious hierarchy. Unlike the Dalai Lama, the tenth Panchen Lama chose to stay in China after the 1959 Tibetan uprising. At the time he urged Tibetans to offer loyalty to the new leadership in Beijing, although he appears to have experienced a change of heart shortly before his curious death. Tibet's "sacrifice far outweighs our development," the Panchen Lama said five days before he died from a "mysterious illness" on January 28, 1989.[22]

The Dalai Lama searched for years for the Panchen Lama's reincarnation, eventually identifying the seven-year-old Gedun Choekyi Nyima as the eleventh Panchen Lama on May 14, 1995. Within hours of the announcement the Chinese press denounced Nyima (the seven-year-old was charged with drowning a dog once) and said his parents were "notorious for speculation, deceit, and scrambling for fame and profit."[23] Nyima disappeared three days later, taken into Chinese custody, and has not been seen since.[24] China then assembled a team of religious scholars to denounce the Dalai Lama's choice and find a new successor. In November 1995, Beijing appointed its own eleventh Panchen Lama, Gyaltsen Norbu.

Nearly twenty years later there remains two competing Panchen Lamas: the Chinese-groomed Norbu and the missing Nyima who, despite not being seen in public since 1995, retains the loyalty of the Dalai Lama and most Tibetans outside China (and likely many within). Gyaltsen Norbu, meanwhile, is disparaged as "the Chinese Panchen Lama" by most Tibetans, says Ajai Shukla.[25]

Norbu has publicly pledged to be a "good living Buddha who loves his motherland, his religion, and serves his country and its people."[26] In March 2013 the Communist Party elevated Norbu to a position on the Standing Committee of the Chinese People's Political Consultative Conference, a "political advisory body that is in charge of minority issues."[27] And Chinese news sources[28] have referred to Norbu as the "highest ranking figure in Tibetan Buddhism."[29]

THE DALAI LAMA SUCCESSION

The struggle over the Panchen Lama was an early harbinger of a larger battle to come. China was laying the political and religious groundwork to rid itself of one of its most persistent irritants, maneuvering itself to choose the next Dalai Lama.

Beijing's campaign began to take form in March 2005, when a new Regulation on Religious Affairs (RRA) passed by the country's State Council took effect. Article 27 sought to allocate to Beijing the right to appoint living Buddhas. The regulations marked a major change in the scope and scale of Chinese involvement in Tibetan religious affairs. Through several centuries of Sino-Tibetan engagement, Beijing had only intervened periodically in the reincarnation of particularly important lamas. An official from the Tibetan Government in Exile in Dharamsala told this author that since occupying Tibet in 1950 Beijing had approved no more than thirty reincarnations, including the eleventh Panchen Lama. "Now," he said, "China will appoint thousands of lamas."

In September 2007, Beijing expanded on its plans to "institutionalize the management of reincarnation."[30] A new decree by the State Administration for Religious Affairs (SARA), stated that *all* reincarnating Buddhas would have to "carry out application and approval procedures" with local and regional religious affairs departments. The appointment of re-incarnated Buddhas with a "particularly great impact" would have to get approval directly from China's cabinet, the State Council. Furthermore, Buddhas would be required to "respect and protect the principles of the unification of the state."

The Golden Urn

The fact that there are no uniform rules for succession of the Dalai Lama has provided Beijing with a path to attempt to co-opt the process. China's strategy was outlined in Article 8 of the 2007 SARA regulations, which stated: "Living Buddhas which have historically been recognized by drawing lots from the golden urn shall have their reincarnating soul children recognized by drawing lots from the golden urn."[31] In effect, Beijing is seizing on a soft precedent set in the late eighteenth century by the Qing Emperor Qianlong. The emperor, says Li Deching, director of religious studies at the China Tibetology Research Center, introduced a golden urn lottery ceremony to select reincarnated lamas in order to "prevent Living Buddhas from appointing their own relatives or people close to them as successors."[32]

The process traditionally involved the inscription of the names of several potential successors ("soul boys") onto plates or slips of paper that were then placed in a special golden urn, sometimes enclosed in silk purses. Under the supervision of local Chinese officials, lamas would draw the successor's name from the urn, which was subsequently sent to the Tibetan National Assembly for approval.[33]

It is a matter of debate how often this process was actually used for selecting Dalai Lamas and other high lamas. China claims it used the golden urn process to select the eleventh Panchen Lama in 1995, and a 1997 White Paper issued by Beijing argues that some "seventy 'soul boys' have been identified by confirmation through lot-drawing from the golden urn."[34] Tibetan scholars concede the practice was used to select the tenth, eleventh, and twelfth Dalai Lamas, but argue it was subsequently rejected by Tibetan religious authorities and applied only sporadically to lower-ranking lamas thereafter.

Emanating a Successor

How would the Dalai Lama respond to China's embrace of the golden urn process to find his reincarnation? What was the succession method preferred by the Tibetan exile movement? Could the next Dalai Lama be chosen outside of China? Could the current Dalai Lama nominate a successor? After China passed the 2007 regulations, neither the TGIE nor the Dalai Lama seemed to have answers. "We've never had to deal with this succession question in exile, so the Dalai Lama will outline a whole new framework soon," Karma Yeshi, a member of the Tibetan parliament in exile told this author.

In September 2011, the Dalai Lama convened a three-day conference in Dharamsala for the heads of all the main Buddhist sects to address the controversy head-on. It was important, says Columbia University's Robert Barnett, for the Dalai Lama to get religious buy-in from all the major Buddhist schools, not just the dominant Gelugpa sect to which he belongs.

The Dalai Lama ultimately left the conferees with as many questions as answers, announcing at the open that the succession question would not be definitively decided until he turned ninety (in 2025), when he would leave "clear written instructions on the issue." He did, however, draw a red line around any attempt by Beijing to influence the succession process. "My reincarnation is to be decided by myself, nobody [else] has the right to decide about that."[35] China's attempts to control the succession process were "outrageous and disgraceful," he said, and "no recognition or acceptance should be given to a candidate chosen for political ends by anyone, including those in the People's Republic of China." [36]

In attempting to keep Beijing out of the succession process, the Dalai Lama had some difficult theological questions to address. Although no uniform rules for succession exist,[37] traditionally the Dalai Lama's reincarnation was identified in a young boy years after his death, either by the second-ranking Panchen Lama, a council of senior lamas, or an appointed Regent. However, the process often created a volatile interregnum of over a decade between the time of the Dalai Lama's death and the years it takes for the reincarnation to first be found, and then to reach an adult age. China would be free to exploit this window of uncertainty, using loyal lamas in Tibet to identify their own reincarnation.

To deal directly with this potential challenge, the Dalai Lama began to build support around a more obscure succession procedure known as "emanation." Unlike reincarnation, emanation has the virtue of granting the Dalai Lama the authority to identify and appoint his own successor before death. The practice, says Columbia's Robert Barnett, "is very well known and is quite common with high lamas, but has never happened with the Dalai Lamas before." [38] As throne holders of the Tibetan state, having more than one living Dalai Lama would have been "politically problematic."

Despite the break with theological precedent, the Dalai Lama's early attempts to promote emanation have not generated any noticeable backlash within the Tibetan community. In an email to this author, an official with the TGIE stated:

> Most of the lineage of the Dalai Lama was done according to reincarnation system but there was a tradition of emanation in the lineage of the Dalai Lama. If His Holiness the fourteenth Dalai Lama emanates rather than reincarnates, from the Tibetan point of view, people will surely respect and believe in emanation. Since Communist China does not believe in religion and being an atheist state, they have no right and authority to appoint the Dalai Lama's successor.

The Dalai Lama added a further wrinkle by announcing the TGIE would not be involved in the succession process, nor would his private office or the Gelugpa school to which he belongs. The Dalai Lama would choose his own successor, with management of the succession going to the Gaden Podrang Trust, a recently constituted body whose managers and trustees will eventually be named by the Dalai Lama.

Robert Barnett notes that in totality, the Dalai Lama's statements were crafted to provide maximum flexibility in the succession process. His successor can be found through reincarnation or emanation; be found inside Tibet or outside Tibet; from within the Dalai Lama's Gelugpa sect or outside it; and can be appointed by a trust that had not yet been established.[39]

The Chinese foreign ministry was quick to condemn the announcement. "The title of Dalai Lama is conferred by the central government and is illegal otherwise. There is a complete set of religious rituals and historical conventions in the reincarnation of the Dalai Lama and a Dalai Lama identifying his own successor has never been the practice."[40] The Dalai Lama and Chinese officials have been sparring over the matter ever since. Speaking to the *Hindu* in July 2012, the Dalai Lama said: "In order for the Chinese government to take responsibility for [my] reincarnation, then the Chinese Communists should first accept religion and particularly Buddhism, and they should accept the theory of rebirth."[41]

Already a controversy has emerged over whether the Dalai Lama's successor will be found inside or outside of Tibet. As far back as 2004 the Dalai Lama stated that "My life is outside Tibet, therefore my reincarnation will logically be found outside [Tibet]."[42] In February 2011, several months before the Dalai Lama's emanation speech, Beijing declared that no Buddhist monk outside China could be recognized as reincarnations of the Dalai Lama.

Early speculation in Delhi is that the Dalai Lama may look to Tawang to find his successor. Of the only two reincarnations ever found outside Tibet proper, one—the sixth Dalai Lama—was found in Tawang. The Tawang Monastery, it is worth noting, belongs to the same Gelugpa sect of Buddhism as the fourteenth Dalai Lama. Jagannath Panda says that if the TGIE wants to maintain legitimacy after the passing of the Dalai Lama, the support of Tawang—an influential source of Buddhist religious authority in India—will be critical.

However, were the Dalai Lama to choose a successor from Tawang, it could have an explosive impact on Sino-Indian relations, further raising the profile of a town that already constitutes one of the most divisive and volatile issues in bilateral relations. The Dalai Lama's trips to Tawang have generated vigorous protests from Beijing and opened India to charges of meddling in China's internal affairs. It would not be unreasonable to assume that a Dalai Lama chosen from Tawang would provide a new and potentially continuous source of tension between Delhi and Beijing.

INDIA AND THE SUCCESSION

Officials in New Delhi are acutely aware of the challenges posed by the Dalai Lama succession issue for Sino-Indian relations. Time and again government officials and security analysts named the succession question as one of the top potential flashpoints in Sino-Indian relations. Chandan Mitra, a serving member of India's parliament, worried the succession question could be the "trigger for a lot of destabilization."[43] "Potentially explosive," was the phrase used by author Mohan Malik. "It could change everything."[44] C. Raja Mohan, meanwhile, worried that China would "go for broke" over the Dalai Lama succession issue. "They will play hard ball. Tibet is so small in terms of population but it has such a hold on their minds."[45]

Why should Indian officials concern themselves with what is essentially a theological dispute between Beijing and the Dalai Lama? First, Indian nationalists see the Dalai Lama as a "powerful ally" and India's "trump card" against China." "If . . . the institution of the Dalai Lama were to get captured by Beijing (like the way it has anointed its own Panchen Lama), India will be poorer by several army divisions against China," explains Brahma Chellaney.[46]

Second, as it has done with the current Dalai Lama, China will almost certainly hold India responsible for any "political activities" from the new Dalai Lama. Should the next Dalai Lama take a more confrontational line toward China or agitate for Tibetan independence, the negative impact on Sino-Indian relations is difficult to quantify.

Third, Tibet watchers have in recent years begun to warn about the building frustration within the Tibetan movement both inside and outside China, and particularly among the youth. There are indications that China's repressive political and religious practices in Tibet proper are leading a growing number of Tibetans to question the utility and efficacy of the Dalai Lama's "Middle Way" approach.

Those frustrations have been further triggered by the collapse of the dialogue between China and the Dalai Lama's representatives in 2010, when the Buddhist leader's two special envoys resigned citing "deteriorating conditions" in Tibet and Chinese intransigence. Begun in 2000, the Dalai Lama's representatives and Chinese officials held nine rounds of largely fruitless talks, with each round stalled on unbridgeable differences over the Dalai Lama's conditions for autonomy for Tibet and China's insistence that the Dalai Lama concede that Tibet has "always" been a part of China. In June 2012 the Dalai Lama himself called the negotiations "futile" unless and until Beijing adopted a "realistic stance."[47]

Tibetan activists frustrated with the progress of the Middle Way have traditionally found a home in the Tibetan Youth Congress (TYC), easily the largest and most influential pro-independence Tibetan organization operating today. Counting some 35,000 members and over seventy-five branches across the world, the TYC has been at the forefront of Tibetan activism since its inception in 1970. The organization has always walked a delicate line between showing deference to the Dalai Lama as the supreme religious authority, and lobbying the Buddhist leader to more explicitly advocate independence.

The TYC's imprint on the Tibetan Government in Exile is enormous: nearly all TGIE officials, including the prime minister, Lobsang Sangay, and several members of parliament, are former TYC members. Karma Yeshi, a former vice president of the TYC and sitting member of parliament, says that all government officials used to be dual members of the TYC, but that now there is a "strict separation."

Unsurprisingly, the TYC is reviled in Beijing. Xinhua has described the group as "an armed spearhead of the fourteenth Dalai Lama group" and the *People's Daily* has accused the TYC of being a "terrorist organization,"[48] blaming it for instigating the deadly rioting in Tibet on March 14, 2008. The "radical separatist organization . . . lacks any understanding of the real national conditions of China and its Tibet region," writes Hua Zi for the *China Daily*.[49]

Despite these accusations, TYC members are adamant about their commitment to nonviolence. "Violence is not an option for us," said current TYC president Tsewang Rigzin in November 2008. "All our campaigns so far have been peaceful." (This writer is unaware of any documented acts of terrorism by the TYC.)

What concerns Indian officials and many inside the Tibetan community is the possibility that the Dalai Lama has served as a unique and potentially irreplaceable check on the passions and excesses of Tibetan activism. Today, even the most ardent proponents of Tibetan independence are loath to criticize the Middle Way in public. Karma Yeshi praised the Dalai Lama as the "best Tibetan ambassador ever" who believed in the Middle Way "deep down in his heart." However, he warned that world pressure on China would wane after the Dalai Lama's passing, and that Tibetans had "waited for too long." "If the issue is not resolved before he passes, then frustration and resentment will definitely build."[50]

The lengthy study on Tibet conducted by IDSA[51] "fears risk of division of Tibetans over the Fifteenth Dalai Lama."[52] "We see a problem after the Dalai Lama goes," says Mohan Guruswamy of India's Centre for Policy Alternatives. "He's containing militancy inside and outside Tibet.[53]

One of the authors of the IDSA report, Jagannath Panda, told this author "Indian policymakers will have to come up with a stronger plan for Tibet in the coming years and prepare for possible destabilizing future Tibetan independence movements."[54] Kanwal Sibal, a former foreign secretary of India says that Delhi will "have to recognize whatever successor is hand-picked by the Dalai Lama."

Whoever succeeds the current Dalai Lama, it will prove virtually impossible to replicate the respect and the cult of personality the fourteenth Dalai Lama has fostered over the past half century. By emanating a successor, the Dalai Lama may be able to confer greater legitimacy on his replacement, but the endeavor remains fraught with uncertainty.

NOTES

1. Institute for Defence Studies and Analyses (IDSA), "Tibet and India's Security: Himalayan Region, Refugees and Sino-Indian Relations," Last modified 2012 (Accessed January 28, 2013): http://www.idsa.in/book/TibetandIndiasSecurity.

2. Jagannath Panda. Author interview. Washington, DC, June 2012.

3. "Central Tibetan Schools Administration," Last Modified 2008–2009 (Accessed June 13, 2013): http://www.ctsa.nic.in/.

4. Amanda Peters, "Education Department Takes Over Running of Central School for Tibetans," *Tibet Post International*, July 11, 2012 (Accessed January 28, 2013): http://www.thetibetpost.com/en/news/exile/2695-education-department-takes-over-running-of-central-school-for-tibetans.

5. "Tibetan Refugee Settlements: India," *Department of Home: Central Tibetan Administration*, 2011 (Accessed February 15, 2013): http://ctrc.tibet.net/settlements-in-india.html.

6. "India: Information on Tibetan Refugees and Settlements," *BCIS Resource Information Center, U.S. Citizenship and Immigration Services*, May 30, 2003 (Accessed January 28, 2013): http://www.uscis.gov/portal/site/uscis/menuitem .5af9bb95919f35e66f614176543f6d1a/?vgnextoid=4e77361cfb98d010VgnVCM10 000048f3d6a1RCRD&vgnextchannel=d2d1e89390b5d010VgnVCM10000048f3d 6a1RCRD.

7. "Tibet and India's Security: Himalayan Region, Refugees, and Sino-Indian Relations," *Institute for Defence Studies and Analyses (IDSA):* 161. May 2012 (Accessed January 28, 2013): http://www.idsa.in/system/files/book_Tibet-India.pdf.

8. Ananth Krishnan, "'Meaningful Autonomy Is the Only Realistic Solution.'" *Hindu.* July 9, 2012 (Accessed June 13, 2013): http://www.thehindu.com/opinion/interview/article3616701.ece.

9. Some 83,000 Tibetan exiles from across the world are registered to vote in elections, with polling stations in over thirty countries.

10. Phurbu Thinley, "TWA to Campaign for Higher Voter Turnout in 2011 Kalon Tripa Elections," *Phayul.com*, March 31, 2010 (Accessed January 28, 2013): http://www.phayul.com/news/article.aspx?id=27018&t=1.

11. Timothy Roemer, "Tibet: Growing Frustration after Latest Round of Talks Between Beijing and The Dalai Lama's Envoys," September 8, 2011 (Accessed January 28, 2013): http://wikileaks.tetalab.org/mobile/cables/10NEWDELHI290.html.

12. Ellen Bork, "Tibet's Transition: Will Washington Take a Stand?" *World Affairs Journal* September/October 2012 http://www.worldaffairsjournal.org/article/tibet%E2%80%99s-transition-will-washington-take-stand.

13. Lalit Mohan, "Lobsang Sangay to be Tibetan Prime Minister," *Tribune*, April 27, 2011 (Accessed January 28, 2013): http://www.tribuneindia .com/2011/20110428/main5.htm.

14. Peter Hartcher, "Dreams of a Leader of a Land He Has Never Seen," *Sydney Morning Herald*, June 26, 2012 (Accessed January 28, 2013): http://www .smh.com.au/opinion/politics/dreams-of-a-leader-of-a-land-he-has-never-seen -20120625-20yh1.html.

15. Agence France Presse, "Tibet Exiled 'PM' admits Dalai Lama's Shoes Hard to Fill," *Himalayan Times Online*, October 20, 2010 (Accessed January 28, 2013): http://thehimalayantimes.com/rssReference.php?headline=Tibet%20 exiled%20PM%20says%20Dalai%20Lama's%20shoes%20hard%20to%20 fill&NewsID=344245.

16. "Dalai Lama's South Africa Visa Delay Unlawful, Court Rules," *Daily Monitor*, November 20, 2012 (Accessed January 28, 2013) http://www.monitor .co.ug/News/World/Dalai-Lama-s-South-Africa-visa-delay-unlawful--court -rules/-/688340/1633370/-/rqc4qkz/-/index.html

17. Linda Feldman, "At White House, The Dalai Lama Sidesteps Trash," *Christian Science Monitor*, February 19, 2010 (Accessed January 28, 2013) http://www .csmonitor.com/USA/Politics/The-Vote/2010/0219/At-White-House-the-Dalai -Lama-sidesteps-trash

18. Dr. Lobsang Sangay, "Occasion of His Inauguration," Inaugural Acceptance Speech, Dharaslama, August 8, 2011.

19. Li Hongmei, "Terrorist Poised to Rule 'Tibetan Government In-Exile'?" *People's Daily Online*, March 22, 2011 (Accessed January 28, 2013): http://english .peopledaily.com.cn/90002/96417/7326988.html.

20. "China Denounces Sangay's Election," *Zeenews.com*, April 28, 2011 (Accessed January 28, 2013): http://zeenews.india.com/news/world/china-denounces-sangay-s-election_702844.html.

21. "Tibet and India's Security: Himalayan Region, Refugees, and Sino-Indian Relations," *Institute for Defence Studies and Analyses (IDSA)*, 159, May 2012 (Accessed January 28, 2013): http://www.idsa.in/system/files/book_Tibet-India.pdf.

22. "Special Topic Paper: Tibet 2008–2009," *Congressional Executive Commission on China*, October 22, 2009 (Accessed January 28, 2013): http://www.cecc.gov/pages/virtualAcad/tibet/tibet_2008-2009.pdf.

23. Schmetzer Uli, "6-Year-Old Tibetan the Incarnation of Chinese Power," *Chicago Tribune*, January 26, 2006 (Accessed January 28, 2013): http://articles.chicagotribune.com/1996-01-16/news/9601160267_1_11th-panchen-lama-tibetan-wei-jingsheng.

24. In 1996 the PRC admitted to holding Nyima in a secret location "at the request of his parents." In 2005, Chinese officials told the UN Special Rapporteur on Freedom of Religion or Belief that Nyima was living a "normal, happy life and receiving a good cultural education."

25. Ajai Shukla, "Ajai Shukla: Remembering India's Capitulation on Tibet," *Business Standard*, August 9, 2011 (Accessed January 28, 2013): http://www.business-standard.com/results/news/ajai-shukla-remembering-indias-capitulation tibet/445212/.

26. "Tibet Marks Panchen Lama's Enthronement Anniversary," *China through a Lens*, December 9, 2005 (Accessed January 28, 2013): http://www.china.org.cn/english/2005/Dec/151352.htm.

27. Ananth Krishnan, "Panchen Lama in Top Chinese Panel," *Hindu*, March 12, 2013 (Accessed June 13, 2013): http://www.thehindu.com/news/international/world/panchen-lama-in-top-chinese-panel/article4501574.ece.

28. "11th Panchen Lama Blesses Buddhists in Tibet," *People's Daily Online*, December 19, 2005 (Accessed January 28, 2013): http://english.peopledaily.com.cn/200512/19/eng20051219_229038.html.

29. In the 1992 White Paper, China had previously referred to the Panchen Lama as the "co-leader of Tibetan Buddhism with the Dalai Lama."

30. "Reincarnation of Tibetan Living Buddhas Must Get Government Approval," *People's Daily Online*, August 3, 2007 (Accessed January 28, 2013): http://english.peopledaily.com.cn/90001/90776/6231524.html.

31. "Human Rights and Rule of Law News and Analysis: Measures on the Management of the Reincarnation of Living Buddhas in Tibetan Buddhism (ICT Translation)," *Congressional Executive Commission on China*, March 14, 2011 (Accessed January 28, 2013): http://www.cecc.gov/pages/virtualAcad/index.phpd?showsingle=98772.

32. "Top Theological Institutes Prepare Living Buddhas," *China News Center*, August 14, 2012 (Accessed January 28, 2013): http://www.chinamedia.com/news/2012/08/14/top-theological-institutes-prepare-living-buddhas/.

33. Jing Wang, *Locating China: Space, Place, and Popular Culture* (New York: Routledge, 2005), 100.

34. "White Paper—Freedom of Religious Belief in China," *Embassy of the People's Republic of China in the United States of America*, October, 1997 (Accessed June 2013): http://www.china-embassy.org/eng/zt/zjxy/t36492.htm.

35. "Will Decide On My Successor When I Am 90, Says Dalai Lama," *India Today*, September 11, 2011 (Accessed January 28, 2013): http://indiatoday.intoday.in/story/dalai-lama-successor-at-90/1/152551.html.

36. "Will Decide On My Successor When I Am 90, Says Dalai Lama," *India Today*, September 11, 2011 (Accessed January 28, 2013): http://indiatoday.intoday.in/story/dalai-lama-successor-at-90/1/152551.html.

37. At the conference the Dalai Lama lamented that there were no "official religious guidelines" on the issue of reincarnation.

38. Robbie Barnett, "Note on the Statement by the Dalai Lama Concerning His Successor," *Columbia*, September 26, 2011 (Accessed January 29, 2013): http://lawprofessors.typepad.com/files/note-on-the-statement-by-hhdl-concerning-his-successor-4.pdf.

39. Robbie Barnett, "Note on the Statement by the Dalai Lama Concerning His Successor," *Columbia*, September 26, 2011 (Accessed January 29, 2013): http://lawprofessors.typepad.com/files/note-on-the-statement-by-hhdl-concerning-his-successor-4.pdf.

40. Didi Kirsten Tatlow, "Dalai Lama Keeps Firm Grip on Reins of Succession," *The New York Times*, October 5, 2011 (Accessed January 29, 2013): http://www.nytimes.com/2011/10/06/world/asia/06iht-letter06.html?pagewanted=all&_r=0.

41. Ananth Krishnan, "Meaningful Autonomy Is the Only Realistic Solution," *Hindu*, July 9, 2012 (Accessed January 29, 2013): http://www.thehindu.com/opinion/interview/article3616701.ece.

42. "Tibet: Time Talks with the Tibetan Spiritual Leader," *Unrepresented Nations and People's Organization*, October 20, 2004 (Accessed January 29, 2013): http://www.unpo.org/article/1321.

43. Chandan Mitra. Author interview. Dew Delhi, August 2012.

44. Mohan Malik. Author interview. Honolulu, April 2012.

45. C. Raja Mohan. Author interview. New Delhi, August 2012.

46. Chellaney Brahma, "Tibet Is at the Core of the India-China Divide," *Stagecraft and Statecraft*, April 2, 2007 (Accessed January 29, 2013): http://chellaney.net/2007/04/02/tibet-is-at-the-core-of-the-india-china-divide/.

47. Mohammed Abbas, "China Unrealistic on Tibet, Talks Futile: Dalai Lama," *Reuters*, June 20, 2012 (Accessed January 29, 2013): http://in.reuters.com/article/2012/06/20/britain-dalailama-idINDEE85J0EZ20120620.

48. Li Hongmei, "Terrorist Poised to Rule 'Tibetan Government In-Exile'?" *People's Daily Online*, March 22, 2011 (Accessed January 28, 2013): http://english.peopledaily.com.cn/90002/96417/7326988.html.

49. Hua Zi, "Central Tibetan Administration Illegitimate," *China Daily*, March 29, 2012 (Accessed January 29, 2013): http://www.chinadaily.com.cn/opinion/2012-03/29/content_14936763.htm.

50. Karma Yeshi. Author interview. Dharamsala, India, August 2012.

51. "Tibet and India's Security: Himalayan Region, Refugees, and Sino-Indian Relations," *Institute for Defence Studies and Analyses (IDSA)*, 151, May 2012 (Accessed January 28, 2013): http://www.idsa.in/system/files/book_Tibet-India.pdf.

52. "Tibet and India's Security: Himalayan Region, Refugees, and Sino-Indian Relations," *Institute for Defence Studies and Analyses (IDSA)*, 151, May 2012 (Accessed January 28, 2013): http://www.idsa.in/system/files/book_Tibet-India.pdf.

53. Guruswamy Mohan. Author interview. New Delhi, November 2011.

54. Jagannath Panda. Author interview. Washington, DC, June 2012.

IV

THIRD PARTIES

Chapter 8

The United States in Sino-Indian Relations

The "Return to Rivalry" chapter of this book traced the evolution of Sino-Indian ties in the twenty-first century through the prism of the border dispute. The narrative implied that the deterioration of bilateral relations from 2006 to 2013 was largely the result of events at the border: China's claims on Tawang, India's military and infrastructure buildup along the Line of Actual Control (LAC), the visit of Indian leaders and the Dalai Lama to Arunachal Pradesh, Chinese intrusions across the LAC, and the stalling of the border negotiations.

However, time and again in interviews conducted with senior officials for this book, it was not the border dispute cited as the principal reason for the general downturn in Sino-Indian relations after 2006, but India's strategic rapprochement with the United States, which began in earnest in 2005. Indeed, there is a case to be made that the development of the Indo-U.S. strategic partnership constitutes the "most important structural development in Sino-Indian relations" in the twenty-first century.[1] Let's explore the facts.

SINCE THE BEGINNING

Washington was a participant in the formative event in the modern history of Sino-Indian relations, the 1962 border war. After welcoming India into the community of democratic nations in 1947, the United States provided Delhi with $75 million a year in developmental aid and a modest arms package through the 1950s. In contrast, the emergence of Communist China in 1949 was seen by Washington as a profound threat to stability in Asia. Those fears were seemingly justified when, within a year of assuming power, Mao Zedong's People's Liberation Army invaded Tibet and was battling American forces in Korea.

When the PLA launched a surprise invasion across the Sino-Indian border on October 20, U.S. President John Kennedy wrote to Indian Prime Minister Jawaharlal Nehru asking "what [America] can do to translate our support into terms that are practically most useful to you as soon as possible."[2] By November 1, U.S. military supplies were arriving in India by air, including antipersonnel mines, .30 caliber machine guns and ammunition, 81mm mortars, 100,000 rounds of ammunition, and radios. By November 14, Washington was preparing to equip five Indian divisions at the combined cost of $50 million.

When China ended the war with the declaration of a unilateral cease-fire on November 21, President Kennedy was considering an Indian request for "modern radar cover" and "twelve squadrons of supersonic all-weather fighters . . . manned by U.S. personnel [to] protect [India's] cities and installations and . . . to assist the Indian Air Force in air battles with the Chinese air force."[3] This early tactical alliance between Washington and Delhi ended abruptly three years later when the Second Indo-Pakistan War of 1965 prompted a suspension of U.S. aid to both countries.

In the 1970s and 1980s America's position in the trilateral triangle shifted. A secret trip to China by U.S. Secretary of State Henry Kissinger in July 1971 began a historic rapprochement between the United States and the People's Republic of China. The deterioration of Sino-Soviet ties in the 1960s had provided the two sides with a common enemy while Pakistan offered them a common friend and interlocutor. Just one month after Kissinger's visit (and a few months before the impending Third Indo-Pakistan War), India signed a Treaty of Friendship and Cooperation with the Soviet Union, helping to solidify a Cold War divide between the USSR and India, on one hand, and China, Pakistan, and the United States on the other.

These alignments remained more or less fixed until the collapse of the Soviet Union in 1991, which dismissed the primary rationale for the U.S.-China entente and removed one of the principal obstacles to improved Indo-U.S. ties. The 1990s saw the trilateral relationship enter a profound state of flux, which is where this story begins.

Not with a Whimper but with a Bang

While China and the United States celebrated the collapse of the Soviet Union in 1991, the end of the Cold War was felt very differently in Delhi. Gone was the superpower that had served as Delhi's principal patron, arms supplier, and political defender over the previous twenty years.

To make matters worse, India was afflicted with a debilitating financial crisis the same year and by the early 1990s Delhi was under mounting pressure from Pakistani-backed terrorists in Kashmir. In 1988 there were just thirty-one fatalities in the disputed region resulting from militancy; by 1993 that number jumped to 2,567.[4]

The spike in Kashmiri militancy paralleled the development of an indigenous Pakistani nuclear weapons capability in the early 1990s, aided in no small part by generous Chinese support. Even today Indian strategists like Commodore C. Uday Bhaskar insist that Pakistan's asymmetric campaign to bleed India through terrorism in Kashmir can be traced to the nuclear deterrent provided by China. "In an indirect way, China's WMD assistance to [Pakistan's military] is enabling terror in South Asia,"[5] Bhaskar argues.

In addition to Pakistan "going nuclear," in 1996 China conducted its own, ultimately final, series of nuclear tests, the same year the UN General Assembly voted to approve a Comprehensive Test Ban Treaty that would impose a global ban on nuclear explosive testing.[6] As it had been nearly a quarter century since India conducted its own "peaceful nuclear test," in 1974, the Bharatiya Janata Party that was brought to power briefly in 1996 feared there would be ambiguity about India's nuclear weapons capability in an era free of nuclear testing. The order to conduct India's first explicit nuclear weapons test would have to wait two years until the BJP returned to power on firmer political footing, but on May 11 and May 13, 1998, five atomic weapons were detonated at the Pokhran site in the deserts of Rajasthan, sixty miles from the Pakistan border.

Amid the relative thaw in Sino-Indian relations in the 1990s, the tests were less surprising to Beijing than the rationale. A week prior to the tests, on the Indian television show "In Focus with Karan," Indian Defense Minister George Fernandez publicly fingered China as "potential threat number one."[7] Shortly after the tests, a private letter from Indian Prime Minister Atal Bihar Vajpayee to the White House outlining India's rationale for the tests was leaked to the public. Without mentioning the country by name, the Indian prime minister implicated China for India's "deteriorating security environment."

Within a week of the test, China's foreign ministry denounced India's "slander of China," and the *PLA Daily* issued a broadside against India's "military expansionist line" and its efforts to "consolidate its hegemonic status in South Asia."[8] China's first-ever White Paper on defense, issued in July 1998, said that India's tests "produced grave consequences on peace and stability in the South Asian region and the rest of the world."[9] But by year's end senior Indian diplomats were welcomed back in Beijing, and the storm quickly passed.

The ease with which China and India navigated the crisis was a welcome surprise. What was not clear to officials at the time was how the nuclear test would serve as an unexpected catalyst for the most substantive diplomatic engagement between the United States and India since the 1960s. Nor could they have foreseen the impact this rapprochement would come to have on the Sino-Indian relationship.

Alarmed at the prospect of nuclear rivalry on the subcontinent, shortly after the May 1998 nuclear tests Washington dispatched U.S. Deputy Secretary of State Strobe Talbott to meet with Indian External Affairs Minister Jaswant Singh. Where previous Indo-U.S. dialogues so often became mired in Cold War acrimony, the Singh-Talbott talks found unexpected traction, with fourteen rounds of dialogue spanning two and a half years from 1998 to 2000.

Tangible results followed. A year after the nuclear test Washington refused to back its longtime ally Pakistan during the abrupt Indo-Pakistan war at Kargil in 1999. The following year President Clinton made a fence-mending visit to India, the first by a U.S. president in twenty-two years, and the two sides established a Joint Working Group on terrorism.

Clinton was succeeded in 2001 by President George W. Bush, who committed his administration to strengthening Indo-U.S. ties and championing India's rise like no U.S. president before him. His foreign policy team believed that it was not a fundamental conflict of interests that divided India and the U.S. during the Cold War, but short-term geopolitical calculations based on the balance-of-power politics of a bygone era. Freed from those artificial constraints, the two governments found their national interests and national values surprisingly congruent.

The terrorist attacks of September 11, 2001 only brought those interests further into alignment, especially as they were followed only two months later by a brazen assault on the Indian parliament building by Pakistani-backed extremists. In the months after 9/11, President Bush waived a series of proliferation-related sanctions on India and established working groups for defense and high technology.

COURTING THE SWING STATE

While Washington and Delhi were turning a new page, in the absence of a common Soviet enemy, China and the United States increasingly came to see each other as strategic competitors, a dynamic reinforced by the 1996 Taiwan Straits Crisis and the 2001 EP-3 incident.[10]

The trilateral relationship entered the new century on very different terms than it entered the 1990s. India, seemingly the great loser at the end of the Cold War, was now in a position to serve as a critical "swing state" in the emerging bipolar order.[11] Shared democratic values made the United States the more natural partner, but their adversarial Cold War relationship had fostered a deep mistrust of the United States among a ruling elite steeped in the principles of Nonalignment.

Few in India doubted that China constituted the more immediate security threat. But a major agreement on the disputed Sino-Indian border in 2003, and an apparent meeting of the Chinese and Indian minds on issues like climate change, the primacy of state sovereignty, and the Doha round of world trade talks kept Sino-Indian ties on a positive trajectory through mid-decade.

In hindsight, the courtship of India reached a zenith in the spring and summer of 2005. U.S. Secretary of State Condoleezza Rice scheduled a trip to Delhi in March 2005, and Chinese Premier Wen Jiabao followed her to India's capital a month later. Both visits held the promise of an ambitious deal that could fundamentally transform India's relationship with each power.

Premier Wen's visit raised expectations in India for a final settlement of the Sino-Indian border dispute. Two years earlier Delhi and Beijing had agreed to appoint high-ranking Special Representatives (SRs) tasked with reaching a final resolution to the dispute, and a snap meeting of the SRs was called just a few weeks prior to Wen's visit to try and reach a last-minute deal.

As the "Return to Rivalry" chapter showed, Premier Wen left New Delhi without the elusive "package deal," instead signing an important but less ambitious protocol on confidence-building measures at the Line of Actual Control. What's worse, Wen's visit marked a turning point in the border negotiations process. A series of crises in the years to follow undermined all momentum toward a border settlement and no substantive agreements were reached in the dozen rounds of border negotiations from 2006 to 2013.

Secretary Rice's March visit to Delhi yielded very different results. It helped to lay the groundwork for two transformative bilateral agreements signed in Washington in June and July that would fundamentally transform relations between the world's largest and oldest democracies. In June 2005 Indian Defense Minister Pranab Mukherjee traveled to Washington to sign a "New Framework for the U.S.-India Defense Relationship" (NFDR) based on "common principles and shared national interests." The ten-year defense agreement pledged increased cooperation in the fields of high technology, missile defense, and military research and development.

"The U.S.-India defense relationship derives from a common belief in freedom, democracy and the rule of law, and seeks to advance shared security interests,"[12] read the document, which promised India a series of exemptions and "ally treatments" regarding the export of U.S. military hardware. Pentagon officials involved in drafting the NFDR told this writer in 2012 that the agreement was "ahead of its time," and that given the political environment in India "it's unlikely the two sides could get such an ambitious deal today."[13]

At the time the NFDR was signed, U.S.-India defense trade over the preceding two decades had been limited to a few dozen jet engines and some Firefinder radar.[14] By 2011, India was the third-largest purchaser of U.S. arms, accounting for some $4.5 billion in sales that year alone.[15] By 2013 India had ordered or purchased sensor-fused bombs, Apache helicopters, P8-I surveillance aircraft, M-777 Howitzers, C-130J and C-17 transport aircraft, and a large amphibious transport dock. In recent years the U.S. conducted more joint military exercises with India—over fifty a year by one estimate[16]—than with any other country, NATO allies included.

Yet, within a month of its signing, the defense pact was overshadowed by a more ambitious and controversial deal on civil nuclear cooperation signed by President George W. Bush and Prime Minister Manmohan Singh in Washington in July 2005.

Much as the border dispute serves as a symbol of the Cold War hostility between China and India, Delhi's international isolation on nuclear issues had long been one of its principal complaints against Washington. China and India both initiated crash nuclear programs in the early 1950s, but Beijing was more effective in its pursuit of an overt weapons capability and was handsomely rewarded for it. China tested its first nuclear weapon in 1964, several years before the Nuclear Nonproliferation Treaty created a two-tiered hierarchy of nuclear "haves" and "have-nots." As it was a full four years after the NPT took effect in 1970 before India conducted its first "peaceful nuclear test," India was relegated to a nuclear pariah and blanketed with international sanctions.

The U.S.-India Nuclear Deal proposed to address this grievance by fundamentally altering the global nonproliferation order and welcoming India, a non-NPT signatory, into the club of accepted nuclear powers.

Despite the favorable terms of the nuclear deal, Indian Prime Minister Manmohan Singh faced a groundswell of domestic opposition from a Left Front opposed to closer integration with the United States and fearful of antagonizing China and Russia. For three years the deal languished in India's parliament (and the U.S. Congress) as the Left threatened to bring down the ruling coalition if the controversial agreement was put to a vote.

In arguably the boldest decision in his decade-long tenure as India's prime minister, Manmohan Singh forced a showdown over the nuclear deal in the summer of 2008. A no-confidence vote was called, and the

anti-deal Indian grps

margins were so tight the two sides "summoned [MPs] from their sick beds and even from prison cells to take part in the vote."[17] Singh's government survived the no-confidence motion by just three votes in the 543-seat parliament[18] and the U.S. Congress passed the necessary legislation to operationalize the deal months later.

Nearly a decade after the nuclear deal was first announced it has been condemned in several corners of Washington as a tactical failure. The lucrative deals promised to American (and other foreign) nuclear companies remain distant promises after India's parliament passed restrictive nuclear liability legislation. In a strategic context, however, the deal cemented a new foundation for Indo-U.S. relations. For India the nuclear deal was, in effect, a referendum on the Indo-U.S. relationship and it represented a crushing defeat for the anti-American left.

THE STRATEGIC TRIANGLE

> Indian politicians these days seem to think their country would be doing China a huge favor simply by not joining the "ring around China" established by the U.S. and Japan.
>
> —*Global Times* OpEd, June 11, 2009[19]

There is no "smoking gun" to demonstrate that India's turn to the United States in 2005 was responsible for the gradual deterioration in Sino-Indian ties that began the following year. And at least one analyst from the Chinese Academy of Social Sciences, China's largest think tank, warned against reading too much into the impact of the Indo-U.S. rapprochement on bilateral ties. "Frankly, we didn't take India very seriously before 2005, and we still don't take India very seriously now. We could care less that India and the U.S. are 'new strategic partners.'"[20]

Yet time and again, Indian and U.S. analysts interviewed for this book argued that the Indo-U.S. rapprochement had a material effect on the paradigm through which China viewed India. Consider that for much of the Cold War Beijing had two principal security concerns vis-a-vis India. The first related to sensitivities over India's intentions in Tibet and its hosting of the Dalai Lama. The second regarded India's ties to superpowers hostile to China (first the United States in the 1960s and then the Soviet Union in the 1970s and 1980s). The latter concern vanished with the collapse of the Soviet Union in 1991, but India's turn to the U.S. in the mid-2000s restored an important dynamic in Sino-Indian relations.

"China wants a post-American, Sino-centric order, and India's turn to the U.S. prevents that reality from taking shape," Ralph Cossa, the head of the CSIS Pacific Forum in Honolulu, explained to this writer. "China perceives India's tilt toward the U.S. as prolonging American hegemony over the global commons."[21]

Di Dongsheng, a professor at Renmin University in Beijing, relayed to this author how the Chinese people are "increasingly seeing India solely through the context of a U.S. effort to contain China in a circle of un-friendly powers."[22] "China wants to see India take a more important role on the global stage. The *only* exception," said Ma Jiali at the China Reform Forum in 2012, "is if India joins some kind of U.S. alliance designed to hedge against China's rise."

BOILING THE FROG

Yet an explicit military alliance between the United States and India is a distant—and perhaps entirely unrealistic—prospect. A powerful coalition of Indian bureaucrats, politicians, and media personalities continue to re-sist efforts at deeper political, military, and institutional cooperation with the U.S. The Indian Ministry of Defense has opposed signing three key "interoperability agreements" (CISMOA, BECA, and LSA) the Pentagon insists are prerequisites to greater military-to-military cooperation. "We want to go steady, but they're still on a first-date mentality," explained a commander at U.S. Pacific Command (PACOM) in Honolulu.

At the political level, public expressions of strategic partnership ea-gerly voiced by U.S. diplomats are often met with uncomfortable silence in Delhi. When U.S. Defense Secretary Leon Panetta described India as a "linchpin" in America's strategic pivot to Asia[23] in June 2012, the state-ment "didn't go over well in India," a Congress Party MP told this author in Washington. "India will not be an adjunct policemen anytime in the next twenty years. Internal consolidation is our priority. Don't start talk-ing to us about burden-sharing."[24] C. Raja Mohan admits that "at the very moment the U.S. moved to an explicit balancing strategy and is urging India to take the leadership role in Asia, India is sending ambiguous sig-nals. Delhi has neither endorsed the U.S. pivot to Asia nor criticized it."[25]

Some have attributed India's apprehension to the enduring legacy of Non-Alignment. Ingrained in Indian strategic thought over the course of the twentieth century, at its core the philosophy instills an aversion to any perceived dependency on another country. Formal alliances are viewed as liabilities that impinge on India's freedom of action and create danger-ous dependencies on self-interested foreign powers.

However, not everyone is convinced that India's "strategic reluc-tance" is the product of an outdated philosophy. There may be a more calculated strategic rationale, says Lt. Col Peter Garretson of the U.S. Air

Force, who spent several years as a fellow at India's Institute for Defense Studies and Analysis:

> India *wants* to move toward the U.S. but fears above all that moving too quickly will unnecessarily provoke China. Delhi's strategy therefore represents a conscious decision to inch toward the U.S. ever-so-slowly, like the euphemism about boiling a frog. Drop the frog in a pot of boiling water and it will jump right out. Increase the temperature too quickly and the frog will know the gig is up. However, if you raise the temperature one degree at a time, the frog doesn't notice until it's too late.[26]

Many Indian strategists are likely to find this formulation too clever by half, noting India's aversion to anything resembling a grand strategy. However, Garretson's metaphor *does* accurately capture the strategic dilemma facing India today. Many Indian strategists believe that China represents their greatest potential security threat. Many also believe that the most effective insurance policy against this threat is a closer strategic partnership with the United States. Yet they also know that pursuing the latter too quickly or too aggressively may unnecessarily provoke Beijing.

"How to achieve a new web of strategic relationships without weakening the present momentum towards better bilateral relations [with China] is the challenge before our diplomacy and military strategists,"[27] explained B. Raman, the former head of India's External Intelligence Agency RAW, in a February 2013 Op-Ed. India can only bridge the "strategic gap" with China through "a combination of internal and external balancing," says C. Raja Mohan. Delhi therefore "seeks simultaneous expansion of security cooperation with the United States while avoiding a needless provocation of Beijing."[28]

EXPLOITING DIVISIONS

> China is working very methodically in the media and among policymakers to promote the message that the U.S. is trying to keep India and China apart.
>
> —Author interview with member of Indian Parliament from the BJP, November 2011.[29]

Though Chinese analysts generally feign indifference toward the Indo-U.S. partnership, official Chinese publications have at times sought to exploit Indian anxieties about aligning too closely with the U.S. and deviating from the principles of Nonalignment. "Will India be courted or forced by the

United States and Japan to join them to contain China?" the *People's Daily* asked on January 22, 2013. Neither, it answered. "India has an independent foreign policy. It never thinks itself the client state of other countries. Instead it has always been proud of its independent foreign policy."[30]

Another theme found in Chinese official media portrays India and China as ancient friends and the United States as engaged in a nefarious strategy to keep Asia's two great powers divided. The editor of the *People's Daily Online*, Li Hongmei, has argued that responsibility for the 1962 Sino-Indian war lay with the United States, which wanted "nothing better than to see the two principal Asian powers locked in military combat, shedding blood and absorbing resources and energies of millions." "Even today," she continued, "some Western powers still choose to side with the right-wing extremist elements in India against China on the decades-long border disputes. Their intention of doing so is abundantly clear to the peace-loving people either in China or in India."[31]

And yet, perhaps the most effective constraint on greater Indo-U.S. ties comes not from China, but from Indian fears of Sino-U.S. collusion. There is a widely held, if misguided, impression in Delhi that America is deeply divided over its approach to Beijing, and is perpetually on the verge of seeking a strategic accommodation with China that would leave America's friends and partners to fend for themselves. The perception is fed by Cold War memories of the abrupt opening to China during the Nixon administration after decades of open hostility.

These anxieties were triggered by talk of a major U.S.-China collaboration or "G2" to manage global economic affairs during President Barack Obama's first term. They resurfaced after the joint statement from the Obama-Hu summit of November 2009 in which the two sides agreed to "strengthen communication, dialogue and cooperation on issues related to South Asia."[32] This led to a U.S.-China subdialogue on South Asia beginning in May 2010, and questions from Delhi about why the United States was colluding with China to keep a balance of power in South Asia.

Fundamentals Strong

> The best shield for peace and stability depends on how India deals with the U.S. There is no other alternative to a valued, trusted, democratic ally.
>
> —Ajit Doval, former head of India's Intelligence Bureau,
> interview with author in New Delhi, November 2011.[33]

While both dynamics have reinforced doubts in Delhi about the costs of moving too swiftly toward the United States, they have not succeeded in stemming the secular improvement in Indo-U.S. relations. The reality is that since the turn of the century, the main impediments to closer Sino-

Indian ties remain fixed or have grown in prominence, while the greatest obstacles to Indo-U.S. collaboration have gradually dissipated. This has put China in an unenviable position in the strategic triangle.

If Beijing proffers more incentives to woo New Delhi, it is likely to find India receptive and willing to collaborate on matters of mutual interest. But it's unlikely to prevent India from pursuing a parallel track of deeper integration with the United States. More important, until India's fundamental security concerns are addressed—namely a resolution of the border dispute and a degrading of China's strategic partnership with Pakistan—the ceiling for growth in the bilateral relationship will remain low and fixed. If, on the other hand, Beijing pursues a more punitive strategy toward India—as it did at times from 2006 to 2013—it is likely to give greater impetus to pro-Western forces in Delhi.

A senior official in India's Ministry of External Affairs told this writer that the Bush administration's outreach in the early-mid-2000s had "widened India's options" with regard to China. "That option [forming a strategic partnership with the U.S.] may have always been there, but the way President Bush approached us made a partnership more amenable to us at a time we needed it most. Until 2005 China had gamed us. President Bush 'de-gamed' us."[34]

NOTES

1. Zorawar Singh, *Himalayan Stalemate: Understanding the India-China Dispute,* London: Straight Forward Publishers, 2012.

2. Foreign Relations of the United States, 1961–1963, Volume XIX, South Asia, Document 187. Telegram from the Department of State to the Embassy in India. October 28, 1962: 1687. Deptel 1677 to New Delhi. March 15, 2013: https://history.state.gov/historicaldocuments/frus1961-63v19/d187.

3. "J.N. to JFK, 'Eyes Only,'" *Indian Express,* November 15, 2010 (Accessed March 11, 2013): http://www.indianexpress.com/olympics/news/j.n.-to-jfk --eyes-only-/711276/0.

4. "Fatalities in Terrorist Violence 1988–2013," http://www.satp.org/satporgtp/countries/india/states/jandk/data_sheets/annual_casualties.htm.

5. "China's WMD assistance to Pakistan is enabling terror in Southeast Asia." *South Asia Terrorism Portal Asian Age,* March 10, 2013: http://www.asianage.comwww.asianage.com/interview-week/china-s-wmd-assistance-pak-enabling-terror-south-asia-372.

6. The CTBT will not enter force until it is ratified by eight "holdout" states listed in Annex 2 of the treaty, including China, Egypt, Iran, Israel, the United States, India, North Korea, and Pakistan (the last three have not signed or ratified the treaty).

7. Stephen Cohen, *Arming without Aiming* (Washington: Brookings Institute Press, 2010), 99.

8. Srikanth Kondapalli, "The Chinese Military Eyes South Asia," *Shaping China's Security Environment: The Role of the People's Liberation Army* (Carlisle, PA: Strategic Studies Institute, U.S. Army War College, 2006), 290.

9. John Garver, *Protracted Contest* (Seattle: University of Washington Press, 2001), 337.

10. Between July 1995 and March 1996 China conducted a series of provocative missile tests in the waters surrounding Taiwan after Taiwan's president was given permission to visit the United States. The United States ordered two aircraft carrier battle groups into the Taiwan Strait in response. In April 2001 a United States EP-3 surveillance aircraft was in a mid-air collision with a Chinese fighter jet. The Chinese pilot was killed and the EP-3 crash-landed on China's Hainan Island. The episode stirred an international crisis, though the twenty-four American pilots were eventually released.

11. C. Raja Mohan, "India and the Balance of Power," *Foreign Affairs:* July/August 2006 (April 8, 2013): http://www.foreignaffairs.com/articles/61729/c-raja-mohan/india-and-the-balance-of-power.

12. S. Amir Latif, "U.S. India Defense Trade: Opportunities for Defending the Partnership," *Center for Strategic and International Studies* (June 2012), 56.

13. Senior Pentagon official. Author interview. Washington, DC, October 2012.

14. S. Amir Latif, "U.S. India Defense Trade: Opportunities for Defending the Partnership," *Center for Strategic and International Studies* (June 2012), 12.

15. "India Is Third Largest Buyer of U.S. Arms," *NDTV* , December 8, 2011 (Accessed April 8,2013): http://www.ndtv.com/article/india/india-is-third-largest-buyer-of-us-arms-156515?pfrom=home-otherstories.

16. S. Amir Latif, "U.S. India Defense Trade: Opportunities for Defending the Partnership," *Center for Strategic and International Studies* (June 2012), v.

17. "Indian Government Survives Vote," *BBC News*, July 22, 2008 (Accessed April 8, 2013): http://news.bbc.co.uk/2/hi/south_asia/7519860.stml.

18. Two hundred seventy two votes were required for a simple majority; the Congress-led coalition earned 275 while the opposition garnered 256.

19. "India's Unwise Military Moves," *People's Daily Online*, June 11, 2009 (Accessed April 8, 2013): http://english.people.com.cn/90001/90777/90851/6676088.html.

20. Analyst from the Chinese Academy of Social Sciences. Author interview. Washington June 2013.

21. Ralph Cossa. Author interview. Honolulu, April 2012.

22. Di Dongsheng. Author interview. Beijing, February 2013.

23. "US Defence Secretary Leon Panetta Identifies India as 'Linchpin' in US Game Plan to Counter China in Asia-Pacific," *India Today*, June 7, 2012 (Accessed April 8, 2013): http://indiatoday.intoday.in/story/leon-panetta-identifies-india-as-linchpin-to-counter-china/1/199505.html.

24. Congress Party MP. Author interview. Heritage Foundation, Washington, DC, September 19, 2012.

25. C. Raja Mohan, "China's Rise, America's Pivot, and India's Asian Ambiguity," *India Seminar*, January 31, 2013: http://carnegieendowment.org/2013/01/31/china-s-rise-america-s-pivot-and-india-s-asian-ambiguity/fdp0.

26. Lt. Col. Peter Garretson. Author interview. Washington, DC, October 2012.

27. B. Raman, "Dragon's New Face," *OutlookIndia.com*, February 3 2013 (Accessed April 8, 2013): http://www.outlookindia.com/article.aspx?283780.

28. C. Raja Mohan, "The New Triangular Diplomacy: India, China and America at Sea," *NamViet News* November 6, 2012 (Accessed April 8, 2013): http://namvietnews.wordpress.com/2012/11/06/the-new-triangular-diplomacy-india -china-and-america-at-sea/.

29. Member of India's Parliament from the Bharatiya Janata Party. Author interview. New Delhi, November 2011.

30. "Will India Join Strategic Containment of China?" *People's Daily Online*, January 22, 2013 (Accessed April 8, 2013): http://english.peopledaily.com.cn/102774/8102712.html.

31. Li Hongmei, "What Is Beyond the Physical Line?" *People's Daily Online*, August 12, 2012 (April 8, 2013): http://english.peopledaily.com.cn/90002/96417/6726134.html.

32. "US China Joint-Statement," *Office of the Press Secretary*, November 17, 2009: http://www.whitehouse.gov/the-press-office/us-china-joint-statement.

33. Ajit Doval. Author interview. New Delhi, November 2011.

34. Senior official in India's Ministry of External Affairs. Author interview. Beijing, April 2013.

Chapter 9

Sweeter than Honey: The Pakistan Factor in Sino-Indian Relations

Higher than mountains, deeper than oceans, stronger than steel, and sweeter than honey.

—Prime Minister Yousef Raza Gilani describing Sino-Pakistan relations at a public press conference, October 2011.[1]

While India has opted for *tactical* partnerships with the world's super-powers to balance against its more powerful Chinese neighbor (first with the United States, then the Soviet Union, and now again with the United States), Beijing has been content to form a sole *strategic* alliance with a smaller power, Pakistan, to guide its regional policy.

Of all the geopolitical alignments to materialize and dissolve in Sino-Indian relations over the past half-century, the China-Pakistan relationship has remained the one constant. As Ye Hailin of the Chinese Academy of Social Sciences notes, "For the last four decades of the twentieth century, China's South Asian policy was based on a single pillar—it's 'all-weather friendship and all-dimensional cooperation' with Pakistan."[2]

Time and again China has proven to be Pakistan's most ardent and consistent ally and arms supplier. While America's economic and military patronage toward Pakistan has frequently eclipsed China's, the Sino-Pakistan relationship lacks the fragility of Pakistan's relationship with the United States, which suffers radical swings and is poisoned by a substantial conflict of national interests and an undercurrent of strategic mistrust.

To date China and Pakistan have no formal military treaty (as China has with North Korea), but in 2006 the two sides ratified the "China-Pakistan Treaty of Friendship, Cooperation, and Good Neighborliness" which prevents either nation from "joining any alliance or bloc which infringes upon the sovereignty, security, and territorial integrity of the other side."[3]

Though the partnership has benefitted both sides, it was only through China's exhaustively documented nuclear, military, and economic assistance that Pakistan has been able to retain a modicum of strategic parity with its larger neighbor and rival, India. In the multilateral arena China has used its permanent, veto-wielding seat on the UN Security Council to shield Pakistan from multilateral sanctions and prevent action against Pakistan-based militant groups. Notably, in 2007 China blocked a U.S.- and Indian-backed initiative to designate the Pakistan-based Jamaat ud Dawa (JuD) as an international terrorist group.[4] One year later, militants affiliated to JuD's sister organization, Lashkar e-Taiba (LeT) launched a horrific terrorist attack in Mumbai that killed 167 people.

Beijing has battled persistent accusations from Delhi that its relationship with Pakistan is exclusively driven by a desire to contain India. "This is old news and an old string the Indians keep harping on," says Dr. Zhao Ganchen of the Shanghai Institute for International Studies. "Our relationship with Pakistan is not directed at India or any other country." Dr. Zhao and others argue—with some justification—that there are legitimate, non-India-centric rationales for the bilateral relationship. Pakistan has provided Beijing with a political gateway to the Muslim world, a physical gateway to the rich energy resources of Central Asia and the Indian Ocean, and a means of keeping a check on Islamist militancy in Xinjiang, the restive, Muslim-majority Chinese province that borders Pakistan.

However, even today Chinese analysts admit that the foundation of their regional policy is built on a desire to "maintain a secure balance" in South Asia. "It will not be good for us if there is a large imbalance between India and Pakistan," admitted the China Reform Forum's Ma Jiali in a conversation in his office in April 2013. Implicit in this rationale is an admission that China does not wish to see India emerge as the unchallenged hegemon in South Asia.

Consequently, many scholars see Pakistan as constituting the main pillar in a Chinese quasicontainment strategy designed to keep India embroiled in regional affairs and occupied by rivalry with its smaller neighbor. Regional analyst Iskander Rehman explains: "China's strategy is to divert India's attention from East Asia and to prevent it from reaching out beyond South Asia, by keeping it focused on the western front, and by using Pakistan as a form of 'proxy deterrent' against India in its own backyard."[5]

This perception is shared by India's senior-most leadership. On September 6, 2010[6] Prime Minister Manmohan Singh told a private a roundtable of journalists that Beijing was tempted to "keep India in low-level equilibrium" by using India's "'soft underbelly,' Pakistan and Kashmir."[7]

Three elements of the Sino-Pakistan relationship remain distinctly threatening to India: the possibility of a two-front war, the provision of Chinese nuclear and military assistance to Pakistan, and Chinese activities in Kashmir.

INTERVENTION

Since the mid-1960s the greatest concern of Indian military strategists has been the prospect of a simultaneous two-front war with China and Pakistan. The fear quickly took tangible form during the Second Indo-Pakistan War of 1965, when China issued India a three-day ultimatum to "dismantle all its military works for aggression" or "bear full responsibility for all the grave consequences arising therefrom."[8] Pakistan ultimately called a ceasefire just hours before the Chinese deadline expired, but the threat again surfaced six years later during the Third Indo-Pakistan War of 1971, when Beijing ordered provocative troop deployments along the Line of Actual Control. Yet this time, China opted against intervening in the conflict, helpless to prevent the division of East and West Pakistan and the creation of Bangladesh.

Indian assessments of the likelihood of a Chinese intervention in a future Indo-Pakistan war vary considerably. This writer has heard several Indian military and civilian officials suggest in private discussions and roundtables that China was today *more* likely to intervene in an Indo-Pakistan conflict than at any time in the twentieth century. The concern was voiced explicitly by a senior official in India's Ministry of External Affairs in November 2011: "Between 1988 and 2005 we could have been confident of no Chinese intervention in a conflict with Pakistan. That is no longer the case today," he argued.

However, little by way of evidence has been offered to support this heightened risk assessment. China has yet to directly intervene in any Indo-Pakistan conflict, and its behavior has become gradually *less* provocative over the course of the past three Indo-Pakistan wars.[9] During the most recent conflict at Kargil in 1999, Chinese President Jiang Zemin reportedly refused Pakistani requests for greater public support[10] and Beijing summoned India's foreign minister to assure him that "China would not back Pakistan's offensive."

Author Mark Frazier has argued another Indo-Pakistan conflict would "serve no purpose from China's perspective."[11] It would, after all, likely result in an Indian victory, likely invite greater U.S. influence in the region, likely destabilize Pakistan, and likely force China to decide between another war with India it doesn't want and another embarrassing failure to back its "all-weather friend." Frazier concludes it "would take a major shift in foreign policy priorities for China to determine that its national interests dictated getting enmeshed in an Indo-Pakistan conflict."[12]

Pakistan's military strategists have slowly come around to this realization, says Stephen Tankel, a Washington-based expert on the region. "At least some members of the Pakistani security establishment appear to have a more clear-eyed and realistic assessment of the type and level of Chinese support they could expect [in an Indo-Pakistan conflict], which is to say significantly less than is often averred publicly by some officials."[13]

Nuclear and Military Transfers

Even if the likelihood of Chinese intervention in an Indo-Pakistan war remains low, the generous nuclear and military assistance Beijing continues to provide its ally remains a source of concern to India. Official Western sources have thoroughly documented Chinese support to Pakistan's conventional military arsenal and its nuclear weapons program in the 1980s and 1990s.[14]

Table 9.1.   Chinese Military Sales to Pakistan 1986–1993

Platform	Year(s)	Numbers
A-5 Fantan-A fighter	1986–88	98
Anza portable Surface to Air missile (SAM)	1989–93	450
Anza-2 SAM	1989–96	750
CSA-1 SAM	1985	20
F-7 jet fighter	1986–90	75
F-7M airguard fighter	1993	20
F-7MP airguard fighter	1985–93	120
FT-7/FT-7P trainer	1991	19
Fuqing-class support ship	1987	1
Hai Ying-2 ShShM/SShM	1984	16
HJ-8 antitank missile	1990–93	200
HN-5A portable SAM	1989–90	200
Hoku class Fast Attack Craft (FAC)	1980	2
Hong Ying-5 portable SAM	1988–90	300
Huangfen-class FAC	1984	4
K-8 Karakorum-8 jet trainer	1994–96	30
Khalid main battle tank	1991	10
M-11 surface-to-surface missile	1991	55
M-11 surface-to-surface missile	1991	20
P-58A patrol craft	1987–90	4
Fantan-A fighter/ground attack	1982–87	148
Red Arrow 8 antitank missile	1990–93	200
T-59 main battle tank	1977–90	987
T-69 main battle tank	1989–91	275
T-69-II main battle tank	1991–95	339
T-85 main battle tank	1993	12

Source: http://www.rand.org/content/dam/rand/pubs/monograph_reports/MR1119/MR1119.appa.pdf

Since the turn of the century the military-to-military relationship has remained equally robust. Beijing has sold Pakistan dozens of F-7MG/PG fighter aircraft and CSS-N-8 antiship cruise missiles, D-30 Towed artillery guns, fire control and air radar, six Panther helicopters, hundreds of air-to-air missiles and guided bombs, self-propelled artillery guns, advanced ZDK-03 AWACS, T-90 tanks, a few dozen K-8 trainer/combat aircraft, four Jiangwei frigates, and potentially several Yuan-class submarines.[15] In mid-2011 China agreed to provide Pakistan with fifty JF-17 fighter jets and Beijing has signaled it will likely export to Pakistan a version of its J-20 fifth generation stealth fighter when it becomes operational in the coming years.

Moreover, Pakistan and China continue an active schedule of annual joint military exercises, including joint naval exercises off the Pakistani coast. Recent highlights include an August 2010 exercise in which the two sides practiced month-long brigade-level war games "barely twenty-five kilometers from the international border with India" in Rajasthan.[16] The following November a joint antiterrorism exercise in Pakistan saw PLA troops parachute into Pakistani territory, demonstrating China's long-range transport capabilities.

China's nuclear assistance to Pakistan has been no less robust in the twenty-first century, though it has gradually migrated from the military to the civilian sphere. China built all three of Pakistan's first nuclear plants—Kahuta, Chashma, and Khushab—and in the 1980s offered Pakistan blueprints for small nuclear weapons that could fit on ballistic missiles, plans Pakistan subsequently shared with Libya and North Korea.[17] China also provided Pakistan "ready-to-launch M-9, M-11, and Dong Feng 21 ballistic missiles,"[18] and may have tested Pakistan's first atomic bomb in 1990.[19]

U.S. officials believe that China's direct assistance to Pakistan's nuclear weapons program receded after China signed the Nuclear Nonproliferation Treaty in 1993 and pledged to halt assistance to "non-safeguarded" nuclear facilities in Pakistan. However, the gesture was partially stripped of its meaning as Pakistan's indigenous nuclear weapons capability was by then already mature.[20] Moreover, since the turn of the century China has *increased* assistance to Pakistan's civil nuclear program, a development covered in greater detail in the chapter titled "Trade and the Global Commons."

KASHMIR

China's diplomatic position on the disputed territory of Kashmir has undergone a welcome evolution from India's perspective. Before 1980 Beijing insisted that the Indo-Pakistan dispute be resolved "in accord with the wishes of the people" of Kashmir, complementing Pakistan's longstanding demand that a referendum be held in the Muslim-majority territory to determine whether it would join India or Pakistan. However, Dr. John Garver notes "after 1980 Chinese officials no longer spoke about the Kashmiri people's right to self-determination, much less endorsed it," and after 1990 China moved even closer to India's position by dropping references to the "relevant UN resolutions," which would ultimately lead to a referendum.[21]

Yet, as China has assumed a more neutral diplomatic position on the Kashmir dispute, it has provoked Indian security concerns with a commercial and, some believe, military presence in the disputed territory. Delhi has repeatedly lodged protests with the Chinese government about the presence of Chinese engineers operating on various infrastructure projects in Pakistan-administered Kashmir, including water-diversion channels, bridges, railways, and telecommunications facilities.[22] Beginning in 2010 some 700 Chinese nationals began work widening the 800-mile Karakoram Highway that crosses the Sino-Pakistan border.

Sporadically, reports have surfaced suggesting China has thousands of soldiers—between 7,000 and 11,000 by one count—operating in Pakistan-controlled Kashmir. "If true, it would be a matter of serious concern and we would do all that is necessary to ensure the safety and security of the nation," Indian government spokesman Vishnu Prakash responded when confronted with one of the reports in 2010.[23]

For their part, Chinese officials have vehemently denied the presence of PLA soldiers inside Kashmir, calling the reports "totally groundless and out of ulterior purpose."[24] Chinese Defense Minister Liang Guanglie saw it fit to directly address the accusation on a rare visit to India in April 2012. "As Minister of National Defense of China, I'd like to take this opportunity to clarify to you once again: the PLA has never deployed a single soldier in Pakistan-controlled Kashmir."[25]

Cracks in the Armor

While the Sino-Pakistan relationship is arguably as sound in 2013 as it has been at any point in their contemporary history, the relationship is not entirely free of discord.[26] One of the more uncomfortable characteristics of the bilateral relationship is the recognition that the Chinese people do not view Pakistan nearly as favorably as Pakistanis view China. In a 2012 Pew Poll[27] 60 percent of Pakistanis reported a "very favorable" view of China while only 4 percent of Chinese reported a "very favorable" view of Pakistan. Ironically, this was almost the exact same number of Chinese that reported a "very favorable" view of India (3 percent). Similarly, the number of Chinese reporting a "somewhat unfavorable" view of Pakistan, 37 percent, was almost identical to the number that reported the same about India, 38 percent.

Second, China has repeatedly proven less charitable to its "all weather friend" than either Pakistanis or outside observers might expect. For example, when Pakistan was hit with a particularly heavy monsoon season in 2010 resulting in nearly 2,000 deaths, America offered $690 million in aid and assistance. China's contribution was a mere $18 million.[28]

Facing an economic crisis at home and a shortage of foreign currency, in October 2008 Pakistani President Asif Ali Zardari traveled to Beijing seeking an economic aid package of $1.5 to $3 billion. Beijing's response was essentially: go ask the IMF. "We have done our due diligence, and [the loan] isn't happening," a Chinese diplomat told Western reporters at the time.[29] Andrew Small of the German Marshall Fund notes that many Chinese find it outrageous that less than 2 percent of Pakistanis pay income taxes[30]: "China is not going to backfill U.S. aid to Pakistan. It is hard for [Beijing] to justify such aid to a skeptical public."[31]

Finally, the subject of Islamist militancy has been a lingering source of tension in the relationship, particularly as it relates to China's restive Xinjiang province. While the Pakistani government has made every effort to insulate China from the tide of militancy spilling from its borders, the relationship has not been free of incidents. According to Jonathan Holslag:[32]

- In 2000, Chinese security forces arrested over 200 heavily armed militants near the Karakoram highway that connects Xinjiang to Pakistan-controlled Kashmir.
- In 2003, Chinese security forces arrested Pakistani nationals in Xinjiang for selling illegal copies of the Koran.
- In 2004, three Chinese nationals were killed in Gwadar, in the restive Pakistani province of Baluchistan.
- In 2006, three Chinese engineers were shot dead in Pakistan and a car bomb targeted Chinese mine workers.
- In 2007, Chinese security forces killed eighteen suspected militants in a raid on a terrorist training camp near the Pakistan border.

When Islamist militants occupied the Lal Masjid mosque in Islamabad in 2006 and 2007, Pakistani officials initially sought negotiations with the hardline group, even after they began launching vigilante raids throughout the capital and kidnapping foreigners. However, when students from the mosque kidnapped nine Chinese nationals from a massage parlor on June 23, 2007,[33] Pakistan's interior minister was dispatched to Beijing two days later and dressed-down for his failure to protect China's citizens. Within a week of his trip to China, Pakistan launched a bloody offensive to retake the mosque that resulted in at least 100 deaths and 200 injuries.

The Chinese leadership has frequently implored Islamabad in private to do more to crack down on Uighur militants operating inside Pakistan, and in August 2011 local Chinese officials in Xinjiang broke precedent and directly accused militants trained in Pakistan for a spate of violence in Xinjiang that left twenty-two people dead. [34]

China's principal concern regards the East Turkestan Islamic Movement (ETIM), an extremist separatist movement linked to al-Qaeda and dedicated to "liberating Xinjiang from Chinese occupation." The ETIM, as well as other Uighur militant groups, is widely believed to operate training camps inside Pakistan, and the group has published videos online seemingly confirming as much.[35] ETIM militants have claimed responsibility for attacks on Chinese citizens inside Pakistan[36] and the Pakistani military has launched raids on ETIM leaders operating in Pakistan's tribal areas.[37] A U.S. drone strike in Pakistan's tribal areas in 2012 reportedly killed a senior ETIM leader, Emeti Yakuf.

All of which has led some analysts to conclude that it is not Chinese affection *for* Pakistan, but Chinese fear *of* Pakistan (or at least of Pakistani instability) that makes stable relations with Islamabad such a high priority for Beijing. "We *must* have good relations with Pakistan because Pakistan harbors terrorism," a noted Chinese scholar on South Asia told this writer in Beijing in April 2013. "If Pakistan decided to take a hands-off approach [to terrorist groups] and 'let it be' we would have tremendous problems."

COMING FULL CIRCLE

It is notable that in surveying the various reasons for the spike in Sino-Indian tensions from 2006 to 2013, the Pakistan factor was noticeably absent. Border issues, India's turn to the United States, and Tibet played major roles in the downturn and, as later chapters will show, maritime security issues, India's turn to the U.S., and friction in the multilateral arena all provided new sources of tension in the bilateral relationship. But the Sino-Pakistan nexus, one of the core legacy disputes in Sino-Indian relations, remained a relative constant.

The relative stability in Indo-Pakistan relations during this period (with the notable exception of the 2008 Mumbai terrorist attacks) no doubt played a major role. The better the state of Indo-Pakistan relations, the less of a source of tension the Sino-Pakistan relationship is for India. And a major factor contributing to the stability in Indo-Pakistan relations over this period was the substantial reduction in the level of terrorist violence in Kashmir. From a pinnacle of 4,057 terrorism-related deaths in the disputed territory 2001, fatalities declined in every year to follow, dropping to 777 in 2007 and 117 in 2012.[38]

It's also true that the China-Pakistan nexus has, in some respects, become genuinely less threatening to India in the twenty-first century.

China's behavior over the course of the last three Indo-Pakistan wars has become progressively less provocative; Beijing's diplomatic position on Kashmir has undergone a welcome evolution from Delhi's perspective; and China has ceased explicit support to Pakistan's nuclear weapons program. "We no longer take sides on Kashmir and we no longer support provocative action by Pakistan," says Dr. Zhao Ganchen of the Shanghai Institute for International Studies. "This has caused us a lot of blowback in Pakistan."[39]

However, there is unlikely to be a dramatic reduction in Indian threat perceptions vis-à-vis the Sino-Pakistan nexus in the short or medium term. Delhi still remains profoundly concerned about the prospects for a "two-front war," still unsure of whether China would enter an Indo-Pakistan conflict on the latter's behalf. China's ongoing conventional military assistance to Pakistan, its support to Pakistan's civilian nuclear program, and its ongoing work in Pakistan-occupied Kashmir are likely to remain sources of tension in the Sino-Indian relationship for the foreseeable future.

NOTES

1. Daniel Bardsley, "Pakistan Flaunts Its Friendship with China in Message to US," *National,* October 3, 2011: http://www.thenational.ae/news/world/asia-pacific/pakistan-flaunts-its-friendship-with-china-in-message-to-us.

2. Ye Hailin, "China and South Asian Relations in a New Perspective," *Yataisuo,* October 23, 2008: http://yataisuo.cass.cn/english/articles/showcontent.asp?id=1111.

3. Iskander Rehman, "Keeping the Dragon at Bay: India's Counter-containment of China in India," *Asian Security.* No. 2 (2009): 119. http://www.militaryphotos.net/forums/showthread.php?159581-Keeping-the-Dragon-at-Bay-India-s-Counter-Containment-of-China-in-Asia.

4. "China Blocked Efforts to Put Sanctions on JuD, Hafiz Saeed," *Times of India,* December 6, 2010: http://articles.timesofindia.indiatimes.com/2010-12-06/india/28240559_1_jud-unsc-taliban-sanctions-committee.

5. Iskander Rehman, "Keeping the Dragon at Bay: India's Counter-containment of China in India," *Asian Security,* No. 2 (2009): 118. http://www.militaryphotos.net/forums/showthread.php?159581-Keeping-the-Dragon-at-Bay-India-s-Counter-Containment-of-China-in-Asia.

6. Tom Wright, "Will Media Setback Silence Mr. Singh?" *Wall Street Journal,* September 8, 2010: http://blogs.wsj.com/indiarealtime/2010/09/08/will-media-setback-silence-mr-singh/.

7. Manmohan Singh, "China Wants India in State of Low-Level Equilibrium: PM," *Times of India,* September 7, 2010: http://articles.timesofindia.indiatimes.com/2010-09-07/india/28215059_1_india-and-pakistan-bilateral-ties-outstanding-issues.

8. John W. Garver, *Protracted Contest* (Seattle: University of Washington Press, 2001), 202.

9. In contrast, most analysts consider it far more likely that Pakistan would intervene on China's behalf in another Sino-Indian war.

10. John W. Garver, *Protracted Contest* (Seattle: University of Washington Press, 2001), 54.

11. Francine Frankel and Harry Harding, *The India-China Relationship: What the United States Needs to Know* (New York: Columbia University Press, 2004), 304.

12. Francine Frankel and Harry Harding, *The India-China Relationship: What the United States Needs to Know* (New York: Columbia University Press, 2004), 304.

13. Stephen Tankel. Author interview. Washington, DC, February 22, 2013.

14. RAND Corporation, "Overview of China's Arms Sales," 1997. http://www.rand.org/content/dam/rand/pubs/monograph_reports/MR1119/MR1119.appa.pdf.

15. SIPRI Arms Database Trade Register, China and Pakistan 1990–2011. Information generated February 20, 2013: http://armstrade.sipri.org/armstrade/page/trade_register.php.

16. Vimal Bhatia, "China-Pakistan War Games along Rajasthan Border," *Times of India*, August 10, 2010: http://articles.timesofindia.indiatimes.com/2011-08-10/india/29871604_1_military-exercise-pakistan-rangers-pakistan-forces.

17. John Tkacik, "The Enemy of Hegemony Is My Friend: Pakistan's De Facto Alliance with China," Congressional testimony, July 26, 2011, House Committee on Foreign Affairs Oversight and Investigations Subcommittee.

18. Iskander Rehman, "Keeping the Dragon at Bay: India's Counter-containment of China in India," *Asian Security*, No. 2 (2009): 117. http://www.militaryphotos.net/forums/showthread.php?159581-Keeping-the-Dragon-at-Bay-India-s-Counter-Containment-of-China-in-Asia.

19. India Defense, "China Tested Nuclear Weapons for Pakistan in 1990: Thomas Reed," January 3, 2009: http://www.india-defence.com/reports-4114.

20. Some analysts have speculated that China waited to join the NPT until it was confident in Pakistan's indigenous nuclear weapons capability.

21. John W. Garver, *Protracted Contest: Sino-Indian Rivalry in the Twentieth Century* (Seattle: University of Washington Press, 2001), 228.

22. "China's Role in PoK on Krishna's Agenda," *Deccan Herald*, April 3, 2013: http://www.deccanherald.com/content/61908/chinas-role-pok-krishnas-agenda.html.

23. "India to Verify Reports of Chinese Presence in PoK, Says Govt," *Times of India*, August 30, 2010: http://articles.timesofindia.indiatimes.com/2010-08-30/india/28301219_1_gilgit-baltistan-chinese-troops-high-speed-rail-and-road.

24. Saibal Dasgupta, "China Calls PoK 'Northern Pakistan,' J&K Is 'India-controlled Kashmir," *Times of India*, September 2, 2010: http://articles.timesofindia.indiatimes.com/2010-09-02/china/28249568_1_gilgit-baltistan-chinese-foreign-ministry-india-s-jammu.

25. Liang Guanglie, "China has no plans for Indian military bases." Interview, *Hindu*: 1–3.

26. Hailin, Le. "China and South Asian Relations in a new perspective" *Yataisuo*. October 23, 2008 http://yataisuo.cass.cn/English/Articles/showcontent .asp?id=1118

27. "Growing Concerns in China about Inequality, Corruption," *Pew Research Center*, October 16, 2012: http://www.pewglobal.org/2012/10/16/chapter-2 -china-and-the-world/.

28. "Sweet As Can Be?" *Economist*, May 12, 2011: http://www.economist .com/node/18682839.

29. Jane Perlez, "Rebuffed by China, Pakistan May Seek I.M.F. Aid," *New York Times*, October 18, 2008: http://www.nytimes.com/2008/10/19/world/ asia/19zardari.html?_r=0.

30. Sabrina Tavernise, "Pakistan's Elite Pay Few Taxes, Widening Gap," July 18, 2011: http://www.nytimes.com/2010/07/19/world/asia/19taxes .html?pagewanted=all&_r=0.

31. Andrew Small. Author interview. Washington, DC, Spring 2011.

32. Jonathan Holslag, *China and India: Prospects for Peace* (New York: Columbia University Press, 2010), 148–150.

33. "Lal Masjid Kidnap Chinese Nationals," *One India News*, June 23, 2007: http://news.oneindia.in/2007/06/23/lal-masjid-brigade-kidnap-chinese-nation als-1182591347.html.

34. "Chinese Media Highlights Pak Angle, Seeks Action on Terror," *Times of India*, August 2, 2011: http://articles.timesofindia.indiatimes.com/2011-08-02/ china/29842091_1_xinjiang-etim-kashgar.

35. Malik Ayub Sumbal, "How the ETIM Enigma Haunts Pakistan-China Relations," *Diplomat*, May 22, 2013: http://thediplomat.com/the -pulse/2013/05/22/how-the-etim-enigma-haunts-pakistan-china-relations/.

36. "Chinese Workers Shot in Pakistan," *BBC News*, July 9, 2007: http://news .bbc.co.uk/2/hi/south_asia/6282574.stm.

37. "Uighur Leader Killed in Pakistan: Rehman Malik," *Dawn.com*, May 7, 2010: http://archives.dawn.com/archives/103175.

38. "Fatalities in Terrorist Violence 1988–2013," *South Asia Terrorism Portal*. http://www.satp.org/satporgtp/countries/india/states/jandk/data_sheets/ annual_casualties.htm.

39. Zhao Ganchen. Author interview. Washington, DC, August 2011.

V
TURF

Chapter 10

The Quest for Energy Independence: China and the Indian Ocean Region

As the relatively weaker states across the region come under the Beijing
shadow, the challenge before India is how to deal with this situation.

—M. K. Narayanan, former Indian National Security Advisor and
Governor of West Bengal, Sixth Rajaji Memorial Lecture on
"China and India: More Rivals than Friends" July 2011.[1]

Previous chapters in this book were dedicated to what Chinese analysts
are fond of calling the "Five Ts of Sino-Indian Relations": threat perceptions, territory (the border dispute), Tibet, Tawang, and third parties (the
United States and Pakistan). The following three chapters will focus on a
sixth category which, in keeping with convention, we will call "turf." This
final component of the Sino-Indian rivalry regards the encroachment of
China and India into each other's traditional sphere of influence, particularly in the maritime arena, and the associated friction this has generated
in bilateral ties.

This component of the Sino-Indian rivalry is both old and new: Since
the 1962 border war China and India have been engaged in a struggle for
access and influence in each other's periphery. For most of the second half
of the twentieth century, this was largely a one-sided struggle, playing
out almost entirely on India's home turf. China was "looking south" long
before India began "looking east," and for the past five decades Delhi has
been engaged in an almost continuous effort to resist Chinese efforts to
cultivate influence in India's immediate neighborhood.

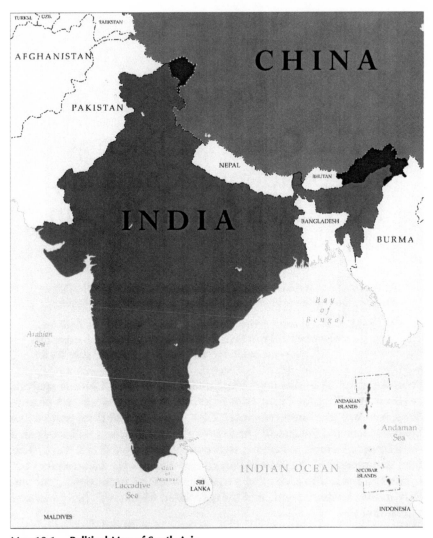

Map 10.1. Political Map of South Asia
Source: American Foreign Policy Council

Were they keeping score in this twentieth century competition, Delhi would take solace in the fact that, with one exception, Pakistan, China has no "client states" in South Asia willing to work openly against Indian interests, and in many regional capitals India's economic and political influence continues to outweigh Beijing's by a wide margin. On the other hand, Beijing successfully cracked the artificial, Monroe Doctrine–like wall India once hoped to construct around the subcontinent and now enjoys cordial ties and booming economic relations with nearly all the region's capitals. As demonstrated in the figure below, Chinese trade with Pakistan, Bangladesh, and Burma has already surpassed India's trade with these countries, while India remains the dominant economic player in Nepal, Sri Lanka, the Maldives, and Bhutan.

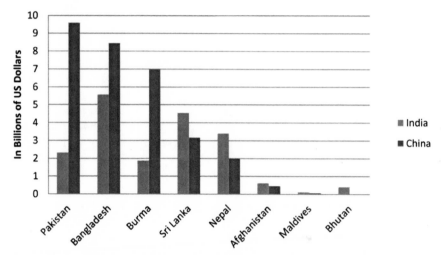

Figure 10.1.   China, India Bilateral Trade with South Asia 2012
Source: IMF Direction of Trade Statistics (accessed June 21, 2013). http://elibrary-data.imf.org

Second, while elements of a containment policy toward India are inherent in China's relationship with Pakistan, it is important to acknowledge that China's success in establishing bonds in South Asia has been as much a function of the pull of regional capitals as it has been a push by Beijing. Indian analysts generally characterize China's South Asia policy as constituting a monolithic, proactive campaign to "keep India boxed in," but India's neighbors have long sought to use China in the same way East Asian countries are now seeking to use India: as a counterbalance to the regional hegemon. "China does not have a policy of countering India by developing a foothold in South Asia. Rather, South Asian countries have a policy of countering India by inviting China to their lands,"[2] observed B. Raman, the former head of India' external intelligence service.

The third distinguishing feature of the Sino-Indian "turf war" in South Asia was that it lacked a maritime component. Until recently, China and India simply had few strategic and economic interests in the other's maritime periphery to speak of and consequently no real conflict of interests at sea. The People's Liberation Army Navy (PLAN) and the Indian Navy had neither the capabilities nor the intent to operate outside their narrow geographic areas of responsibility and only rarely ventured into each other's maritime domain.

Thirteen years in the new century, much has changed. The center of focus in these regional competitions is now shifting to the maritime arena. The PLAN now has a semipermanent presence in the Indian Ocean to fight piracy off the Horn of Africa, and the Indian Navy has sent aircraft carriers through the Strait of Malacca as part of its regular forays into the Western Pacific to exercise with friendly navies. As China's dependence on foreign energy imports has surged, the security of its sea lines of communication through the Indian Ocean have become a paramount concern. For its part, India has a growing number of energy investments in the Western Pacific and a growing number of regional allies at odds with Beijing.

Will these changes herald a new era for Sino-Indian competition in the maritime arena? India's national security advisor, Shivshankar Menon, believes talk of a maritime rivalry between the two powers is both "overdone" and "not inevitable." Speaking at a public forum in March 2013, he argued: "Over the last decade an Indian presence in the waters east of Malacca and Chinese presence west of Malacca have become the new norm. Both have happened simultaneously and without apparent friction."[3]

That's only partially true. As the following chapters will show, the structural changes in these parallel regional competitions *have* generated new friction in the relationship, albeit at a level the two capitals have thus far been able to effectively manage.

PHASE TWO

In the twenty-first century, China's South Asia policy has become an Indian Ocean policy. For Beijing the region no longer represents an arena for a regional competition with India, but the focal point in a global quest for energy security. The U.S. Energy Information Administration (EIA) provides a broad roadmap for understanding China's energy calculus and the increasingly prominent role of the Indian Ocean in that calculus.

Like the United States, China is richly endowed with natural resources, but in recent years the explosive rise in China's energy demand—which is expected to surge an additional 60 percent between 2010 and 2035—has outpaced the domestic supply and production of fossil fuels. China became a net importer of oil in 1993,[4] a net importer of natural gas in 2007,[5] and a net importer of coal in 2009.[6]

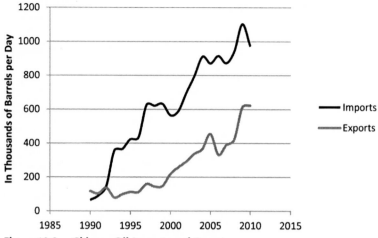

Figure 10.2.   Chinese Oil Imports and Exports

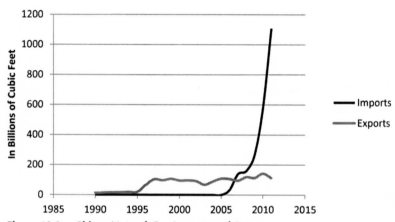

Figure 10.3.   Chines Natural Gas Imports and Exports

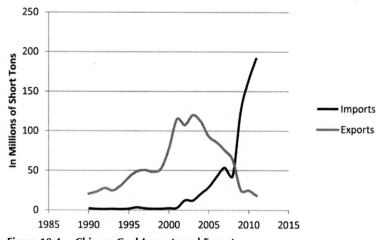

Figure 10.4.   Chinese Coal Imports and Exports

Also like the United States, China relies heavily on coal to meet its energy needs: coal was responsible for two-thirds of China's total energy consumption, with oil at around 19 percent, hydroelectric and natural gas at about 5 percent each, and nuclear 1 percent. China benefits from the third-largest coal reserves in the world and produced 3.7 billion tons of coal in 2012. However, imports began exceeding exports in 2009,[7] and while coal is expected to make up a shrinking part of China's energy portfolio—dropping from two-thirds in 2010 to half in 2035—China will have to bridge the gap largely by importing other fossil fuels.

China is also reasonably well endowed with oil, with perhaps the highest reserves in East Asia (as much as twenty-five billion barrels). But here too China has already become a net importer; the second-largest importer of oil in the world after the United States. China consumes almost ten million barrels of oil per day (mbpd), but produces only 4 mbpd, forcing it to import over half of its oil needs.

In 2007 China became a net importer of natural gas and by 2013 was importing over 29 percent of its natural gas needs. Half of those imports came in the form of liquefied natural gas (LNG), which travels via ships on commercial shipping lanes.

Finally, nuclear power generation is expected to grow rapidly in the coming decades: from 14 gigawatt capacity in 2013 to 130 gigawatt capacity in 2035. But as nuclear only accounts for 1 percent of China's energy portfolio today, even a significant spike in nuclear power capacity will not mitigate China's overwhelming dependence on fossil fuels.

In sum, after spending much of the twentieth century virtually energy independent, China is now importing nearly 8 percent of its coal, 22 percent of its natural gas, and 60 percent of its oil needs. It should come as no surprise, then, that the security of China's energy imports have become a paramount concern of the Chinese leadership.

And while a sizeable share of China's natural gas and coal imports come via pipeline or originate in East Asia (as seen in the chart below), most of China's oil suppliers lie west of the Strait of Malacca in the Middle East or Africa (Saudi Arabia, Angola, and Iran being the top three, joined by Iraq, Sudan, and Kuwait in the top 10). A full 80 percent of China's oil imports now transit the Strait of Malacca.[8]

It was Chinese President Hu Jintao that initially coined the term "Malacca Dilemma" in a 2003 speech to a Communist Party conference to describe China's dependence on the critical naval chokepoint that connects the Indian Ocean to the Western Pacific. A much-publicized article in the China Youth Daily the following year argued "It is no exaggeration to say that whoever controls the Strait of Malacca will also have a stranglehold on the energy route of China."[9]

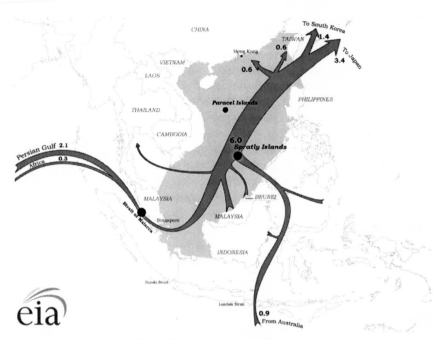

Map 10.2.   Natural Gas Flows Through the Strait of Malacca

Source: "The South China Sea is an important world energy trade route." U.S. Energy Information Administration. Last modified April 4, 2013. http://www.eia.gov/todayinenergy/detail.cfm?id=10671#

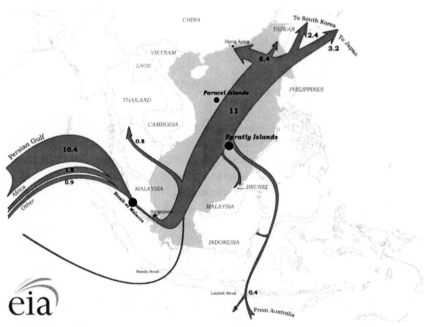

Map 10.3.   Oil Flows Through the Strait of Malacca

Source: "The South China Sea is an important world energy trade route." U.S. Energy Information Administration. Last modified April 4, 2013. http://www.eia.gov/todayinenergy/detail.cfm?id=10671#

Indeed, the Malacca Dilemma has loomed so large in China's strategic thinking that securing and diversifying China's energy imports was one of the premier foreign policy and energy initiatives of the Hu Jintao administration. The past decade saw China rapidly raise its energy efficiency standards by setting hard targets for cuts in carbon and energy intensity; undertake major efforts to begin exploiting its sizable but technically challenging shale gas reserves; and invest in oil and gas projects across the globe. China has constructed strategic petroleum reserves on its eastern seaboard and in Xinjiang, with storage capacity of around 140 million barrels as of 2012, with plans to expand that to 500 million barrels by 2020, along with an additional several hundred million barrels of commercial storage capacity.[10]

Most important, though, China has constructed (and plans to construct) an elaborate network of oil and natural gas pipelines from Central Asia, Pakistan, Russia and Burma, and within China itself. By 2015, China is projected to double the 50,000 kilometers of domestic oil and gas pipelines it had in 2010.

Table 10.1. **Chinese External Oil and Gas Pipelines**

Type	Countries Participating	Capacity	Completion Date
Oil	Kazakhstan	200,000 bbl/d	May 2006
Oil	Russia	300,000 bbl/d	January 2011
Oil	Burma	440,000 bbl/d	September 2013
Gas	Turkmenistan, Kazakhstan, Uzbekistan	1.4 Tcf/year	December 2009
Gas	Burma	12 Bcf/year	October 2013

And while some of the foreign pipeline projects in the table above have a legitimate economic rationale, as importing gas and oil directly to China's remote western provinces can be more cost-effective than transporting it inland from China's coasts, others seem to be driven primarily by the desire to reduce China's dependence on the Strait of Malacca, and lack justification on purely economic grounds.

However, Andrew Erickson and Gabriel Collins argue that as an energy security strategy China's pipeline plans may be "largely a pipe dream."[11] Many of the pipelines under construction or recently constructed are not new supply routes but, in the case of Pakistan and Burma, simply "shortcut" routes in which oil will still have to be carried by tanker from the country of origin. The oil pipeline from Russia, meanwhile, is simply a substitute for oil exports that previously traveled by rail. Erickson and Collins conclude: "The pipelines are not likely to increase Chinese oil import security in quantitative terms, because additional volumes they bring in will be overwhelmed by China's demand growth; *the country's net reliance on seaborne oil imports will grow over time, pipelines notwithstanding.*"[12]

All of which presents Chinese policymakers with three uncomfortable conclusions: (1) China's energy consumption and energy imports will continue to grow; (2) despite Beijing's best efforts those imports will in large part continue to be transported by sea, and; (3) a large share of those sea-borne imports will continue to come from suppliers west of the Strait of Malacca, leaving China with relatively long and relatively vulnerable sea lines of communication.

STRING OF WHAT?

These three conclusions help explain why China's South Asia policy has transformed from a continental policy to a maritime strategy focused on energy security and protecting its sea lines of communication. And it is in the context of this quest for energy security that we must examine the much-publicized debate over China's "String of Pearls."

The term is the product of a clever play on words from a 2004 study by U.S. consulting firm Booz Allen Hamilton for the Department of Defense titled "Energy Futures in Asia." The study effectively encapsulated growing concerns about a series of Chinese investments in Indian Ocean littoral countries—ports, listening posts, radar stations, and container terminals in Pakistan (Gwadar), Sri Lanka (Hambantota), Burma (Sittwe), Bangladesh (Chittagong), and elsewhere—that some feared would carry explicit military arrangements for the PLA Navy (PLAN) and offer China a threatening strategic presence in the Indian Ocean.

Beijing responded to the String of Pearls debate by insisting that its investments in Indian Ocean littoral countries are exclusively commercial in nature; that China *has* never and *will* never seek military bases abroad; and that China's relationship with South Asian countries will never come at India's expense. At least initially, these assurances fell on deaf ears.

However, there has been a maturation of the debate over China's String of Pearls in India in recent years, and an acknowledgement that the worst fears driving the discussion have been inflated. The more closely officials scrutinized China's Indian Ocean Rim investments, the more they appeared to be genuine commercial ventures that carried no explicit military agreements or basing rights. Some of the "pearls," like reported

Chinese listening posts on Burma's Coco Islands, "turned out to be more media tales than actual projects."[13]

"None of the formal agreements related to these [Chinese] ventures included access assurances for the Chinese navy,"[14] concluded Jonathan Holslag in his 2009 study of Sino-Indian relations. "The rationale behind these developments is more economic than strategic," explains the Center for Naval Analysis' Nilanthi Samarnayake. "Beijing is trying to connect its western provinces to the globalized economy by constructing lines of communication south to the Bay of Bengal."[15]

THE PLAN ENTERS THE INDIAN OCEAN

Just as Indian strategists have recognized that China's regional investments are driven primarily by Beijing's quest for energy security, Indian security concerns have been partially rekindled in the form of the PLAN's first quasipermanent deployment to the Indian Ocean.

The PLAN's entry into the region is a relatively new phenomenon, though the young service's first foreign port calls were to South Asia, from November 1985 to January 1986, when a handful of PLAN warships visited Karachi, Colombo, and Chittagong. One year later, the Indian Coast Guard interdicted three Chinese trawlers near the Andaman and Nicobar Islands carrying advanced survey equipment and detailed military charts and maps.

In 2000 a Chinese guided missile destroyer dropped anchor in Malaysia for a four-day stay and then headed west to Dar Es Salaam, Tanzania in the first full transit of the Indian Ocean by a PLAN warship. The following year a PLAN submarine made an unannounced, unpublicized port call to Myanmar,[16] and in 2005 two PLAN ships arrived in Kochi, India, to conduct joint exercises with the Indian Navy.

It was not until 2008, however, that the PLAN would conduct its first-ever long-term foreign naval deployment in the Indian Ocean. The origins of the mission can be traced, unexpectedly, to the Somali capital of Mogadishu in 2006. The seizure of the city that year by Islamist militants during Somalia's civil war precipitated a surge in piracy off the Horn of Africa.

As part of the U.S. war effort in Afghanistan, the U.S. Navy, and the navies of Spain, France, Germany, and the UK had formed Combined Task Force-150[17] to conduct maritime security operations in the Indian Ocean. It was charged with combating drug smuggling and weapons trafficking, but from 2006 to 2008 intervened directly to thwart several pirate attacks in the Gulf of Aden. On August 22, 2008, the CTF-150 established a Maritime Security Patrol Area aimed at deterring piracy through a narrow corridor in the Gulf of Aden.

Then Russia and India joined suit, deploying their own warships to the region in October 2008 to operate separately from combined task force.[18] Finally, following two high-profile piracy attacks on Chinese merchant ships in the Gulf of Aden, on December 26, 2008, China dispatched a PLAN flotilla to participate in its own escort missions off the Horn of Africa, marking "the first out-of-area operations for the Chinese military in more than 600 years."[19]

Five years later the Chinese flotilla has become a regular presence in the Indian Ocean, by China's official statistics escorting over 5,046 Chinese and foreign ships and rescuing or assisting over fifty ships as of February 2013.[20] Comprising two frigates or destroyers and a supply ship, the rotating warships of the flotilla are commanded by a Rear Admiral who reports directly to PLAN headquarters.

The deployment has provided an "ideal chance for the PLAN to practice and evaluate various blue water tactics, techniques, and procedures in an environment far from the Chinese periphery, without generating significant political or military alarm,"[21] explains Brig. Gen. Mandip Singh of India's Institute for Defense Studies and Analysis. Perhaps most important, the task force is dependent on—and has given the PLAN valuable experience operating in—ports in Djibouti, Oman, Yemen, and Pakistan for resupply and refueling.

Agreements with the host nations offer China access to port facilities to obtain essential supplies such as fuel, food, and fresh water for deployed forces. Such agreements can also involve reciprocal guarantees of military support in such areas as training, equipment, and education.

India Reacts

The PLAN's deployment in the Indian Ocean has elicited mixed responses from Delhi. Officially, the government has welcomed the Chinese antipiracy mission: "The sustainable contribution of the PLA Navy to combating the scourge of piracy in the Gulf of Aden is something that we are well aware of and highly appreciate," notes a statement from the Indian Embassy in Beijing.[22]

The Chinese deployment has given the PLAN and the Indian Navy a rare forum to cooperate at an operational level. India has also deployed a warship to the Gulf of Aden to combat piracy and, like China and Japan, has opted not to submit to the command of the international coalition coordinating piracy patrols. In 2011, the three outliers entered into a Shared Awareness and Deconfliction (SHADE) pact to "share data and achieve the most efficient use of Naval Forces" that took effect January 1, 2012.

A convoy coordination group shares information about each country's warship movements and escort schedules to avoid "bunching up" their

patrols and leaving the Gulf of Aden without protection for long periods
of time. On May 6, 2011, a Chinese vessel was attacked by pirates 450
nautical miles off India's western coast, and the Indian Navy answered
the ship's distress call and thwarted the attack.

However, the PLAN's presence in the Indian Ocean Region is also generating its fair share of consternation in Delhi and has already led to at
least one miniconfrontation at sea. In January 2009 there was reportedly
a "tense stand-off" when Chinese warships forced an Indian Kilo-class
submarine that had been trailing the Chinese flotilla to surface. The submarine "tried to evade the Chinese warships by diving deeper," writes
C. Raja Mohan in *Samudra Manthan*, "but the warships continued the
chase [and] sent an antisubmarine helicopter to track the submarine,
which had tried to jam the Chinese warships' sonar system."[23] Eventually the two PLAN destroyers forced the Indian submarine to surface
in an episode that was widely reported in the Chinese press and not
refuted by Delhi.

In 2013 news reports pointed to the increasingly active presence of
Chinese submarines in the Indian Ocean. Subsurface contact data col-
lected by the U.S. military and subsequently shared with India sug-
gested twenty-two contacts with foreign navies (not identified but
suspected to be mostly PLAN submarines from China's Hainan Island–
based South Sea Fleet) had been made in the Indian Ocean in 2012.[24]
One contact in 2012 reportedly took place ninety kilometers from India's
Andaman and Nicobar Islands, six contacts northwest of the Strait of
Malacca, thirteen contacts south of Sri Lanka, and two in the Arabian
Sea. An Indian government report on the matter, *Perceived Threats to
Subsurface Deterrent Capability and Preparedness,* said the implicit focus of
the PLAN appeared to be to "control highly sensitive sea lines of com-
munication within the region."

Commodore C. Uday Bhaskar (ret.), former head of India's National
Maritime Foundation, told this author China was "looking for excuses to
be in the Indian Ocean. It's more to mark their presence than actually to
fight piracy."[25] Similarly, this writer witnessed an illustrative exchange by
senior Indian and Chinese naval strategists at an international conference
on maritime security. "We understand that you came to the Indian Ocean
to combat piracy, and we believe in that mission," the Indian strategist
said to his Chinese counterpart. "But you've done your job. Piracy is under control. *Now go home.*"[26]

The candid exchange underscores Indian concerns that the PLAN is not
simply conducting a temporary, counterpiracy mission but is laying the
groundwork for a more durable and permanent presence in the Indian
Ocean. The Indian media frequently reference a 1993 quote attributed

to Zhao Nanqi, the head of the PLA General Staff Logistics Department, in which he said: "We can no longer accept the Indian Ocean as only an ocean of the Indians."[27] And several reports suggest that in 2009, Chinese officials told the U.S. Pacific Fleet commander that the Indian Ocean should be recognized as a part of China's sphere of influence.[28]

These concerns have been fed by an increasingly public debate within China about the utility and necessity of overseas military commitments to protect Chinese interests abroad. Daniel Kostecka documents statements by active and retired PLA officers that offer a window into this discussion.[29]

In February 2009, Senior Colonel Dai Xu argued that establishing military bases overseas was a logical extension of the PLAN's new mission in the Gulf of Aden. "If we make things difficult for ourselves in this matter by maintaining a rigid understanding of the doctrines of nonalignment and the nonstationing of troops abroad, then it will place a lot of constraints on us across the board."[30] Others have touted the utility of overseas supply facilities in East Africa, and the need for a "stable and permanent supply and repair base" in the Indian Ocean.[31]

Suspicions of China's designs on the Indian Ocean were further stoked by Vice Admiral Su Zhiqian, commander of the PLAN East China Sea Fleet, when he seemed to hint at a more permanent presence for the PLAN in the Indian Ocean during a speech at the Galle Dialogue in Sri Lanka December 13, 2012. "The freedom and safety of the navigation *in the Indian Ocean* play a very important role in the recovery and development of global economy *and the Chinese navy will actively maintain the peace and stability of the Indian Ocean* [emphasis added]."[32]

THE FUTURE OF CHINA IN THE INDIAN OCEAN REGION

One can expect that as China becomes increasingly reliant on SLOCs through the Indian Ocean to feed its growing economy, it will become decreasingly content to depend on foreign navies to provide security for those SLOCs. Conversely, as the PLAN continues to field the capabilities of a true "blue water navy" to match China's global interests, Chinese strategists are likely to find it increasingly difficult to dismiss the utility of overseas military bases.

For many Indian strategists this seems to be a foregone conclusion. For while fears over the "String of Pearls" have abated, they have been replaced by concerns over the PLAN's presence in the Indian Ocean. Chandan Mitra, a member of parliament from the BJP, says "It's only a matter of time—perhaps ten to fifteen years—before the Chinese Navy asserts itself in the Indian Ocean. And we must be prepared."[33]

NOTES

1. "China's Growing Influence in Asia Poses Challenge," *Economic Times*, July 28, 2011: http://articles.economictimes.indiatimes.com/2011-07-28/news/29824658_1_china-and-india-gwadar-pakistan.

2. B. Raman, "Dragon's New Face," *OutlookIndia.com*, 2013: http://www.out lookindia.com/article.aspx?283780.

3. Samudra Manthan, "Sino Indian Rivalry in the Indo-Pacific," Speech, March 4, 2013: http://www.orfonline.org/cms/export/orfonline/documents/Samudra-Manthan.pdf.

4. International Energy Agency, "People's Republic of China," *Oil and Gas Security Emergency Response of IEA Countries 2012*, 2012: http://www.iea.org/publications/freepublications/publication/China_2012.pdf.

5. International Energy Agency, "People's Republic of China," *Oil and Gas Security Emergency Response of IEA Countries 2012*, 2012: http://www.iea.org/publications/freepublications/publication/China_2012.pdf.

6. World Coal Association, "Coal's Vital Role in China," *Ecoal*, Vol. 74. May 2011: http://www.worldcoal.org/resources/ecoal-archive/ecoal-current-issue/coals-vital-role-in-china/.

7. Juan Du, "China Coal Imports to Continue Affecting Global Prices: Platts," May 22, 2013. http://www.chinadaily.com.cn/bizchina/2013-05/22/content_16518558.htm.

8. 2011 Office of the Secretary of Defense DOD Annual Report to Congress Military and Security Developments Involving the People's Republic of China, 2011, 20: http://china.usc.edu/App_Images//2011-defense-report-china.pdf.

9. "China's Energy Strategy: The Impact on Beijing's Maritime Policies," edited by Gabriel B. Collins, 120: http://www.army.forces.gc.ca/caj/documents/vol_11/iss_3/CAJ_Vol11.3_25_e.pdf.

10. International Energy Agency, "People's Republic of China," *Oil and Gas Security Emergency Response of IEA Countries 2012*, 2012: http://www.iea.org/publications/freepublications/publication/China_2012.pdf.

11. Andrew S. Erickson and Gabriel B. Collins, "China's Oil Security Pipe Dream: The Reality and Strategic Consequences of Seaborne Imports," *Naval War College Review*, 2010: 89–104.

12. Andrew S. Erickson and Collins Gabriel B. "China's Oil Security Pipe Dream The Reality, and Strategic Consquences, of Seaborne Imports." *Naval War College Review*, 2010: 89–104.

13. Jonathan Holslag, *China and India: Prospects for Peace* (New York: Columbia University Press, 2010), 135.

14. Jonathan Holslag, *China and India: Prospects for Peace* (New York: Columbia University Press, 2010), 135.

15. Nilanthi Samaranayake, "The Long Littoral Project: Bay of Bengal: A Maritime Perspective on Indo-Pacific Security," Center for Naval Analysis, September 2012: http://www.cna.org/sites/default/files/research/IRP-2012-U-002319-Final percent20Bay percent20of percent20Bengal.pdf.

16. John W. Garver, "The Security Dilemma in Sino-Indian Relations," *India Review*, Vol. 1 no 4: 14.

17. Later reconstituted as Combined Task Force-151.

18. In January 2009, the U.S. established Combined Task Force-151, dedicated solely to combating piracy, allowing CTF-150 to return to its normal duties.

19. Christian Le Miere, "China's Unarmed Arms Race," *Foreign Affairs*, July 29, 2013: http://www.foreignaffairs.com/articles/139609/christian-le-miere/chinas-unarmed-arms-race?

20. Xinhua, "China's Escort Fleet to Join Exercise in Pakistan," *Xinhuanet .com*, February 17, 2013: http://news.xinhuanet.com/english/china/2013-02/17/c_132174099.htm.

21. Mandip Singh, "Chinas Military in 2011: Modernization on Track," May, 2012: http://www.idsa.in/system/files/book_Chinayear2011.pdf.

22. "Warm Reception to Indian Naval Ships in China," *ZeeNew*, June 13, 2012: http://zeenews.india.com/news/world/warm-reception-to-indian-naval-ships -in-china_781647.html.

23. C. Raja Mohan, *Samudra Manthan: Sino-Indian Rivalry in the Indo-Pacific* (Washington, DC: Carnegie Endowment for International Peace, 2012), 202.

24. In 2006 the U.S. registered six "extended patrols" by Chinese submarines outside their territorial waters and an additional 12 in 2008.

25. C. Uday Bhaskar. Author interview. New Delhi, August 2012.

26. Maritime Security Conference, April 2013.

27. Youssef Bodansky, "The PRC Surge for the Strait of Malacca and Spratly Confronts India and the U.S.," International Strategic Studies Association, Defense and Foreign Affairs Strategic Policy, September 30, 1995: 6–13.

28. G. Parsatharathy,"Games Neighbours Play," *Times of India*, June 29, 2009: http://articles.timesofindia.indiatimes.com/2009-06-29/edit-page/28191796_1_southern-tibet-sino-indian-people-s-daily.

29. Daniel J. Kostecka, "Places and Bases: The Chinese Navy's Emerging Support Network in the Indian Ocean," Naval War College Review, Vol. 64, No. 1. Winter 2011: 70.

30. Michael C. Chase and Andrew S. Erickson, "Changes in Beijing's Approach to Overseas Basing?" *China Brief*, September 24, 2009: http://www.jamestown.org/programs/chinabrief/single/?tx_ttnews[tt_news]=35536&cHash=1e7c04ad8f.

31. "PRC Expert: PLA Navy May Contemplate Setting up Supply Bases Abroad," *Beijing China National Radio*, December 26, 2009: www.cnr.cn/.

32. Che Hongliang, "Chinese Navy to Actively Maintain Peace and Stability in Indian Ocean" December 17, 2012: http://english.people.com.cn/90786/8060266 .html.

33. Chandan Mitra. Author interview. New Delhi, November 2011.

Chapter 11

Securing India's Ocean: The Andaman and Nicobar Islands

India has adopted what is essentially a three-pronged strategy in response to Chinese engagement in the Indian Ocean Region. First, it is undertaking an accelerated modernization and expansion of the Indian Navy, investing in platforms with the ability to confront a large conventional naval force in the Indian Ocean and allow it to more effectively project power abroad.

Second, India is working to diplomatically counteract Chinese influence in the region through renewed engagement with Indian Ocean littoral countries, as well as fortify its defenses in the Indian Ocean; a "Necklace of Diamonds" to match China's "String of Pearls."

Third, India is finally adding a strategic and military component to the Look East policy it adopted in 1991. Delhi is prioritizing better relations with Vietnam, Australia, Japan, and Singapore and has become a vocal proponent of the concept of freedom of navigation, and it has invested in controversial offshore energy projects off Vietnam's coast in waters claimed by China.

While India's Look East policy will be addressed in the chapter to follow, we will now turn our attention to the Indian Navy and the key link in India's "Necklace of Diamonds," the Andaman and Nicobar Islands.

INDIA GOES TO SEA

Surrounded on three sides by the Indian Ocean with over 7,500 kilometers of coastline, one might expect the country to have a rich maritime tradition.

Some 90 percent of India's trade by volume now moves by sea, serviced by thirteen major and 185 minor ports and over 1,000 merchant vessels.[1]

Yet, like China, for most of its history India's strategic attention has been fixed on continental Asia and overland threats to the north and west. This was the path taken by multiple Muslim invasions between the eighth and sixteenth centuries, and at the birth of modern India this familiar threat was reconstituted in the form of a hostile Pakistani state. The bias toward continental defense was further reinforced by the 1962 war with China, when India's traditionally secure Himalayan border to the northeast became a second source of vulnerability.

As a consequence, India's navy was long treated as the "Cinderella service." Relegated to only marginal roles in India's half-dozen twentieth-century conflicts, the Indian Navy has long played third fiddle to the Indian Army (which still commands roughly half of Indian military spending) and the Indian Air Force. The Indian Navy received a windfall from the 1971 Indo-Soviet defense pact, benefitting mightily from Soviet "friendship prices," through which it acquired missile boats, frigates and destroyers, and even a nuclear submarine (on lease). But the 1991 Indian financial crisis preceded a "lost decade" of general neglect in which the service ordered no new warships.

At the beginning of this century several developments turned India's attention seaward. Among these were the rapid growth of sea-based commerce (India had two container ships in 1988 and 328 in 2012)[2]; the evolution of the concept of a 200-nautical-mile Exclusive Economic Zone (giving India economic domain over two million square kilometers of Indian Ocean); the 1999 Kargil War with Pakistan (which forced a fundamental reassessment of India's military spending and priorities); and a belated recognition of the blossoming strategic value of the Indian Ocean.

Perhaps most important, by the turn of the century the economic reforms prompted by the 1991 Indian financial crisis unshackled India from the 3 to 5 percent "Hindu rate of growth" that had limited its strategic potential for the better half of the twentieth century. The 7 to 10 percent annual GDP growth more befitting a large developing country provided the government with sufficient revenues to begin its most ambitious military modernization in decades, and in recent years the Indian Navy has become the prime benefactor.

As of 2013 the Indian Navy's budget is not only ballooning in absolute terms, it is demanding a larger share of the Indian defense budget. An analysis by the Delhi-based Institute for Defense Studies and Analysis shows that in the 2012 and 2013 defense budget, the Indian Navy's allocation increased by an astonishing 74 percent year-over-year from $2.74 billion to $4.77 billion, while the Indian Air Force's budget increased by only 0.5 percent and the Indian Army's *decreased* by 3 percent[3] (the Navy took a modest reduction in the 2014 defense budget). And whereas the budget of the Indian army is saddled with massive manpower and operating expenses, the capital-intensive navy spends twice as much on force modernization.

Moreover, the new capital is flowing into a service that has received high marks from impartial observers. U.S. military officials interviewed at the headquarters of Pacific Command in Honolulu offered praise for the Indian Navy, calling it "very forward-leaning and aggressive."[4] "The [Indian] navy's seamanship," writes the Brookings Institute's Stephen Cohen, "is rated as NATO-quality by U.S. Navy officers who participated in joint exercises or who sailed alongside Indian Navy vessels."[5]

China on the Mind

India's naval modernization is a powerful symbol of its national security priorities. As Walter Ladwig explains, "If the Indian Navy were primarily concerned with Pakistan or littoral defense, then a localized fleet of short-range surface combatants supplemented by land-based naval aviation assets would be most appropriate."[6] Instead, the Indian Navy is devoting its resources to aircraft carriers, nuclear submarines, long-range sea-launched ballistic missiles, and expeditionary capabilities—all of which suggest India is preparing to meet a challenge from a large conventional force in the Indian Ocean, and that it is developing the capabilities to sustain operations further abroad, in the Western Pacific.

The Indian Navy plans to have 150 ships under its command by the late 2020s, including fifteen stealth frigates, twelve guided missile destroyers, eighteen to twenty submarines (three of them nuclear-powered), 500 aircraft and, most important, three aircraft carriers, allowing it to operate two carrier groups at any given time.[7]

Given the troubled history of Indian defense procurement, it is an ambitious goal. A report from the Indian comptroller and auditor general (CAG) reveals that the Indian Navy today "has just sixty-one, forty-four, and twenty percent respectively of these frigates, destroyers, and corvettes that it has projected as its minimum requirement."[8] Ravi Vohra, former director of India's National Maritime Foundation, has identified critical capability shortages in antisubmarine warfare, long-range missile technology, and net-centric warfare.[9]

To bridge these gaps, India currently has some forty-three naval vessels under construction domestically, and an additional three being built in Russia. Recently retired Naval Chief Admiral Nirmal Verma says the Indian Navy plans to induct five platforms a year between 2012 and 2017.

Table 11.1. Indian Naval Forces

Ship Type	In Service	Under Construction/On Order
Frigates *Nine operational* *(Seven under* *construction)*	Six Russian-origin Talwar- class frigates, the last of which was commissioned in June 2013. Three Indian-origin Shivalik- class stealth frigates.	Seven domestically-produced Project 17A frigates to be inducted from 2017 onward.
Destroyers *Eight (Seven)*	Five Russian-origin Rajput- class destroyers. Three Delhi-class Project 15 destroyers.	Three Kolkata-class Project 15A destroyers to be inducted by 2014. Four additional Project 15B destroyers are expected after the 15A destroyers are complete.
Aircraft Carriers *One* *(Three–Four)*	INS *Viraat*, aging 1950s-era, Centaur-class, 24,000-ton, British-origin carrier. It will be decommissioned in 2018–2019.	India will take delivery of the 44,000-ton, Russian-origin *Admiral Gorshkov* in December 2013, purchased in 2004 and several years behind schedule and over cost. At least two Indigenous non- nuclear Aircraft Carriers (IACs) under construction: the 44,000- ton *Vikrant* and the 60,000-ton *Vishaal*. The first is expected before 2020. A third IAC is rumored.
Surveillance *Aircraft* *Thirteen (Eight–* *Twelve)*	Five Soviet-era IL-38 and eight Tu-142 surveillance aircraft.	In 2006 India purchased eight advanced P8-I Neptune surveillance aircraft from the U.S. The first Neptune was delivered to Delhi in May 2013. India may order an additional four.
Naval Combat *Aircraft* *Twenty-eight* *(Twenty-nine)*	A dozen aging Mk.51 Sea Harriers (for use on the *Viraat*) and sixteen MiG- 29K Fulcrums (for use on the *Admiral Gorshkov*).	India has already purchased an additional twenty-nine MiG- 29Ks, with delivery underway. A naval version of the indigenous Tejas fighter is being developed for carrier use.
Conventional *Submarines* *Fifteen* *(Twenty-four)*	Fourteen diesel-electric submarines including four aging Shishumar-class German-origin submarines and ten Russian-origin Kilo-class subs.	Six French-origin Scorpene submarines under construction in India. Expected delivery date 2015-2018. Six Air-Independent Propulsion (AIP) subs to be built under Project-75I. Twelve more indigenous submarines planned thereafter.

Ship Type	In Service	Under Construction/On Order
Nuclear Submarines One (Three)	One Russian-origin Akula-II SSN nuclear submarine on ten-year lease beginning April 2012. India may lease a second Russian submarine for $1.5 billion.	Three SSBNs dubbed Advanced Technology Vehicles (ATV) under construction in India. The first, INS *Arihant*, launched sea trials in 2009, and its reactor in 2013. The ATVs will carry a dozen K-15 Sagarika Sea-Launched Ballistic Missiles (SLBMs) with a range of 700–750 kilometers with K-4 SLBMs under development with a range of 4000 kilometers.
Amphibious Warfare and Transport Sixteen (Twelve)	Fifteen landing ship tanks and landing craft utility ships. One U.S.-origin, 17,000-ton Landing Platform Dock acquired in 2007.	Eight more landing craft utility ships and four large Landing Platform Docks to be purchased or built indigenously.

India's Eastern Naval Command (ENC), with responsibility for the eastern Indian Ocean, has traditionally been the junior partner to the Pakistan-focused Western Naval Command (WNC). That is changing, with a major transfer of naval assets underway from the WNC to the Vishakhapatnam-based ENC. A full fifty warships—over a third of India's naval fleet—are now under the ENC's command. [10]

All five of India's Rajput-class guided missile destroyers have been transferred to ENC from the Western fleet, as has the Russian-leased nuclear submarine (SSN) *Chakra*. India's three Shivalik-class stealth frigates are headed to the ENC along with P8-I Neptune maritime patrol craft on order from the U.S. and a new Italian-origin fleet tanker, INS *Shakti*. When India takes delivery of the Russian-origin aircraft carrier *Admiral Gorshkov* in 2013, the carrier *Viraat* will be transferred to the ENC until India's two Indigenous Aircraft Carriers (IACs) are pressed into service sometime after 2015. When the full contingent of three carriers is operational, the ENC will command two of them. ENC will also take command of India's first indigenous nuclear submarine (SSBN), the INS *Arihant*, when it enters service sometime around 2015.

A new military base is now under construction in Andhra Pradesh on India's eastern coast near Rambilli, forty kilometers south of ENC headquarters in Vishakhapatnam. Codenamed Project Varsha, the new base will reportedly host underground pens to protect nuclear submarines from spy satellites and air attack.

To be sure, it is not just the Indian Navy's capabilities and force structure that are changing, but its doctrine as well. In 2004 and 2009 India for the first time released two important Maritime Doctrine documents, as well as a Maritime Strategy document in 2007. The documents, Iskander Rehman notes, "only mention China in passing, with fleeting—albeit foreboding—references to 'some nations' attempting to 'gain a strategic toehold in the Indian Ocean Rim.'"[11]

They do, however, prioritize a stronger deterrent capability against foreign intervention by nonlittoral navies, and the 2009 Maritime Doctrine defines primary and secondary zones of interest, the latter of which includes the South China Sea. The documents also outline a more expansive view of India's maritime security interests than previously articulated; interests which now explicitly include economic and energy security. "The protection of our coast, our 'sea lines of communication' and the offshore development areas is a major prerequisite of our nation's development," said Indian President Pratibha Patil during the President's Fleet Review in 2011.[12]

C. Raja Mohan notes that "like many other developing countries, India [initially] sought to limit the activities of major powers near its waters." However, with the expanding concept of its maritime interests, "India needs open seas to protect its national sovereignty." Delhi's new conception of the seas, says Mohan, "is in violation of China's maritime philosophy." [13]

THE ANDAMAN AND NICOBAR ISLANDS

It has become almost cliché to suggest that while China holds the military advantage over India at their disputed border, this advantage is negated by India's qualitative edge in the maritime domain. On the surface this may seem peculiar: the Indian Navy is no better equipped than the Chinese Navy, holding distinct advantages in some areas (aircraft carrier operations) and obvious disadvantages in others (submarine warfare). Rather, India's advantage in the maritime arena derives from one exceptional factor: geography.

Like an "unsinkable aircraft carrier," watching guard over the Indian Ocean, the Indian subcontinent is positioned between China and most of its energy suppliers in the Persian Gulf and Africa. As the previous chapter showed, many of the critical sea lines of communication (SLOCs) that feed China's voracious appetite for natural resources must pass through the Indian Ocean en route to the Western Pacific.

This alone puts India in a favorable geographic position, but the advantage is magnified by an obscure chain of Indian islands straddling arguably the most important naval chokepoint in the world, the Strait of Malacca. Constituting the shortest navigable route from the Indian

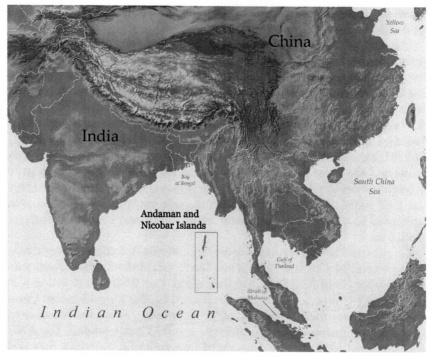

Map 11.1.   The Andaman and Nicobar Islands
Source: American Foreign Policy Council

Ocean to the Pacific Ocean for commercial traffic, sixty thousand vessels transit the Strait every year, carrying as much as one-third of the world's seaborne trade. As much as fifteen million barrels of oil pass through the Strait each day.

A Latent Asset

If India is forming a "Necklace of Diamonds" to counter China's String of Pearls, the Andaman and Nicobar Islands (ANI) are the key link in that necklace. A distant and long-neglected "sentinel outpost" in the eastern Indian Ocean, the ANI represent India's land bridge to Southeast Asia and a latent strategic asset that could play a pivotal role in any maritime competition between India and China in the Indo-Pacific.

A chain of 572 islands (just over thirty inhabited) stretching over 500 miles north to south at the western mouth of the Strait of Malacca, the ANI's population numbers just under 400,000, a majority of whom are Hindu. The islands—lush with thick tropical vegetation and India's only active volcano—constitute just 0.2 percent of India's landmass but account for 30 percent (600,000 square kilometers) of the country's 200-nautical-mile Exclusive Economic Zone.[14]

The ANI were periodically occupied by Indian empires in the first millennia before European colonial powers began jockeying for control of the islands in the eighteenth century. The Dutch colonized the islands in the 1750s, eventually ceding them to the British in the nineteenth century, who incorporated them into British India.

Three years after Indian independence the ANI became a part of the Indian Union and were upgraded to the status of "Union Territory" in 1957. In 1963–1964 a small naval garrison was established on the islands and the coast guard followed in the 1970s, when the islands were brought under the domain of the Eastern Naval Command. In the 1980s the first naval air station, *INS Utkrosh*, was commissioned[15] and was upgraded to a three-star command in the 1990s and known as Fortress Andaman or FORTRAN.

Yet the islands were reduced to a marginal role in India's strategic consciousness until October 2001, when Delhi established a new Andaman and Nicobar Command (ANC) in the capital, Port Blair. The decision was the product of a series of recommendations by the Kargil Review Committee[16] and was made amid widespread reporting about the presence of Chinese monitoring centers in Burma's nearby Coco Islands.[17] The ANC was designed to act as the flagship of integration: it is India's first and only joint tri-service command, with rotating three-star commanders-in-chief from the Army, Navy, and Air Force reporting directly to the chairman of the Chiefs of Staff Committee.

Today the command serves as the focal point for Indian engagement with regional navies in Southeast Asia. This includes biannual coordinated patrols with the navies of Thailand (Indo-Thai Corpat) and Indonesia (Ind-Indo Corpat), the annual SIMBEX bilateral maritime exercises with Singapore (beginning in 2007), and the biennial multilateral naval conglomeration *Milan* (beginning in 1995).[18]

The ANC's jurisdiction is limited to the islands' 200-nautical-mile Exclusive Economic Zone (EEZ) and it has no formal responsibility for the South China Sea. Its official responsibilities include maritime surveillance, humanitarian assistance and disaster relief, as well as suppressing gun running, narcotics smuggling, piracy, and poaching in India's EEZ.

Sainik Samachar, a magazine published by the Indian Ministry of Defense, notes the ANC's mandate also includes "ensuring that the *eastern* approaches to the Indian Ocean comprising the three straits—Malacca, Lombok and Sunda—remain free from threats for shipping" as well as "monitor[ing] ships passing through the Six Degree and Ten Degree Channels."[19]

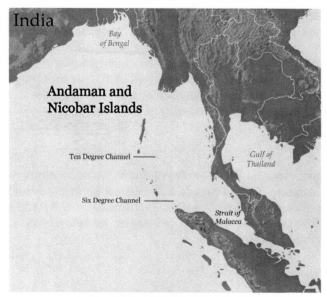

Map 11.2. The Six and Ten Degree Channels
Source: American Foreign Policy Council

This last responsibility is critical, as the ANI enjoy domain over two important channels west of the Strait of Malacca. The vast majority of international trade transiting the Strait of Malacca also passes through the 200-kilometer-wide Six Degree Channel between the Indonesian island of Aceh and Great Nicobar, home to the Indian Navy's newest air base. This means the vast majority of container traffic through the Strait of Malacca also passes through India's Exclusive Economic Zone.

To the north the 150-kilometer-wide Ten Degree Channel (named after the tenth parallel) separates the Nicobar Islands from the Andaman Islands and is used by a much smaller volume of ships bound for the Bay of Bengal. The Indian Coast Guard established a new station on the Hut Bay Islands straddling the Ten Degree Channel in 2010.[20]

Capabilities

Details on the capabilities under the ANC must be pieced together through scattered open-source material. By all accounts the command is only modestly equipped. The *Times of India* reports "force-levels have unfortunately remained largely static in the tri-Service command since it came into existence in October 2001."[21]

The ANC hosts just one infantry brigade, around fifteen small warships, and a handful of Dornier-228 maritime patrol aircraft, as well as

Mi-8 and Chetak helicopters,[22] though reports suggest two Indian Navy warships are regularly deployed to patrol the northern and southern islands.[23] The command hosts no unmanned aerial vehicles (UAVs), despite requests from ANC commanders for Israeli-origin Heron UAVs. A former ANC commander told this writer that the UAVs are "long past due" and that UAVs based in Car Nicobar would give India the capability to "monitor all traffic through the Strait of Malacca."

Army

The *Amphibians*, the 108 Mountain Brigade (3,000 soldiers), is based at Birchgunj military station outside Port Blair. It consists of three infantry battalions, including a locally raised Territorial Army battalion. The Indian Army is said to be planning to increase force levels to at least two brigades totaling 8,000 soldiers.

Naval Forces

The ANC at present does not have major surface combatants among the fifteen ships permanently based there.[24] The flotilla (ANFLOT) mostly consists of amphibious landing ship tanks and small landing craft. In January 2013 the Indian Navy commissioned its largest offshore patrol vessel at the ANC for maritime surveillance and patrolling India's EEZ.[25]

Commodore B. C. Sethi says the fleet is projected to go up to thirty-two ships by 2022.[26] And a force established in 2009 to protect Indian naval ports, the Sagar Prahari Bal, is reportedly being provided with twelve fast interception boats and 100 personnel for use at the ANC.[27]

Air Stations

Indian Naval Air Station INS Utkrosh Port Blair, South Andaman Island. (NAVY)—Located in the capital, Port Blair, this naval air base shares facilities with Vir Savarkar International Airport (IXZ). It is one of the two airstrips on the island over 10,000 feet. The air station reportedly houses three Dornier aircraft (INAS 318) and three Chetak helicopters (INAS 321) from the navy and a similar number from the coast guard. It also handles air traffic control over Port Blair, including six to twelve civilian flights daily.[28] Sukhoi30-MKIs have operated from Port Blair, but there are no squadrons permanently stationed there.

Car Nicobar or Carnic Air Force Station (AIR FORCE)—The only Air Force base on the islands is on the northernmost of the Nicobar islands. It is host to the 37 Wing Air Force station, the ANI's second 10,000-foot runway, and a squadron of Mi-8 helicopters and Dornier aircraft.[29] In May 2012,

India landed its first C-130J Hercules at the Car Nicobar airbase,[30] and exercises involving Sukhoi-30MKI squadrons have been held at the air force station.

INS Baaz, Campbell Bay, Great Nicobar (NAVY)—INS *Baaz* is the newest air base on the islands, inaugurated on July 31, 2012. It is located on Great Nicobar, the southernmost island in the chain, and 300 kilometers closer to the Strait of Malacca than the next closest base on Car Nicobar. The airstrip is only 3,000 feet in length but is being extended to 12,000 feet and being equipped for night operations.

Naval Airstrip at Shibpur, North Andaman (NAVY)—This small air strip is 3,000 feet long but is reportedly being expanded to 12,000 feet and being equipped with facilities for night operations. [31]

Additionally there are naval forward operating bases on Kamorta Island, INS Kardip, and at Diglipur in the north Andamans. The Coast Guard operates a network of surface radar facilities[32] and maintains bases in Port Blair, Diglipur, Campbell Bay,[33] and Hut Bay. A new coast guard station was commissioned in Mayabunder in December 2012 with air assets and eight ships.[34]

Future plans to upgrade the military capabilities of the ANC reportedly include stationing an additional Army brigade, a combat aircraft squadron, and a new squadron of amphibious surveillance aircraft on the islands, as well as upgrading of the ANC's submarine warfare capabilities,[35] and establishing an amphibious warfare training facility[36] and a missile testing site at Rutland Island.[37]

A policy paper for the Institute for Defense Studies and Analysis by Iskander Rehman suggests the ANC's capabilities could be bolstered by "stationing one or two large warships there on a permanent basis, by setting up Brahmos cruise missile silos on some of the larger islands, and by providing the ANC with its own separate budget so that its platform acquisition efforts no longer fall victim to inter-service turf wars."[38]

Gen. Aditya Singh, a former commander in chief of the Andaman and Nicobar Command, agrees with some of these recommendations, but cautions that stationing a large permanent force structure on the islands is not in the cards anytime soon. He considers the requirements of housing a larger force—accommodations, schools, food and water supply—to be cost prohibitive. Instead, Gen. Singh argues that India should build capacity to host temporary three to four month deployments.

THE FUTURE OF THE ANI

Western observers might expect the ANI to be a cornerstone in India's maritime strategy; a firewall against threats to the east and a power-projection platform serving India's interests in the Pacific. The ANI have been likened to America's Indian Ocean military outpost at Diego Garcia; however, the comparison is inadequate. The ANI are in a far more valuable location, are 200 times the size of Diego Garcia (8,000 square kilometers compared to forty-four square kilometers), and enjoy a more solid foundation of volcanic soil than the British-owned coral atoll.

And yet, as we have seen, the command has only modest capabilities at its disposal and was long shunned by the Indian military hierarchy as a desolate sentinel post. An Indian parliamentary report pointed out that among civilian support staff, "no one wants to go there."[39] Delhi has not "outlined a bold geo-economic vision for the island chain," says C. Raja Mohan[40] which "can no longer be neglected as a group of islands suitable at best for the transportation of criminals and political offenders."[41] Several factors have traditionally contributed to neglect of the ANI:

Distance

Though the islands are just a two-hour flight from either Kolkata or Chennai, they are 1,200 kilometers from India's eastern coast (but only fifty-seven kilometers from Burma's Coco Island and 163 kilometers from Indonesia) and have long been viewed by the Indian establishment as too distant and too vulnerable to be of much strategic value. Indian analyst Srikanth Kondipalli is not surprised Delhi has moved so slowly to equip the islands. "It's simply too far away. It's closer to the [Chinese province of] Yunnan than Mumbai."[42]

Natural Disasters

The islands are vulnerable to natural disasters, a reality vividly illustrated by the 2004 tsunami that terrorized the Indian Ocean region, whose epicenter was just 160 kilometers from the ANI. The Nicobar group in particular was devastated with over 3,000 dead and 60,000 homeless, while the Andaman group suffered only minor damage, in part because Greater Andaman is ringed and protected by a series of smaller islands. The ANC was praised by outside observers for organizing the entire rescue, relief, and rehabilitation effort, including the construction of 10,000 shelters, and the command returned to full operational status within three months of the tsunami.

ASEAN

India's contentious relationship with ASEAN in the twentieth century may have played a role in India's reluctance to arm and equip the ANI.

The western-aligned countries of ASEAN long viewed India as a Soviet client whose influence in the region was unwelcome. They particularly deplored India's support of the Soviet-backed Vietnamese regime's invasion of Cambodia in 1978. In the past, an arms buildup at ASEAN's doorstep likely would have unnecessarily provoked Indonesia and Malaysia.

Doctrine

The eastern Indian Ocean and the Pacific waters beyond simply had not captured the imagination of Indian strategists until very recently. India fought a half-dozen wars in the twentieth century, none of which involved any substantial naval engagements, and none took the Indian military farther east than neighboring Bangladesh.

Many of these obstacles are fading in prominence in the twenty-first century. In particular, India's relationship with ASEAN has dramatically improved since the end of the Cold War, and Indian strategists are beginning to call for a greater utilization of the ANC. Indian Air Marshal Dhiraj Kukreja says India needs to "grow out of its earlier thinking" and "develop the islands as a hub or 'spring board' for power projection in the region," warning that the islands "can serve as a bridgehead for any country wishing to either attack mainland India or carry out subversive activities."[43]

More recently, at the commissioning ceremony of the new air station, *INS Baaz*, Navy Chief Admiral Nirmal Verma said the islands "offer a vital geo-strategic advantage to India. Not only do they provide the nation with a commanding presence in the Bay of Bengal, the Islands also serve as our window into East and South East Asia."[44]

HOW MUCH OF AN ASSET?

At least in private, some Indian strategists have begun touting the value of the ANC as a "trump card" in any potential confrontation with China. "If China tries something in the South China Sea or at the border, we will grab them by the balls in the Strait of Malacca," one Indian naval commander relayed to this author, voicing a sentiment heard in multiple interviews with this book. Shashank Joshi of the Royal United Services Institute has documented several recent assessments by Indian and Western scholars which concluded that the Indian Navy "can shut down the Indian Ocean shipping lanes whenever it chooses."[45] A retired rear admiral in the Indian Navy, Raja Menon, argues that China's "weakness lies in the Indian Ocean." He continues, "Today they are merely SLOCs; tomorrow they will be the Chinese jugular. . . . [$10 billion] spent on strengthening the Indian Navy's SLOC interdiction capability would have given us a stranglehold on the Chinese routes into the Indian Ocean."[46]

However, these assessments appear to have overlooked the practical challenges associated with any single country attempting to "cut off" China's oil supplies, even one as favorably positioned as India. A 2008 article for the *Naval War College Review*[47] by Gabriel Collins and William Murray took a detailed look at this very question and ultimately concluded that while attractive in theory, in practice a campaign to sever China's energy SLOCs would offer nearly insurmountable challenges to a country like India, and may even be untenable for a group of countries working in concert. "China," they concluded, "is not fundamentally vulnerable to a maritime energy blockade in circumstances other than global war." Let's examine why.

There are several strategies a state like India could pursue to affect the supply of oil to China in wartime: (1) to close the Strait of Malacca to all container traffic; (2) to enforce a near-in blockade of China close to its shores and ports, and; (3) to selectively target ships carrying oil to China and confiscate the ships and crew, or deter them from continuing their voyage.

Option one, closing the Strait of Malacca to all container traffic, may be the least-attractive option. Even a temporary closure of the Strait could have a devastating effect on the global economy and would almost certainly provoke a backlash—and likely intervention—by any number of third parties. The littoral states of the Malacca Strait—Singapore, Malaysia, Indonesia—have been fiercely protective of their sovereignty over the strait's waters. One would have to assume that any unilateral military intervention in the strait could provoke an armed confrontation with one or more of the littoral powers, as well as any number of third parties powers dependent on the strait for trade and commerce.

If this weren't enough of a deterrent, any force attempting to cut China's energy lifeline from the Indian Ocean would have to deal with three naval chokepoints, not one. There are two alternative passages from the Bay of Bengal to the South China Sea that could handle considerably more traffic—albeit at a greater financial cost—in the event of a closure of the Malacca Strait: the Sunda and Lombok Straits.

The fifty-mile-long Sunda Strait has "highly irregular bottom topography" as well as "a tricky channel, depth limitations, and a live volcano, and is not favored by oil tankers."[48] However, it is much shorter and a full fifteen miles wide at its narrowest point, though dangerous currents and shallow stretches have dissuaded heavy use.

The Lombok Strait would add 1,600 nautical miles (or three and a half days) to a ship's journey, but at eleven miles wide and 150 meters deep at its shortest and narrowest points, the Lombok Strait is "wider,

Map 11.3. Lombok and Sunda Straits
Source: American Foreign Policy Council

deeper, and less congested" than the Strait of Malacca and, unlike Malacca and Sunda, ships of over 100,000 dead weight tons can transit the Lombok Strait.

Option two, a close-in blockade or a ban on all maritime shipping in and out of China, would avoid many of the practical challenges associated with selective interdiction and the closure of the Malacca Strait. But such an operation would play precisely to China's strengths in anti-access area denial (A2/AD). Arguably the principal aim of China's military modernization over the past two decades has been to field platforms and capabilities—antiship ballistic and cruise missiles, cyber warfare capabilities, integrated air defense systems, a large submarine force—that would allow it to deny the U.S. Navy access to the Western Pacific in the event of a confrontation over Taiwan. As Indian naval strategists would readily admit, the Indian Navy is in no position to engage China in a "naval and aerial war of attrition" on its own turf.

Option three, selectively interdicting container ships bound for China, would allow India to leverage its advantageous geographic position. It would be less hazardous than confronting the PLA Navy in the Western Pacific, and less likely to provoke a conflict with a third power than closing the strait entirely.

However, the practical challenges of selective interdiction are manifold. Only 10 percent of China's energy imports are carried on domestic ships. The other 90 percent are transported on foreign-flagged commercial vessels, meaning a large number of tankers would have to be boarded and their shipping documents examined. Simply identifying the destination of these tankers would present its own set of challenges. As Collins and Murray note, "some oil cargoes are resold on the spot market as many as thirty times while the tankers carrying them are still at sea."[49]

Finally, the effects of any SLOC interdiction strategy would likely be slow to develop. China could lengthen the timeframe further by the rationing of energy, the use of strategic petroleum reserves, and an increase in imports via rail, road, and pipeline. Most important, China would have a window to launch retaliatory measures at the Sino-Indian border, where it still holds major advantages in terms of military power and infrastructure, as well as a robust ballistic missile and air force. There would be a high likelihood China could achieve limited military objectives at the border—like seizing Tawang—long before a maritime interdiction strategy would have a decisive effect.

The only conditions under which a sustained operation to "cut" China's SLOCs would be effective is in the event of a large-scale, multicountry conflict with the Indian Navy operating in conjunction with the U.S. Navy, the littoral states in the Strait of Malacca, and others. In a confined Sino-Indian war, for the time being India could at best impose costs on China in the maritime arena, but the impact would be limited and likely pale in comparison to the type of pressure China could apply at their land border.

NOTES

1. Ajai Shukla, "The Great Game in the Indian Ocean," *Business Standard*, September 1, 2012 (Accessed July 2, 2013): http://www.business-standard.com/article/beyond-business/the-great-game-in-the-indian-ocean-112090100019_1.html.

2. United Nations, "Review of Maritime Transport," 2011 (Accessed July 2, 2013): http://unctad.org/en/Docs/rmt2011_en.pdf.

3. Laxman K. Bahara, "India's Defence Budget 2012–13," Institute for Defense Studies and Analysis, March 20, 2012 (Accessed July 2, 2013): http://www.idsa.in/idsacomments/IndiasDefenceBudget2012-13_LaxmanBehera_200312.

4. U.S. military officials (Pacific Command). Author interview. Honolulu, April 2012.

5. Stephen Cohen, *Arming without Aiming* (Washington: Brookings Institute Press, 2010), 95: http://www.brookings.edu/research/books/2010/armingwithoutaiming.

6. Walter Ladwig, "Delhi's Pacific Ambition: Naval Power, "'Look East,' and India's Emerging Influence in the Asia-Pacific Asian Security," Vol. 5, No. 2, June 2009.

7. Rajeev Anantaram, "Rearmament of India," *Business Standard*, July 9, 2011: http://www.business-standard.com/article/beyond-business/rearmament-of -india-111070900006_1.html.

8. Ajai Shukla, "A Helicopter from INS Shivalik Lands on PLA Navy War-ship, Ma'anshaan during Exercises in June 2011," *Broadsword*, December 17, 2012: http://ajaishukla.blogspot.com/2012/12/indias-ocean.html.

9. Vivek Raghuvanshi, "China Threat Inspires Indian Navy's Plans," *Defense News*, October 20, 2008: http://www.iss.europa.eu/uploads/media/op77.pdf.

10. Sudha Ramachandran, "Indian Navy Pumps Up Eastern Muscle," *Asian Times*, August 21, 2011: http://www.atimes.com/atimes/South_Asia/MH20Df02 .html.

11. Iskander Rehman, *Shaping the Emerging World Order: India and Multilateralism* (Washington, DC: Brookings Institute, 2013), 138–39.

12. "India's President Wants Improved Maritime Security," *Defense News*, December 20, 2011 (Accessed April 15, 2013): http://www.defensenews.com/article/20111220/DEFSECT03/112200307/India-s-President-Wants-Improved -Maritime-Security.

13. C. Raja Mohan, "India's New Role in the Indian Ocean," *India Seminar*, January 2011 (Accessed April 15, 2013): http://www.india-seminar .com/2011/617/617_c_raja_mohan.htm.

14. C. Raja Mohan, "India's New Role in the Indian Ocean," *India Seminar*, January 2011 (Accessed April 15, 2013): http://www.india-seminar .com/2011/617/617_c_raja_mohan.htm.

15. "Andaman and Nicobar Command," *Global Security*, 2011: http://www .globalsecurity.org/military/world/india/anc.htm.

16. The Kargil Review Committee was established in the aftermath of the Kargil War with Pakistan to determine what went wrong and how to best reorganize the Indian military.

17. Nilanthi Samaranayake, "The Long Littoral Project: Bay of Bengal: A Maritime Perspective on Indo-Pacific Security," Center for Naval Analysis, September 2012: http://www.cna.org/sites/default/files/research/IRP-2012-U-002319-Final%20 Bay%20of%20Bengal.pdf.

18. Sainik Samachar, "Andaman and Nicobar Command Saga of Energy," October 12, 2011: http://www.sainiksamachar.nic.in/englisharchives/2011/oct16 -11/h5.htm.

19. Sainik Samachar, "Andaman and Nicobar Command Saga of Energy," October 12, 2011: http://www.sainiksamachar.nic.in/englisharchives/2011/oct16 -11/h5.htm.

20. "Coast Guard Drops Anchor at 10 Degree Channel," *webindia123*, January 20, 2010. http://news.webindia123.com/news/articles/India/20100125/14320 99.html.

21. Rajai Pandit, "IAF Conducts First Ever Landing of 'Super Hercules' Military Aircraft at Car Nicobar Airbase." *Times of India*, May 28, 2012: http://articles

.timesofindia.indiatimes.com/2012-05-28/india/31876848_1_car-nicobar-hindon
-airbase.

22. Rajai Pandit, "Strategically-Important A&N Command to Get a Boost." *Times of India,* February 6, 2010: http://articles.timesofindia.indiatimes.com/2010-02-06/india/28115911_1_anc-airfield-andamans.

23. Sainik Samachar, "Andaman and Nicobar Command Saga of Energy" October 16, 2011: http://www.sainiksamachar.nic.in/englisharchives/2011/oct16-11/h5.htm

24. "India to Plug Gaps in Security of Andaman & Nicobar Islands," *DNA India.*

25. "INS Saryu Commissioned for Maritime Surveillance." *Times of India.* January 21, 2013 (Accessed May 13, 2013): http://articles.timesofindia.indiatimes.com/2013-01-21/india/36462455_1_andaman-and-nicobar-islands-ins-saryu-ships-and-fleet-support.

26. Sainik Samachar, "Andaman and Nicobar Command Saga of Energy," October 12, 2011: http://www.sainiksamachar.nic.in/englisharchives/2011/oct16-11/h5.htm.

27. Sainik Samachar, "Andaman and Nicobar Command Saga of Synergy," October 16, 2011: http://www.sainiksamachar.nic.in/englisharchives/2011/oct16-11/h5.htm.

28. Sainik Samachar, "Andaman and Nicobar Command Saga of Synergy," October 16, 2011: http://www.sainiksamachar.nic.in/englisharchives/2011/oct16-11/h5.htm.

29. Sainik Samachar, "Andaman and Nicobar Command Saga of Synergy," October 16, 2011: http://www.sainiksamachar.nic.in/englisharchives/2011/oct16-11/h5.htm.

30. Rajat Pandit, "IAF conducts first ever landing of 'Super Hercules' military aircraft at Car Nicobar airbase," May 28, 2013: http://articles.timesofindia.india times.com/2010-02-06/india/28115911_1_anc-airfield-andamans.

31. "India to Reinforce Security in Andaman & Nicobar," *Brahmand.com,* February 9, 2010. http://www.brahmand.com/news/India-to-reinforce-security-in-Andaman--Nicobar/3132/1/12.html.

32. "India to Reinforce Security in Andaman & Nicobar," *Brahmand.com,* February 9, 2010. http://www.brahmand.com/news/India-to-reinforce-security-in-Andaman--Nicobar/3132/1/12.html.

33. Indian Coast Guard, "Coast Guard Region (Andaman & Nicobar)," http://www.indiancoastguard.nic.in/Indiancoastguard/org/rhqan.html.

34. Sainik Samachar, "Andaman and Nicobar Command Saga of Energy," October 16, 2011. http://www.sainiksamachar.nic.in/englisharchives/2011/oct16-11/h5.htm.

35. "Navy Unveils Plans, Puts Andamans in Forefront of its Strategy." *Rediff.com,* October 17, 2011: http://www.rediff.com/news/special/navy-unveils-plans-puts-andamans-in-forefront-of-its-strategy/20111017.htm.

36. Home to amphibious platforms, naval offshore patrol vessels, and fast attack craft.

37. "India to Establish 2 Additional Missile Test Sites," *Defensenews.com*, February 27, 2013 (Accessed May 13, 2013): http://www.defensenews.com/article/20130227/DEFREG03/302270018.

38. Iskander Rehman, "China's String of Pearls and India's Enduring Tactical Advantage," *IDSA COMMENT*: http://www.idsa.in/idsacomments/ChinasString ofPearlsandIndiasEnduringTacticalAdvantage_irehman_080610.

39. Nilanthi Samaranayake, "The Long Littoral Project: Bay of Bengal: A Maritime Perspective on Indo-Pacific Security," Center for Naval Analysis, September 2012: http://www.cna.org/sites/default/files/research/IRP-2012-U-002319 -Final%20Bay%20of%20Bengal.pdf.

40. C. Raja Mohan. *Samudra Manthan: Sino-Indian Rivalry in the Indo-Pacific* (Washington, DC: Carnegie Endowment for International Peace, 2012), 181.

41. C. Raja Mohan. *Samudra Manthan: Sino-Indian Rivalry in the Indo-Pacific* (Washington, DC: Carnegie Endowment for International Peace, 2012), 179.

42. Srikanth Kondipalli. Author interview. New Delhi, August 2012.

43. Dhiraj Kukreja, "Andaman and Nicobar Islands: A security challenge for India," *Indian Defence Review*, Vol. 28. No. 1, 2013: http://www.indiandefencereview .com/news/andaman-and-nicobar-islands-a-security-challenge-for-india/.

44. "INS Baaz Commissioned as First Naval Air Station in Nicobar Islands," IDR News Network, August 10, 2012: http://www.indiandefencereview.com/ news/ins-baaz-commissioned-as-first-naval-air-station-in-nicobar-islands/.

45. Shashank Joshi, "Can India Blockade China?" *Diplomat*. August 12, 2013: http://thediplomat.com/flashpoints-blog/2013/08/12/can-india-blockade -china/

46. Raja Menon, "A Mountain Strike Corps Is Not the Only Option." *Hindu*. July 29, 2013: http://www.thehindu.com/opinion/lead/a-mountain-strike -corps-is-not-the-only-option/article4963979.ece?ref=relatedNews

47. Gabriel B. Collins and William S. Murray, "No Oil for the Lamps of China?" *Naval War College Review*, Spring 2008, Vol. 61, No. 2.

48. Mokhzani Zubir, "The Strategic Value of Malacca Strait," April 15, 2013: http://www.aspirasi-ndp.com/en/archive/ThestrategicvalueoftheStraitof Malacca.pdf

49. Gabriel B. Collins and William S. Murray, "No Oil for the Lamps of China?" *Naval War College Review*, Spring 2008, Vol. 61, No. 2: 8.

Chapter 12

India Looking East:
Freedom of Navigation
and the South China Sea

The year 1991 was a challenging one for India. The collapse of the Soviet Union that December deprived Delhi of its longtime superpower benefactor, a trauma magnified by the onset of a debt crisis that sent the Indian currency into free fall. Delhi responded, rather uncharacteristically, by turning the economic crisis into a strategic opportunity. A substantial devaluation of the Indian rupee in the summer of 1991 preceded an economic liberalization campaign shepherded by then–Finance Minister Manmohan Singh that drove a fundamental reorientation not only of Indian economic policy, but its foreign policy as well.

While domestic economic reforms were the initiative's main focus, the crisis prompted a broad recognition that the insular, Nonaligned foreign policy that had guided India through the Cold War had also limited India's strategic and economic potential. India, and much of the South Asian subcontinent, missed the economic miracle that gripped East Asia in the 1980s. As the Asian Tigers galloped into modernity, the Indian subcontinent seemed frozen in time—even today it remains among the poorest, least integrated, and most unstable regions in the world.[1]

A "Look East" policy was born as a framework for India to expand its economic horizons beyond the confines of South Asia, and specifically to engage with the economically dynamic countries of the Association of Southeast Asian Nations (ASEAN).[2] India had been virtually locked out of the region during the Cold War: its 1971 defense pact with the Soviet Union served it poorly in a part of the world dominated by Western-leaning governments. The collapse of the USSR in 1991 removed that obstacle to engagement, however, and India became a "Sectoral Dialogue Partner" of ASEAN the following year.

1992

Singapore, it should be noted, played a leading role in shepherding India into the political economy of Southeast Asia over the ensuing decade. The country's founding father and geopolitical savant, Lee Kuan Yew, was personally committed to deepening Indo-ASEAN engagement, and India became a full dialogue partner of ASEAN at the fifth ASEAN summit in 1995, and a member of the ASEAN Regional Forum (ARF) the following year. In the mid-1990s, Singapore became the first country to conduct regular joint naval exercises with India (SIMBEX), and to this day, Singapore, with nearly 10 percent of its population ethnic Indians, remains Delhi's largest trade and investment partner in ASEAN.[3]

By the turn of the century, two developments heralded a new era for India's Look East policy. First, buoyed by the economic reforms of the early 1990s, by 2003 the Indian economy began growing at near-double-digit rates, piquing the interest of the business-minded elites of Southeast Asia. Second, China's rise began to spark a new wave of security concerns in the region that opened a strategic opportunity for India, which came to be seen as a friendly counterbalance to China. In 2002 Goh Chok Tong, the Prime Minister of Singapore, compared ASEAN to a jumbo jet, with China as its one wing and India as the other. Both were needed to bring balance to the organization and the region.[4]

That year ASEAN made India a summit partner, and the following year the two sides began work on Free Trade Agreement which took effect January 2010 following years of tough negotiations. As Indo-ASEAN economic relations gained steam, Delhi began to conceptually and geographically broaden the horizons of its regional engagement.

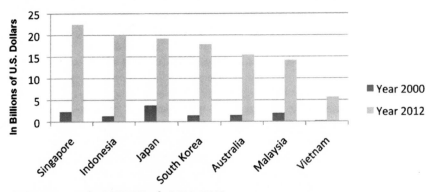

Figure 12.1.   Indo-ASEAN Trade 2000, 2012
Source: IMF Direction of Trade Statistics (accessed June 21, 2013), http://elibrary-data.imf.org

Beginning in the mid-2000s, Delhi began enthusiastically courting security ties with East Asian nations, holding a series of multilateral naval exercises with Indonesia, Singapore, Sri Lanka, and Thailand in the eastern Indian Ocean. This new phase of Look East, declared External Affairs Minister Yaswant Sinha in 2003, marked "a shift from trade to wider economic and security issues including joint efforts to protect the sea lanes and coordinate counter-terrorism activities." It was also "characterized by an expanded definition of 'East,' extending from Australia to East Asia, with ASEAN at its core."[5]

Perhaps most important, India began to rejuvenate its stagnant relationship with Japan. India has been the largest foreign recipient of Japanese aid over the past thirty years,[6] but Tokyo had long been estranged from Delhi as a result of its refusal to sign the Nuclear Nonproliferation Treaty and its cozy relationship with the Soviet Union. However, Michael Green argues that by the 1990s "conservative Japanese politicians on the right . . . found common cause with conservative, anti-Chinese Indian political figures."[7]

A visit to India by Japanese Prime Minister Yoshi Mori in August 2000 produced an "Indo-Japanese Partnership for the twenty-first century" and that year Japanese aid to India was restored after having been suspended following India's 1998 nuclear test. From 2000 to 2012 Indo-Japanese trade quadrupled, though $18 billion in bilateral trade in 2012 was dwarfed by the $340 billion in Sino-Japanese trade that year.

Table 12.1. Indo-Japan Security Milestones

2000	Indo-Japanese partnership for the twenty-first century
2000	Coast guards from both countries begin holding joint exercises
2005	Japan-India partnership in a New Asian Era
2006	Relationship elevated to "Strategic and Global Partnership"
2008	Joint Declaration on Security Cooperation
2009	Action Plan to advance security cooperation
2009	Comprehensive Economic Partnership Agreement
2011	First U.S.-India-Japan trilateral dialogue held
2012	India signs contract to provide Japan with rare earths after China reduces exports
2013	Pact signed for regular bilateral military exercises; Japan agrees to sell India two advanced amphibious aircraft

Secure in its relationship with Japan, ASEAN, and the United States, India began taking tentative steps toward expanding its military reach into the western Pacific, and toward reengaging with traditional allies in the region such as Vietnam.

- 2000: India conducts its first naval exercises in the South China Sea, "a low-level, unstructured exercise" with Vietnam.[8]
- 2002: The Indian Navy, granted port access by Singapore, escorts American ships through the Strait of Malacca as part of Operation Enduring Freedom.[9]

- 2004: After a massive tsunami wreaks havoc in large parts of South and Southeast Asia, Indian rescue efforts extend to the South China Sea under the aegis of the "Regional Core Group": the United States, India, Japan, and Australia.
- 2005: The Indian aircraft carrier *Viraat* makes its first voyage into the South China Sea, transiting the Strait of Malacca and making port calls in Malaysia, Singapore, and Indonesia. For the first time the Indo-Singapore SIMBEX exercises are held in the South China Sea.
- 2007: India sends three guided-missile destroyers, a missile corvette, and a fleet tanker on a two-month deployment to the Pacific to participate in first-ever trilateral naval drills with the U.S. and Japan off the Japanese coast. Two Indian destroyers later conduct a five-day exercise with the PLA Navy off Qingdao, before exercising with the Russian navy. On its return, the Indian naval flotilla conducts additional exercises with Vietnam and the Philippines.

THE QUAD INITIATIVE

By 2007 growing anxieties about China's rise were pushing Australia, Japan, the United States, and India toward more institutionalized security cooperation. The Japanese prime minister at the time, Shinzo Abe, had become a vocal proponent of forming an "arc of freedom" in the Pacific, later arguing that Australia, India, Japan, and the U.S. state of Hawaii should form a "democratic diamond" to "safeguard the maritime commons stretching from the Indian Ocean region to the western Pacific."[10]

The first step toward this vision came in 2004, when the United States, Australia, Japan, and India joined hands to establish the "Regional Core Group" under U.S. Joint Task Force 536 to provide relief to victims of the Indian Ocean tsunami that year.

Two years later, the United States merged its two bilateral security dialogues with Japan and Australia into a Trilateral Security Dialogue. In March 2007, Australia signed its own individual security pact with Tokyo and India conducted its first "Strategic Dialogue" with Japan. One month later, the United States, Japan, and India conducted their first-ever trilateral military exercises off Tokyo Bay featuring four guided-missile destroyers from Japan, two destroyers from the United States, and a destroyer, corvette, and tanker from India.

Amid this deepening web of strategic engagement, in May 2007 assistant secretary-level representatives of the four democracies held the inaugural meeting of a new Quadrilateral Initiative on the sidelines of an ASEAN Regional Forum meeting in Manila. The meeting prompted Beijing to send demarches to all four countries inquiring about the purpose of their gathering while the *People's Daily* signaled China's discomfort with the democratic conclave: "It is absolutely not new for Japan and the U.S. to sit down and plot conspiracies together but it is rather intriguing to get India involved."[11]

Six months after the inaugural meeting of the Quad, the initiative took a bold step forward. Since 1993 the United States and India had been conducting low-level joint naval exercises under the Malabar Exercise moniker. After being suspended for several years following India's nuclear test of 1998, the exercises resumed in 2002 with a relatively small naval contingent and routine maneuvers. Over the ensuing five years the exercises grew gradually more robust: in 2004 the U.S. sent a nuclear-powered *Los Angeles*–class submarine to participate in the Malabar drills, and in 2005 the United States and India both sent aircraft carriers. However the Malabar exercise of September 2007 were something altogether different.

First, unlike previous Malabar exercises, the drills of 2007 involved not only U.S. and Indian naval forces, but those of Australia, Singapore, and Japan. Second, while all the previous iterations of the Malabar exercises were held in the Indian Ocean, the ninth Malabar exercise of 2007 was held in the Pacific waters off Okinawa. The third distinguishing factor was the size and potency of the armada: over twenty-five vessels including *three* aircraft carriers (two U.S., one Indian); a nuclear-powered submarine; a dozen cruisers, frigates, and destroyers; and more than 20,000 personnel.

However, it would be the last time the four democracies would join hands in such a grand show of force. In the months following the exercise, right-wing governments in Japan and Australia gave way to new leadership from the left intent on pursuing better relations with Beijing. A report from the National Bureau of Asian Research says the Quadrilateral Initiative "was effectively neutralized, and eventually jettisoned, by domestic political developments in Australia and Japan."[12]

"After we stuck our neck out the Australians broke the contract," a senior official in the MEA told this author over lunch in Delhi. "It left a bad taste in our mouth." For many in India, this large, multilateral show of force with U.S.-allied navies in an exercise perceived as overtly hostile to China was a clear violation of the principles of "Nonalignment." And in the short term the collapse of the Quad strengthened the hand of critics who had warned against participating in the exercises in the first place.

"Demonstrations against the [Malabar] exercise by the communist party [of India] put the Congress Party on the defensive and the new naval headquarters had to take a step back," notes C. Raja Mohan.[13] India temporarily scaled back its maritime activism and "shifted toward a more traditional Indian foreign policy posture of non-alignment."[14] In 2008, the Malabar exercise was a lower-key affair, held in the Arabian Sea and involving just the United States and India.

MALABAR EXERCISES

By 2009 India was again inching toward greater security cooperation with the Pacific democracies, albeit at a more subdued pace. The 2009 Malabar exercise was again joined by Japan and held off Japanese waters, but involved a smaller contingent of forces and notably excluded Australia. In November 2009 India signed its first Joint Declaration on Security Cooperation with Australia, paving the way for a series of breakthroughs in Indo-Australian relations.

Table 12.2. Malabar Exercises

2002	Arabian Sea	India, U.S.	First Malabar exercise since 1996 (first three held in 1992, 1995, 1996). Four days of joint exercises; relatively small naval contingent (two U.S. and two Indian warships) and routine maneuvers, antisubmarine exercises, replenishment-at-sea drills.
2003	Arabian Sea	India, U.S.	U.S. and Indian frigates, submarines, and aircraft conduct antisubmarine warfare tactics.
2004	Indian Ocean off southwest coast of India	India, U.S.	U.S. sends nuclear-powered *Los Angeles*–class submarine SSN *Alexandria*; P-3C Orion maritime patrol aircraft; India sends destroyer, frigate, and submarine. 2,000 personnel total.
2005	Indian Ocean off southwest coast of India	India, U.S.	U.S. and India both send aircraft carriers; U.S. Carrier Strike Group 11 with the USS *Nimitz* joins INS *Viraat*; joint salvage operation; twenty-four-hour "mock war" exercise.
2006	Indian Ocean off coast of Goa	India, U.S., Canada	Canadian frigate HMCS *Ottawa* joins exercise for first time, along with U.S. Expeditionary Strike Group 5. Eleven warships, two submarines, two Coast Guard ships, a U.S. nuclear-powered submarine, and guided missile frigates and destroyers from both the U.S. and India. Practiced amphibious landing.
2007	Off the coast of Okinawa	India, Australia, Japan, Singapore, U.S.	Over twenty-five vessels including *three* aircraft carriers (two U.S., one Indian), a nuclear powered submarine, a dozen cruisers, frigates and destroyers, and more than 20,000 personnel. Surface and antisubmarine warfare, counterpiracy, and counterterrorism exercises.

2008	Off the coast of India	India, U.S.	U.S. sends Carrier Strike Group 7 led by USS *Ronald Reagan*, nuclear submarine USS *Springfield*, P3C Orion aircraft. India sends two destroyers, four guided-missile frigates, replenishment tanker and a diesel-electric submarine. Maritime interdiction, counterpiracy and counterterrorism operations.
2009	Off the coast of Okinawa	India, U.S., Japan	Surface, subsurface, and air operations, including helicopters from each navy landing and taking off from the other navy's ships. U.S. sends guided missile destroyers, fast-attack submarines, P-3C Orion and SH-60 Seahawk aircraft. India sends two guided missile destroyers, a guided missile corvette, and a replenishment tanker. Japan sends a guided missile destroyer and frigate.
2010	Indian Ocean	India, U.S.	U.S. sends guided missile cruisers, destroyers, and frigates, nuclear submarines, P-3 Orion aircraft, SH-60 helicopters, and a SEAL detachment. Indian Navy sends guided-missile destroyers, two frigates and a submarine. Surface and antisubmarine warfare, coordinated gunnery exercises, air defense and visit, board, search, and seizure drills.
2011	Off the coast of Okinawa	India, U.S. Japan forced to back out after March 2011 tsunami	U.S. sends two guided-missile frigates, nuclear submarine; India sends three guided-missile destroyers, a corvette, and a replenishment tanker. Surface action group exercise operations; formation maneuvering; helicopter cross-deck evolutions; underway replenishments; humanitarian assistance and disaster relief; gunnery exercises; visit, board, search, and seizure; maritime strike; air defense; screen exercise and antisubmarine warfare.
2012	Bay of Bengal, and waters west of Nicobar Islands	India, U.S.	U.S. sends aircraft carrier, submarine, guided, missile destroyer and cruiser and a logistics ship. India sends two destroyers, corvette, and replenishment tanker. Ten days of exercises in communications, surface action group (SAG) operations, helicopter cross-deck evolutions, and gunnery exercises. Both on shore and off shore exercises.
2013	Bay of Bengal	India, U.S.	U.S. sends a guided missile destroyer; India sends a guided missile destroyer and a frigate. On-shore and at sea exercises.

Though Australia particpated in the Quad Initative in 2007, the two democracies had long been estranged over Canberra's refusal to export uranium to India, a condition of India's refusal to sign the 1970 Nuclear Nonproliferation Treaty (NPT). However, prompted by the passage of the U.S.-India nuclear deal in 2008, Australia, with 40 percent of the world's known uranium reserves, lifted its longstanding ban on exports to non-signatories of the NPT in December 2011. In the process, Canberra removed the greatest obstacle to deeper political engagement with India. The following year India and Australia began talks on a civil nuclear deal and launched a Dialogue on Energy Security. The year 2013 saw the first trip to Australia by an Indian defense minister, where he reached an agreement to establish the first Indo-Australian bilateral maritime exercises, likely in 2015.

Elsewhere, between 2010 and 2013 India held four rounds of trilateral dialogue with the United States and Japan (November 2011, October 2012, March 2013, May 2013); established its first Foreign Policy and Security Dialogue with South Korea and purchased eight antimine ships from Seoul; renewed a ten-year Defense Agreement with Singapore; signed a deal with Japan to institutionalize bilateral naval exercises and purchase two amphibious search and rescue craft from Tokyo; and extended Vietnam a $100 million credit line to purchase four Indian patrol boats. The initiatives signal a new commitment to strategic engagement with the Pacific democracies. And in tandem, they symbolize a waning commitment to philosophy of Nonalignment, or at least a less rigid interpretation of its strictures.

China Responds

Beijing's initial reaction to India's Look East policy was simply to try to discourage India from joining East Asia's plethora of regional institutions—or at least to ensure that where India was granted a seat at the table, so too was Pakistan (part of China's policy of seeking "balance" in South Asia).

"As Indian Ambassador to Thailand, I know from first-hand personal knowledge that amongst China's regional priorities was thwarting the emergence of any significant Indian role in Southeast Asia," lamented Ambassador Ranjit Gupta at a public lecture in November 2011. "China was absolutely livid when India was invited to become a full Dialogue Partner of ASEAN ahead of China." Additionally, China "tried very hard to prevent India from being included in the [ASEAN Regional Forum]" and made "strong but ultimately unsuccessful attempts" at excluding India from the East Asia Summit."[15]

As that strategy failed to blunt India's steady integration into the region, and the Sino-Indian rivalry sharpened in the late 2000s, Chinese

Table 12.3. Multilateral Organizations of India and China

Organization	Acronym	India (Status & Entry Date)		China (Status and Entry Date)	
Asia Cooperation Dialogue	ACD	Member	2002	Member	2002
Asian-Pacific Economic Cooperation	APEC			Member	1991
ASEAN Plus Three	APT			Member	1997
ASEAN Regional Forum	ARF	Member	1994	Member	1994
Asian Development Bank	ADB	Member	1966	Member	1986
Association of Southeast Asian Nations	ASEAN	Dialogue Partner	1992	Dialogue Partner	1991
Brazil, South Africa, India, and China	BASIC	Member	2009	Member	2009
Bay of Bengal Initiative for Multi-Sectorial Technical and Economic Cooperation	BIMSTEC	Member	1997		
Brazil, Russia, India, China, South Africa	BRICS	Member	2009	Member	2009
Comprehensive Economic Partnership for East Asia	CEPEA	Member	2008	Member	2006
East Asia Summit	EAS	Member	2005	Member	2005
Group of Twenty Finance Ministers and Central Bank Governors	G-20	Member	2003	Member	2003
International Monetary Fund	IMF	Member	1945	Member	1980
Nonproliferation Treaty	NPT			Member	1992
Shanghai Cooperation Organization	SCO	Observer		Member	2001
South Asian Association for Regional Cooperation	SAARC	Member	1985	Observer	2005
World Bank		Member	1945	Member	1980
World Health Organization	WHO	Member	1948	Member	1972
World Trade Organization	WTO	Member	1995	Member	2001

*Chart includes entry by the People's Republic of China (PRC) only

pundits were given greater freedom to take aim at India's new engagement in China's periphery.

In 2010 the editor of the *People's Daily Online* opined: "History is a great teacher. India's 'Look East policy' was born out of failure—the failure of India's Cold War strategy of 'playing both ends against the middle,' today, India is harping on the same string, but should wisely skip the out-of-tune piece."[16]

A year later Xinhua warned that if India intends to "antagonize its neighbor by taking it as an imaginary enemy and get unwisely involved in affairs which fall within other's backyards, it would hold its national strategies as hostage and put at stake its own national interests. It is highly advisable for New Delhi to think twice about the pitfalls in making its foreign policies."[17]

In February 2012, a retired PLA officer expressed irritation to this writer at the growing number of closed-door security meetings between India and the U.S.-allied countries of the region. He suggested that if India wanted to discuss security matters with the countries of East Asia, it should only do so with China present at the table. "Does China invite India into its security discussions with Pakistan?" this writer asked.

The retired officer dismissed the question with a comment about the need for "risk analysis" if India's intentions in East Asia were "malignant." Later in the conversation this writer began a question: "If you are concerned about Indian activities in the South China Sea, why don't . . ." "*Concerned!?*" he interrupted. "*We are not concerned with anything; we would crush them!*" the officer barked before going silent for the duration of the dinner.

To be sure, such sentiments are not necessarily representative of the views China's diplomatic corps, or even its political elite. Other Chinese scholars interviewed for this book expressed profound ambivalence about India's engagement in East Asia, noting that India's activities in the region were of little consequence compared to its territorial disputes with Japan, Vietnam, and the Philippines. "Frankly speaking, we don't care what India is doing in the South China Sea," says Ye Hailin of the Chinese Academy of Social Sciences. "We are concerned about the U.S., ASEAN, and Japan; no one else. It is not worth wasting our time on an irrelevant player."[18]

What the retired officer's outburst does represent is growing irritation among *Chinese nationalists* inside and outside the PLA at India's Look East policy. Their principal concern is that India will gradually become part of a loose confederation of U.S.-allied countries collaborating to contain China or deter the country's rise. But beyond this broad concern, two related elements of India's engagement in the region are problematic from Beijing's perspective: Indian oil exploration in the contested waters off Vietnam, and Delhi's increasingly vocal support for the principle of "freedom of navigation."

FREEDOM OF NAVIGATION

Supporting the concept of "freedom of navigation" became synonymous with opposing Chinese hegemony in the South China Sea. The turn of phrase was met in Beijing with equal parts confusion and irritation. "Freedom and safety of navigation in the South China Sea is assured. . . . There is no issue currently in this area, nor will there ever be issues in that area

Table 12.4.   Maritime Boundary Definitions Under the UN Convention on the Law of the Sea

Category	Area	Definition
Territorial Sea	Up to twelve nautical miles from a country's baseline (low-water coastline)	Sovereign territory of the state. Foreign vessels have right to innocent passage.
Contiguous Zone	Up to twenty-four nautical miles from the baseline	State may exercise control necessary to prevent infringement of its customs, fiscal, immigration or sanitary laws.
Exclusive Economic Zone (EEZ)	Up to 200 nautical miles from baseline	Sovereign rights for exploring and exploiting resources; preserving marine environment; establishing artificial islands and structures
Continental Shelf	Up to 350 nautical miles from baseline (when it extends beyond 200 nautical miles)	Sovereign rights for exploring and exploiting natural resources
High Seas	All parts of the sea that are not included in the EEZ, the territorial sea, or in the internal waters of a state. No exclusive rights.	

Source: The National Oceanic and Atmospheric Administration (NOAA), http://www.gc.noaa.gov/gcil_maritime.html

in the future," Chinese Foreign Minister Yang Jiechi stated in September 2012.[19] Dr. Wu Shicun, director of China's National Institute for South China Sea Studies, explained in January 2013 that "freedom of navigation in the South China Sea has been used as an excuse to carry out military activities while the fact is, freedom of navigation has not been a problem at all in the South China Sea."[20]

Dr. Wu is correct insofar as China has done nothing to violate the principal of freedom of navigation for commercial vessels in internationally recognized high seas. However, China *does* restrict the economic activities of foreign vessels operating in its 200–nautical mile Exclusive Economic Zone (EEZ) This is problematic insofar as China's claims to all of the territory within the imprecisely defined "9-dash line," for example, would extend its EEZ—and its ability to restrict the economic activities of foreigners—across virtually all of the South China Sea. It is in this context that Chinese vessels have engaged in dangerous confrontations with Filipino and Vietnamese fishing vessels in waters claimed by China.

The second concern relates to military activities in China's EEZ. Under Beijing's interpretation of UNCLOS, coastal states have the right to restrict the military activities of foreign warships operating in their EEZ. This interpretation has already led to several miniconfrontations at sea between U.S. and Chinese ships, with the latter seeking to prevent U.S. surveillance vessels from operating in China's Exclusive Economic Zone. Here too the concern is that China's claims to all of the territory within the South China Sea would grant it a virtual veto over surveillance and other military activities by foreign nations.[21]

India gave an early indication on how it would come down on this debate when it released a Maritime Military Strategy in 2007. The document's title—"Freedom to Use the Seas"—was a political declaration in its own right.

Then, amid a year of rising tensions between China and its neighbors over competing territorial claims, in 2010 Indian Minister of State for External Affairs Preneet Kaur joined eleven other countries at an ASEAN Regional Forum conference to declare that the South China Sea should remain open for international navigation.[22] However, the call was ultimately overshadowed by a more forceful declaration by U.S. Secretary of State Hillary Clinton at the same forum. "The United States, like every nation, has a national interest in freedom of navigation, open access to Asia's maritime commons, and respect for international law in the South China Sea."[23]

 It was not until 2011, following an incident in the South China Sea, that Indian officials began to regularly and publicly voice support for freedom of navigation there. In July 2011 an Indian amphibious assault vessel, the *INS Airavat*, was on a routine visit to Vietnam. On its journey to the northern port of Haiphong it was contacted over an open radio channel some forty-five nautical miles off the coast of Vietnam: "You are entering Chinese waters. Move out of here," said an unidentified caller. No Chinese ships were present on the horizon, and the *Airavat* ignored the warning.[24]

The episode was dismissed by both capitals as a hoax, but it seemed to focus Delhi's attention on the implications of Chinese hegemony over the South China Sea. Shortly after the episode became public, the Ministry of External Affairs issued a statement saying: "India supports freedom of navigation in international waters, including in the South China Sea, and the right of passage in accordance with accepted principles of international law."[25] Senior Indian naval officials have noted that India's position is similar to that articulated by Washington, but that unlike the United States, Delhi has not yet said that freedom of navigation is "in India's national interest."[26] Former Indian Navy Chief Admiral Sureesh Mehta told this writer not to read too much into the distinction: "for practical purposes our positions on this issue are one and the same."[27]

Indian Defense Minister A. K. Antony provided further substance to India's position at the Shangri La security dialogue held in Singapore from June 1 to 4, 2012:

> Unlike in previous centuries, maritime freedoms cannot be the prerogative of a few. Large parts of the common seas cannot be declared exclusive to any one country or group. We must find the balance between the rights of nations and the freedoms of the world community in the maritime domain. Like individual freedoms, the fullness of maritime freedoms can be realized only when all states, big and small, are willing to abide by universally agreed laws and principles.[28]

Weeks after Antony's speech, Indian warships bound for the Philippines from South Korea received a call—"Welcome to the South China Sea, Foxtrot-47"—and an "unexpected escort" from a Chinese frigate for twelve hours as they traveled through international waters.[29] The message from China, says C. Raja Mohan, was essentially: "Nice to see you here, but you are in our territorial waters and within them there is no right to 'freedom of navigation' for military vessels. You are here at our sufferance."[30]

Finally, on December 3, 2012, India's Navy Chief of Staff Admiral D. K. Joshi declared: "Freedom of navigation is the concern of the whole world, not just ours. If the navy is not to protect national assets [in the South China Sea] then what are we there for?"[31] The statement was enough to earn India a rebuke from China a few weeks later. At the Galle Dialogue 2012 in Sri Lanka, Vice Admiral Su Zhiqian, the commander of China's East Sea Fleet, stated: "The freedom and safety of navigation *in the Indian Ocean* play a very important role in the recovery and development of global economy and *the Chinese navy will actively maintain the peace and stability of the Indian Ocean.*"[32]

ONGC AND INDIA'S ECONOMIC STAKE
IN THE SOUTH CHINA SEA

India's increasingly vocal support for freedom of navigation in the South China Sea is directly linked to its expanding economic interests in the region. The focal point of this engagement, and one of its principal sources of friction with Beijing, are a series of investments in Vietnamese offshore energy blocks by the Indian Company ONGC Videsh.

ONGC has been operating in Vietnam's coastal waters since the late 1980s, when it acquired an exploration license for Block 06.1 some 370 kilometers southeast of Vung Tau. The block still contributes some 50 percent of Vietnam's domestic gas needs, and through March 2012 India had invested $342 million in the project and maintained a 45 percent stake.[33]

In May 2006 ONGC signed a production-sharing contract with Petro-Vietnam granting it exploration rights in two additional offshore deep-water blocks—127 and 128—in the Phu Kanh basin. In July 2009 ONGC invested $68 million and drilled a well in Block 127 but it abandoned the block shortly after for economic reasons. [34]

The more controversial block was 128, which fell inside waters China was claiming as part of its Exclusive Economic Zone. There was little protest from Beijing when the original deal was signed in 2006. But when ONGC and PetroVietnam inked a three-year agreement in October 2011 to promote long-term cooperation in the oil and gas industry in the South China Sea, China began to push back.

China's foreign ministry issued a statement claiming it was "opposed to any country engaging in oil and gas exploration and development activities in waters under China's jurisdiction."[35] Days later, Indian External Affairs Minister S. M. Krishna was in Hanoi insisting that ONGC would move forward with its plans for Block 128.

This earned India a sharp rebuke from a *People's Daily* publication, *China Energy News*: India's "energy strategy is slipping into an extremely dangerous whirlpool," the article warned.[36] On September 17, 2011, the hawkish *Global Times* added:

> Reasoning may be used first, but if India is persistent in this, China should try every means possible to stop [it] from happening. . . . India should bear in mind that its actions in the South China Sea will push China to the limit. China cherishes the Sino-Indian friendship, but this does not mean China values it above all else . . . China has been peaceful for so long that some countries doubt whether it will stick to its stated bottom line. China should remind them of how clear this line really is.[37]

A day after this article printed, China announced that it planned to expand seabed mineral exploration in the Indian Ocean. Beijing had received approval from the International Seabed Authority (ISA) in July 2011 to explore 10,000 square kilometers of seabed in the southwest Indian Ocean to mine for polymetallic sulphide ore. But China waited until September 18 to announce that it would sign a fifteen-year exploration contract with the ISA, giving it exclusive rights to develop ore deposits there. India's Directorate of Naval Intelligence responded with a warning that the contract would provide China an excuse to operate its warships in India's backyard.[38]

Six months later signs emerged that India was considering abandoning its South China Sea stakes under the weight of Chinese pressure. In May 2012 India's junior oil minister, RPN Singh, announced to parliament that ONGC would be vacating oil block 128 because it wasn't commercially viable. Indian officials privately insisted the block was abandoned for techno-economic reasons and ONGC "had failed to start drilling activity as per the timeline worked out in the original contract."[39] ONGC's website says the company "had difficulty anchoring at the location due to the hard carbonate sea bottom."[40]

However, there was a widespread assumption that this was a geopolitical decision taken in deference to China. The assumption was seemingly confirmed when, a month later, ONGC announced it had signed an agreement with the Chinese firm China National Petroleum Corporation (CNPC) to cooperate in oil exploration, crude oil refining, and building oil and gas pipelines.[41] China's state-owned China National Offshore Oil Company (CNOOC), then opened nine blocks for energy exploration in disputed waters for global bidding, including the area containing block 128. [42]

By June 2012 Vietnam was publicly courting ONGC to retain its contract in Block 128 and offered to provide additional data to ONGC to "help make future exploration economically feasible."[43] A month later ONGC appeared to do an about face, with PetroVietnam announcing ONGC had accepted a two-year extension of its contract. ONGC's website confirms that the contract has been extended "to find a solution to the anchoring problem."[44] In the fall of 2012, over lunch in Washington, a member of parliament from India's Congress Party insisted that the Indian parliament had supported ONGC's decision to remain in block 128. "We live cheek to jowl with China. It was a strategic choice for us and it has important implications for the Indo-Pacific."[45]

"We cannot just be picked up and thrown out," noted Bhaskar Roy, an Indian strategic affairs analyst. "There is public interest in India on this issue: where are we going, are we giving up our sovereignty because of Chinese pressure. It shows that we also have capabilities and also determination to protect our own interest."[46]

The last chapter in this continuing saga came in December 2012 when India's Navy chief, Admiral D. K. Joshi, got somewhat ahead of Delhi in vowing to protect India's economic interests in the South China Sea by force if necessary: "Not that we expect to be in those waters very, very frequently, but when the requirement is there, for example, in situations where our country's interests are involved, for example ONGC. . . . we will be required to go there and we are prepared for that. . . . Are we having exercises of that nature? The short answer is yes."[47]

CHINA AND THE FUTURE OF INDIA'S LOOK EAST POLICY

Admiral Joshi's remarks are a window into the public debate taking place in India about the appropriate role for India in the South China Sea, and the extent to which it is willing to go to protect its interests there. The question is directly linked to the broader intent of India's Look East policy: is it designed simply to expand India's economic horizons, or should it be leveraged as a strategic asset against China?

Some nationalist commentators have become vocal proponents of the latter. Former External Affairs Minister Jaswant Singh has said India and others should contend with Chinese assertiveness by heeding Sun Tzu's counsel: "Contain an adversary through the leverage of converting the neighborhood of the adversary into hostiles."[48] The Indian Policy document *Non-Alignment 2.0* notes partnerships in East Asia "may help delay, if not deter, the projection of Chinese naval power in the Indian Ocean. . . . It is in our interest that China remains preoccupied with the first-tier, more immediate maritime theater [Yellow Sea, the Taiwan Straits, the East China Sea, and the South China Sea.]"[49]

Indian national security hawk Bharat Karnad has implored Delhi to cultivate ties to Vietnam the way China has done with Pakistan so "India can pay Beijing back in the same coin."[50] "It is time India joined Japan, ASEAN, and Taiwan to impose on Beijing the costs of living dangerously," he has argued. "The process of reversing the heat to cook the Chinese frog in the South China Sea waters is long overdue."[51] Other Indian analysts have called for basing options in Vietnam's Cam Ranh Bay, and suggested India should supply Vietnam with nuclear-capable Brahmos cruise missiles.

However, authoritative figures in the Indian establishment have gone to great lengths to emphasize the limits of India's ability to project power in the South China Sea. Admiral Joshi was explicitly rebuffed by the political establishment for saying the Indian Navy was prepared to venture into the South China Sea to protect ONGC's investments. And former Navy Chief Admiral Arun Prakash has argued that "the Pacific and the South China Sea are of concern to us, but activation in those areas is not on the cards."[52] "A distant location like the South China Sea," he said, "is hardly an ideal setting to demonstrate India's maritime or other strengths."[53]

In the end, a great deal of uncertainty looms of the future of India's engagement in the South China Sea and the Western Pacific. One can expect India to continue courting stronger military and economic relations with the U.S.-allied countries of the region, though it will proceed cautiously on measures perceived as overtly hostile to China, such as selling Vietnam the Brahmos cruise missile or participating in large, multilateral displays of force in the Western Pacific. India seems to have set a ceiling at trilateral engagements, allowing Japan to participate in the Malabar exercises when they are held off the coast of Okinawa.

Iskander Rehman predicts that while India will never engaged in a "formalized alliance given New Delhi's profound attachment to its continued diplomatic maneuverability, one can well envision the emergence of a 'tacit security compact' or 'an informal balancing arrangement of some type.'"[54] C. Raja Mohan largely concurs, noting that India is "in no position to become a counterweight to China in Southeast Asia," but acting in concert with the United States and Japan, "India can contribute to a more stable balance of power" there.[55]

NOTES

1. "South Asia Least Integrated Region in World," *Nation*, December 3, 2012: http://www.nation.com.pk/pakistan-news-newspaper-daily-english-online/business/03-Dec-2012/south-asia-least-integrated-region-in-world.

2. ASEAN includes Brunei, Cambodia, Indonesia, Laos, Malaysia, Myanmar, the Philippines, Singapore, Thailand, Vietnam.

3. "India—Singapore Bilateral Relations," January 2013, Indian Ministry of External Affairs: http://www.mea.gov.in/Portal/ForeignRelation/Brief__for_MEA_s_website_-_Jan_2013-1.pdf.

4. "Speech by Mr. Goh Chok Tong, Senior Minister, at the Global Action Forum for Arab and Asian Dialogue," *Ministry of Foreign Affairs: Singapore*, April 27, 2007 (Accessed April 15, 2013): http://www.mfa.gov.sg/content/mfa/media_centre/press_room/sp/2007/200704/speech_20070427.html.

5. Yaswant Sinha Speech at Harvard University, Cambridge, September 23, 2003: www.mea.gov.in.

6. "Japan-India Relations" Japanese Ministry of Foreign Affairs: http://www.mofa.go.jp/region/asia-paci/india/index.html?ef642a70.

7. Michael J. Green, "Japan, India, and the Strategic Triangle with China," *Strategic Asia 2011–12*: 132–147.

8. Bharat Verma, *Threat from China* (New Delhi: Lancer Publishers and Distributers, 2011), 178.

9. C. Raja Mohan, *Samudra Manthan: Sino-Indian Rivalry in the Indo-Pacific* (Washington DC: Carnegie Endowment for International Peace, 2012), 98.

10. Shinzo Abe, "Asia's Democratic Security Diamond," *Project Syndicate*, November 2012: http://www.project-syndicate.org/commentary/a-strategic-alliance-for-japan-and-india-by-shinzo-abe.

11. "A 'Goodwill' Joint Naval Drill?" *People's Daily Online* editorial, April 21, 2007: http://english.peopledaily.com.cn/200704/21/eng20070421_368521.html.

12. William Tow, "The Trilateral Strategic Dialogue: Facilitating Community Building or Revisiting Containment?" *National Bureau of Asian Research* December 2008 (Accessed April 15, 2013): http://www.nbr.org/publications/special report/pdf/Preview/SR16_preview.pdf.

13. C. Raja Mohan, *Samudra Manthan: Sino-Indian Rivalry in the Indo-Pacific* (Washington D.C.: Carnegie Endowment for International Peace, 2012), 98.

14. William Tow, "The Trilateral Strategic Dialogue: Facilitating Community Building or Revisiting Containment?" *National Bureau of Asian Research* December 2008 (Accessed April 15, 2013): http://www.nbr.org/publications/special report/pdf/Preview/SR16_preview.pdf

15. Ambassador Ranjit Gupta. Public lecture, Thiruvananthapuram TMCA Hall hosted by Kerala International Center November 9, 2011, India's ambassador in residence at JNU, secretary, Ministry of External Affairs 1999–2000. Ambassador to Yemen, Venezuela, Oman, Thailand, Spain, Head of Office in Taiwan.

16. Li Hongmei, "China's 'Look East Policy' Means 'Look to Encircle China'?" *People's Daily*, October 27, 2010 (Accessed April 15, 2013): http://english.peopl edaily.com.cn/90002/96417/7179404.html.

17. Li Hongmei, "India Needs Pause When Driving East," xinhua.net, November 8, 2011 (Accessed April 15, 2013): http://news.xinhuanet.com/ english2010/indepth/2011-11/08/c_131235363.htm.

18. Ye Hailin. Author interview. Washington, DC, June 2013.

19. Shaun Tandon, "China Says South China Sea Freedom of Navigation 'Assured,'" *ABS CBN News*, September 5, 2012 (Accessed April 15, 2013): http:// www.abs-cbnnews.com/global-filipino/world/09/05/12/china-says-south -china-sea-freedom-navigation-assured.

20. "Increased Military Presence in South China Sea a Concern for All Nations," *Observer Research Foundation*, January 11, 2013 (Accessed April 15, 2013): http://www.orfonline.org/cms/sites/orfonline/html/interview/wu.html.

21. Ironically, like twenty-five other nations, India takes the same position as China regarding home-state consent for foreign military vessels in its EEZ, but has not taken provocative actions to challenge foreign warships, instead lodging diplomatic protests.

22. Indrani Bagchi, "India to Discuss China with US Later This Month," *Economic Times*, September 4, 2010 (Accessed April 15, 2013): http://articles .economictimes.indiatimes.com/2010-09-04/news/27606150_1_core-interests -south-china-sea-exercises.

23. "Travel Diary: Secretary Clinton Participates in ASEAN Regional Forum" *DipNote: U.S. Department of State Official Blog*, July 23, 2010 (Accessed April 15, 2013): http://blogs.state.gov/index.php/site/entry/travel_diary_secretary_ asean_regional_forum.

24. Indrani Bagchi, "China Harasses Indian Naval Ship on South China Sea," *Times of India*, September 2, 2011 (Accessed April 15, 2013): http://articles.times ofindia.indiatimes.com/2011-09-02/india/30105514_1_south-china-sea-spratly -ins-airavat.

25. Indrani Bagchi, "China Harasses Indian Naval Ship on South China Sea," *Times of India*, September 2, 2011 (Accessed April 15, 2013): http://articles.times ofindia.indiatimes.com/2011-09-02/india/30105514_1_south-china-sea-spratly -ins-airavat.

26. Senior Indian naval officials. Author interview. New Delhi, November 2011.

27. Mehta Sureesh. Author interview. Honolulu, May 2013.

28. Abhijit Iyer-Mitra, "India Stops Hedging, Backs American Naval Strategy," *Atlantic Sentinel*, June 18, 2012 (Accessed April 15, 2013): http://atlanticsentinel.com/2012/06/india-stops-hedging-backs-american-naval-strategy/.

29. Ananth Krishnan, "In South China Sea, a Surprise Chinese Escort for Indian Ships," *Hindu*, June 14, 2012 (Accessed April 15, 2013): http://www.thehindu.com/news/national/article3524965.ece.

30. Raja Mandala and Raja Mohan, "Indian Navy in South China Sea: Beijing's Unwelcome Escort," June 14, 2012: http://www.indianexpress.com/news/indian-navy-in-south-china-sea-beijing-s-unwelcome-escort/962011/.

31. "Indian Navy Prepared to Defend its Interest in South China Sea, says Admiral DK Joshi," *India Today*, December 3, 2012 (Accessed April 15, 2013): http://indiatoday.intoday.in/story/india-prepared-to-intervene-in-south-china-sea-navy-chief/1/235881.html.

32. Che Hongliang, "Chinese Navy to Actively Maintain Peace and Stability of Indian Ocean," *Chinese Military Online*, December 14, 2012 (Accessed December 14, 2012): http://eng.chinamil.com.cn/news-channels/china-military-news/2012-12/14/content_5142763.htm.

33. "ONGC Videsh Pens Pact with PetroVietnam," *Rigzone*, October 12, 2011 (Accessed April 15, 2013): http://www.rigzone.com/news/oil_gas/a/111765/ONGC_Videsh_Pens_Pact_with_PetroVietnam.

34. "CIS and Far East Assets," *ONGC Videsh Limited*, 2010 (Accessed April 15, 2013): http://www.ongcvidesh.com/Assets.aspx?AspxAutoDetectCookieSupport=1.

35. Ananth Krishnan, "China Warns India on South China Sea Exploration projects," *Hindu*, September 15, 2011: http://www.thehindu.com/news/international/china-warns-india-on-south-china-sea-exploration-projects/article2455647.ece.

36. "Not as Close as Lips and Teeth," *Economist*, October 22, 2011: http://www.economist.com/node/21533397/print.

37. Greg Terode, "Beijing Pressure Intense in South China Sea Row," *South China Morning Post*, August 14, 2011: http://www.scmp.com/article/979876/beijing-pressure-intense-south-china-sea-row.

38. "China Announces Plan to Expand Seabed Mining in Indian Ocean," *Economic Times*, September 17, 2011: http://articles.economictimes.indiatimes.com/2011-09-17/news/30169240_1_polymetallic-sulphide-ocean-mineral-resources-research-state-oceanic-administration.

39. Pranab Dhal Samanta. "China Puts Indian Oil Block Up for Auction," *Indian Express*, July, 17, 2012: http://www.indianexpress.com/news/china-puts-indian-oil-block-up-for auction/975480/.

40. "ONGC Ltd. Assets," 2010: http://www.ongcvidesh.com/(X(1)S(j510jd45p2p41mepsypgkjey))/Assets.aspx?AspxAutoDetectCookieSupport=1.

41. "ONGC, China National Petroleum Corp Ink JV," *Indian Express*, June 19, 2011: http://www.indianexpress.com/news/ongc-china-national-petroleum-corp-ink-jv/964034.

42. Harsh Pant, "The South China Sea: A New Area in Chinese-Indian Rivalry," *Nation*, June 20, 2012: http://www.nationmultimedia.com/opinion/The-South-China-Sea-A-new-area-in-Chinese-Indian-r-30208644.html.

43. Rakesh Sharma, "ONGC to Continue Exploration in South China Sea," *Wall Street Journal*, July 19, 2012: http://online.wsj.com/article/SB1000087239639044446430457753618276315566.html.

44. "ONGC Ltd. Assets," 2010: http://www.ongcvidesh.com/(X(1)S(j510jd45p2p41mepsypgkjey))/Assets.aspx?AspxAutoDetectCookieSupport=1.

45. Member of Parliament from India's Congress Party. Lunch discussion. Heritage Foundation, September 19, 2012.

46. "India Vows to Protect S. China Sea Interests" *Voice of America*, December 4, 2012: http://www.voanews.com/content/india-vows-to-protect-south-china-sea-interests/1558070.html.

47. "India Vows to Protect S. China Sea Interests" *Voice of America*, December 4, 2012: http://www.voanews.com/content/india-vows-to-protect-south-china-sea-interests/1558070.html.

48. Jaswant Singh, "Asia's Giants Colliding at Sea?" *Project Sydicate*: http://www.project-syndicate.org/commentary/asia-s-giants-colliding-at-sea.

49. Sunil Khilnani, et al., *Nonalignment 2.0: A Foreign and Strategic Policy in the Twenty First Century*, 2012: http://www.cprindia.org/sites/default/files/Non-Alignment%202.0_1.pdf.

50. Bharat Karnad, "China Uses Pak, Vietnam to Open India," *Indian Express*, October 3, 2005: http://expressindia.indianexpress.com/news/fullstory.php?newsid=55789.

51. "'First Mover' Disadvantage," *Security Wise*, October 1, 2011: http://bharatkarnad.com/7.

52. Ajai Shukla, "Navy Chief Says Indian Ocean Is Priority, Not South China Sea," *Business Standard*, August 8, 2008: http://www.business-standard.com/article/economy-policy/navy-chief-says-indian-ocean-is-priority-not-south-china-sea-112080802019_1.html.

53. Arun Prakash, "India Must Pause before Entering into Choppy Waters," *Rediff News*, September 26, 2011. http://www.rediff.com/news/column/column-india-must-pause-before-venturing-into-choppy-waters/20110926.htm.

54. Iskander Rehman, *Shaping the Emerging World Order: India and Multilateralism* (Washington, DC: Brookings Institute, 2013), 144 and 147.

55. C. Raja Mohan, *Samudra Manthan: Sino-Indian Rivalry in the Indo-Pacific* (Washington DC: Carnegie Endowment for International Peace, 2012), 31.

VI

TRADE

Chapter 13

Trade and the Global Commons

It is often said that that Sino-Indian rivalry is sharpest closest to home. Bilateral issues of regional significance—the border dispute, Tibet, the China-Pakistan relationship—generate the most friction, while the multilateral arena provides the best forum for cooperation. Proponents of this theory point to Sino-Indian coordination at the Doha round of global trade talks and on their common agendas for climate change and distaste for foreign military interventions. India's voting record at the United Nations, they note, is far more congruent with China's than the United States'.

And yet, upon examination the case for a convergence of Chinese and Indian interests at the global level is quite thin. Ask Chinese and Indian officials to elaborate on their mutual global interests and the response is generally unenthusiastic and nonspecific. As Ashley Tellis argues, "The conventional wisdom about a Sino-Indian convergence on transnational issues vis-à-vis the West is considerably exaggerated. . . . The divide between Beijing and New Delhi may be just as significant on matters of global magnitude [as it is on bilateral regional matters]."[1]

True to form, as tensions between China and India spiked in the late 2000s, their rivalry broke out of the confines of the bilateral relationship and spilled into the multilateral arena. Indian analysts interviewed for this book identified Chinese attempts to thwart Indian initiatives at the Asian Development Bank (ADB) and the Nuclear Suppliers Group (NSG) as a material escalation of their regional competition. This chapter will briefly survey the minidisputes at the ADB and NSG before turning to two issues of materially greater significance to the Sino-Indian rivalry: water security and trade.

THE ASIAN DEVELOPMENT BANK (ADB)

The ADB is a sixty-seven-member regional institution modeled after the World Bank and created to help finance development projects in Asia. At a March 2009 board meeting of the ADB, the bank was to consider the merits of a $2.9 billion "country plan" loan to India. One of the largest recipients of ADB funds, India had never had a proposal blocked before.[2]

However, China, a board member of the bank and the institution's third-largest donor (India is the fourth-largest), objected to this particular loan as it included $60 million for a flood management, water supply, and sanitation project in Arunachal Pradesh. Beijing noted that the loan would have financed a project in territory claimed by China, and Chinese officials succeeded in postponing a vote until June.

India's mainstream newspapers called the dispute a "major confrontation,"[3] and Indian officials blasted China's position as "outrageous."[4] In anticipation of the June vote, Delhi sent demarches to sixty-six countries to cultivate support for the loan and insisted it would withdraw the entire proposal before dropping the project in Arunachal Pradesh. The *Indian Express* reported that the turning point at the ADB came when the United States, which holds the maximum voting share at the bank, rallied board members to support the loan. Save for China, all board members ultimately voted to approve the loan, including Pakistan, which feared backing a precedent that would deny ADB funds to "disputed areas."[5]

A Chinese foreign ministry spokesman said the bank's approval "cannot change the existence of the China-Indian territorial disputes,"[6] and a few months later China scored a small victory when it mustered enough votes to pass a "disclosure agreement" which prevented the ADB from formally acknowledging Arunachal Pradesh as a part of India. This time, Japan, Australia, and several ASEAN countries voted with China.[7]

In isolation, the ADB dispute may have been dismissed as a routine diplomatic spat. But following on the heels of a similar controversy at the Nuclear Suppliers Group a year earlier, China's attempt to block the ADB loan to India seemed to confirm suspicions that, while Beijing has mastered the diplomatic language of Sino-Indian comity, its actions and policies revealed a country working actively against India's interests.

THE NUCLEAR SUPPLIERS GROUP

The boldest expression of the twenty-first-century U.S.-India partnership was the nuclear deal signed by President Bush and Prime Minister Singh in 2005. However, obtaining the signatures of the two leaders that July was just the first in a long series of domestic and international hurdles that had to be cleared in order to operationalize the deal. Specifically, as a nonsignatory to the Nuclear Nonproliferation Treaty, India was forced to obtain waivers or exemptions from two international nuclear regulatory bodies: the International Atomic Energy Agency (IAEA) and Nuclear Suppliers Group (NSG).

India obtained the necessary safeguards agreement from the IAEA with relative ease in the summer of 2008. But when the issue moved to the forty-seven-member NSG the following month to consider a "full-scope safeguards exemption," China opposed the waiver. During tense negotiations the evening of September 5, Chinese representatives walked out of the meeting. U.S. President George W. Bush personally phoned Chinese President Hu Jintao to lobby in support of the waiver, and the next morning, and "after it became clear that no other country would block [the resolution] and in the wake of U.S. and Indian diplomacy," Beijing relented, supporting the waiver.[8]

In a sign of Delhi's outrage at China's position, when Chinese Foreign Minister Yang Jiechi visited India days later to inaugurate a new Chinese consulate in Kolkata, he was denied a visit with Congress Party President Sonia Gandhi. C. Raja Mohan argues that of all China's provocations in the late 2000s, its "attempt to undermine the U.S. effort to secure a waiver for India" at the NSG was "Beijing's worst transgression."[9]

One year after the U.S-India nuclear deal was signed, speaking at a public forum Pakistani Prime Minister Shaukat Aziz "referred to Newton's third law of motion—every action has an equal and opposite reaction—and explained a strong Sino-Pak relationship is a natural reaction of the Indo-U.S. relationship."[10] The comments foreshadowed China's response to the U.S.-India nuclear deal, revealed in the summer of 2010. Beijing would have a nuclear deal of its own with Pakistan, constructing two new nuclear plants in Pakistan at the Chashma facility, where it had already helped finance and build twin pressurized heavy water reactors,[11] Chashma I and II (online in 2000 and 2011).[12]

The Sino-Pakistan nuclear deal was controversial for a number of reasons. Unlike India, Pakistan hosted an abysmal nuclear proliferation record. Its top nuclear scientist, A. Q. Khan, is charged by U.S. and other Western intelligence agencies with running a world-class proliferation ring that exported nuclear weapons-related materials to Libya, Iran, and North Korea.[13]

Moreover, rather than pursue a similar set of exemptions for Pakistan at the IAEA and NSG, China chose simply to bypass the NSG by claiming the nuclear plants had been "grandfathered in" when China joined the NSG in 2004. The U.S. State Department countered that the construction of Chashma III and IV would be inconsistent with China's commitments to the NSG.[14] And nonproliferation experts deemed Beijing's "grandfather" rationale dubious, as "Beijing's 2004 explanations to the NSG did not mention grandfathering any more reactors" to Pakistan.[15]

Yet there was little India or the United States could do to force China to seek a waiver from the NSG, where it likely would have faced stiff resistance. As if to underscore this point, in June 2013 China announced it would build two new 1,100 megawatt nuclear reactors for Pakistan at Karachi (KANUPP 2 and 3). And again Chinese officials indicated they would not seek an NSG waiver. "The Chinese say all the right things and do all the wrong things," a senior Indian diplomat serving in Beijing told this author. "At a time when the world is deeply concerned about Pakistan's nuclear weapons, China is giving them more nukes."[16]

WATER

Though not yet a principal point of friction between China and India, bilateral concerns relating to water security have a potentially high upside risk for tension and conflict in the future.

Per capita, Asia is the most water-scarce region of the world. North America, for example, has more than four times the water per person, and South America over nine times as much. Yet, as Indian water security analyst Brahma Chellaney explains: "Water shortages were relatively unknown in Asia until the 1970s or even until the 1980s. It's only the last quarter of a century that water shortages have become apparent. So this is a new phenomenon; a phenomenon that has arisen because of the economic boom in Asia."[17]

India and China, the two most populous countries in the world, are particularly affected by regional water scarcity. India has 17.3 percent of the world's population but only 4.3 percent of the world's water supply, and its groundwater supplies—which make up eighty percent of its domestic water use[18]—are in rapid decline. A World Bank study warns 60 percent of India's aquifers could be in critical condition by 2030. By 2025 Indian per capita water availability may decline by 26 percent relative to 2001 levels.[19] China has only marginally more water per capita than India: 6.5 percent of global water resources for nearly 20 percent of the world's population. More important, China's water is unevenly distributed and of poor quality: as much as 40 percent of its water is unsuitable for drinking, industry, or agriculture, and over a third of Chinese provinces are "water scarce."[20] Meanwhile, China's north and northeast, with nearly a third of the country's population, have only 7 percent of its surface water.[21] In 1999, Wen Jiabao, then vice-premier, told a meeting of Chinese scientist and engineers that water scarcity threatened the "very survival of the Chinese nation."[22]

China has responded to this potential water crisis with some of the most ambitious and costly water-diversion and water-storage projects in the world. The 22,500 megawatt (MW) Three Gorges Dam, the world's largest hydropower project, is the most infamous of China's projects. But the most ambitious and technically-challenging may be the less-publicized Great South-North Water Transfer Project. Fifty years in the making, the project was formally launched in 2002 and as much as $34 billion has been invested as of early 2013.[23] The project envisions three lines to move water from China's south and west to the water-scarce north and east.

And it is this project which may have a direct bearing on India, for China's water-rich southwest provides freshwater not only to China, but to much of the Indian subcontinent as well. Most of China's fresh water supplies are located on what is sometimes referred to as the "third pole," the Tibetan plateau, whose 12,000 cubic kilometers of freshwater are the largest reserves on the six populated continents.[24] This gives China control over the headwaters of ten of Asia's largest and most essential rivers—including the Indus, Ganges, Brahmaputra, Irrawaddy, Salween, Mekong, Yellow, Yangtze, Tarim, and Amu Darya. India is particularly dependent on the Ganges, Brahmaputra, and Indus: one-third of India's water supply—and over half of the water supply of India's north—originates in Tibet.

As it stands today, the Great South-North Water Transfer Project poses little threat to India's water supply. Neither the Eastern Route (which is expected to be completed in 2013), nor the Middle Route (due to be completed in late 2014) divert water from Tibet. The proposed Western Route (still in the developmental phase) would transfer water from the Yangtse River to the Yalong River and from the Yalong and Dadu rivers to the Yellow River, none of which would, in theory, affect India's water supply.

However, several Chinese academics have proposed different variations on a western water diversion scheme which could impact the Brahmaputra River, which flows into India's northeast from Tibet.[25] Yet the Western Route remains by far the most challenging and controversial of the proposed routes, and may well never come to fruition. In 2006 China's own water resources minister bluntly admitted that the Western Route was "unnecessary, unscientific and not feasible."[26]

However, even in the absence of a water-diverting Western Route, India has expressed concerns over more conventional Chinese dam projects on the Brahmaputra River. China is, in short, on a damming spree: over half of the 50,000 large dams in the world are in China, which is expected to spend $600 billion on water infrastructure development through 2020.[27]

This is problematic insofar as China does not have a single water-sharing arrangement with any of its neighbors, and has demonstrated a troubling lack of transparency in its dam-building. Beijing, for instance,

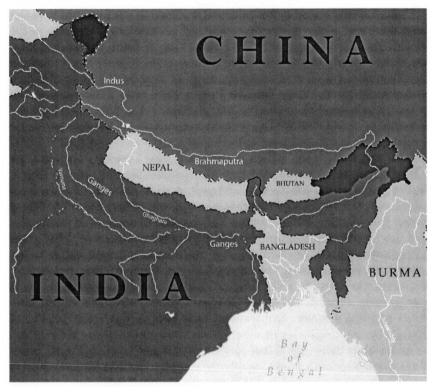

Map 13.1. China and India Cross-Border Rivers
Source: American Foreign Policy Council

denied the construction of a dam on the Brahmaputra river at Zangmu for years, despite being provided with satellite images clearly indicating the construction of a dam at the site. Then, in 2010, Chinese officials made an about-face and admitted they had constructed a 510 MW run-of-the-river dam at Zangmu.[28]

Beijing, it should be noted, *does* have a handful of modest information-sharing agreements with India. In 2002 the two countries signed a five-year Memorandum of Understanding (MoU) in which China agreed to provide India twice-daily email reports on water flows on the Brahmaputra during the flood season (June 1 to October 15).[29] The MoU was renewed in 2008 for an additional five years and again for an equal term in June 2013.[30] Similar MoUs on the Sutlej River were signed in 2005 and 2010.[31] However, India is pressing China for the creation of more substantive institutional mechanisms like a water commission or intergovernment dialogue, of which China has so far proven unreceptive.

Absent these institutional mechanisms, the Zangmu episode has fed speculation in India that China will begin a damming spree on the Brahmaputra—as many as twenty-eight dams have been proposed by Chinese hydropower lobbying groups[32]—giving it the power to cut off the water supply to India's northeast. These fears were further stoked in January 2013 when China's State Council approved plans for three additional dams on the Brahmaputra, at Dagu, Jiacha, and Jiexy.[33]

However, the proposal that has sparked the most feverish speculation in India is a rumored plan by Sinohydro, a state-owned hydropower company, to build a gigantic 38,000 MW dam on the "Great Bend" of the Brahmaputra where the river takes a sharp U-turn where water falls over steep gorges for 1,000 meters near the Indian border. The proposed dam is said to have nearly double the capacity of the Three Gorges Dam.

Yet there are three reasons that the immediate water-security concerns of Indian analysts may be overblown.

First, most experts agree that the steep technical, financial, and environmental challenges associated with building a dam at the "Great Bend" have, at least for the time being, rendered the project untenable.

Second, all of the current dams planned by China on the Brahmaputra are run-of-the-river (RoR) projects. Unlike conventional hydroelectric dams, RoR dams typically involve no—or very limited—water storage. In other words, their ability to impact water flows downstream is negligible. Indian Prime Minister Manmohan Singh has publicly acknowledged that current Chinese plans to dam the Brahmaputra would not affect water flows.[34]

Perhaps more important—and often overlooked—is the recognition that most of the water that feeds the Brahmaputra enters the river *after* it has crossed the Indian border in Arunachal Pradesh. Though the Brahmaputra flows for 1,625 kilometers in Tibet and only 918 kilometers in India,[35] "almost eighty percent of the catchment of Brahmaputra river is in India," Indian External Affairs Minister S. M. Krishna observed in 2009.[36]

As they currently stand, China's dam projects are not poised to affect water flow into India, and the ones with the potential to do so—variations on the western line of the Great South-North Water Transfer project and a massive dam at the "Great Bend" of the Brahmaputra—remain pipe dreams. Nevertheless, in the short term one can expect the Indian media to continue to stir fear and speculation about China's water plans, and China to continue to fuel that speculation by stonewalling more formal institutional agreements on water-sharing with India.

THE FAILURE OF ECONOMIC INTERDEPENDENCE

This book is primarily concerned with the elements of geopolitical rivalry in Sino-Indian relations. A comprehensive examination of the bilateral economic relationship not only falls outside the limited focus of this work, but is a task better handled by a trained economist.

However, one question regarding the economic relationship has a direct bearing on this project: namely, why has the rapid growth in bilateral trade and investment not done more to ameliorate the political and security tensions that shadow the relationship? After all, China is now India's largest trading partner, up from seventh place at the turn of the century. After a surge from $1 billion in trade in 1998 to $74 billion in trade in 2011, a commitment by both capitals to expand trade to $100 billion by 2015 looked like a conservative estimate before trade took a modest downturn in 2012.

Students of political economy would predict that this deepening economic integration should have raised the costs of conflict and rivalry, and created powerful constituencies in each country lobbying for a more harmonious political relationship. And yet, elements of rivalry are as prevalent today as they were two decades ago, when bilateral trade was negligible.

Officials and analysts from both countries interviewed for this book suggested that while the growth in trade and investment was undoubtedly a positive development, the unbalanced nature of the economic relationship ensured that it has remained as much a source of tension as a pacifying agent.

Terms of Trade

India was running minor trade surpluses with China as late as 2004–2005, before the trade balance began to tilt decisively in China's favor. Since 2006, China's trade surplus with India has ballooned, principally because Indian imports from China have substantially outpaced Chinese imports from India. In 2012, China's exports to India totaled $48 billion while India's exports to China totaled only $19 billion.[37] This represented a proportionally large trade deficit of $29 billion and one that is growing by the year.

China, in other words, exports more than two and a half times as much to India as India does to China. Excluding oil imports, China now accounts for half of India's global trade deficit.[38] The problem, notes the *Economist*, is that "India does not produce much that China wants to buy" while "investment flows are negligible."[39]

Though economists rightly caution against viewing modest trade deficits and surpluses as inherently negative or positive, there is a strong correlation between trade imbalances and political tensions. "Although the manifold increase in trade has been a lubricant to the overall relationship, the increasing adverse trade imbalance . . . has been a matter of concern to India," writes Indian security analyst Rup Narayan Das.[40] A former In-

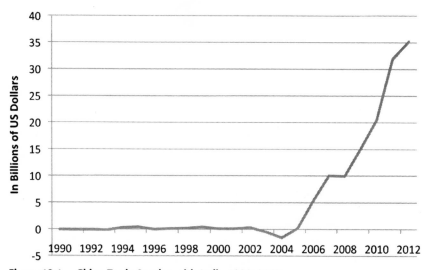

Figure 13.1.   China Trade Surplus with India 1990–2012
Source: IMF Direction of Trade Statistics (accessed August 5, 2013).http://elibrary-data.imf

dian Foreign Secretary put it more bluntly in a presentation to South Asia experts at the Heritage Foundation in October, 2012: "Trade with China is so imbalanced it is not useful for us."[41]

For its part, China has acknowledged the political costs of the growing trade deficit and insists it is taking active measures to correct the imbalance. "There exists a trade imbalance between China and India, but China does not purposefully seek a trade surplus and has been actively expanding imports from India," said Chinese Commerce Minister Chen Deming in 2008.[42] However, the deficit has continued to soar since Minister Chen's remarks, and the lopsided trade relationship continues to be a top agenda item for India at bilateral meetings.

"We are waiting for our Chuck Schumer to appear and start railing against Chinese trade practices and making threats," a senior Indian diplomat explained to this writer, referring to the U.S. Senator from New York who has been an outspoken critic of Chinese trade practices. "It will happen. It's inevitable. The Chinese are completely insensitive to trade issues."[43]

Composition of Trade

Over three-quarters of Indian exports to China consist of raw materials and intermediate products. Copper and iron ore, slag and ash, cotton, plastics, synthetic fibers, and lead round out some of India's top exports to China.[44]

China's exports to India, in contrast, constitute a wide variety of sophisticated capital goods with higher profit margins. China's top exports to India in 2012 were telecom equipment, industrial equipment and heavy machinery, computers and computer parts, iron and steel, fertilizers, and air conditioners. "We are exporting primary raw materials to China, while it is exporting semi-finished products to us. . . . The trade with China is definitely skewed," Commerce Minister Anand Sharma told India's Upper House of Parliament in 2011.[45]

Relative Importance of Trade

Bilateral trade is far more important to India's economy than China's. Where China is now India's largest trading partner, in 2011–2012 India was only the ninth largest trading partner of China (counting ASEAN and the EU as single trading partners).[46]

China simply does not place a great deal of value on its trading relationship with India. At a relatively minor $48 billion, China's exports to India are one-tenth of the value of its annual exports to the United States, which reached $411 billion in 2011.[47] India accounts for just 2.5 percent of China's total world exports, which touched $2 trillion in 2012. Contrast this with the relatively high importance China places on sensitive political and security dynamics in the relationship—including Tibet, the Dalai Lama, and India's partnership with the United States—where cooperation is often overshadowed by competition.

And while Indian exports to China represent a more substantial 7 percent of its total foreign exports, Chinese investments in India are almost negligible. Between 2000 and 2012, Chinese investments in India totaled $135 million, while Japanese investments in India over that period were $13 billion.[48]

Market Access/Trade Friction

Finally, China and India regularly charge each other with erecting barriers to market access. India has accused China of flooding its market with cheap goods and has been a leading critic of Chinese dumping practices. In fact, no country has filed more complaints against China at the World Trade Organization than India. In December 2011, India's minister of state for commerce and industry told the Upper House of Parliament (Rajya Sabha) that seventy-seven antidumping measures were currently in force against China and that, of the 272 anti-dumping cases India had filed at the WTO since 1992, 149 were directed against China.[49] The *Wall*

Street Journal notes that from 2010 to 2012, India issued thirty-five dumping[50] complaints against Chinese firms and imposed duties twenty-two times to protect Indian goods.[51]

Delhi has frequently complained about the fact that IT and pharmaceutical companies—two areas of comparative advantage for India—have been "frozen out of the Chinese market." While Indian exports of pharmaceuticals to Western markets soared in the late 2000s, exports to China dropped by 12 percent between 2007 and 2012. India's ambassador to China says "registration processes are a deterrence to pharmaceutical exports" and "the Chinese duty structure is hard on value-added engineering products that are India's forte."[52]

China's principal complaints against India tend to focus on barriers to investment. This author recalls a Chinese professor from Renmin University drawing a back-of-the-envelope chart over dinner in Beijing. "If we estimate that the American economy is 90 percent open to trade, and the Chinese economy being 75 percent open, we would say India's is only 15 percent open. It is not at all a free market."[53]

In particular, China has complained of the extraordinary measures Delhi has taken to block investments from Chinese companies in sensitive infrastructure and telecommunications projects. China is said to be on a "blacklist" of countries posing unique security concerns whose investments have to go through a special process of examination and approval. In recent years the Indian government has intervened to veto Chinese proposals to set up hydro-electric plants in Himachal Pradesh and a tender for dredging of the Mazagon Dockyard. And former Chinese Ambassador to India Zheng Ruxiang says Delhi has banned telecom operators from purchasing equipment from Chinese telecom giants Huwaei Technologies and ZTE Corporation.[54]

A COMPLEX PICTURE

The quasiofficial Indian policy document *Nonalignment 2.0* succinctly summarized the China-India economic relationship as "present[ing] a complex and somewhat ambiguous picture."[55] The absolute, secular growth in the Sino-Indian economic relationship is likely to continue well into the twenty-first century, creating new avenues for cooperation, new personal and economic bonds, and marginally greater costs to conflict. However, given the record of the previous fifteen years, there is little evidence to suggest that the continued growth in trade and investment will materially affect the strategic mistrust that pervades the political and security spheres.

NOTES

1. Ashley J. Tellis and Sean Mirski, "Crux of Asia: China, India, and the Emerging Global Order," Carnegie Endowment: http://carnegieendowment .org/2013/01/10/crux-of-asia-china-india-and-emerging-global-order/f0gw.

2. Sudha Ramachandran, "Chinese Antics Have India Fuming," *Asia Times,* May 5, 2009 (Accessed April 24, 2013): http://www.atimes.com/atimes/South_ Asia/KE05Df01.html.

3. Pranab Dhal Samanta, "India-China Face-off Worsens over ADB Loan for Arunachal," *Indian Express,* May 15, 2009: http://www.indianexpress.com/ news/indiachina-faceoff-worsens-over-adb-loan-for-arunachal/459910/.

4. "India Lashes Out on China for Blocking ADB Loan" *Siasat Daily,* July 1, 2009: http://www.siasat.com/english/content/india-lashes-out-china-blocking -adb-loan.

5. Pranab Dhal Samanta, "China Says No but US, Japan Help ADB Clear India's Plan," *Times of India,* June 16, 2009 (Accessed April 24, 2013): http://www .indianexpress.com/news/china-says-no-but-us-japan-help-adb-clear-indias -plan/477252/.

6. Saurabhi Joshi, "China Blasts ADB approval for Arunachal Loan: Report," *StratPost,* June 18, 2009 (Accessed April 24, 2013): http://www.stratpost.com/ china-blasts-adb-approval-for-arunachal-loan-report.

7. Roy Shubhajit, "Aussie Vote Not Anti-India, Just Pro-ADB: New Envoy," *Indian Express,* September 25, 2009 (Accessed April 24, 2013): http://www.indian express.com/news/aussie-vote-not-antiindia-just-proadb-new-envoy/521250.

8. M. Taylor Fravel, "China Views India's Rise: Deepening Cooperation, Managing Differences," *Strategic Asia 2011–12* (September 2011) 87.

9. C. Raja Mohan, *Sumdra Manthan: Sino-Indian Rivalry in the Pacific* (Washington, DC: Carnegie Endowment for International Peace, 2012), 222.

10. John Tkacik, "The Enemy of Hegemony Is My Friend: Pakistan's *de facto* 'Alliance' with China," Testimony before the House Committee on Foreign Affairs Oversight and Investigations Subcommittee, July 26, 2011: http://www. strategycenter.net/research/pubID.257/pub_detail.asp.

11. Pakistan has had a third Canadian-origin nuclear plant in operation near Karachi since 1971.

12. "Nuclear Power in Pakistan," *World Nuclear Association,* May 2012 (Accessed April 24, 2013): http://www.world-nuclear.org/info/inf108.html.

13. "The Khan Network," paper by David Sanger submitted to the Conference on South Asia and the Nuclear Future, June 4–5, Stanford University: http:// iis-db.stanford.edu/evnts/3889/Khan_network-paper.pdf.

14. Daniel Horner, "Chinese-Pakistani Reactor Deal Moves Ahead," *Arms Control Association,* April 2011 (Accessed April 24, 2013): http://www.armscontrol .org/print/4783.

15. Fred McGoldrick, "Road Ahead for Export Controls: Challenges for the Nuclear Suppliers Group," *Arms Control Association,* January/February 2011 (Accessed April 24, 2013): http://www.armscontrol.org/act/2011_01-02/McGoldrick.

16. Senior Indian diplomat. Author interview. Beijing, February 2012.

17. The Brookings Institute, "Water: Asia's New Battleground," transcript Brahma Chellaney, January 24, 2013.

18. Kenneth Pomeranz, "The Great Himalayan Watershed: Agrarian Crisis, Mega-Dams and the Environment," *New Left Review*, Vol. 58, July–August 2009: 8.

19. "India Groundwater: A Valuable but Diminishing Resource," March 6, 2012: http://www.worldbank.org/en/news/feature/2012/03/06/india-ground water-critical-diminishing.

20. Brahma Chellaney, *Water: Asia's New Battleground* (Washington, DC: Georgetown University Press, 2011).

21. Kenneth Pomeranz, "The Great Himalayan Watershed: Agrarian Crisis, Mega-Dams and the Environment," *New Left Review*, Vol. 58, July–August 2009: 8.

22. Kenneth Pomeranz, "The Great Himalayan Watershed: Agrarian Crisis, Mega-Dams and the Environment," *New Left Review*, July 26, 2011, Vol. 58, July–August 2009: 8.

23. "Costly Drops," *Economist*, February 7, 2013: http://www.econo mist.com/news/china/21571437-removing-salt-seawater-might-help-slake -some-northern-chinas-thirst-it-comes-high.

24. Sophie le Clue, "Geopolitical Risks: Transboundary Rivers," *China Water Risk*, February 9, 2012.

25. Zhe Kang, "Diversion Debate," *ChinaDialogue*, June 13, 2011: http://www .chinadialogue.net/article/show/single/en/4349-Diversion-debate.

26. "China Turns to Salt Water to Ease Drought," *ChinaDaily.com*, November 31, 2006: http://www.chinadaily.com.cn/china/2006-10/31/content_720980.htm.

27. Wai-Shin Chan, Nick Robins, and Zoe Knight, "HSBC Global Research, No Water, No Power," *HSBC Global Research*, September 2012.

28. Indrani Bagchi, "China Admits to Brahmaputra Project," *Times of India*. April 21, 2010: http://articles.timesofindia.indiatimes.com/2010-04-22/india/ 28126091_1_zangmu-brahmaputra-india-and-china.

29. "South Asia's Waters: Unquenchable Thirst," *Economist*, November 16, 2011: http://www.economist.com/node/21538687.

30. Gargi Parsai, "India, China Renew Flood Data Pact on Brahmaputra," *The Hindu*, May 20, 2013: http://www.thehindu.com/news/national/india-china -renew-flood-data-pact-on-brahmaputra/article4732965.ece.

31. Avilash Roul,"India-China Hydro Diplomacy: Beyond Information Sharing MoUs," SSPC, March 22, 2013: http://sspconline.org/opinion/IndiaChinaHydro Diplomacy_22032013.

32. Ananth Krishan, "China's Tourism Plan Quells Brahmaputra Dam Fears," *Hindu*, June 24, 2012: http://www.thehindu.com/news/international/ chinas-tourism-plan-quells-brahmaputra-dam-fears/article3566337.ece.

33. Ananth Krishan,"China Gives Go-Ahead for Three New Brahmaputra Dams," *Hindu*, January 30, 2013: http://www.thehindu.com/news/international/china -gives-goahead-for-three-new-brahmaputra-dams/article4358195.ece.

34. "PM Allays Fears on Chinese Dam-Building on Brahmaputra," *Times of India*, March 29, 2013: http://articles.timesofindia.indiatimes.com/2013-03-29/ india/38124666_1_brics-brahmaputra-new-chinese-president.

35. Saurabh Dubey, "Chinese Dam on Brahmaputra India Outraged. But the Government Reacts Meekly," *Tibet Third Pole*: http://tibet.org/tibet3rdpole .org/?p=548.

36. "'China Building Airstrips along LAC,' Govt Says No Need to Worry," *Times of India*, December 1, 2009: http://articles.timesofindia.indiatimes.com/2009-12 -01/india/28094065_1_airstrips-line-of-actual-control-china.

37. Sutirtho Patranobis, "India's Iron Ore Export to China Falls, Decreases Bilateral Trade," *Hindustan Times*, January 21, 2013 (Accessed April 15, 2013): http://www.hindustantimes.com/world-news/China/India-s-iron-ore-export -to-China-falls-decreases-bilateral-trade/Article1-997781.aspx.

38. "Friend, Enemy, Rival, Investor," *Economist*, June 30, 2012 (Accessed April 15, 2013): http://www.economist.com/node/21557764.

39. "Friend, Enemy, Rival, Investor," *Economist*, June 30, 2012 (Accessed April 15, 2013): http://www.economist.com/node/21557764.

40. R. N. Das, "Sino-Indian Trade: Smoothing the Rough Edges," Institute for Defence Studies Analyses, September 27, 2011 (Accessed April 15, 2013): http:// www.idsa.in/idsacomments/SinoIndianTradeSmootheningtheRoughEdges_rnd as_270911#footnoteref2_6byynby.

41. Roundtable conference at the Heritage Foundation, October 5, 2012.

42. Ding Qingfen, "China, India to Narrow Trade Gap," *China Daily*, August 30, 2012 (Accessed April 15, 2013): http://usa.chinadaily.com.cn/business/ 2012-08/30/content_15718053.htm.

43. Senior Indian diplomat. Author interview. Beijing, February 2012.

44. Global Trade Information Services Inc., *Global Trade Atlas* (Accessed August 5, 2013): http://www.gtis.com/GTA/.

45. Mandip Singh, "China Year Book 2011," Institute for Defence Studies and Analyses, May 2012 (Accessed April 15, 2013): http://www.idsa.in/system/ files/book_Chinayear2011.pdf.

46. "Statistical Communiqué on the 2011 National Economic and Social Development," National Bureau of Statistics of China, February 22, 2012 (Accessed April 15, 2013): http://www.stats.gov.cn/english/newsandcomingevents/ t20120222_402786587.htm.

47. "The People's Republic of China," Office of the United States Trade Representative, April 15, 2013: http://www.ustr.gov/countries-regions/china -mongolia-taiwan/peoples-republic-china.

48. Prasenjit Bhattacharya, "China Looks to Increase India Investments," *Wall Street Journal, India Real Time*, November 27, 2012: http://blogs.wsj.com/india realtime/2012/11/27/china-looks-to-increase-india-investments/.

49. "149 Anti-Dumping Cases against China Highest among Foreign Nations: Govt," *Economic Times*, December 21, 2011 (Accessed April 15, 2013): http:// articles.economictimes.indiatimes.com/2011-12-21/news/30542669_1_anti -dumping-measures-dgad-anti-dumping-probes.

50. "Dumping" is when a country exports products at below-market rates or at a cheaper price than it charges in its home market

51. "Trade Gap Strains India-China Ties," *Wall Street Journal*, August 3, 2012 (Accessed April 15, 2013): http://online.wsj.com/article/SB100008723963904436 87504577563542149677000.html.

52. Ambassador S. Jaishankar, Institute of South Asian Studies, "Special Address by Dr. S. Jaishankar, India's Ambassador to China, at the Institute of South Asian Studies (ISAS) Symposium on India-China Relations, held on November 23, 2012, 10.00 am at the National Library Building," 2013: http://www.isas.nus.edu.sg/Attachments/PublisherAttachment/Address_by_Amb_S_Jaishankar_Address_(23Nov12)FINAL_30112012133458.pdf.

53. Renmin University professor. Author interview. Beijing, February 2012.

54. Heather Timmons, "India Tells Mobile Firms to Delay Deals for Chinese Telecom Equipment," *New York Times*, April 30, 2010 (Accessed April 15, 2013): http://www.nytimes.com/2010/05/01/business/global/01delhi.html?_r=0 .

55. Sunil Khilnani, Rajiv Kumar, and Pratap Bhanu Mehta, "Nonalignment 2.0: A Foreign and Strategic Policy for India in the 21st Century," January 30, 2012: 14 (Accessed April 15, 2013): http://www.cprindia.org/sites/default/files/NonAlignment percent202.0_1.pdf.

Executive Summary

The Sino-Indian relationship bears little resemblance to the conventional inter-state rivalry epitomized by the United States and the Soviet Union during the Cold War. It lacks even the passion and sharp edges of the modern Sino-Japanese or Indo-Pakistan rivalries. Yet the trappings of rivalry are still an important—and at times predominant—feature of bilateral relations. The most apt comparison is likely the contemporary Sino-U.S. relationship, where economic and diplomatic ties flourish despite the prevalence of geopolitical tensions and strategic mistrust.

Also like the Sino-U.S. relationship, the Sino-Indian relationship is characterized by asymmetry and imbalance, only in this case China holds nearly all the material advantages. In measurements of comprehensive national power China is as far ahead of India as the U.S. is ahead of China, underscoring a stark imbalance in threat perceptions.

However, India holds a soft power advantage with the potential to one day offset China's hard power advantages. China and India are both billion-person-plus Asian giants with expanding spheres of economic and geopolitical interests. Both have a history of regional hegemony and both are fielding new aircraft carriers, new nuclear submarines, and longer-range ballistic missiles. Yet each country's spectacular rise is being received by the world and the international system very differently.

Despite its vocal commitment to a "peaceful rise" and burgeoning economic relations with all its neighbors, China's ascent has sparked a wave of security concerns across the Indo-Pacific. As a result, despite decades of relative peace and prosperity, Asia has quietly slipped into the world's most active arms race. In 2012, for the first time ever, military expenditures in Asia exceeded those of the European Union. In fact, every one of top five arms importers between 2007 and 2012 were Asian countries.[1]

This phenomenon reflects regional anxieties about China, but it also emphasizes how differently the world perceives China and India: It was not Beijing that was the world's largest importer of arms from 2007 to 2012, but Delhi.[2] And yet, outside of Pakistan, India's robust military modernization has not provoked any major security concerns; quite the opposite. India is arguably enjoying a more favorable position in the international court of public opinion today than at any point since independence in 1947.

The irony of India's soft power windfall is that it is less the product of any Indian initiative than the way in which China's rise (and the collapse of the Soviet Union) has altered the paradigm in which the international community has come to view India. For much of the Cold War India was derided in the West as a cantankerous overlord of the subcontinent; a virtual client of the USSR locked in an intractable rivalry with Pakistan. However, viewed in the post–Cold War context of an Indo-Pacific region falling under the shadow of China's rise, India has come to be seen as the passive, friendly, multiethnic democracy that could serve as a valuable external balancer to the Middle Kingdom.

How effectively Delhi will leverage this soft power to achieve its objectives regarding China remains an open question. In fact, Delhi has yet to properly define its objectives vis-à-vis Beijing; its China policy has always been reactive rather than proactive. To date, Indian policy has been defined by what it *doesn't* want China to do, and that list has grown larger in the young twenty-first century.

- Stop claims to the border town of Tawang, stop stonewalling the border negotiations process by refusing to exchange maps, and stop the policy of aggressive border patrolling.
- Stop stapling visas to residents of Arunachal Pradesh and denying visas to officials from Arunachal Pradesh.
- Stop strategic assistance to Pakistan and infrastructure projects in Pakistan-occupied Kashmir.
- Stop undermining Indian authority in neighboring countries.
- Stop the antipiracy mission in the Indian Ocean once the threat from piracy has abated.
- Stop being the only member of the UN Security Council to refuse to endorse a permanent seat for India at the council.
- Stop challenging India at multilateral forums like the Asian Development Bank and Nuclear Suppliers Group, and stop demanding that Pakistan get a seat at the table whenever India is granted one.

- Stop the onslaught of cyber-attacks, cyber-spying, and cyber-theft that stem from within China's borders.
- Stop stonewalling a water-sharing treaty, and be more transparent in plans to build dams on the Brahmaputra river.
- Stop trade practices that have hindered Indian exports to China and caused severe imbalances in the trading relationship.

WHAT DOES CHINA WANT FROM INDIA?

What will most define Sino-Indian relations in the twenty-first century is not what India does and wants, but China. China has always been the independent variable and the driver of events in contemporary Sino-Indian relations. And India has always struggled to interpret and react to Chinese policies.

So what does China want from India? Officials in Beijing insist their principal aspiration is to pursue a qualitatively improved relationship with Delhi through cooperation, consultation, enhanced trust and mutual understanding. Asia, they say, will only prosper if China and India rise together. On paper it is a commendable goal, and at times Beijing has supported this rhetoric with action. But is a better relationship with Delhi an authentic objective of Chinese policy, or merely a diplomatic slogan to disguise less benign intentions?

This author believes that improved ties with India *are* a genuine goal for many of China's political and economic elite. However, this assumption carries two caveats. First, the desire for better relations does not necessarily extend to China's increasingly influential nationalists, for whom India is an irritant and a troublemaker. They believe India—a second-rate power—has not shown sufficient deference to China on its core interests, and they may one day come to covet Tawang and "Southern Tibet" with the same fervor they are now directing at China's maritime territorial disputes.

Second, even those in China who genuinely want a better working relationship with India do so under the condition that Delhi acknowledge its place in what China's elite see as the natural Asian hierarchy, and adjust its policies accordingly. "A leading regional power, India intends to assume a bigger role in South Asia. But that raises the question of how India is going to use its increasing power," noted an OpEd in the *Global Times* in 2012. "*The dominance India is seeking has to be conducive to the equilibrium of the current international order* [emphasis added]."[3]

For many Chinese elite, India's place in that order is several rungs below China's, and given its rank as a middle-tier power Chinese officials expect India to:

- Stop allowing the Dalai Lama and the Tibetan Government in Exile to conduct "political activities."
- Stop exploring for energy in Pacific waters claimed by China.
- Stop the trend toward closed-door security dialogues and multilateral military exercises with the U.S. and its allies in East Asia.
- Stop trade protectionist practices.
- Stop the Indian media from provoking anti-Chinese sentiments and from sensationalizing everything from border incursions to China's "String of Pearls."
- Stop adding new military forces and infrastructure along the disputed Line of Actual Control.
- Stop offering moral support for the Tibetan cause, and put a stop to any talk of playing the "Tibet card."
- Stop trying to prevent neighboring countries from establishing stronger political, economic, and military ties to Beijing.
- Stop laying claim to Aksai Chin, and prepare to cede at least part of Arunachal Pradesh—including Tawang—to China in a package deal to resolve the border dispute.

THE POTENTIAL FOR CONFLICT

It is unlikely the twenty-first century will witness a large-scale conflict between China and India. Nuclear weapons, economic interdependence, cautious political leadership, and geography all raise formidable barriers to military conflict.

For the time being, neither the political elite nor the general public in either country has any appetite for conflict. Even if they did, the practical constraints are manifold. Neither military is capable of sustaining a major land offensive deep into the other's territory for a prolonged period of time. Such an operation would require maintaining long ground-lines-of-communication (GLOCS) vulnerable to air assault across Himalayan passes rendered impassable for several months out of the year.[4]

Similarly, neither the Chinese nor the Indian Navy is in a position to challenge the other in their opponent's immediate neighborhood, where each state enjoys a considerable "home-field advantage" in terms of air support, land-based missiles, and logistics. Both navies lack the "blue water" resupply and logistics capabilities to sustain large-scale operations thousands of kilometers from their shores. Perhaps most important, these limitations are well-understood by the political and military leadership in both countries.

However, if the bar to total war is almost inconceivably high, the possibility of localized or limited conflict is not, and the prospect for increased tensions on multiple fronts is not only possible but likely. What follows is a list of the scenarios most likely to produce limited conflict in the near- to mid-term, followed by a table outlining potential triggers of further tensions.

Table 14.1.   Potential Limited Conflict Scenarios

Scenario	Threat Level
Chinese intervention in another Indo-Pakistan War	Low
A limited Chinese offensive at the border, possibly to seize Tawang	Low
An accidental or unexpected clash by patrols at the LAC leading to an escalation	Low-Medium
A naval incident in the South China Sea or Indian Ocean leading to an escalation	Low-Medium
The succession of the Dalai Lama or a turn toward militancy from the Tibetan exile community in India sparking retaliatory measures from China	Low-Medium

Table 14.2.   Potential Triggers of Further Tensions

Scenario	Potential to Trigger Tensions
The Dalai Lama succession issue, including potential for heightened Tibetan militancy, and the next Dalai Lama being picked in Tawang	High
New Indian energy exploration projects in waters claimed by China	Medium-High
The establishment of formal basing arrangements for the PLA Navy in the Indian Ocean	Medium
Continued disturbances and intrusions at the Line of Actual Control	High
Increased defense collaboration and multilateral security between India and the United States, Japan, Australia, and others in East Asia	Medium-High
Increased defense collaboration and multilateral security exercises between China and Pakistan, Nepal, Sri Lanka, and Bangladesh	Medium-High
Continued sparring in the global commons: cyber, space, water, multilateral forums (UNSC, ADB, NSG, WTO)	High
New trade tensions	High
Continued or accelerated unrest on the Tibetan plateau	Medium-High
Heightened Chinese nationalism pushing China toward a harder line on the border dispute	Medium-High
Heightened tensions over water security stemming from Chinese dams on the Brahmaputra or reduced water supply due to climate change	Medium-High

THE DANGER OF COMPLACENCY

It should be encouraging to both sides that despite the prevalence of competition and rivalry, the risk of major conflict remains quite low. This is due in no small part to one of the most encouraging dynamics in Sino-Indian relations: the commitment of the political elite in both countries to manage and mitigate tensions in the relationship. In India, where anti-Chinese sentiments are more prevalent, the phenomenon is even more pronounced, with the political elite serving as important restraining agents, downplaying tensions and dismissing talk of rivalry.

However, in its current form this trend carries downside risks as well. This analyst witnessed a troubling ambivalence among officials from both countries regarding the prevalence of anti-Chinese and anti-Indian sentiments, which were all too often dismissed as minority views with little impact on policy and those who craft it. They seemed content that a handful of diplomats would be capable of managing the contentious relationship behind closed doors in perpetuity, irrespective of popular sentiments.

Yet, in India in particular, the roots of anti-Chinese sentiments run deep and permeate nearly all sectors of Indian society, including the military. "Our intellectuals keep talking about 'deep civilizational links' that can't be broken. They use polite excuses each time China provokes us, dismissing it as a 'normal phenomenon.' The [Indian] military doesn't believe that for a second," a lieutenant general in the Indian Army told this writer over lunch, expressing a cynicism heard in multiple interviews for this book.[5]

Dismissing this level of hostility as inconsequential—73 percent of Indians surveyed in a 2013 poll saw China as a "big threat"[6]—may prove costly. Chapter 4, "The Elusive Settlement," demonstrated how public animus was already materially restricting the flexibility of *both* governments to pursue territorial concessions and, by consequence, resolving the world's largest border dispute. And while anti-Indian sentiment is comparatively less pronounced in China, nearly two-thirds of Chinese polled by Pew in 2012 reported an "unfavorable" view of India.[7] Among China's influential nationalists, disdain for India is more widespread, and more intensely felt.

The risk is that the mistrust simmering just beneath the surface leaves the two countries with a dangerously thin margin for error. China and India have crafted mature and sophisticated mechanisms for managing their rivalry, and a framework that allows them to pursue low-cost, mutually beneficial cooperation despite it. But it's unclear how durable that framework will prove if seriously tested in the future, under different leadership in either country.

chan policy back fire?

The two sides have at times struggled to contain the rivalry *with* committed and practical leadership in both capitals. But as China and India ascend the development ladder faster than any two countries of their size before them, history suggests a turbulent ride awaits them. It is inevitable each will face challenges in the form of civil and social unrest, terrorism, separatism, religious strife, demographic challenges, income inequality, water scarcity and economic downturns. If these forces result in the emergence of more nationalist or xenophobic leadership in either country, the margin for error in Sino-Indian relations grows even thinner, and the temptation to channel negative energy toward perceived external enemies grows stronger. And as each country's expanding spheres of interest and influence increasingly come to occupy the same space, the lure of rivalry is likely to grow stronger.

Stonewalling an exchange of maps and shelving the border dispute for "future generations" to decide, avoiding signing a water-sharing agreement, failing to reach a modus vivendi on the Dalai Lama and Tibetan Government in Exile, and failing to come up with cooperative mechanisms on maritime security in anticipation that conditions will prove more conducive in the future may prove a costly error in judgment. Time, in this case, may not be on their side.

SINO-INDIAN RELATIONS IN THE TWENTY-FIRST CENTURY

- China and India are more politically and economically engaged than at any point in contemporary history. Chinese President Hu Jintao and Indian Prime Minister Manmohan Singh had twenty-six face-to-face meetings during Hu's term in office (2002–2012) and the two countries now have thirty-six separate dialogues in place. Trade expanded 74-fold from 1998 to 2012, and the Chinese and Indian armies held joint exercises for the first time in history in 2007, 2008, and 2013. The two capitals have begun to cooperate on issues of mutual interest at the global level, most notably on world trade talks, climate change negotiations, the primacy of state sovereignty, and the need to reform global governance institutions.

- Yet, like the Sino-U.S. relationship, China-India relations do not exist in a zero-sum universe: cooperation and competition coexist side by side, at times advancing in tandem on parallel tracks. And the competitive aspect of Sino-Indian relations is in some arenas advancing even faster the than cooperative aspect.

- After a period characterized by cooperation and confidence-building from 2000 to 2005, elements of rivalry returned to the forefront of China-India relations from 2006 to 2013. The stalling of negotiations over their longstanding border dispute, Chinese insecurities in Tibet, the Chinese ambassador to India's claims on "all of Arunachal Pradesh," and an Indian arms and infrastructure buildup at the border, combined with other developments to undermine at least some of the progress made in the early 2000s.

- The traditional "core disputes"—the disputed border, Tibet, China's support for Pakistan—have been joined by a host of new friction points, including India's strategic partnership with the United States, a growing conflict of interests in the maritime arena, Indian oil exploration in waters claimed by China, water security, the People's Liberation Army Navy's antipiracy mission in the Indian Ocean, the Dalai Lama succession issue, and jousting at multilateral forums, among others.

- The Sino-Indian relationship is characterized by asymmetry and imbalance. In most relevant indicators, the gap between China and India is as large or larger than the gap between China and the United States. Measured by Gross Domestic Product (GDP), China's economy was over four times the size of India's in 2012. China's official military budget of $119 billion was over three times larger than India's $38 billion defense budget in 2013. India has over double the poverty rate (29.8 percent versus 13.4 percent) and only two-thirds the literacy rate (61 percent versus 92 percent).

- Favorable demographics are likely to put India in a position to close the strategic gap with China by mid-century. In 2012 India's working-age population grew by twelve million while China's shrank by three million and a June 2013 UN report on world population prospects predicts India's population will surpass China's by 2028.

- The current disparity in "comprehensive national power" underscores a yawning gap in threat perceptions. While public polling suggests Pakistan still narrowly edges out China as the top threat in the eyes of the Indian public, among many in India's national security establishment China has comfortably surpassed Pakistan as the country's principal security threat. India, by contrast, ranks considerably lower in China's threat matrix, though there are indications it is making a gradual climb up the ranks of China's strategic priorities.

- Though Indian leaders speak the diplomatic language of Sino-Indian comity, their actions reveal a country deeply concerned about China's rise. For the past five years India has been the world's largest importer of arms, despite an overwhelming superiority over Pakistan in conventional arms. Nearly all the major initiatives to improve India's military infrastructure are taking place at India's border with China, not Pakistan.

- In 2009 India added two new mountain infantry divisions to the Eastern Sector, followed by an announcement in 2013 that India would raise its first 50,000-person offensive Strike Corps, also to be deployed in the Eastern Sector. India's naval modernization is geared toward power projection capabilities and the ability to meet a challenge from a large conventional force. And in the strategic arms arena, India is developing longer-range ballistic missiles capable of reaching targets upward of 5,000 kilometers, despite having all of Pakistan covered by its short- and medium-range missile arsenal.
- The Chinese and Indian people still hold overwhelmingly negative views toward one another. A Lowy Institute Poll released in May 2013 reports less than a third of Indians (31 percent) felt China's rise had been good for India, while 65 percent felt India should "join other countries to limit China's influence." Some 73 percent of Indians surveyed thought war with China was a "big threat" and 70 percent thought China's aim was "to dominate Asia." Meanwhile, a 2012 Pew Research poll found 62 percent of Chinese respondents with an unfavorable view of India versus only 32 percent reporting a favorable view. Less than a third of Chinese respondents thought bilateral ties were defined by cooperation.

CHINA-INDIA-U.S. STRATEGIC TRIANGLE

- India, seemingly the great loser at the end of the Cold War, entered the twenty-first century in a position to serve as a critical "swing state" in the emerging bipolar order. The United States and China both appeared to be courting New Delhi between 2000 and 2005, before Delhi seemingly bet on the United States with its decision to sign a ten-year defense agreement and civil nuclear deal in Washington that summer. The transformation of India's relationship with the U.S. represents arguably the most important structural change in Sino-Indian relations in the young century.
- Since the turn of the century, the main impediments to closer Sino-Indian ties remain fixed or have grown in prominence, while the greatest obstacles to Indo-U.S. collaboration have gradually dissipated. China is now in an unenviable position in the strategic triangle.
- If Beijing pursues incentives to woo New Delhi, it is likely to find India receptive and willing to collaborate on matters of mutual interest. But it will not prevent India from pursuing a parallel track of deeper integration with the United States More important, until India's fundamental security concerns are addressed, the ceiling for

growth in the bilateral relationship will remain low and fixed. If, on the other hand, Beijing pursues a more punitive strategy toward India, it is likely to prove counterproductive in the long term, giving even greater impetus to pro-Western forces.

- A senior official in India's Ministry of External Affairs told this writer that the Bush administration's outreach in the early-mid-2000s had "widened India's options" with regard to China. "That option [forming a strategic partnership with the U.S.] may have always been there, but the way President Bush approached us made a partnership more amenable to us at a time we needed it most. Until 2005 China had gamed us. President Bush 'de-gamed' us."

- While an explicit military alliance between the United States and India is a distant—and perhaps entirely unrealistic—prospect, by 2011 India was the third-largest purchaser of U.S. arms, accounting for some $4.5 billion in sales that year alone. By 2013 India had ordered or purchased sensor-fused bombs, Apache helicopters, P8-I surveillance aircraft, M-777 Howitzers, C-130J and C-17 transport aircraft, and a large amphibious transport dock. In recent years the U.S. conducted more joint military exercises with India than with any other country, NATO allies included.

- Though Chinese analysts generally feign indifference toward the Indo-U.S. partnership, official Chinese publications have at times sought to exploit Indian anxieties about aligning too closely with the United States and deviating from the principles of Nonalignment. U.S. and Indian officials interviewed this book believed India's rapprochement with the United States was among the most important factors influencing China's less-charitable approach toward India after 2006.

- Perhaps the most effective constraint on greater Indo-U.S. ties comes not from China, but from Indian fears of Sino-U.S. collusion. These anxieties were triggered by talk of a major U.S.-China collaboration or "G2" to manage global economic affairs during President Barack Obama's first term and by the initiation of a U.S.-China subdialogue on South Asia.

BORDER DISPUTE

- The territorial dispute remains a considerable and continuous source of tension in the relationship, as evidenced by the minicrisis over the month-long intrusion by a Chinese border patrol nineteen kilometers across the Line of Actual Control in April 2013.

- A great deal of confusion continues to cloud the debate over the Sino-Indian border dispute. The two sides have yet to agree on even the length of their shared border: Indian media reports and authoritative figures frequently peg the border at 4,057 kilometers, but the official figure from the Indian Home Ministry and Indo-Tibetan Border Police is 3,380 kilometers. China, meanwhile, claims the border is 2,000 kilometers in length.
- China's claims in the Eastern Sector remain similarly obscure. Though the two sides exchanged maps for the Middle Sector in 2001, China has stonewalled an exchange of maps in the Eastern and Western Sectors which would define each side's claims. It is unclear whether China is claiming all or part of Arunachal Pradesh, and whether it is also claiming a small tract of land in Assam. Furthermore, it is unclear why the contemporary literature suggests China is claiming 90,000 square kilometers in India's northeast, when its claim appears to be closer to 70,000 square kilometers and no more than 85,000 square kilometers.
- China's enthusiasm for a grand bargain "package deal" which would enshrine the status quo along the Line of Actual Control has declined dramatically since Beijing last (informally) proposed such a deal in the early 1980s. Since that time, China has emphasized its claim on the Eastern Sector and the strategically vital border town of Tawang in particular.
- After two important border agreements signed in 2003 and 2005, a surge of Indian optimism regarding a final resolution to the dispute was underpinned by the assumption that China had dropped its claim to Tawang as part of a provision of the 2005 border protocol in which the two sides agreed not to disturb "settled populations." The realization that China had not dropped its claims to Tawang in the years to follow contributed to the stalling of the negotiations process.
- Indian and Chinese analysts interviewed for the book expressed profound pessimism about the prospects for a border solution in the near term *or the long term*, reflecting the paralysis that has seized the border negotiations process since 2005. Several officials warned not to expect a resolution in the next fifteen years, and Chinese officials and analysts have suggested the issue should be shelved "for future generations to decide."
- Perhaps the biggest emerging obstacle to a border dispute stem from domestic constraints from the relative weakness of the political leadership in both capitals, and the relative unwillingness of both publics to stomach territorial concessions. The greater constraints exist on the Indian side, both politically and institutionally, but China

is facing constraints of its own in the form of increasingly influential nationalist interest groups who are taking a harder line on China's territorial disputes. The vice president of the PLA's Academy of Military Science recently warned that nationalist PLA commentators were "inciting public sentiment and *causing some interference with our high-level policy decision-making and deployments* [emphasis added]."

- Over the past two decades China has gained a considerable advantage over India in terms of infrastructure and logistics capabilities along the Line of Actual Control (LAC). In 2006 Delhi sought to address this widening gap when it abruptly reversed a longstanding border doctrine which counseled against building infrastructure along the LAC, fearing it would aid an invasion force. India is now upgrading and adding thousands of kilometers of road and rail in its border states and drilling tunnels through mountain passes rendered impassable due to inclement weather for nearly half the year.

- However, seven years after it was first announced, the border infrastructure modernization plan remains a distant promise. Bureaucratic hurdles (most notably environmental and inter ministerial clearances), local protests, a lack of skilled labor and modern equipment, and corruption have all been blamed for the glacial pace of progress in road-building. Many of India's forward positions along the Himalayan border are still supplied by helicopter or via a grueling, multiday hike.

- In addition to the infrastructure modernization plan, India is currently engaged in the largest permanent buildup of military forces along the border with China in decades, including adding two new mountain infantry divisions to the northeast in 2009, and announcing raising of a new offensive Strike Corps in 2013—the first offensive corps dedicated to the China border. Additionally, India is upgrading dozens of airfields and forward operating bases near the border and stationing its most advanced fighter/strike aircraft, the Sukhoi-30MKI, and its most advanced cruise missile, the Brahmos, at positions near the border.

- Sikkim, the tiny Himalayan enclave wedged between China and India, is not a settled issue in Sino-Indian relations. China refused to recognize Indian sovereignty over Sikkim when it voted to join the Indian Union in 1975. Beijing seemed to reverse this policy in 2003, when it agreed to reopen a historic trading post at the Sikkim-China border—a move Indian analysts and officials deemed sufficient to put the issue to rest. However, no Chinese official has ever explicitly recognized Indian sovereignty over Sikkim, and still active on the Chinese foreign ministry's website (as of July 2013) is a page titled "China and Sikkim" which contains one line of text:

"The Chinese Government does not recognize India's illegal annexation of Sikkim."

- Border incursions remain a recurring point of contention in bilateral relations and a regular feature of criticism in Indian press. Indian government figures report over 200 Chinese "transgressions" across the border every year, and Chinese analysts suggest Indian patrols transgress the Line of Actual Control with similar frequency, though China keeps no official count and Chinese media outlets rarely report on incursions. In 2008 reports of Chinese border incursions in the "Finger area" of Sikkim prompted India to move T-72 battle tanks to the area in response.

TIBET AND TAWANG

- Tibet remains a core dispute in Sino-Indian relations, and India's proximity to Tibet and its hosting of the Dalai Lama and Tibetan Government in Exile remain major irritants for Beijing. Domestic unrest on the plateau since 2008 has raised Chinese sensitivities in Tibet at a time when Indian strategists are calling for greater assertiveness on Tibet issues.
- Beijing was unsettled by the series of ethnic riots that killed nineteen and injured 300 in 2008. Even more problematic from China's perspective has been the wave of self-immolations that have seized the plateau since 2009, resulting in over 100 fatalities as Buddhist monks have set themselves on fire to protest Chinese rule.
- India has only ever played the "Tibet card" once, when it tacitly facilitated CIA assistance to Tibetan rebels in the late 1950s and early 1960s. However, there are growing calls within India to become more assertive on matters relating to Tibet. Delhi dispatched several senior officials and allowed the Dalai Lama to visit the disputed territory of Tawang during a spike in Sino-Indian tensions in 2009 and in 2010 for the first time withheld recognition of China's "One China" policy in a joint statement with China. When India's Exernal Affairs Minister and Prime Minister visited Beijing in May and October 2013, respectively, both joint statements again excluded mention of the "One China" policy, potentially signaling a new precedent.
- China's foremost demand on India is that it prevent the Dalai Lama, whose permanent residence is in Dharamsala, Himachal Pradesh, from engaging in "political activities." And while India has in principle agreed to those terms, the two sides have never properly defined—and they clearly have different perceptions of—what constitutes "political activities." Some Chinese analysts

insist that *any* public activities of the Dalai Lama are inherently political, while others have charged Delhi with using the Dalai Lama
and Tibetan Government in Exile as a tool to provoke China with
plausible deniability.

- The Tibetan Government in Exile elected its first prime minister in
2001 and reelected him in 2006, though he was vested with largely
symbolic powers. In 2011, the Dalai Lama announced that he was
granting the supreme political authority bestowed on all his predecessors to the position of prime minister. Interest in that year's vote
surged, and Lobsang Sangay, a Harvard-educated Bostonite was
elected with 55 percent of the vote. While he is committed to the
Dalai Lama's "Middle Way," he has been more confrontational in his
rhetoric toward China than His Holiness.

- A great deal of uncertainty surrounds the future of the Tibetan Government in Exile. Some of the greatest questions are: Can Lobsang
Sangay emerge from the Dalai Lama's shadow? Can he cultivate
legitimacy with world leaders at a time fewer and fewer dignitaries
are willing to meet with the Dalai Lama?

- Time and again in interviews for this book, the question of who will
succeed the seventy-six-year-old Dalai Lama was cited as a decisive—and potentially explosive—issue in Sino-Indian relations. At
stake is the future of a global religion, but the issue has potentially
profound implications for the China-India relationship.

- The Dalai Lama succession question has already sparked a fierce
competition between the institution of the Dalai Lama and Beijing
for the right to name a successor. The fact that there are no uniform
rules for succession has provided Beijing with a path to attempt to
co-opt the process. In March 2005 and September 2007 Beijing's State
Council passed new regulations granting it greater authority over
the appointment of living Buddhas and laying out its plans to "institutionalize the management of reincarnation."

- Beijing is attempting to seize on a precedent set by Qing Dynasty
Emperor Qianlong, who introduced a "golden urn" lottery process
that was used to select a handful of Dalai Lamas but was subsequently abandoned by Tibetans.

- In September 2011, the Dalai Lama convened a three-day conference
in Dharamsala for the heads of all the main Buddhist sects where he
addressed the succession controversy. He said it would not be definitively decided until he turned ninety (in 2025) and began to build
support around a more obscure succession procedure known as "emanation," which would give the Dalai Lama the right to choose his own
successor, rather than have him identified by a Regent, council, or the
Panchen Lama after his death, as per the usual custom.

- Early speculation in Delhi is that the Dalai Lama may look to Tawang to find his successor. Of the only two reincarnations ever found outside Tibet proper, one—the sixth Dalai Lama—was found in Tawang. And in 2008 the Dalai Lama reversed his longstanding position that Tawang had historically been a part of Tibet, insisting that it was an integral part of India.
- Beijing seems to be banking on the fact that the Tibetan movement will fragment and fracture in the Dalai Lama's absence, and that they can score a victory by simply "waiting him out."
- In Delhi the concern is that current Dalai Lama has served as a powerful restraining agent on the passions of the Tibetan exile movement. Some Indian strategists fear that in his absence, Tibetan youth could take a turn toward militancy. There are signs that they have grown increasingly resentful toward China, particularly after the collapse of the dialogue between Beijing and the Dalai Lama's representatives in 2010. If a new Dalai Lama or a new generation of Tibetan leaders begin agitating for independence, it would pose a serious challenge to China-India relations.

PAKISTAN

- While India has opted for *tactical* partnerships with superpowers to balance against its more powerful Chinese neighbor (first with the U.S., then the Soviet Union, and now again with the U.S.), Beijing has been content to form a sole *strategic* alliance and "all-weather friendship" with a smaller regional power, Pakistan, to guide its regional policy over the last five decades. Unlike China's other relationships in South Asia, there are explicit elements of a containment strategy vis-à-vis India inherent in its relationship with Pakistan.
- While the Sino-Pakistan relationship remains a "core concern" of India's, in surveying the motivations for the spike in Sino-Indian tensions from 2006–2013, the Pakistan factor was noticeably absent. The relative stability in Indo-Pakistan relations during this period (with the notable exception of the 2008 Mumbai terrorist attacks) no doubt played a major role. This was reinforced by the relative decline in violence in Kashmir: From a pinnacle of 4,057 terrorism-related deaths in the disputed territory in 2001, fatalities declined in every year to follow, dropping to 777 in 2007 and 117 in 2012.
- For India, the China-Pakistan nexus has in some respects become less threatening in the twenty-first century. China's behavior over the course of the last three Indo-Pakistan wars has grown progressively less provocative, its diplomatic position on Kashmir has assumed a

level of neutrality, and China has ceased explicit support to Pakistan's nuclear weapons program.

- However, there has not yet been a substantial reduction in Indian threat perceptions vis-a-vis the China-Pakistan nexus. Delhi still remains profoundly concerned about the prospects for a "two-front war," unsure of whether China would enter an Indo-Pakistan conflict on the latter's behalf. China's ongoing conventional military assistance to Pakistan, its support to Pakistan's civilian nuclear program, and its ongoing work in Pakistan-occupied Kashmir all remain persistent concerns and sources of tension in bilateral relations.
- Indian assessments of the likelihood of a Chinese intervention in a future Indo-Pakistan war vary considerably. This writer heard several Indian military and civilian officials suggest in private discussions and roundtables that China was today *more* likely to intervene in an Indo-Pakistan conflict than at any time in the twentieth century. However, little was offered by way of evidence to corroborate this threat assessment. As author Mark Frazier argues, another Indo-Pakistan conflict would likely "serve no purpose from China's perspective."
- The Sino-Pakistan military-to-military relationship remains robust and since the turn of the century Beijing has sold Pakistan dozens of F-7MG/PG fighter aircraft and CSS-N-8 antiship cruise missiles, D-30 Towed artillery guns, fire control and air radar, six Panther helicopters, hundreds of air-to-air missiles and guided bombs, self-propelled artillery guns, advanced ZDK-03 AWACS, T-90 tanks, a few dozen K-8 trainer/combat aircraft, four Jiangwei frigates, and potentially several Yuan-class submarines. In mid-2011 China agreed to provide Pakistan with fifty JF-17 fighter jets, and Beijing has signaled it will likely export to Pakistan a version of its J-20 fifth generation stealth fighter when it becomes operational in the coming years.
- China's direct assistance to Pakistan's nuclear weapons program receded after China signed the Nuclear Nonproliferation Treaty in 1993 and pledged to halt assistance to "nonsafeguarded" nuclear facilities in Pakistan. However, since the turn of the century China has *increased* assistance to Pakistan's civil nuclear program, agreeing to build two new nuclear plants at Chashma in 2010 and two new nuclear plants near Karachi in 2013.
- China has decided not to submit the agreements to the Nuclear Suppliers Group for a waiver, where the international regulatory body would likely challenge the nuclear sales. Beijing has argued the reactors were "grandfathered in" when China joined the NSG in 2004—a rationale most U.S. experts deem dubious.
- Not all is rosy in the Sino-Pakistan relationship. A 2012 Pew Poll found that while 60 percent of Pakistanis reported a "very favor-

able" view of China, only 4 percent of Chinese reported a "very favorable" view of Pakistan. Ironically, this was almost the exact same number of Chinese that reported a "very favorable" view of India (3 percent).

- When Pakistan was hit with a particularly heavy monsoon season in 2010 resulting in nearly 2,000 deaths, America offered $690 million in aid and assistance. China's contribution was a mere $18 million. Chinese find it outrageous that less than two percent of Pakistanis pay income taxes and Andrew Small says "China is not going to backfill U.S. aid to Pakistan. It is hard for [Beijing] to justify such aid to a skeptical public."
- Perhaps the greatest source of discord in bilateral relations stems from the subject of Islamist militancy. Extremists have targeted and killed Chinese workers inside Pakistan, but Beijing's principal concern regards the presence of extremist Uighur groups like the East Turkestan Islamic Movement finding support, refuge, and training in Pakistan's lawless tribal regions.
- Some analysts have concluded that it is not Chinese affection *for* Pakistan, but Chinese fear *of* Pakistan (or at least of Pakistani instability) that makes stable relations with Islamabad such a high priority for Beijing. "We *must* have good relations with Pakistan because Pakistan harbors terrorism," one Chinese analyst told this writer over lunch in Beijing.

WATER

- Water security is poised to become an issue of increasing significance to Sino-Indian relations. Asia is the most water-scarce continent on earth, and India and China are both affected by water scarcity. India has 17.3 percent of the world's population but only 4.3 percent of the world's water supply, and its groundwater supplies—which make up 80 percent of its domestic water use—are in rapid decline. A World Bank study warns 60 percent of India's aquifers could be in critical condition by 2030.
- China has only marginally more water per capita than India: 6.5 percent of global water resources for nearly 20 percent of the world's population. However, China's water is unevenly distributed and of poor quality: as much as 40 percent of its water is unsuitable for drinking, industry or agriculture, and over a third of Chinese provinces are "water scarce." China's north and northeast, with nearly a third of the country's population, have only 7 percent of its surface water.
- In contrast, China's southwest—and the Tibetan plateau in particular—hold the largest freshwater reserves on the six populated con-

tinents. Three rivers whose headwaters begin in Tibet—the Ganges, Brahmaputra, and Indus—also provide over one-third of India's water supply and over half of the water supply to India's north.

- The principal source of friction relating to water issues stem from Indian concerns that Chinese efforts to divert and store water from Tibet's rivers will negatively affect India's water supply. China is currently engaged in the some of the most ambitious, expensive, and technically challenging water diversion and storage projects in the world, most notably the Three Gorges Dam and the Great South North Water Transfer Project. It is also on a damming spree: over half of the 50,000 large dams in the world are now in China.

- Indian concerns have been stoked by China's refusal to sign a water-sharing agreement (China has no water-sharing treaties with any of its neighbors), and by a lack of transparency in Chinese dam-building. Beijing denied the construction of a dam on the Brahmaputra River at Zangmu for years before abruptly making an about-face in 2010 and admitting they had constructed a 510 MW run-of-the-river dam at Zangmu.

- The Zangmu episode fed speculation that China will begin a damming spree on the Brahmaputra: as many as twenty-eight dams have been proposed by Chinese hydropower lobbying groups. These fears were further stoked in January 2013 when China's State Council approved plans for three additional dams on the Brahmaputra, at Dagu, Jiacha, and Jiexy.

- All of the current dams planned by China on the Brahmaputra are run-of-the-river (RoR) projects, which do not affect water supply downriver. It is also true that most of the water that feeds the Brahmaputra enters the river *after* it crosses the Indian border in Arunachal Pradesh.

- As they currently stand, China's dam and water diversion projects (including the Eastern and Middle Routes of the Great South North Water Diversion Project) are not poised to affect water flow into India. The proposals with the potential to do so—the Western line of the Great South North Water Transfer project and a massive dam 38,000 MW dam at the "Great Bend" of the Brahmaputra—appear unlikely to ever come to fruition.

MARITIME SECURITY

- China and India had few conflicts of interests at sea before the turn of the century. Before 2000 Chinese warships made few voyages into the Indian Ocean, and Indian warships only rarely ventured into the Western Pacific.

- Thirteen years into the twenty-first century, the People's Liberation Army Navy (PLAN) has a semipermanent presence in the Indian Ocean to fight piracy off the Horn of Africa, and the Indian Navy has sent aircraft carriers through the Strait of Malacca as part of its regular forays into the Western Pacific. As China's dependence on foreign energy imports has surged, the security of its sea lines of communication through the Indian Ocean have become a paramount concern. For its part, India has a growing number of energy investments in the Western Pacific and a growing number of regional allies at odds with Beijing.
- India's Look East policy was born out of the 1991 financial crisis and a desire to expand India's economic and strategic horizons, not out of any compulsion to contain China. Similarly, China's thrust into the Indian Ocean is more about protecting its sea lines of communication and diversifying its energy imports than it is about containing India. Both are essentially defensively and economically motivated initiatives. Yet both are increasingly being seen as, and assuming characteristics of, an offensive strategy.

LOOK EAST

- In recent years India has begun adding more strategic and defense components to its Look East policy. Indian strategists recognize the limits of their ability to project power into the Western Pacific and acknowledge they are in no position to pose a strategic challenge to China or defend their economic interest there by force. On the other hand, Delhi has increasingly come to see its growing diplomatic and military capital in the region as a useful but limited point of leverage over China.
- India has successfully reinvigorating its longstanding partnership with Vietnam, infused new energy in Indo-Japanese ties, and transformed its long-stagnant relationship with Australia. Delhi has shown a new willingness to engage in bilateral and multilateral security dialogues and military exercises with the Pacific democracies, though it is proceeding tentatively and has capped its multilateral engagement at trilateral dialogues/exercises after the massive 2007 Malabar Exercise.
- Chinese concerns about India's Look East policy rank far below its other priorities in East Asia, yet Chinese nationalists are unsettled by what they see as India drifting toward a loose coalition of Indo-Pacific democracies collaborating on security matters with negative implications for Chinese interests. Beyond that, they are irritated by Indian investments in energy projects off the coast of Vietnam in

waters claimed by China, and by India's vocal support for "Freedom of Navigation" in the South China Sea—a phrase that has become a buzzword for opposing Chinese hegemony in the Western Pacific.

- Following an incident in the South China Sea in 2011 Indian officials began to regularly and publicly voice support for freedom of navigation. In July 2011 an Indian amphibious assault vessel, the *INS Airavat*, was on a routine visit to Vietnam. It was contacted over an open radio channel some forty-five nautical miles off the Vietnamese coast: "You are entering Chinese waters. Move out of here," said an unidentified caller. No Chinese ships were present on the horizon and the *Airavat* ignored the warning.

- A year later, Indian warships bound for the Philippines from South Korea received a call—"Welcome to the South China Sea, Foxtrot-47"—and an "unexpected escort" from a Chinese frigate for twelve hours as they traveled through international waters. The message from China, says C. Raja Mohan, was essentially: "Nice to see you here, but you are in our territorial waters and within them there is no right to 'freedom of navigation' for military vessels. You are here at our sufferance."

CHINA AND THE INDIAN OCEAN

- In the twenty-first century, China's South Asia policy has become an Indian Ocean policy. For Beijing the region no longer represents an arena for a regional competition with India, but the focal point in a global quest for energy security.

- In 2011 coal was responsible for two-thirds of China's total energy consumption, with oil at around 19 percent, hydroelectric at 6 percent, natural gas at 4 percent, and nuclear 1 percent. China became a net importer of oil in 1993, a net importer of natural gas in 2007, and a net importer of coal in 2009. After spending much of the twentieth century virtually energy independent, China is now importing nearly 8 percent of its coal, 22 percent of its natural gas, and 60 percent of its oil needs.

- While a sizeable share of China's natural gas imports come via pipeline or originate in East Asia, most of China's oil suppliers lie west of the Strait of Malacca in the Middle East or Africa (Saudi Arabia, Angola, and Iran being the top three, joined by Iraq, Sudan, and Kuwait in the top ten). A full 80 percent of China's oil imports now transit the Strait of Malacca.

- Securing and diversifying China's energy imports was one of the premier foreign policy and energy initiatives of the Hu Jintao administration. The past decade saw China rapidly raise its energy efficiency; begin trying to exploit its sizable but technically challenging shale gas reserves; and invest in oil and gas projects across the globe. China has constructed strategic petroleum reserves on its eastern seaboard and in Xinjiang with storage capacity of around 140 million barrels as of 2012, with plans to expand that to 500 million barrels by 2020, along with an additional several hundred million barrels of commercial storage capacity.

- Most important, China has constructed (and plans to construct) an elaborate network of oil and natural gas pipelines from Central Asia, Pakistan, Russia and Burma, and within China itself. By 2015, China is projected to double the 50,000 kilometers of domestic oil and gas pipelines it had in 2010.
- However, as Andrew Erickson and Gabriel Collins argue, as an energy security strategy China's pipeline plans may be "largely a pipe dream." "The pipelines are not likely to increase Chinese oil import security in quantitative terms, because additional volumes they bring in will be overwhelmed by China's demand growth; *the country's net reliance on seaborne oil imports will grow over time, pipelines notwithstanding* [emphasis added]."
- One can expect that, as China becomes increasingly reliant on SLOCs through the Indian Ocean to feed its growing economy, it will become decreasingly content to depend on foreign navies to provide security for those SLOCs. Conversely, as the PLAN fields the capabilities of a true "blue water navy" to match China's global interests, Chinese strategists are likely to find it increasingly difficult to dismiss the utility of overseas military bases.
- There has been a maturation of the "String of Pearls" debate inside India—specifically a recognition that China's investments in Indian Ocean Rim countries have not carried any explicit military or basing arrangements, and have instead been legitimate commercial ventures. And while China has not established any "client states" in the subcontinent outside of Pakistan, Chinese trade with Pakistan, Bangladesh, and Burma has already surpassed India's trade with these countries, though Delhi remains the dominant economic player in Nepal, Sri Lanka, the Maldives, and Bhutan.
- Just as Indian strategists have recognized that China's "String of Pearls" are driven primarily by its quest for energy security, Indian security concerns have been partially rekindled in the form of the PLAN's first quasipermanent deployment to the Indian Ocean: on December 26, 2008, China dispatched a PLAN flotilla to participate in its own escort missions off the Horn of Africa, marking "the first out-of-area operations for the Chinese military in more than 600 years."
- The deployment has given the PLAN valuable experience operating in ports in Djibouti, Oman, Yemen, and Pakistan for resupply and re-

fueling and provided an "ideal chance for the PLAN to practice and evaluate various blue water tactics, techniques and procedures in an environment far from the Chinese periphery, without generating significant political or military alarm." It has also fed an increasingly public debate within China about the utility of overseas military deployments to protect Chinese interests abroad.

SECURING INDIA'S OCEAN

- At the beginning of the century several developments turned India's attention seaward. Among these were: the rapid growth of sea-based commerce (India had two container ships in 1988 and 328 in 2012); the evolution of the concept of a 200 nautical-mile Exclusive Economic Zone (giving India economic domain over two million square kilometers of Indian Ocean); the 1999 Kargil War with Pakistan (which forced a fundamental reassessment of India's military spending and priorities); and a belated recognition of the blossoming strategic value of the Indian Ocean.
- India is engaged in an accelerated modernization and expansion of the Indian Navy, investing in platforms with the ability to confront a large conventional naval force in the Indian Ocean and allow it to more effectively project power abroad. The Indian Navy's budget is ballooning in absolute terms, and is demanding a larger share of the defense budget. In the 2012–2013 budget the Indian Navy's allocation increased by 74 percent year over year from $2.74 billion to $4.77 billion, before taking a modest reduction in the 2013–2014 budget.
- It plans to have 150 ships under its command by the late 2020s, including fifteen stealth frigates, twelve guided missile destroyers, eighteen to twenty submarines (three of them nuclear powered), 500 aircraft and, three aircraft carriers, allowing it to operate two carrier groups at any given time.
- India is undertaking a major transfer of naval assets from the Pakistan-focused Western Naval Command to the more China-focused Eastern Naval Command. A full fifty warships—over a third of India's naval fleet—are now under the ENC's command. The ENC will control two of India's three carriers and India's first indigenous nuclear submarine. India is also building a new base on its coast to accommodate nuclear submarines.
- India is working to diplomatically counteract Chinese influence in the region through renewed engagement with Indian Ocean littoral countries, and fortifying its defenses; a "Necklace of Diamonds" to match China's "String of Pearls."

- The key link in India's Necklace of Diamonds are the Andaman and Nicobar Islands (ANI), a chain of 572 islands strategically positioned at the western entrance of the Strait of Malacca. The ANI are 200 times the size of Diego Garcia (8,000 square kilometers compared to forty-four square kilometers), and enjoy a more solid foundation of volcanic soil than the British-owned coral atoll.
- India established a new triservice command on the Andaman and Nicobar Islands in 2001 but force levels have remained largely static in the dozen years since its inception. The ANC hosts just one infantry brigade, around fifteen small warships and a handful of Dornier-228 maritime patrol aircraft, as well as Mi-8 and Chetak helicopters, though reports suggest two Indian Navy warships are regularly deployed to patrol the northern and southern islands. The command hosts no unmanned aerial vehicles (UAVs).
- In Delhi the islands have traditionally been viewed as too distant, too vulnerable, and too expensive to maintain (they are 1,200 kilometers from India's eastern coast but only fifty-seven kilometers from Burma's Coco Island and 163 kilometers from Indonesia). And though some Indian strategists are calling for greater utilization of the islands, there has not yet been a paradigm shift regarding the need to more robustly equip the command as a power-projection platform into the Western Pacific.
- The ANI enjoy domain over two important channels west of the Strait of Malacca. The vast majority of international trade transiting the Strait of Malacca also passes through the 200-kilometer-wide Six Degree Channel between the Indonesian island of Aceh and Great Nicobar, home to the Indian Navy's newest air base. As a consequence the vast majority of container traffic through the Strait of Malacca also passes through India's Exclusive Economic Zone. The islands have domain over the Ten Degree Channel to the north, through which container traffic headed for the Bay of Bengal passes.
- Some Indian strategists have suggested that the ANI gives India an opportunity to "retaliate in the Indian Ocean if China provokes us at the border." And while India's position astride China's vital sea lines of communication put it in a strategically advantageous position, the practical challenges associated any country attempting to "cut off" China's oil supplies are manifold.

TRADE

- Bilateral trade surged 67-fold between 1998 and 2012. The two sides have targeted $100 billion in bilateral trade by 2015.

- Students of political economy would predict that this deepening economic integration should have raised the costs of conflict and rivalry and created powerful constituencies in each country lobbying for a more harmonious political relationship. Yet, elements of rivalry are as prevalent today as they were two decades ago, when bilateral trade was negligible.
- The trading relationship is profoundly unbalanced: India was running minor trade surpluses with China as late as 2004–2005, before the trade balance began to tilt decisively in China's favor. In 2012, China's exports to India totaled $48 billion while India's exports to China totaled only $19 billion.
- Both countries regularly charge each other with erecting barriers to market access. No country has filed more "antidumping" complaints against China at the World Trade Organization than India. China, meanwhile, charges the Indian government with unfairly but frequently intervening to block Chinese investments in sensitive sectors of the Indian economy like telecom and infrastructure.
- The absolute, secular growth in the Sino-Indian economic relationship is likely to continue into the twenty-first century, creating new avenues for cooperation, new personal and economic bonds, and marginally greater costs to conflict. However, there is little evidence to suggest that the continued growth in trade and investment will begin to degrade the strategic mistrust that pervades the political and security spheres.

NOTES

1. Rodion Ebbinghausen,"The New Arms Race in Asia," *Deutsche Welle*, March 18, 2013 (Accessed July): http://www.dw.de/the-new-arms-race-in-asia/a-16681158.

2. China's overall military spending still outpaced India's by a factor of four.

3. "India's Surprising but Welcome Message," *Global Times*, February 22, 2010 (Accessed July 2013): http://www.globaltimes.cn/opinion/editorial/2010-02/506893.html.

4. This was no doubt a major factor in China's decision to abruptly end the Sino-Indian border war of 1962 in late November, just one month after the outbreak of hostilities. It also may have played a role in China's decision not to intervene in the 1971 Third Indo-Pakistan War, which Delhi timed to coincide with the closure of the Himalayan passes in December.

5. Lieutenant-General in the Indian Army. Author interview. Washington, DC, May, 2013.

6. Lowy Institute for International Policy India Poll 2013. May 20, 2013. 13 (Accessed June 12, 2013): http://www.lowyinstitute.org/publications/india-poll-2013.

7. "Growing Concerns in China about Inequality, Corruption," *Pew Research Global Attitudes Project*, October 16, 2012 (Accessed April 10, 2013): http://www.pewglobal.org/files/2012/10/Pew-Global-Attitudes-China-Report-FINAL-October-10-20122.pdf.

Bibliography

"11th Panchen Lama Blesses Buddhists in Tibet." *People's Daily Online*, December 19, 2005 (Accessed January 28, 2013): http://english.peopledaily.com.cn/200512/19/eng20051219_229038.html.

"149 Anti-Dumping Cases against China Highest among Foreign Nations: Govt." *Economic Times*, December 21, 2011 (Accessed April 15, 2013): http://articles.economictimes.indiatimes.com/2011-12-21/news/30542669_1_antidumping-measures-dgad-anti-dumping-probes.

"96% Chinese against Indian Visits to Arunachal." *NDTV*, October 14, 2009 (Accessed April 24, 2013): http://www.ndtv.com/article/india/96-chinese-against-indianvisits-to-arunachal-10025.

2011 Office of the Secretary of Defense DOD Annual Report to Congress Military and Security Developments Involving the People's Republic of China, 2011. http://china.usc.edu/App_Images//2011-defense-report-china.pdf.

2012 Revision of the World Population Prospects. Population Division of the United Nations Department of Economic and Social Affairs of the United Nations Secretariat. http://esa.un.org/wpp/.

"A 'Goodwill' Joint Naval Drill?" *People's Daily Online* editorial. April 21, 2007 http://english.peopledaily.com.cn/200704/21/eng20070421_368521.html.

"A Himalayan Rivalry." *Economist*, August 19, 2010 (Accessed April 22, 2013): http://www.economist.com/node/16843717.

Abbas, Mohammed. "China Unrealistic on Tibet, Talks Futile: Dalai Lama." *Reuters*, June 20, 2012 (Accessed January 29, 2013): http://in.reuters.com/article/2012/06/20/britain-dalailamaidINDEE85J0EZ20120620.

Abe, Shinzo. "Asia's Democratic Security Diamond." *Project Syndicate*, November 2012. http://www.project-syndicate.org/commentary/a-strategic-alliance-for-japan-and-india-by-shinzo-abe.

"After Dalai Lama's Rebuke, China Breathes Fire." *Times of India,* November 9, 2009 (Accessed January 30, 2013): http://www.timesnow.tv/After-Dalai -Lamas-rebuke-China-breathes-fire/articleshow/4331672.cms.

"Aksai Chin." *Princeton.edu,* February 6, 2013: http://www.princeton .edu/~achaney/tmve/wiki100k/docs/Aksai_Chin.html.

Allcock, John B. *Border and Territorial Disputes,* 3rd Ed. Harlow: Longman Current Affairs, 1992.

"America's Image Remains Strong: Indians See Threat from Pakistan, Extremist Groups." *Pew Research Global Attitudes Project.* October 20, 2012 (Accessed April 10, 2013) http://www.pewglobal.org/2010/10/20/indians-see-threat-from -pakistanextremist-groups/.

Anantaram, Rajeev. "Rearmament of India." *Business Standard,* July 9, 2011. http://www.business-standard.com/article/beyond-business/rearmament -of-india111070900006_1.html.

Analyst from the Chinese Academy of Social Sciences. Author interview. Washington, DC, June 2013.

Andaman and Nicobar Command, *Global Security.* 2011. http://www.global security.org/military/world/india/anc.htm.

Arpi, Claude. "A New Road to Bhutan." *Claude Arpi's Blogspot,* November 24, 2012 (Accessed January 30, 2013): http://claudearpi.blogspot.com/2012/11/ a-new-road-to-bhutan.html.

"Arunachal Pradesh Is Our territory: Chinese Envoy." *Rediff India Abroad,* November 14, 2006 (Accessed July 8, 2013). http://www.rediff.com/news/2006/ nov/14china.htm.

"Arunachal: Tawang Trek." *Wild World India.* January 28, 2013:http://www.wild worldindia.com/treks/tawang.asp.

"Background Note: India," U.S. Department of State, 2012 (Accessed April 22, 2013): http://www.state.gov/r/pa/ei/bgn/3454.htm.

Bagchi, Indrani. "China Admits to Brahmaputra Project." *Times of India,* April 21, 2010 http://articles.timesofindia.indiatimes.com/2010-04-22/india/28126091_1_ zangmu-brahmaputra-india-and-china.

Bagchi, Indrani. "China Harasses Indian Naval Ship on South China Sea." *Times of India,* September 2, 2011 (Accessed April 15, 2013): http://articles .timesofindia.indiatimes.com/2011-09-02/india/30105514_1_south-china-sea -spratly-ins-airavat.

Bagchi, Indrani. "Finally, Pranab Calls China a Challenge." *Times of India,* November 5, 2008 (Accessed April 10, 2013): http://articles.timesofindia .indiatimes.com/2008-11-05/india/27900493_1_india-and-china-india-china -chinese-president-hu-jintao.

Bagchi, Indrani. "India Declines to Affirm 'One China' Policy." *Times of India,*December 17, 2010 (Accessed April 24, 2013): http://articles.timesofindia .indiatimes.com/2010-1217/india/28261765_1_stapled-china-india-india-and -china.

Bagchi, Indrani. "India to Discuss China with US Later This Month." *The EconomicTimes,* September 4, 2010 (Accessed April 15, 2013): http://articles .economictimes.indiatimes.com/2010-0904/news/27606150_1_core-interests -south-china-sea-exercises.

Bagchi, Indrani. "Keep Off Pok, India Warns China." *Times of India*, September 16, 2011 (Accessed April 16, 2013): http://articles.timesofindia.indiatimes.com/2011 -0916/india/30164512_1_stapled-visas-karakoram-highway-china-issues.

Bahara, Laxman K. Institute for Defense Studies and Analysis. *India's Defence Budget 2012–13*, March 20, 2012 (Accessed July 2, 2013): http://www.idsa.in/ idsacomments/IndiasDefenceBudget201213_LaxmanBehera_200312.

Bajaj, Vikas. "India Measures Itself against a China That Doesn't Notice." *New York Times*, August 31, 2011 (April 13, 2013): http://www.nytimes.com/2011/09/01/ business/global/india-looks-to-china-as-aneconomic-model.html?_r=2&.

Barnett, Robbie. "Note on the Statement by the Dalai Lama Concerning His Successor." *Columbia*, September 26, 2011 (Accessed January 29, 2013): http:// lawprofessors.typepad.com/files/note-on-the-statement-by-hhdl-concerning -his-successor-4.pdf.

Bardsley, Daniel. "Pakistan Flaunts Its Friendship with China in Message to US." *National*, October 3, 2011. http://www.thenational.ae/news/world/asia pacific/pakistan-flaunts-its-friendship-with-china-in-message-to-us.

Beech, Hannah. "As Tibetans Burn Themselves to Protest Chinese Rule, Communists in Beijing Stress Happiness in Tibet." *Time World*, November 10, 2012 (Accessed January 30, 2013): http://world.time.com/2012/11/10/as-tibetans -burn-themselves-to-protest-chinese-rule-communists-in-beijing-stress-happi ness-in-tibet/.

Bhaskar, C. Uday. Author interview. New Delhi, August 2012.

Bhaskar, C. Uday. Author interview. Honolulu, Hawaii, May 22, 2013.

Bhatia, Vimal. "China-Pakistan war games along Rajasthan border." *Times of India*, August 10, 2010. http://articles.timesofindia.indiatimes.com/2011-0810/ india/29871604_1_military-exercise-pakistan-rangers-pakistan-forces.

Bhattacharya, Prasenjit. "China Looks to Increase India Investments." *Wall Street Journal, India Real Time*, November 27, 2012. http://blogs.wsj.com/indiareal time/2012/11/27/china-looks-to-increase-indiainvestments/.

"Bilateral Relations with the U.S. Truly Multi-Faceted." *Deccan Herald*, April 13, 2013. http://www.deccanherald.com/content/36818/bilateral-relations-us -truly multi.html.

"BJP National Spokesperson and MP, Shri Tarun Vijay." *Bharatiya Janata Party*, January 8, 2012 (Accessed April 2013): http://www.bjp.org/index .php?option=com_content&view=article&id=7526:pres-bjp-national-spokes person-and-mp-shri-tarun-vijay&catid=68:pressreleases&Itemid=494.

Blecher, Marc. "China in 2008: Meeting Olympian Challenges." *Asian Survey*, Vol. 49, No. 1, 2009.

Bodansky, Youssef. "The PRC Surge for the Strait of Malacca and Spratly Confronts India and the U.S." International Strategic Studies Association. Defense and Foreign Affairs Strategic Policy, September 30.

"Border Conflict Stirs Old Resentments Over 'Incursions' in Indian Media." *Global Times*, May 13, 2013 (Accessed June 12, 2013): http://www.globaltimes.cn/ content/781259.shtml.

Bork, Ellen. "Tibet's Transition: Will Washington Take a Stand?" *International Campaign for Tibet*, September 26, 2012 (February 27, 2013): http://www.savetibet .org/media-center/tibet-news/tibets-transition-will-washington-take-stand.

Bose, Manilal. *History of Arunachal Pradesh.* New Delhi: Concept Publishing Company, 1997.

Burke, Dennis J. "Tibetans in Exile in a Changing Global Political Climate." *Economic and Political Weekly.*

Central Tibetan Administration. "UN Urges China to Urgently Address Longstanding Grievances of Tibetans." *Central Tibetan Administration,* November 2, 2012 (January 30, 2013): http://tibet.net/2012/11/02/un-says-china-must-urgentlyaddress-longstanding-grievances-of-tibetans/.

"Central Tibetan Schools Administration," 2008–2009 (Accessed June 13, 2013): http://www.ctsa.nic.in/.

Chakravarti, Prithwis Chandra. *India's China Policy.* Bloomington: Indiana University Press, 1962.

Chan, Wai-Shin, Robins, Nick, and Knight, Zoe. "HSBC Global Research, No Water, NoPower." *HSBC Global Research.* September 2012.

Chase, Michael C., and Erickson, Andrew S. "Changes in Beijing's Approach to Overseas Basing?" *China Brief,* September 24, 2009. http://www.jamestown.org/programs/chinabrief/single/?tx_ttnews[tt_news]=3556&cHash=1e7c04ad8f.

Chellaney, Brahma. *Water: Asia's New Battleground.* Georgetown University Press, 2011.

Chellaney, Brahma. "Tibet Is at the Core of the India-China Divide." *Chellanay.net,* 2007 (Accessed January 30,2013): http://chellaney.net/2007/04/02/tibet-is-at-the-core-of-the-india-china-divide/.

Cheng, Dean. "China: No Sequestration for Chinese Military Spending." *Heritage Network, The Foundry Blog,* March 6, 2013 (Accessed June 12, 2013): http://blog.heritage.org/2013/03/06/no-sequestration-for-chinese-military-spending/.

"China Aims to Dominate Tech Industry; Asks for India's Help." *Newsmax.com,* April 10, 2005 (April 22, 2013): http://archive.newsmax.com/archives/articles/2005/4/10/82600.shtml.

"China and Sikkim." *Ministry of Foreign Affairs of the People's Republic of China,* August 25, 2003 (Accessed April 22, 2013): www.fmprc.gov.cn/eng/wjb/zzjg/yzs/gjlb/2772/t16190.htm.

"China Announces Plan to Expand Seabed Mining in Indian Ocean" *Economic Times,* September 17, 2011. http://articles.economictimes.indiatimes.com/2011-09 17/news/30169240_1_polymetallic-sulphide-ocean-mineral-resources-researchstate-oceanic-administration.

"China Biggest Enemy of India, Pakistan No Threat: Mulayam" *Daily Press,* April 29, 2013 (Accessed June 18, 2013): http://india.nydailynews.com/politicsarticle/32439a4b041e4c7af5c321904de0b5 8/china-biggest-enemy-of-india-pakistan-no-threat-mulayam.

"China Blocked Efforts to Put Sanctions on JuD, Hafiz Saeed." *Times of India,* December 6, 2010. http://articles.timesofindia.indiatimes.com/2010-1206/india/28240559_1_jud-unsc-taliban-sanctions-committee.

"'China Building Airstrips along LAC,' Govt Says No Need to Worry." *Times of India,* December 1, 2009. http://articles.timesofindia.indiatimes.com/2009-12 01/india/28094065_1_airstrips-line-of-actual-control-china.

"China Denounces Sangay's Election." *Zeenews.com*, April 28, 2011 (Accessed January 28, 2013): http://zeenews.india.com/news/world/china-denounces -sangay-selection_702844.html.

"China Grants Visa to Arunachal Pradesh Academician." *Times of India*, December 6, 2007 (Accessed April 24, 2013): http://articles.timesofindia .indiatimes.com/200712 06/india/27984868_1_ganesh-koyu-visa-arunachal -pradesh.

"China Incursion to Be Raised, Sikkim Is a Closed Chapter: India." *The Indian Express*, June 20, 2008 (Accessed June 12, 2013): http://www.indianexpress.com/ news/china-incursionto-be-raised-sikkim-is-a-closed-chapter-india/325132/.

"China, India Have Great Wisdom to Handle Sensitive Issues." *People's Daily Online*, May 10, 2013 (Accessed June 12, 2013): http://english.peopledaily.com .cn/90883/8239797.html.

China, India Hold Border Talks, Pledge to Safeguard Peace." *English.news.cn*, March 3, 2012 (Accessed February 6, 2013): http://news.xinhuanet.com/ english/china/201203/06/c_131450604.htm.

"China-India Ties Fragile, Need Special Care: Chinese Envoy," *Times of India* December 14, 2010. http://articles.timesofindia.indiatimes.com/2010-12 14/ india/28213836_1_chinese-envoy-zhang-yan-china-india.

"China Issuing 'Invalid' Stapled Visas to Arunachal Pradesh Residents." *Times of India*, February 25, 2012 (Accessed April 24, 2013): http://articles.timesof india.indiatimes.com/2011-01-12/india/28374355_1_stapled-visas-techi-china -weightlifting-grand-prix.

"China 'Ready to Work' on Stapled Visa Issue with India." *Indian Express*, April 12, 2011 (Accessed April 24, 2013): http://www.indianexpress.com/news/ chinaready-to-work-on-stapled-visa-issue-with-india/775244/.

"China Reiterates Its Claim to Arunachal Pradesh." *Dawn the Internet Edition*, November 15, 2006 (Accessed April 22, 2006): http://archives.dawn .com/2006/11/15/top7.htm.

"China Retorts to India on Arunachal Issue." *News Track India*, November 12, 2008 (Accessed April 24, 2013): http://www.newstrackindia.com/newsdetails/3664.

"China Rules Out Early Sikkim Resolution." *Dawn the Internet Edition*, June 27, 2003 (April 22, 2013): http://archives.dawn.com/2003/06/28/top6.htm.

"China Says No Change in Its Arunachal Pradesh Policy." *Economic Times*, January 17, 2011 (Accessed April 24, 2013): http://articles.economictimes.india times.com/2011-01 17/news/28432458_1_stapled-visas-weightlifting-grand -prix-indian-immigration officials.

"China Should Respect India's Sensitivities: SM Krishna." *Daily News and Analysis*, October 15, 2010 (Accessed April 14, 2013): http://www.dnaindia.com/ india/report_china-should-respect-india-s-sensitivitiessm-krishna_1452946.

"China to Pump $47 Bln into Tibet to 2015," *Reuters*, September 14, 2011 (Accessed January 20, 2013): http://www.reuters.com/article/2011/09/14/china -tibet idUSL3E7KE24W20110914.

"China Turns to Salt Water to Ease Drought." *China Daily.com*, November 31, 2006: http://www.chinadaily.com.cn/china/2006-10/31/content_720980.htm.

"China Voices 'Strong Dissatisfaction' over Indian Leader's Visit to Disputed Region." *China View*, October 13, 2009 (Accessed April 24, 2013): http://news .xinhuanet.com/english/2009-10/13/content_12222106.htm.

"China Violated LAC 505 Times since January 2010." *Tribune*, May 16, 2012: http://www.tribuneindia.com/2012/20120517/main6.htm.

"China: Visa Regime Unchanged for Arunachal Pradesh." *Stratfor*, January 14, 2011 (Accessed April 24, 2013): http://www.stratfor.com/sitrep/20110114 -china-visaregime-unchanged-arunachal-pradesh.

"China Was the Aggrieved; India the Aggressor in '62." *OutlookIndia.com*, October 22, 2009 (Accessed June 13, 2013) http://www.outlookindia.com/article .aspx?282579.

"China Wins Approval to Explore Indian Ocean" *2point6billion.com*, August 3, 2011. http://www.2point6billion.com/news/2011/08/03/china-wins-approval-to -exploreindian-ocean-9894.html.

"China's Growing Influence in Asia Poses Challenge," *Economic Times*, July 28, 2011. http://articles.economictimes.indiatimes.com/2011-07-28/news/298246 58_1_china-and-india-gwadar-pakistan.

"China's Role in PoK on Krishna's Agenda." *Deccan Herald*, April 3, 2013. http:// www.deccanherald.com/content/61908/chinas-role-pok-krishnasagenda.html.

"China's WMD Assistance to Pakistan Is Enabling Terror in Southeast Asia." Asian Age, March 10, 2013: http://www.asianage.comwww.asianage.com/interview week/china-s-wmd-assistance-pak-enabling-terror-south-asia-372.

Chinese analysts. Author interview. Beijing, February 2012.

"Chinese Media Highlights Pak Angle, Seeks Action on Terror." *Times of India*, August 2, 2011. http://articles.timesofindia.indiatimes.com/2011-08-02/ china/29842091_1_xinjiang-etim-kashgar.

"Chinese Media Mock India's 'Dwarf' Missile." *BBC News Asia-Pacific*, April 10, 2013 (Accessed April 20, 2012): http://www.bbc.co.uk/news/world-asia -pacific17784779.

"Chinese Workers Shot in Pakistan." *BBC News*, July 9, 2007. http://news.bbc .co.uk/2/hi/south_asia/6282574.stm.

Ching Ching Ni, "China Steps Up Criticism of Dalai Lama over Tibet." *Los Angeles Times*, March 20, 2008. http://articles.latimes.com/2008/mar/20/world/ fg-tibet20.

"CIS and Far East Assets." *ONGC Videsh Limited*, 2010 (Accessed April 15, 2013): http://www.ongcvidesh.com/Assets.aspx?AspxAutoDetectCookieSupport=1.

"Coast Guard Drops Anchor at 10 Degree Channel." *webindia123*, January 20, 2010. http://news.webindia123.com/news/articles/India/20100125/1432099.html.

Cohen, Stephen. *Arming Without Aiming*. Washington: Brookings Institute Press, 2010. http://www.brookings.edu/research/books/2010/armingwith outaiming.

Collins, Gabriel B., ed."China's Energy Strategy: The Impact on Beijing's Maritime Policies." http://www.army.forces.gc.ca/caj/documents/vol_11/iss_3/ CAJ_Vol11.3_25_e.pdf.

Collins, Gabriel B., and Murray, William S., "No Oil for the Lamps of China?" *Naval War College Review*, Spring 2008, Vol. 61, No. 2.

Conboy, Kenneth, and Morrison, James. *The CIA's Secret War in Tibet*. University Press of Kansas, 2002.

"Confidence-Building Measures along the Line of Actual Control in the India-China Border Areas." *The Stimson Center*, 2013 (Accessed February 6, 2013): http://www.stimson.org/research-pages/confidence-building-measures-along-the-line-of-actual-control-in-the-india-china-border-areas/.

Congress Party MP. Author interview. Heritage Foundation, Washington, DC, September 19, 2012.

Cossa, Ralph. Author interview. Honolulu, Hawaii, April 2012.

"Costly Drops." *Economist*, February 7, 2013 http://www.economist.com/news/china/21571437-removing-salt-seawater-might-help-slake-some-northern-chinas-thirst-it-comes-high.

"Countries in the Region." *Ministry of Foreign Affairs of the People's Republic of China*, 2005 (Accessed April 22, 2013): www.fmprc.gov.cn/eng/wjb/zzjg/yzs/gjlb/default.htm.

Curtis, Lisa, and Cheng, Dean. "The China Challenge: A Strategic Vision for U.S.-India Relations." *Heritage Foundation*, July 18, 2012 (Accessed February 6, 2013): http://www.heritage.org/research/reports/2011/07/the-china-challenge-astrategic-vision-for-us-india-relations.

Dalai Lama. *My Land and My People*. New York: Warner Books, 1997.

Das, R. N. "Sino-Indian Trade: Smoothing the Rough Edges." Institute for Defence Studies Analyses, September 27, 2011 (Accessed April 15, 2013): http://www.idsa.in/idsacomments/SinoIndianTradeSmootheningtheRoughEdgesndas_270911#footnoteref2_6byynby.

Dasgupta, Saibal. "China Calls PoK 'Northern Pakistan,' J&K Is 'India-controlled Kashmir." *Times of India*, September 2, 2010. http://articles.timesofindia.indiatimes.com/2010-09-02/china/28249568_1_gilgitbaltistan-chinese-foreign-ministry-india-s-jammu.

Dasgupta, Saibal. "India, China Decide to Ramp Up Ties." *Times of India*, May 11, 2013 (Accessed June 12, 2013): http://articles.timesofindia.indiatimes.com/201305/11/china/39185699_1_khurshid-border-dispute-recent-chinese-incursion.

Dash, Dipak K. "Govt Plans 11 Tunnels on Pak, China Borders." *Times of India*, January 6, 2012 (Accessed April 22, 2013): http://articles.timesofindia.indiatimes.com/2012-0106/india/30597365_1_tunnels-strategic-roads-highways-ministry.

"Dignitaries Met: 2005–2010." *Dahlilama.com*. 2012 (Accessed January 30, 2013): http://www.dalailama.com/biography/dignitaries-met.

Dongsheng, Di. Author interview. Beijing, China, February 2013.

Doval, Ajit. Author interview. New Delhi, November 2011.

Du, Juan. "China Coal Imports to Continue Affecting Global Prices: Platts." May 22, 2013. http://www.chinadaily.com.cn/bizchina/2013-05/22/content_16518558.htm.

Dubey, Saurabh. "Chinese Dam on Brahmaputra India outraged. But the Government Reacts Meekly." *Tibet Third Pole*. http://tibet.org/tibet3rdpole.org/?p=548.

Ebbinghausen, Rodion. "The New Arms Race in Asia." Deutsche Welle, March 18, 2013 (Accessed July): http://www.dw.de/the-new-arms-race-in-asia/a-16681158.

Erickson, Andrew S., and Collins, Gabriel B. "China's Oil Security Pipe Dream The Reality and Strategic Consquences of Seaborne Imports." *Naval War College Review*, 2010.

ET Bureau. "Beijing Uneasy as Rao Meets Dalai Lama." *Economic Times (India Times)*. Accessed July 14, 2010 (January 20, 2013): http://articles.economic times.indiatimes.com/2010-07-14/news/28400948_1_tibet-related-issues-dalai -lama-china-political-activities.

"Fatalities in Terrorist Violence 1988–2013," *South Asia Terrorism Portal*. http:// www.satp.org/satporgtp/countries/india/states/jandk/data_sheets/annual_ caualties.htm.

Foreign Relations of the United States, 1961–1963. Volume XIX, South Asia, Document187. Telegram from the Department of State to the Embassy in India. October 28, 1962: 1687. Deptel 1677 to New Delhi. March 15, 2013. https://history. state.gov/historicaldocuments/frus1961-63v19/d187.

"'First Mover' Disadvantage." *Security Wise*, October 1, 2011. http://bharat karnad.com/7.

"Foreign Ministry Spokesperson Liu Jianchao's Press Conference on May 18, 2004. *Ministry of Foreign of Affairs of the People's Republic of China*, May 18, 2004 (Accessed April 22, 2013): www.fmprc.gov.cn/eng/xwfw/2510/t112578.htm.

"Forgotten: The Man Who Won Us Tawang." *The Pioneer*, March 10, 2012 (Accessed 30, 2013): http://www.dailypioneer.com/home/online-channel/top -story/48702forgotten-the-man-who-won-us-tawang.html.

Francine, Frankel and Harding, Harry. *The India-China Relationship: What the United States Needs to Know*. New York: Columbia University Press, 2004.

Fravel, M. Taylor. "China Views India's Rise: Deepening Cooperation, Managing Differences." *Strategic Asia*, 2011–2012.

Fravel, M. Taylor. "Regime Insecurity and International Cooperation: Explaining China's Compromises on Territorial Disputes." *International Security*, Vol. 30 Issue 2: 46–83, fall 2005 (Accessed Feburary 8, 2013): http://belfercenter.hks. harvard.edu/files/is3002_pp046-083_fravel.pdf.

"Friend, Enemy, Rival, Investor." *Economist*, June 30, 2012 (Accessed April 15, 2013): http://www.economist.com/node/21557764.

French, Patrick. *Tibet, Tibet: A Personal History of a Lost Land*. Random House Digital Inc., 2009.

Ganchen, Dr. Zhao. Author interview. Washington, DC, August 2011.

Ganchen, Dr. Zhao. Author interview. Washington, DC, May 16, 2012.

Ganchen, Dr. Zhao. Email correspondence. January 16, 2013.

Garretson, Lt. Col Peter. Author interview. Washington, DC, October 2012.

Garver, John W. *Protracted Contest: Sino-Indian Rivalry in the Twentieth Century*. Seattle: University of Washington Press, 2001.

Garver, John. "The Security Dilemma in Sino-Indian Relations." *India Review*, Vol. 1, No. 4 (2012): 33.

Geens, Stefan. "Google Maps' Arunachal Pradesh Place Names Turn Chinese, Google Admits Error." *Ogle Earth*, August 9, 2009 (February 6, 2013):

http://ogleearth.com/2009/08/google-maps-arunachal-pradesh-place-names
-turnchinese-google-admits-error/.

George, Narmala. "Chinese Incursion Leaves India on Verge of Crisis." *Associated Press,* May 2, 2013: http://world.time.com/2013/05/02/chinese-incursion
-leavesindia-on-verge-of-crisis/.

Global Trade Information Services, Inc. Global Trade Atlas (Accessed August 5, 2013): http://www.gtis.com/GTA/.

Goldstein, Melvyn. *A History of Modern Tibet: The Calm Before the Storm: 1951–1955.* Los Angeles: University of California Press, 2009.

Goldstein, Melvyn. "The Dalai Lama's Dilemma." *Foreign Affairs,* Vol. 77, No. 1: 86, January/February 2008 (Accessed February 6, 2013): http://c2.hbs.boellnet.de/downloads/Link_Goldstein.pdf.

Goldstein, Melvyn. *The Snow Lion and the Dragon.* Berkeley: University of California Press, 1997.

"Government to Expedite Road Infrastructure Works along China Border." *Economic Times,* September 8, 2010 (Accessed April 22, 2013): http://articles.economictimes.indiatimes.com/2010-0811/news/27589064_1_road-infrastructure-border-areas-km.

"Gov't Says Arunachal Integral Part of India after Chinese Protest." *Times of India,* October 13, 2009 (Accessed April 24, 2013): http://articles.timesofindia.indiatimes.com/2009-10-13/india/28077010_1_china-claims-arunachal
-pradesh-ma-zhaoxu.

Green, Michael J. "Japan, India, and the Strategic Triangle with China." *Strategic Asia 2011–12.*

"Growing Concerns in China about Inequality, Corruption." *Pew Research Center,* October 16, 2012: http://www.pewglobal.org/2012/10/16/chapter-2-china
-and-the-world/.

Guanglie, Liang. "China Has No Plans for Indian Military Bases." *Hindu:* 1

Gupta, Ambassador Ranjit. Public lecture at Thiruvananthapuram TMCA Hall-hosted by Kerala International Center, November 9, 2011. India's ambassador in residence at JNU, Secretary, Ministry of External Affairs 1999–2000. Ambassador to Yemen, Venezuela, Oman, Thailand, Spain, Head of Office in Taiwan.

Gurpeet, Cdr, and Khurana, S. "China-India Maritime Rivalry." *Indian Defence Review,* Vol. 23, No. 4.

Guruswamy, Mohan. Author interview. Delhi, November 2011.

Guruswamy, Mohan. Email correspondence. December 5, 2012.

Hailin, Ye. Author interview. Washington, DC, June 27, 2013.

Hailin, Ye. "China and South Asian Relations in a New Perspective." *Yataisuo,* October 23, 2008: http://yataisuo.cass.cn/english/articles/showcontent.asp?id=1111.

Hartcher, Peter. "Dreams of a Leader of a Land He Has Never Seen." *Sydney Morning Herald,* June 26, 2012 (Accessed January 28, 2013): http://www.smh.com.au/opinion/politics/dreams-of-a-leader-of-a-land-he-hasnever
-seen-20120625-20yh1.html.

Hazarika, Sanjoy. Author interview. New Delhi, August 2012.

Hessler, Peter. "Tibet through Chinese Eyes." *The Atlantic,* January 30, 2013 (Accessed June 13, 2013): http://www.theatlantic.com/magazine/archive/1999/02/tibet-through-chinese-eyes/306395/?single_page=true.

"History of Tibet." *China.org.cn.* March 21, 2008 (Accessed January 28, 2013): http://www.china.org.cn/china/2008-03/21/content_13268563.htm.

Hoffman, Steven A. *India and the China Crisis.* Los Angeles: University of California Press, 1990.

Hongliang, Che. "Chinese Navy to Actively Maintain Peace and Stability of Indian Ocean." *Chinese Military Online.* December 14, 2012 (Accessed December 17 2012): http://eng.chinamil.com.cn/news-channels/china-military-news/201212/14/content_5142763.htm.

Hongmei, Li. "China's 'Look East Policy' Means 'Look to Encircle China'?" *People's Daily*, October 27, 2010 (Accessed April 15, 2013): http://english.people daily.com.cn/90002/96417/7179404.html.

Hongmei, Li. "India Needs Pause When Driving East." *Xinhua*, November 8, 2011 (Accessed April 15, 2013): http://news.xinhuanet.com/english2010/indepth/2011-11/08/c_131235363.htm.

Hongmei, Li. "Terrorist Poised to Rule 'Tibetan Government In-Exile'?" *People's Daily Online*, March 22, 2011 (Accessed January 28, 2013): http://english.peopledaily.com.cn/90002/96417/7326988.html.

Hongmei, Li. "What Is Beyond the Physical Line?" *People's Daily Online.* August 12, 2009 (Accessed January 30, 2013): http://english.people.com.cn/90002/96417/6726134.html.

Horner, Daniel. "Chinese-Pakistani Reactor Deal Moves Ahead." *Arms Control Association*, April 2011 (Accessed April 24, 2013): http://www.armscontrol.org/print/4783.

Hui, Lu. "Commentary: Seven Questions to the 14th Dalai Lama." *Xinhua*, February 24, 2012 (Accessed April 2013): http://news.xinhuanet.com/english/indepth/2012-03/24/c_131487143.htm.

"Human Rights and Rule of Law News and Analysis: Measures on the Management of the Reincarnation of Living Buddhas in Tibetan Buddhism (ICT Translation)." *Congressional Executive Commission on China*, March 14, 2011 (Accessed January 28, 2013): http://www.cecc.gov/pages/virtualAcad/index.phpd?showsingle=98772.

"Increased Military Presence in South China Sea a Concern for All Nations." Observer Research Foundation, January 11, 2013 (Accessed April 15, 2013): http://www.orfonline.org/cms/sites/orfonline/html/interview/wu.html.

"India: Information on Tibetan Refugees and Settlements." *BCIS Resource Information Center, U.S. Citizenship and Immigration Services*, May 30, 2003 (Accessed January 28, 2013): http://www.uscis.gov/portal/site/uscis/menuitem.5af9bb959 19f35e66f61417654 6d1a/?vgnextoid=4e77361cfb98d010VgnVCM10000048f3d 6a1RCRD&vgnextcannel=d2d1e89390b5d010VgnVCM10000048f3d6a1RCRD.

"India and China: A Himalayan Rivalry." *Economist*, August 19, 2010 (Accessed June 19, 2013): http://www.economist.com/node/16843717.

"India Being Swept Up by Missile Delusion." *Global Times*, April 19, 2012 (Accessed April 10, 2013): http://www.globaltimes.cn/NEWS/tabid/99/ID/705627/India being-swept-up-by-missile-delusion.aspx.

"India, China to Set-Up Border Mechanism." *Hindustan Times*, January 17, 2012 (Accessed April 24 2013): http://www.hindustantimes.com/India news/NewDelhi/India-China-sign-border-management-pact/Article1798623.aspx.

"India Covets Dalai Lama's Visit." *Global Times*, November 9, 2009 (Accessed April 24, 2013): http://world.globaltimes.cn/asia-pacific/2009-11/483521.html.

India Defense. "China tested nuclear weapons for Pakistan in 1990: Thomas Reed." January 3, 2009. http://www.india-defence.com/reports-4114.

"India Groundwater: A Valuable but Diminishing Resource." March 6, 2012. http://www.worldbank.org/en/news/feature/2012/03/06/india-ground water-critical-diminishing.

"India Lashes Out on China for Blocking ADB Loan" *Siasat Daily*, July 1, 2009. http://www.siasat.com/english/content/india-lashes-out-china-blocking -adbloan.

"India Is Third Largest Buyer of U.S. Arms." *NDTV*, December 8, 2011 (Accessed April 8, 2013): http://www.ndtv.com/article/india/india-is-third-largest -buyer-of-us arms156515?pfrom=home-otherstories.

"India Ready to Work for a Fair and Reasonable Solution to Border Dispute with China." *Rediff on the Net* 1997, April 10, 2013. http://www.rediff.com/news/1996/2811chin.htm.

"India Should Not 'Stir Up' Border Trouble, Says PLA General Ahead of Antony Visit." *Hindu*, July 4, 2013. http://www.thehindu.com/news/interna tional/world/indiashould-not-stir-up-border-trouble-says-pla-general-ahead -of-antony visit/article4881266.ece?mstac=0.

"India—Singapore Bilateral Relations." January 2013 Indian Ministry of External Affairs. http://www.mea.gov.in/Portal/ForeignRelation/Brief__for_MEA_s_website__Jan_2013-1.pdf.

"India to Establish 2 Additional Missile Test Sites." *Defensenews.com*. February 27, 2013 (Accessed May 13, 2013): http://www.defensenews.com/article/20130227/DEFREG03/302270018.

"India to Reinforce Security in Andaman & Nicobar." *Brahmand.com*, February 9, 2010. http://www.brahmand.com/news/India-to-reinforce-security-in -AndamanNicobar/3132/1/12.html.

"India to Verify Reports of Chinese Presence in PoK, Says Govt." *Times of India*, August 30, 2010. http://articles.timesofindia.indiatimes.com/2010-0830/india/28301219_1_gilgit-baltistan-chinese-troops-high-speed-rail-and-road.

"India Vows to Protect S. China Sea Interests" *Voice of America*. December 4, 2012. http://www.voanews.com/content/india-vows-to-protect-south-china -seainterests/1558070.html.

"India Upholds Freedom of Navigation in International Waters." *Times of India*, November 4, 2011 (Accessed April 15, 2013): http://articles.timesof india.indiatimes.com/2011-1104/india/30358765_1_navigation-indian-war ship-south-china-sea.

"India's Gandhi Calls for Dialogue with China." *Reuters*, October 27, 2007 (Accessed April 10, 2013): http://www.reuters.com/article/2007/10/27/us -china-india-gandhiidUSPEK13281820071027.

"India's President Wants Improved Maritime Security." *Defense News*, December 20, 2011 (Accessed April 15, 2013): http://www.defensenews.com/article/20111220/DEFSECT03/112200307/India-sPresident-Wants-Improved -Maritime-Security.

"India's Surprising but Welcome Message." *Global Times*, February 22, 2010 (Accessed July 2013): http://www.globaltimes.cn/opinion/editorial/2010 -02/506893.html.

"India's Unwise Military Moves." *People's Daily Online*, June 11, 2009 (Accessed April 8, 2013): http://english.people.com.cn/90001/90777/90851/6676088 .html.

Indian Coast Guard. "Coast Guard Region (Andaman & Nicobar)." http://www .indiancoastguard.nic.in/Indiancoastguard/org/rhqan.html.

"Indian Government Survives Vote." *BBC News* July 22, 2008 (Accessed April 8, 2013): http://news.bbc.co.uk/2/hi/south_asia/7519860.stml.

"Indian Navy Prepared to Defend its Interest in South China Sea, says Admiral DK Joshi," *India Today*, December 3, 2012 (Accessed April 15, 2013) http:// indiatoday.intoday.in/story/india-prepared-to-intervene-in-south-china-sea -navy-chief/1/235881.html.

Indian officials. Author interview. Washington, March 2012.

"Indian, Pakistani, and Chinese Border Disputes: Fantasy Frontiers." *Economist Online*, February 8, 2012 (Accessed February 6, 2013): http://www.economist .com/blogs/dailychart/2011/05/indian_pakistani_and_chinse_border_ disputes.

"Indian Tanks Move in Sikkim after Chinese Activities." *India Today*, July 28, 2009 (Accessed June 12, 2013): http://indiatoday.intoday.in/story/Indian+tanks+ move+in+Sikkim+after+Chineseactivities/1/53856.html.

"INS Baaz Commissioned as first Naval Air Station in Nicobar Islands." IDR News Network, August 10, 2012. http://www.indiandefencereview.com/ news/ins-baaz-commissioned-as-first-naval-air-station-in-nicobar-islands/.

"INS Saryu Commissioned for Maritime Surveillance." *Times of India*. January 21, 2013 (Accessed May 13, 2013). http://articles.timesofindia.indiatimes .com/2013-01-21/india/36462455_1_andaman-and-nicobar-islands-ins-saryu -ships-and-fleetsupport.

Institute for Defence Studies and Analyses (IDSA). "Tibet and India's Security: Himalayan Region, Refugees and Sino-Indian Relations," 2012 (Accessed January 28, 2013): http://www.idsa.in/book/TibetandIndiasSecurity.

International Energy Agency. "People's Republic of China." *Oil and Gas Security Emergency Response of IEA Countries 2012*, 2012. http://www.iea.org/publications/freepublications/publication/China_2012.pdf.

Iyer-Mitra, Abhijit. "India Stops Hedging, Backs American Naval Strategy." *Atlantic Sentinel*, June 18, 2012 (Accessed April 15, 2013): http://atlanticsentinel .com/2012/06/india-stops-hedging-backs-american-naval-strategy/.

Jaishankar, S. Indian Ambassador to China. Author interview. Beijing, April 2013.

"Japan-India Relations." Japanese Ministry of Foreign Affairs. http://www.mofa .go.jp/region/asia-paci/india/index.html?ef642a70.

Jethmalani, Ram. "China Threat Cannot Be Ignored." *Sunday Guardian*, February 8, 2013 (Accessed June 13, 2013): http://www.Sundayguardian.com/analysis/ china-threat-cannot-be-ignored.

Jintao, Hu. "Working Together to Expand Cooperation and Create a Bright Future." *Embassy of the People's Republic of China in India*, November 26, 2006 (Accessed

April 10, 2013): http://in.china-embassy.org/eng/embassy_news/2006en/
t282088.htm.

"JJ Clarifies: Remarks on India-China Border Personal." *Indian Express,* April 21,
2012 (Accessed February 8, 2013): http://www.indianexpress.com/news/
jjclarifies-remarks-on-indiachina-border-personal/939599\.

"J.N. to JFK, 'Eyes Only.'" *The Indian Express,* November 15, 2010 (Accessed March
11, 2013): http://www.indianexpress.com/olympics/news/j.n.-to-jfk--eyes
-only /711276/0.

Johnson, Jo, and McGregor, Richard. "China Raises Tension in India Dispute."
Financial Times, June 10, 2007 (Accessed April 22, 2013): http://www.ft.com/
cms/s/0/2606bb64-176e11dc-86d1000b5df10621.html#axzz27snGlnfl.

Joshi, Saurabhi. "China Blasts ADB Approval for Arunachal Loan: Report." *Strat-
Post,* June 18, 2009 (Accessed April 24, 2013): http://www.stratpost.com/china
-blastsadb-approval-for-arunachal-loan-report.

Joshi, Saurabhi."India to Double Troops in Arunachal." *StratPost,* June 8, 2009
(Accessed April 22, 2013): http://www.stratpost.com/india-to-double-troops
-in-arunachal.

Joshi, Shashank. "Can India Blockade China?" *Diplomat,* August 12, 2013 (Accessed
August 12, 2013): http://thediplomat.com/flashpoints-blog/2013/08/12/can-
india-blockade-china/

Kalha, R. S. "The Chinese Message and What Should the Reply Be?" IDSA Comment, May 21, 2013. http://www.idsa.in/idsacomments/TheChineseMessage
Indiareply_rskalha_210513

Kang, Zhe. "Diversion Debate." *ChinaDialogue,* June 13, 2011: http://www.china
dialogue.net/article/show/single/en/4349-Diversion-debate.

Kapoor, Naveen. "PM Manmohan Singh Says India Greatly Values Friendship
with China." *Yahoo News,* November 19, 2012 (Accessed April 10, 2013): http://
in.news.yahoo.com/pm-manmohan-singh-says-india-greatly-values-friend
ship-070223951.html.

Karnad, Bharat. "China Uses Pak, Vietnam to Open India." *Indian Express,* October 3, 2005. http://expressindia.indianexpress.com/news/fullstory.php?news
id=55789.

Khilnani, Sunil, et al. "Nonalignment 2.0: A Foreign and Strategic Policy in the
21st Century." 2012. http://www.cprindia.org/sites/default/files/NonAlign
ment%202.0_1.pdf.

"Know Your Own Strength." *The Economist,* March 20, 2013 (April 10, 2013):
http://www.economist.com/news/briefing/21574458-india-poised-become
-one-four-largest-military-powers-worldend?zid=306&ah=1b164dbd43b0cb27
ba0d4c3b12a5e227.

Kondipalli, Srikanth. Author interview. New Delhi, August 2012.

Kondapalli, Srikanth. "Military Seminar Report #204." Institute of Peace and Conflict Studies. December 27, 2006 (Accessed February 8, 2013): http://ipcs.org/
seminar/military/india-china-border-issue-763.html.

Kondapalli, Srikanth. "The Chinese Military Eyes South Asia." *Shaping China's
Securit Environment: The Role of the People's Liberation Army.* Carlisle: Strategic
Studies Institute, US Army War College, 2006.

Kostecka, Daniel J. "Places and Bases: The Chinese Navy's Emerging Support Network in the Indian Ocean." *Naval War College Review*. Vol. 64, No. 1. Winter 2011: 70.

Krishan, Ananth. "China Gives Go-Ahead for Three New Brahmaputra Dams," *Hindu*, January 30, 2013. http://www.thehindu.com/news/international/china-gives-goahead-for-three-new-brahmaputra-dams/article4358195.ece.

Krishnan, Ananth "China Sees a Newly Assertive India." *Hindu*, November 30, 2011 (Accessed April 24, 2013): http://www.thehindu.com/news/national/article2672222.ece.

Krishnan, Ananth. "China Will Not Accept LAC as Solution for Border Dispute, Says Commentary." *Hindu* citing *Jiafang Daily/Liberation Daily*, October 25, 2012 (Accessed February 8, 2013): http://www.thehindu.com/news/national/china-will-not-accept-lac-assolution-to-border-dispute-says-commentary/article4031786.ece.

Krishnan, Ananth. "China Warns India on South China Sea Exploration Projects." *Hindu*, September 15, 2011. http://www.thehindu.com/news/international/china-warns-india-on-south-china-sea-exploration-projects/article2455647.ece.

Krishan, Ananth. "China's Tourism Plan Quells Brahmaputra Dam Fears" *Hindu*, June 24, 2012. http://www.thehindu.com/news/international/chinas-tourism-plan-quells-brahmaputra-dam-fears/article3566337.ece.

Krishnan, Ananth. "Chinese Visa Policies Cast a Shadow over Ties." *Hindu*, July 22, 2011 (Accessed April 24, 2013): http://www.thehindu.com/news/national/article2282599.ece.

Krishnan, Ananth. "In South China Sea, a Surprise Chinese Escort for Indian Ships," *Hindu*, June 14, 2012 (Accessed April 15, 2013) http://www.thehindu.com/news/national/article3524965.ece.

Krishnan, Ananth. "Meaningful Autonomy Is the Only Realistic Solution." *The Hindu*. July 9, 2012: http://www.thehindu.com/opinion/interview/article3616701.ece.

Krishnan, Ananth. "Month after Border Talks, Chinese Paper Says Aksai Chin is Closed Chapter." *Hindu*, Februay 16, 2012. http://www.thehindu.com/todays-paper/tp-international/article 2898189.ece.

Krishnan, Ananth."Officials Dismiss China's Kashmir Border Claims." *Hindu*, December 2010 (Accessed February 6, 2013). http://www.thehindu.com/news/national/article963655.ece.

Krishnan, Ananth "Panchen Lama in Top Chinese Panel." *Hindu*, March 12, 2013 (Accessed June 13, 2013): http://www.thehindu.com/news/international/world/panchen-lama-in-top-chinese-panel/article4501574.ece.

"Kuan-san, Tan, and Dalai Lama." 1959 (Accessed January 30, 2013): http://www.claudearpi.net/maintenance/uploaded_pics/Letters_Tan_Dalailama.pdf.

Kukreja, Dhiraj. "Andaman and Nicobar Islands: A security challenge for India." *Indian Defense Review*. 28. No. ,1 2013.http://www.indiandefencereview.com/news/andaman-and-nicobar-islands-a-security-challenge-for-india/.

Kuna. "China Illegally Claiming 90,000 km of Our Territory—India." TwoCircles.ne, February 28, 2008. http://twocircles.net/node/50808.

Ladwig, Walter. "Delhi's Pacific Ambition: Naval Power, 'Look East,' and India's Emerging Influence in the Asia-Pacific Asian Security." Vol. 5, No. 2, June 2009.

Lal, Dinesh. *Indo-Tibet-China Conflict* (Delhi: Kalpaz Publications, 2008).

"Lal Masjid kidnap Chinese Nationals." *One India News,* June 23, 2007. http://news.oneindia.in/2007/06/23/lal-masjid-brigade-kidnap-chinese-nation als1182591347.html.

Lancaster, John. "India, China Hoping to 'Reshape the World Order' Together." *Washington Post,* April 12, 2005 (Accessed July 24, 2013): http://www.washingtonpost.com/wp-dyn/articles/A43053-2005Apr11.html.

Latif, S. Amir. "U.S. India Defense Trade: Opportunities for Defending the Partnership." *Center for Strategic and International Studies* (June 2012).

le Clue, Sophie. "Geopolitical Risks: Transboundary Rivers." *China Water Risk.* February 9, 2012.

Le Miere, Christian. "China's Unarmed Arms Race." *Foreign Affairs.* July 29, 2013. http://www.foreignaffairs.com/articles/139609/christian-le-miere/chinas-unarmed-arms-race?

Li, Li. *Security Perception and China-India Relations.* New Delhi: KW Publishers, 2009.

Lieutenant-General in the Indian Army. Author interview. Washington, DC, May, 2013.

"Lieutenant-General Wang Hongguang Blasts PLA Pundits' 'Interference' in Decisions and Deployments." *South Sea Conversations,* April 29, 2013. http://south seaconversations.wordpress.com/.

Liu, Xuechang. "Look Beyond the Sino-Indian Border Dispute." *China Institute of International Studies,* August 11, 2011 (Accessed January 30, 2013): http://www.ciis.org.cn/english/2011-08/11/content_4401017.htm.

Lowy Institute for International Policy India Poll 2013. May 20, 2013. 13 (Accessed June 12, 2013): http://www.lowyinstitute.org/publications/india-poll-2013.

Machar, Sainiksa. "Andaman & Nicobar Command Saga of Synergy." October 16, 2011. http://www.sainiksamachar.nic.in/englisharchives/2011/oct1611/h5.htm.

Malik, Mohan. Author interview. Honolulu, April 2012.

Malik, Mohan. "Historical Fiction: China's South China Sea Claims." *World Affairs Journal,* May/June 2013.

Malik, Mohan."India-China Competition Revealed in Ongoing Border Disputes." *Power and Interest News Report,* October 9, 2007 (Accessed April 10, 2013): http://www.gees.org/documentos/Documen-02608.pdf.

Malik, Mohan. "War Talk: Perpetual Gap in Chindia Relations." *Association for Asian Research,* October 7, 2009 (Accessed April 22, 2013): http://www.asian research.org/articles/3224.html.

Mandala, Raja and Mohan, Raja. "Indian Navy in South China Sea: Beijing's Unwelcome Escort," June 14, 2012. http://www.indianexpress.com/news/indian-navy-in-south-china-sea-beijing-s-unwelcome-escort/962011/.

Manthan, Samudra. "Sino Indian Rivalry in the Indo-Pacific." Speech. March 4, 2013. http://www.orfonline.org/cms/export/orfonline/documents/Samudra-Manthan.pdf.

"Many Chinese Think India Greatest Security Threat after US: New Poll." *Indian Express,* December 2, 2009 (April 22, 2013): http://www.indianexpress.com/news/many-chinese-think-india-greatest-security-t/548808/.

Marcello, Patricia Cronin. *The Dalai Lama: A Biography*. Greenwood Publishing Group, 2003.

Maritime Security Conference, April 2013.

Marshall, Julie. *Britain and Tibet: 1765–1947*. New York: Taylor & Francis, 2007.

Maxwell, Neville Maxwell. "Whose Tawang? A Dispute within the Sino-Indian Boundary Dispute," January 30, 2013 (Accessed June 13, 2013): http://china indiaborderdispute.files.wordpress.com/2010/07/nmaxwelltawangse nsister spostnov2011.pdf.

McGoldrick, Fred."Road Ahead for Export Controls: Challenges for the Nuclear Suppliers Group." *Arms Control Association,* Jan/Feb 2011 (Accessed April 24, 2013): http://www.armscontrol.org/act/2011_01-02/McGoldrick.

Member of India's Parliament from the Bharatiya Janata Party. Author interview. New Delhi, November 2011.

Member of Parliament from India's Congress Party. Lunch discussion. Heritage Foundation, September 19, 2012.

Menon, Raja. "A Mountain Strike Corps Is Not the Only Option." *Hindu,* July 29, 2013. http://www.thehindu.com/opinion/lead/a-mountain-strike-corps -is-not-the-only-option/article4963979.ece?ref=relatedNews

Miles, James Miles. "Transcript: James Miles Interview on Tibet." *CNN Asia,* March 20, 2008 (Accessed January 30, 2013): http://www.cnn.com/2008/ WORLD/asiapcf/03/20/tibet.miles.interview/.

Ministry of External Affairs New Delhi. Author interview. South Block, New Delhi, November 2011.

Mitra, Chandan. Author interview. New Delhi, November 2011.

Mohan, C. Raja. "China's Rise, America's Pivot, and India's Asian Ambiguity." *India Seminar,* January 31, 2013. http://carnegieendowment.org/2013/01/31/ china-srise-america-s-pivot-and-india-s-asian-ambiguity/fdp0.

Mohan, C. Raja. "India and the Balance of Power." *Foreign Affairs,* July/August 2006 (April 8, 2013): http://www.foreignaffairs.com/articles/61729/c-raja -mohan/india-and-the-balance-of-power.

Mohan, C. Raja. "India's New Role in the Indian Ocean." *India Seminar,* January 2011 (Accessed April 15, 2013): http://www.india seminar.com/2011/617/617_c_ raja_mohan.htm.

Mohan, C. Raja. "The New Triangular Diplomacy: India, China and America at Sea." *NamViet News,* November 6, 2012 (Accessed April 8, 2013): http://nam vietnews.wordpress.com/2012/11/06/the-new-triangular-diplomacyindia -china-and-america-at-sea/.

Mohan, C. Raja. *Samudra Manthan: Sino-Indian Rivalry in the Pacific*. Washington DC: Carnegie Endowment for International Peace, 2012.

Mohan, Guruswamy. Author interview. New Delhi, November 2011.

Mohan, Guruswamy. "50 Years after 1962: Will India and China Fight a War Again," *South Asia Monitor*, 1–3.

Mohan, Lalit. "Lobsang Sangay to be Tibetan Prime Minister." *Tribune,* April 27, 2011 (Accessed January 28, 2013): http://www.tribuneindia .com/2011/20110428/main5.htm.

Mukherjee, Pranab. ". . . Arunachal Pradesh is an Integral Part of India." *Outlook India,* November 11, 2008 (Accessed April 14, 2013): http://www.outlookindia .com/article.aspx?238923.

Narayanan, Ram. "Should India Make Up with China Now?" *Freedom First,* Monthly No. 513, March 2010 (Accessed February 8, 2013): http://www.wired .com/beyond_the_beyond/2010/02/freedom-first-and-chinalast/.

"Navy Unveils Plans, Puts Andamans in Forefront of its Strategy." *Rediff.com.* October 17, 2011. http://www.rediff.com/news/special/navy-unveils-plans -puts-andamans-in-forefront-of-its-strategy/20111017.htm.

"No Mention of 'One China Policy' in India-China Joint Statement." *Phayul.com,* December 17, 2010 (Accessed April 24, 2013): http://www.phayul.com/news/ article.aspx?id=28767&t=1.

Noorani, A. G. "Only Political Leaders Can Resolve the Boundary Dispute between India and China, Not Officials." *Frontline,* Vol. 25, Issue 21, October 11–24, 2008 (Accessed February 6, 2013): http://www.frontlineonnet.com/ fl2521/stories/20081024252108000.htm.

Noorani, A. G. "The Truth." *Frontline.* November 30, 2013 (Accessed January 30, 2013): http://pay.hindu.com/ebook%20-%20ebfl20121130part1.pdf.

"Not as close as Lips and Teeth." *Economist,* October 22, 2011: http://www .economist.com/node/21533397/print.

"Now India, China in Map Row over Arunachal Pradesh, Aksai Chin." *India Today,* November 23, 2012 (February 6, 2013): http://indiatoday.intoday.in/ story/india-china-map-row-arunachal-pradesh/1/230544.html.

"Nuclear Power in Pakistan." *World Nuclear Association,* May 2012 (Accessed April 24, 2013): http://www.world-nuclear.org/info/inf108.html.

Olesen, Alexa."China, India Resolving Sikkim Dispute." *Associated Press,* October 8, 2003 (Accessed April 22, 2013): www.tibet.ca/en/newsroom/wtn/arhive/ old?y=2003&m=10&p=8_4.

One official from the Tibetan Government in Exile. Author interview. Dharamsala, India, August 2012.

"ONGC, China National Petroleum Corp Ink JV." *Indian Express,* June 19, 2011. http://www.indianexpress.com/news/ongc-china-national-petroleum -corp-ink jv/964034.

"ONGC Ltd. Assets," 2010. http://www.ongcvidesh.com/(X(1)S(j510jd45p2p41 mepsypgkjey))/Assets.aspx?spxAutoDetectCookieSupport=1.

"ONGC Videsh Pens Pact with PetroVietnam." *Rigzone,* October 12, 2011 (Accessed April 15, 2013): http://www.rigzone.com/news/oil_gas/a/111765/ ONGC_Videsh_Pens_Pact_wit_PetroVietnam.

"Origins of So-Called 'Tibetan Independence.'" *People's Daily Online,* January 28, 2013 (Accessed June 13, 2013): http://english.peopledaily.com.cn/whitepaper/ 6%282%29.html.

"Pakistan to Start Work on Chinese Aided Nuclear Power Plant." *Kyodo News International,* June 13, 2001. http://www.globalpost.com/dispatch/news/ kyodonews-international/130613/pakistan-start-work-chinese-aided-nuclear -powerplant.

Panda, Jagannath P. Author interview. Washington, DC, June 2012.

Panda, Jagannath P. "China's Designs on Arunachal Pradesh." *Institute for Defence Studies and Analyses,* March 12, 2008.

Pandit, Rajat. "Army Reworks War Doctrine for Pakistan, China." *The Times of India,.* December 30, 2009 (Accessed April 22, 2013): http://articles.tim

india.indiatimes.com/200912-30/india/28104699_1_war doctrine-new-doctrine -entire-western-front.

Pandit, Rajai. "IAF Conducts First Ever Landing of 'Super Hercules' Military Aircraft at Car Nicobar Airbase." *Times of India*, May 28, 2012. http://articles .timesofindia.indiatimes.com/2012-05-28/india/31876848_1_car nicobar-hin don-airbase.

Pandit, Rajai, "Strategically-important A&N Command to Get a Boost." *Times of India*, February 6, 2010. http://articles.timesofindia.indiatimes.com/2010-02 -06/india/28115911_1_ancairfield-andamans.

Pandya, Shree, and Wallentine, Kevin. "An Interview with Melvyn Goldstein." *Claremont Mckenna University*, January 30, 2013.

Pant, Harsh. "The South China Sea: A New Area in Chinese-Indian Rivalry." *Nation*, June 20, 2012. http://www.nationmultimedia.com/opinion/The -South-China-SeaA-new-area-in-Chinese-Indian-r-30208644.html.

Parsai, Gargi. "India, China Renew Flood Data Pact on Brahmaputra." *Hindu*, May 20, 2013. http://www.thehindu.com/news/national/india-china-renew -flood-datapact-on-brahmaputra/article4732965.ece.

Parsatharathy, G. "Games Neighbours Play." *Times of India*, June 29, 2009. http:// articles.timesofindia.indiatimes.com/2009-06-29/edit page/28191796_1_ southern-tibet-sino-indian-people-s-daily.

Patranobis, Sutirtho. "India's Iron Ore Export to China Falls, Decreases Bilateral Trade." *Hindustan Times*, January 21, 2013 (Accessed1April 15, 2013): http:// www.hindustantimes.com/world-news/China/India-s-iron-ore-export-to -China-falls-decreases-bilateral-trade/Article1-997781.aspx.

Perlez, Jane. "Rebuffed by China, Pakistan May Seek I.M.F. Aid." *New York Times*, October 18, 2008. http://www.nytimes.com/2008/10/19/world/ asia/19zardari.html?_r=0.

Peters, Amanda. "Education Department Takes Over Running of Central School for Tibetans." *Tibet Post International*, July 11, 2012 (Accessed January 28, 2013): http://www.thetibetpost.com/en/news/exile/2695-education-department-takesover-running-of-central-school-for-tibetans.

"PM Allays Fears on Chinese Dam-Building on Brahmaputra" *Times of India*, March 29, 2013. http://articles.timesofindia.indiatimes.com/2013-0329/ india/38124666_1_brics-brahmaputra-new-chinese-president.

Polgreen, Lydia. "India Digs Under Top of the World to Match Rival." *New York Times*, July 31, 2010 (Accessed April 22, 2013): http://www.nytimes .com/2010/08/01/world/asia/01pass.html?pagewanted=all.

Pomeranz, Kenneth. "The Great Himalayan Watershed: Agrarian Crisis, Mega-Dams and the Environment." *New Left Review*, Vol. 58, July–August 2009.

Prakash, Arun. "India Must Pause before Entering into Choppy Waters." *Rediff News*. September 26, 2011. http://www.rediff.com/news/column/column -india-must-pause-before-venturing-into-choppy-waters/20110926.htm.

"PRC Expert: PLA Navy May Contemplate Setting up Supply Bases Abroad." *Beijing China National Radio*, December 26, 2009. www.cnr.cn/.

Press Trust of India. February 8, 2010. "India to Plug Gaps in Security of Andaman and Nicobar Islands." http://www.dnaindai.com/india/report-india-to-plug-gaps-in-security-of-andoman-and-nicobar-islands-1345128.

Presse, Agence France. "Tibet Exiled 'PM' Admits Dalai Lama's Shoes Hard to Fill." *Himalayan Times Online*, October 20, 2010 (Accessed January 28, 2013): http://thehimalayantimes.com/rssReference.php?headline=Tibet%20 exiled%20M%20says%20Dalai%20Lama's%20shoes%20hard%20to%20 fill&NewsID=34245.

Public Lecture by Ambassador Ranjit Gupta. At Thiruvananthapuram TMCA Hall, hosted by Kerala International Center, November 9, 2011.

Qingfen, Ding. "China, India to Narrow Trade Gap." *China Daily*, August 30, 2012 (Accessed April 15, 2013): http://usa.chinadaily.com.cn/business/2012x08/30/ content_15718053.htm.

Rabgey, Tashi, and Sharlho, Tseten Wangchuk. "Sino-Tibetan Dialogue in the Post-Mao Era: Lessons and Prospects." *East-West Center*, Policy Studies No. 12. 2004 (Accessed June 13, 2013): http://www.eastwestcenter.org/publications/ sinotibetan-dialogue-post-mao-era-lessons-and-prospects.

Raghavan, B. S. "India China Confluence, Ushering in a New Golden Era." *Hindu Business Line*, July 6, 2009 (Accessed February 6 2013): http://www.the hindubusinessline.in/bline/2009/07/06/stories/2009070650390900.htm.

Raghavan, Srinath. "The Fifty Year Crisis: India and China Since 1962." *India Seminar*, January 2013 (Accessed April 15, 2013): http://www.indiaseminar .com/2013/641/641_srinath_raghavan.htm.

Raghuvanshi, Vivek. "China Threat Inspires Indian Navy's Plans." *Defense News*, October 20, 2008. http://www.iss.europa.eu/uploads/media/op77.pdf.

Raghuvanshi, Vivek. "India to Modernize Road Networks in Border Areas." *Defense News*, May 7, 2010 (April 22, 2013): http://www.defensenews.com/ article/20100507/DEFSECT02/5070304/India-Modernize-Road-Networks -Border-Areas.

Rajagopalan, Rajeswari Pillai, and Prasad, Kailash. "Sino-Indian Border Infra-structure: Issues and Challenges." *ORF Issue Brief*, August 2010 (Accessed January 30, 2013): http://www.observerindia.com/cms/sites/orfonline/modules/ issuebrief/attachment /Ib_231283150074942.pdf.

Rajan, D. S. "China Should Break Up the Indian Union, Suggests a Chinese Strate-gist." *Chennai Centre for China Studies*, August 9, 2009 (Accessed April 22, 2013): http://www.c3sindia.org/india/719.

Rajeswar, T. V. "India-China Border Dispute: What Can Be a Possible Solu-tion." *Tribune*, January 30, 2013 (Accessed June 13, 2013): http://www.tribune india.com/2012/20121103/edit.htm#4.

Ramachandran, Sudha. "China Plays Long Game on Border Disputes." *Asia Times Online*, June 27, 2008 (Accessed February 8, 2013): http://www.atimes.com/ atimes/China/MA27Ad02.html.

Ramachandran, Sudha. "China Toys with India's Border." *Asia Times Online*, June 27, 2008 (Accessed 30, 2013): http://www.atimes.com/atimes/South_Asia/ JF27Df01.html.

Ramachandran, Sudha. "Chinese Antics have India Fuming," *Asia Times*, May 5, 2009 (Accessed April 24, 2013): http://www.atimes.com/atimes/South_Asia/ KE05Df01.html.

Ramachandran, Sudha. "Indian Navy Pumps Up Eastern Muscle." *Asian Times*, August 21, 2011. http://www.atimes.com/atimes/South_Asia/MH20Df02.html.

Raman, B. "An Assessment: Brajesh Mishra (1928–2012)." *OutlookIndia.com*, September 29, 2012. http://www.outlookindia.com/article.aspx?282419.

Raman, B. "Dragon's New Face." *OutlookIndia.com*, 2013 (Accessed February 27, 2013): http://www.outlookindia.com/article.aspx?283780.

RAND Corporation, "Overview of China's Arms Sales," 1997. http://www.rand.org/content/dam/rand/pubs/monograph_reports/MR1119/MR119.appa.pdf.

"Reincarnation of Tibetan Living Buddhas Must Get Government Approval." *People's Daily Online*, August 3, 2007 (Accessed January 28, 2013): http://english.peopledaily.com.cn/90001/90776/6231524.html.

Rehman, Iskander. "China's String of Pearls and India's Enduring Tactical Advantage" *Idsa Comment*. http://www.idsa.in/idsacomments/Chinas StringofPearlsandIndiasEnduringTactic lAdvantage_irehman_080610.

Rehman, Iskander. "Keeping the Dragon at Bay: India's Counter-containment of China in India." *Asian Security*. No. 2, 2009. http://www.militaryphotos.net/forums/showthread.php?159581-Keeping-the Dragon-at-Bay-India-s-Counter-Containment-of-China-in-Asia.

Rehman, Iskander. *Shaping the Emerging World Order: India and Multilateralism*. Washington, DC: Brookings Institute, 2013.

Renmin University professor. Author interview. Beijing, February 2012.

"Return Tawang to China to Resolve Boundary Dispute." *Rediff News*. March 7, 2007 (Accessed January 30, 2013): http://www.rediff.com/news/report/china/20070307.htm.

Roemer, Timothy. "Tibet: Growing Frustration after Latest Round of Talks Between Beijing and The Dalai Lama's Envoys." September 8, 2011 (Accessed January 28, 2013): http://wikileaks.tetalab.org/mobile/cables/10NEWDELHI290.html.

Roul, Avilash. "India-China Hydro Diplomacy: Beyond Information Sharing MoUs." SSPC, March 22, 2013. http://sspconline.org/opinion/IndiaChina HydroDiplomacy_22032013.

Roundtable conference at the Heritage Foundation, October 5, 2012.

"Round Table Discussion on Indo-China Border Impasse." *Observer Research Foundation*, August 4, 2007 (Accessed February 6, 2013): http://www.observerindia.com/cms/sites/orfonline/modules/report/ReportDetail.ml?cmaid=9806&mmacmaid=9807.

Samachar, Sainik. "Andaman and Nicobar Command Saga of Energy," October 12, 2011. http://www.sainiksamachar.nic.in/englisharchives/2011/oct16-11/h5.htm.

Samanta, Pranab Dhal. "China Puts Indian Oil Block up for Auction." *Indian Express*, July, 17, 2012. http://www.indianexpress.com/news/china-puts-indian-oil-blockup-for auction/975480/.

Samanta, Pranab Dhal. "China Says No but US, Japan Help ADB Clear India's Plan," *Times of India*, June 16, 2009 (Accessed April 24, 2013): http://www.indianexpress.com/news/china-says-no-but-us-japan-help-adb-clearindias-plan/477252/.

Samanta, Pranab Dhal. "India-China Face-Off Worsens over ADB Loan for Arunachal," *Indian Express*, May 15, 2009. http://www.indianexpress.com/news/indiachinafaceoff-worsens-over-adb-loanfor-arunachal/459910/.

Samaranayake, Nilanthi. "The Long Littoral Project: Bay of Bengal: A Maritime Perspective on Indo-Pacific Security." Center for Naval Analysis, September

2012. http://www.cna.org/sites/default/files/research/IRP-2012-U-002319 Final%20Bay%20of%20Bengal.pdf.

Sangay, Dr. Lobsang. "Occasion of His Inauguration." Inaugural Acceptance Speech, Dharaslama. August 8, 2011.

Saran, Shyam. "China in the Twenty-First Century: What India Needs to Know about China's World View." Second Annual K. Subrahmanyam Memorial Lecture.

Scholar at the Shanghai Institute for International Studies. Author interview. Washington, DC, May 2012.

"Security Perception and China-India Relations" Li Li (KW Publiushers New Delhi 2009).

Senior Indian naval officials. Author interview. New Delhi, November 2011.

Senior official in India's Ministry of External Affairs. Author interview. Beijing, April 2013.

Senior Pentagon official. Author interview. Washington, DC, October 2012.

Sethi, Manpreet. "The Agni-V: A Dragon's Response." *Diplomat*, April 10, 2013 (Accessed April 2012): http://the-diplomat.com/flashpoints-blog/2012/04/27/theagni-v-%E2%80%93-a-dragons-response/.

Shah, Giriraj. *Tibet: Himalayan Region: Religion, Society, and Politics*. Delhi: Kalpaz Publications, 2003.

Shakabpa, W. D. *Tibet: A Political History*. New Haven: Yale University Press, 1967.

Shanshan, Zhu. "90% in Online Poll Believe India Threatens China's Security." *Global Times*, June 11, 2009 (Accessed April 22, 2013): www.globaltimes.cn/china/topphoto/200906/436320.html.

Sharma, Rakesh. "ONGC to Continue Exploration in South China Sea." *The Wall Street Journal*, July 19, 2012. http://online.wsj.com/article/SB10000872396390444464304577536182763155 6.html.

Shen, Simon. "Exploring the Neglected Constraints on Chindia: Analysing the Online Chinese Perception of India and Its Interaction with China's Indian Policy." *China Quarterly* Vol. 207, September 2011.

Sheridan, Michael. "Chinese Sure No One Will Rain on Their Parade." *Australian*, September 28, 2009 (Accessed April 22, 2013): http://www.theaustralian.com.au/news/world/chinese-make-sure-no-one-willrain-on-their-parade/story-e6frg6so-1225780181859.

Shisheng, Hu. Author interview. Beijing, February 2012.

Subhajit, Roy. "Incursion an Acne, Can Be Cured with Ointment, Says Kurshid." *Indian Express*, April 26, 2013 (Accessed June 18, 2013): http://www.indianexpress.com/news/incursion-acne-can-be-cured-with-ointment-says-khurshid/1107855/.

Shukla, Ajai. "A Helicopter from INS Shivalik Lands on PLA Navy Warship, Ma'anshaan during Exercises in June 2011." *Broadsword*, December 17, 2012. http://ajaishukla.blogspot.com/2012/12/indias-ocean.html.

Shukla, Ajai. "Ajai Shukla: Remembering India's Capitulation on Tibet." *Business Standard*, August 9, 2011 (Accessed January 28, 2013): http://www.businessstandard.com/results/news/ajai-shukla-remembering-indias-capitulation-tibet/445212/.

Shukla, Ajai. Author interview. New Delhi, November 2011.

Shukla, Ajai. "China's Third Confrontation with India's Border Build Up." *Broadsword*, April 26, 2013 (Accessed June 13, 2013): http://ajaishukla.blogspot .com/2013/04/chinasthird-confrontation-with-indias.html.

Shukla, Ajai. "Navy Chief Says Indian Ocean Is Priority, Not South China Sea." *Busines Standard*, August 8, 2008. http://www.business-standard.com/ article/economypolicy/navy-chief-says-indian-ocean-is-priority-not-south -china-sea112080802019_1.html.

Shukla, Ajai. "The Great Game in the Indian Ocean." *Business Standard*, September 1, 2012 (Accessed July 2, 2013): http://www.business-standard.com/article/ beyondbusiness/the-great-game-in-the-indian-ocean-112090100019_1.html.

Shukla, Ajai. "The LAC Is Not the LoC." *Broadsword*, September 19, 2012 (Accessed February 8, 2013): http://ajaishukla.blogspot.com/2012/09/the-lac-is-not-loc .html.

Shukla, Saurabh. "China Plays the Bully on Arunachal: Beijing Tells Delhi to Work Out Eastern Sector Formula." *Mail Online*, January 20, 2012 (April 24, 2013): http://www.dailymail.co.uk/indiahome/indianews/article-2092841/China -plays-bully-Arunachal-Beijing-tells-Delhi-work-Eastern-sector-formula.html.

Singh, Jaswant. "Asia's Giants Colliding at Sea?" *Project Syndicate*. http://www .projectsyndicate.org/commentary/asia-s-giants-colliding-at-sea.

Singh Mandip, "China Year Book 2011." Institute for Defence Studies and Analyses, May 2012 (Accessed April 15, 2013): http://www.idsa.in/system/files/ book_Chinayear2011.pdf.

Singh, Mandip, "Chinas Military in 2011: Modernization on Track," May, 2012. http://www.idsa.in/system/files/book_Chinayear2011.pdf.

Singh, Manmohan. "China Wants India in State of Low-Level Equilibrium: PM." *Times of India*, September 7, 2010. http://articles.timesofindia.indiatimes .com/2010-0907/india/28215059_1_india-and-pakistan-bilateral-ties-outstand ing-issues.

Singh, Rahul. "China Now Bigger Threat than Pakistan, Says IAF Chief." *Hindustan Times*, May 23, 2009 (Accessed April 22, 2013): http://www.hindustan times.com/NewsFeed/India/China-now-bigger-threat-thanPakistan-says -IAF-chief/Article1413933.aspx.

Singh, Zorawar. *Himalayan Stalemate: Understanding the India-China Dispute*. London: Straight Forward Publishers, 2012.

Sinha, Yaswant. Speech at Harvard University, Cambridge, September 23, 2003. www.mea.gov.in.

SIPRI Arms Database Trade Register, China and Pakistan 1990–2011, February 20, 2013. http://armstrade.sipri.org/armstrade/page/trade_register.php.

Small, Andrew. Author interview. Washington, DC, March 14, 2012.

Smith, Jeff. "China and Pakistan's Nuclear Collusion." *Wall Street Journal*, April 2, 2013. http://online.wsj.com/article/SB100014241278873232965045783981442 4810024.html.

"South Asia Least Integrated Region in World." *Nation*, December 3, 2012. http://www.nation.com.pk/pakistan-news-newspaper-daily-english online/ business/03-Dec-2012/south-asia-least-integrated-region-in-world.

"South Asia's Waters: Unquenchable Thirst." *Economist*. November 16, 2011. http://www.economist.com/node/21538687.

Speaker of Tibetan government. Author interview. Dharamsala, India, August 2012.

"Special Topic Paper: Tibet 2008–2009." *Congressional Executive Commission on China*, October 22, 2009 (Accessed January 28, 2013): http://www.cecc.gov/pages/virtualAcad/tibet/tibet_2008–2009.pdf.

"Speech by Mr. Goh Chok Tong, Senior Minister, at the Global Action Forum for Arab and Asian Dialogue," *Ministry of Foreign Affairs: Singapore*, April 27, 2007 (Accessed April 15, 2013): http://www.mfa.gov.sg/content/mfa/media_centre/press_room/sp/2007/200704/seech_20070427.html.

"Statement of the Indian Government." *Indian Government*. January 30, 2013. http://fnvaworld.org/download/india-tibet/1965IndianStatementatUN.pdf.

"Statistical Communiqué on the 2011 National Economic and Social Development." National Bureau of Statistics of China, February 22, 2012 (Accessed April 15, 2013): http://www.stats.gov.cn/english/newsandcomingevents/t20120222_40278587.htm.

Shubhajit, Roy. "Aussie Vote Not Anti-India, Just Pro-ADB: New Envoy." *Indian Express*, September 25, 2009 (Accessed April 24, 2013): http://www.indianexpress.com/news/aussie-vote-not-antiindia-just-proadb-newenvoy/521250.

Sumbal, Malik Ayub. "How the ETIM Enigma Haunts Pakistan-China Relations." *Diplomat*, May 22, 2013. http://thediplomat.com/the-pulse/2013/05/22/how-the-etim-enigma-haunts-pakistan-china-relations/.

Sureesh, Mehta. Author interview. Honolulu, May 2013.

Suryanarayana. "China's Gesture." *Frontline*. Vol. 21, No. 11, April 22, 2013 (Accessed June 22, 2013): www.frontlineonnet.com/fl2111/stories/20040604001905100.

Svensson, Jesper. "Managing the Rise of a Hydro-Hegemon in Asia: China's Strategic Interests in the Yarlung-Tsangpo River." *IDSA Occasional Paper No. 23*, April 2012.

"Sweet as can be?" *Economist*, May 12, 2011. http://www.economist.com/node/18682839.

Tandon, Shaun. "China Says South China Sea Freedom of Navigation 'Assured,'" *ABS CBN News*, September 5, 2012 (Accessed April 15, 2013): http://www.abscbnnews.com/global-filipino/world/09/05/12/china-says-south-china-sea-freedom-navigation-assured.

Tankel, Stephen. Author interview. Washington, DC, February 22, 2013.

Tanner, Murray Scot. "Distracted Antagonists, Wary Partners: China and India Assess Their Security Relations." *CNA*, September 2011 (Accessed February 8, 2013): http://www.cna.org/sites/default/files/research/Distracted%20Antagonists%2C%20Wary%20Partners%20D0025816%20A1.pdf.

Tatlow, Didi Kirsten. "Dalai Lama Keeps Firm Grip on Reins of Succession." *New York Times*, October 5, 2011 (Accessed January 29, 2013): http://www.nytimes.com/2011/10/06/world/asia/06ihtletter06.html?pagewanted=all&_r=0.

Tavernise, Sabrina. "Pakistan's Elite Pay Few Taxes, Widening Gap." July 18, 2011. http://www.nytimes.com/2010/07/19/world/asia/19taxes.html?pagewanted=all&r=0.

"Tawang, Other Areas of Arunachal Integral Parts of India: Chidambaram." *Daily News and Analysis, India.com*, April 2, 2010 (Accessed January 30, 2013): http://www.dnaindia.com/india/report_tawang-other-areas-of-arunachal-integral-parts-of-india-chidambaram_1366623.

Tellis, Ashley J., and Mirski, Sean. "Crux of Asia: China, India, and the Emerging Global Order." Carnegie Endowment. http://carnegieendowment .org/2013/01/10/crux-of-asia-china-india-andemerging-global-order/f0gw.

Terode, Greg. "Beijing Pressure Intense in South China Sea Row." *South China Morning Post*, August 14, 2011. http://www.scmp.com/article/979876/beijing -pressure-intense-south-china-sea-row.

Tharoor, Ishaan. "Beyond India vs. China: The Dalai Lama's Agenda." *Time World*, November 5, 2009 (Accessed January 30, 2013): http://www.time.com/ time/world/article/0,8599,1934948,00.html.

The Brookings Institute "Water: Asia's New Battleground." Transcript Brahma Chellaney, January 24, 2013.

"The Khan Network." Paper by David Sanger submitted to the Conference on South Asia and the Nuclear Future, June 4–5. Stanford University. http://iisdb .stanford.edu/evnts/3889/Khan_network-paper.pdf.

The Lowy Institute New India Poll 2013, May 20, 2013. http://www.lowy institute.org/publications/india-poll-2013.

"The People's Republic of China." Office of the United States Trade Representative, April 15, 2013. http://www.ustr.gov/countries-regions/china-mongolia taiwan/peoples-republic-china.

"The World Factbook: India." *Central Intelligence Agency*, January 29, 2013 (Accessed February 5, 2013): https://www.cia.gov/library/publications/the-world factbook/geos/in.html.

Thinley, Phurbu. "TWA to Campaign for Higher Voter Turnout in 2011 Kalon Tripa Elections." *Phayul.com*, March 31, 2010 (Accessed January 28, 2013): http://www.phayul.com/news/article.aspx?id=27018&t=1.

"Tibet and India's Security: Himalayan Region, Refugees, and Sino-Indian Relations." *Institute for Defence Studies and Analyses (IDSA)*, May 2012 (Accessed January 28, 2013): http://www.idsa.in/system/files/book_Tibet-India.pdf.

"Tibet Marks Panchen Lama's Enthronement Anniversary." *China through a Lens*, December 9, 2005 (Accessed January 28, 2013): http://www.china.org.cn/ english/2005/Dec/151352.htm.

"Tibet: Time Talks with the Tibetan Spiritual Leader." *Unrepresented Nations and People's Organization*, October 20, 2004 (Accessed January 29, 2013): http:// www.unpo.org/article/1321.

"Tibetan Refugee Settlements: India." *Department of Home: Central Tibetan Administration*, 2011 (Accessed February 15, 2013): http://ctrc.tibet.net/settlements -in-india.html.

Timmons, Heather. "India Tells Mobile Firms to Delay Deals for Chinese Telecom Equipment." *New York Times*, April 30, 2010 (Accessed April 15, 2013): http:// www.nytimes.com/2010/05/01/business/global/01delhi.html?_r=0 .

Tkacik, John. "The Enemy of Hegemony Is My Friend: Pakistan's De Facto Alliance with China." Congressional testimony, July 26, 2011. House Committee on Foreign Affairs Oversight and Investigations Subcommittee.

"Top Theological Institutes Prepare Living Buddhas." *China News Center*, August 14, 2012 (Accessed January 28, 2013): http://www.chinamedia.com/ news/2012/08/14/top-theological-institutes-prepare-living-buddhas/.

Tow, William. "The Trilateral Strategic Dialogue: Facilitating Community Building or Revisiting Containment?" *National Bureau of Asian Research*, December 2008 (Accessed April 15, 2013): http://www.nbr.org/publications/special report/pdf/Preview/SR16_preview.pdf.

"Trade Gap Strains India-China Ties," *Wall Street Journal*, August 3, 2012 (Accessed April 15, 2013): http://online.wsj.com/article/SB1000087239639044368 750457756354214967700.html.

"Travel Diary: Secretary Clinton Participates in ASEAN Regional Forum." *DipNote: U.S. Department of State Official Blog*, July 23, 2010 (Accessed April 15, 2013): http://blogs.state.gov/index.php/site/entry/travel_diary_secretary_ asean_reginalforum.

Tzou, Byron. *China and International Law: The Boundary Disputes*. New York: Praeger Publishers, 1990.

"Uighur Leader Killed in Pakistan: Rehman Malik." *Dawn.com*, May 7, 2010. http://archives.dawn.com/archives/103175.

Uli, Schmetzer. "6-Year-Old Tibetan the Incarnation of Chinese Power." *Chicago Tribune*, January 26, 2006 (Accessed January 28, 2013): http://articles.chicago tribune.com/1996-01-16/news/9601160267_1_11th panchen-lama-tibetan-wei-jingsheng.

United Nations. "Review of Maritime Transport," 2011 (Accessed July 2, 2013): http://unctad.org/en/Docs/rmt2011_en.pdf.

Upreti, Deepak K. "LAC Airbases to Be Upgraded." *Deccan Herald*, March 11, 2012 (Accessed April 22, 2013): http://www.deccanherald.com/content/233718/ lacairbasesupgraded.html.

"US China Joint-Statement." Office of the Press Secretary, November 17, 2009. http://www.whitehouse.gov/the-press-office/us-china-joint-statement.

"US Defence Secretary Leon Panetta Identifies India as 'linchpin' in US Game Plan to Counter China in Asia-Pacific." *India Today*, June 7, 2012 (Accessed April 8, 2013): http://indiatoday.intoday.in/story/leon-panetta-identifies-india-as -linchpin-to-counter-china/1/199505.html.

U.S. Military Officials (Pacific Command). Author interview. Honolulu, April, 2012.

Vardarajan, Siddharth. "India Tells China: Kashmir Is to Us What Tibet, Taiwan Are to You," November 15, 2010 (Accessed April 24, 2013): http://www.thehindu .com/news/national/article886483.ece.

Verma, Bharat. *Threat from China*. New Delhi: Lancer Publishers and Distributers, 2011.

Wang, Jing. *Locating China: Space, Place, and Popular Culture*. New York: Routledge, 2005.

"Warm Reception to Indian Naval Ships in China." *ZeeNews*, June 13, 2012. http://zeenews.india.com/news/world/warm-reception-to-indian-naval -ships-inchina_781647.html.

"West Bengal Governor Ignores China's 'Advice,' Attends Dalai Lama Meet," *Times of India*, December 1, 2011 (Accessed April 24, 2013): http://articles .timesofindia.indiatimes.com/2011-12-01/india/30462526_1_dalai-lama-west -bengal-governor-spiritual-leader.

"Will Decide On My Successor When I Am 90, Says Dalai Lama." *India Today,* September 11, 2011 (Accessed January 28, 2013): http://indiatoday.intoday.in/story/dalai-lama-successor-at-90/1/152551.html.

"Will India Join Strategic Containment of China?" *People's Daily Online,* January 22, 2013 (Accessed April 8, 2013): http://english.peopledaily.com.cn/102774/8102712.html.

"What a Waste." *Economist,* May 11, 2013 (Accessed July 8, 2013): http://www.economist.com/news/leaders/21577372-how-india-throwing-away-worlds-biggest-economic-opportunity-what-waste.

"White Paper—Freedom of Religious Belief in China." Embassy of the People's Republic of China in the United States of America, October 1997 (Accessed June, 2013): http://www.china-embassy.org/eng/zt/zjxy/t36492.htm.

World Coal Association. "Coal's Vital Role in China." World Coal Association. *Ecoal.,* Vol. 74, May 2011. http://www.worldcoal.org/resources/ecoal-archive/ecoalcurrent-issue/coals-vital-role-in-china/

Wright, Tom. "Will Media Setback Silence Mr. Singh?" *Wall Street Journal,* September 8, 2010. http://blogs.wsj.com/indiarealtime/2010/09/08/will-media-setback-silence-mr-singh/.

Xiaohua, Li. "India's Provocation Irritates Chinese Netizens." *China.org.cn,* June 15, 2009 (Accessed April 22, 2013) http://www.china.org.cn/international/2009 06/15/content_17951232.htm.

Xiaojun, Li. "Muddying the Waters." *Hindu,* July 10, 2010 (Accessed January 30, 2013): http://www.thehindu.com/opinion/letters/article3621384.ece.

Xinhua. "China's Escort Fleet to Join Exercise in Pakistan." *Xinhuanet.com,* February 17, 2013. http://news.xinhuanet.com/english/china/2013-02/17/c_132174099.htm.

Yeshi, Karma. Author interview. Dharamsala, India, August 2012.

Zi, Hua. "Central Tibetan Administration Illegitimate." *China Daily,* March 29, 2012 (Accessed January 29, 2013): http://www.chinadaily.com.cn/opinion/2012 03/29/content_14936763.htm.

Zude, He, and Wei, Fang. "India's Increasing Troop May Go Nowhere." *People's Daily Online,* November 15, 2011 (Accessed April 10, 2013) http://english.peopledaily.com.cn/102774/7644826.html.

Index

About the Author

Jeff M. Smith is the Director of South Asia Programs and Kraemer Strategy Fellow at the American Foreign Policy Council, a Washington, DC–based think tank. He has traveled extensively throughout India and China and provided briefings and consulted for the Pentagon, the State Department, Congress, and the Directorate of National Intelligence on Asian security issues. His writings have appeared in the *Wall Street Journal*, *Harvard International Review*, CNN, and the *Diplomat*, among others. Smith is also the managing editor of the *World Almanac of Islamism*, and editor of AFPC's *South Asia Security Monitor* and *Eurasia Security Watch*. His expert commentary can be seen on Fox News, CNBC, the BBC, and the *Voice of America*.

Indian debate, 383, 120-21

CPSIA information can be obtained at www.ICGtesting.com
Printed in the USA
BVOW02*2232101213

338746BV00002B/8/P

India re One China: p 94

Australia 184-7

Indian debate: 120-26 383